A4

진짜녀석들

OPIc

IM3-AL

진짜녀석들 OPIc IM3-AL

2쇄 발행	2023. 01. 02
지은이	박영진
펴낸이	박영진
기획팀	진짜녀석들 기획팀
편집팀	진짜녀석들 편집팀
관리팀	진짜녀석들 관리팀
주 소	서울시 송파구 법원로 4길 5, 226호
전 화	(02) 6956 0549
홈페이지	www.jinjja-eng.com
email	cs@jinjja-eng.com
ISBN	ISBN 979-11-970507-7-0 (13740)
저작권자	박영진

www.jinjja-eng.com

A4
한 장 암기로
획득하는

진짜녀석들
OPIc

IM3-AL

Contents

OPIc의 이해

진짜녀석들 OPIc IM3 - AL

APPENDIX

OPIc 의 이해

OPIc이란?

OPIc이란?

- OPIc(Oral Proficiency Interview computer)은 iBT 기반의 외국어 말하기 평가입니다.
- OPIc은 개인 맞춤형 평가로서, 응시자가 수십가지 항목 중에서 일정 개수를 선택한 후, 응시자의 실력에 따른 난이도를 선택합니다.
- 여러 가지 다양한 토픽의 질문들을 듣고 음성을 녹음하여 채점자가 평가를 하는 시스템입니다.
- 단순히 문법 및 어휘만을 측정하는 시험이 아닌, 해당되는 질문에 명확하고 풍부한 답변을 얼마나 유창하게 하는가에 집중이 되어 있는 시험입니다.

OPIc 시험 구성

- OPIc은 총 1시간의 시험으로 Orientation(20분) & 실제 시험시간(40분)으로 구분되어 있습니다.
- 실제 시험시간은 40분이며, 40분을 모두 채우지 않아도 괜찮습니다.
- 또한 OPIc은 답변의 제한 시간이 없기에 15개 문제를 모두 마치면 종료 후, 퇴실하시면 됩니다.

Orientation 20분

Background Survey
- 평가문항을 위한 사전 질문

Self Assessment
- 시험의 난이도 결정을 위한 자기평가

Overview of OPIc
- 화면구성, 청취 및 답변방법 안내

Sample Question
- 실제 답변 방법 연습

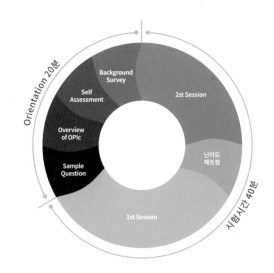

시험시간 40분

1st Session
- 개인 맞춤형 문항
- 질문 청취 2회
- 문항별 답변시간 제한 無
- 약 7문항 출제

난이도 재조정
- Self Assessment (2차 난이도 선택)
- 쉬운질문/비슷한 질문 /어려운 질문 中 선택

2nd Session
- 개인 맞춤형 문항
- 질문 청취 2회
- 문항별 답변시간 제한 無
- 약 7문항 출제

OPIc 평가 영역

OPIc은 아래의 5가지 영역이 충족되어야 보다 더 높은 등급을 획득할 수 있습니다.

Language Control	Function Global Tasks	Text Type	Contents Contexts	Comprehen-sibility
Grammar Vocabulary Fluency Pronunciation	일관적으로, 편하고 꾸준하게, 즉흥적으로 대처할 수 있는 언어 과제 수행 능력	어문의 길이와 구성능력 (단위 : 단어, 구, 문장, 접합된 문장들, 문단)	주제와 상황에 대한 표현 능력	질문 의도 파악 (Interviewer의 질문을 제대로 파악하였는가?)
출중한 영어 실력! 꾸준하게 학습한 영어실력이 바탕이 되어야 해요!	**탁월한 센스!** 어떤 문제가 나와도 순발력 있게 대처 할 수 있는 센스가 바탕이 되어야 해요!	**든든한 암기량!** 다양한 문제 답변을 대비한 탄탄한 암기가 바탕이 되어야 해요!	**짱짱한 훈련!** 다양한 상황의 문제들의 답변에 대비한 연습이 바탕이 되어야 해요!	**리스닝 파악!** 문제를 제대로 알아들을 수 있도록 수도 없이 질문을 듣는 리스닝이 바탕이 되어야 해요!

OPIc 등급

OPIc은 총 9개의 등급으로 나누어져 있습니다.

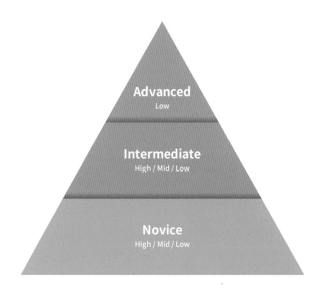

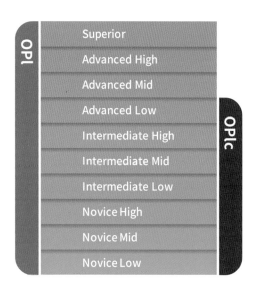

Background Survey 설정

OPIc은 개인 맞춤형 평가입니다. 응시자가 수십가지의 설문 항목에서 일정 개수의 주제를 선택하게 됩니다. 출제 주제와 질문을 최대한 예상하고 그에 맞는 답변을 제공하기 위해서 **진짜녀석들 OPIc**은 아래와 같은 Background Survey 선택을 추천합니다.

1. 현재 귀하는 어느 분야에 종사하고 계십니까?

☐ 사업/회사
☐ 가사
☐ 교사/교육자
☐ 군복무
■ 일 경험 없음

'사업/회사,재택 근무/재택 사업' 선택 시 추가 질문
1.1. 현재 귀하는 직업이 있으십니까?

☐ 네
☐ 아니오

'네' 선택 시 추가 질문
1.1.1. 귀하의 근무 기간은 얼마나 되십니까?

☐ 첫 직장 – 2개월 미만
☐ 첫 직장 – 2개월 이상
☐ 첫 직장 아님 – 경험 많음

'첫 직장 – 2개월 이상, 첫 직장 아님 – 경험 많음' 선택 시 추가 질문
1.1.1.1. 귀하는 부하 직원을 관리하는 관리직을 맡고 있습니까?

☐ 네
☐ 아니오

2. 현재 귀하는 학생이십니까?

☐ 네
■ 아니오

'아니오' 선택 시 추가 질문
2.2. 예전에 들었던 강의 목적은 무엇입니까?

☐ 학위 과정 수업
☐ 전문 기술 향상을 위한 평생 학습
☐ 어학 수업
■ 수강 후 5년 이상 지남

3. 현재 귀하는 어디에서 살고 계십니까?

■ 개인 주택이나 아파트에 홀로 거주
☐ 친구나 룸메이트와 함께 주택이나 아파트에 거주
☐ 가족(배우자/자녀/기타 가족 일원)과 함께 주택이나 아파트에 거주
☐ 학교 기숙사
☐ 군대 막사

4. 귀하는 여가 활동으로 주로 무엇을 하십니까?
(두 개 이상 선택)

☐ 영화보기
☐ 클럽/나이트클럽 가기
☐ 공연 보기
■ 콘서트 보기
☐ 박물관 가기
■ 공원 가기
☐ 캠핑하기
■ 해변 가기
☐ 스포츠 관람
☐ 주거 개선
■ 술집/바에 가기
■ 카페/커피전문점 가기
☐ 게임하기 (비디오, 카드, 보드, 휴대폰 등)
☐ 당구 치기
☐ 체스 하기
☐ SNS에 글 올리기
☐ 친구들에게 문자 보내기
☐ 시험대비과정 수강하기
☐ TV 보기
☐ 리얼리티 쇼 시청하기
☐ 뉴스를 보거나 듣기
☐ 요리 관련 프로그램 시청하기
■ 쇼핑하기
☐ 차로 드라이브하기
☐ 스파/마사지 샵 가기
☐ 구직 활동하기
☐ 자원봉사하기

5. 귀하의 취미나 관심사는 무엇입니까?
(한 개 이상 선택)

☐ 아이에게 책 읽어 주기
■ 음악 감상하기
☐ 악기 연주하기
☐ 글쓰기 (편지, 단문, 시 등)
☐ 그림 그리기
☐ 요리하기
☐ 애완동물 기르기
☐ 독서
☐ 춤추기
☐ 주식투자 하기
☐ 신문 읽기
☐ 여행 관련 블로그나 잡지 읽기
☐ 사진 촬영하기
☐ 혼자 노래 부르거나 합창하기

6. 귀하는 주로 어떤 운동을 즐기십니까?
(한 개 이상 선택)

☐ 농구
☐ 야구/소프트볼
☐ 축구
☐ 미식축구
☐ 하키
☐ 크리켓
☐ 골프
☐ 배구
☐ 테니스
☐ 배드민턴
☐ 탁구
☐ 수영
☐ 자전거
☐ 스키/스노우 보드
☐ 아이스 스케이트
■ 조깅
■ 걷기
☐ 요가
☐ 하이킹/트레킹
☐ 낚시
☐ 헬스
☐ 태권도
☐ 운동 수업 수강하기
☐ 운동을 전혀 하지 않음

7. 귀하는 어떤 휴가나 출장을 다녀온 경험이 있습니까?
(한 개 이상 선택)

☐ 국내 출장
☐ 해외 출장
■ 집에서 보내는 휴가
■ 국내 여행
■ 해외여행

Self Assessment 선택

OPIc은 개인 맞춤형 평가입니다. 6개의 난이도 중, 한 가지를 선택하시게 됩니다. 실제 시험에서는 각 난이도의 샘플 답변을 들어 보실 수 있습니다. 단, 실력과 무관하게 너무 높은 난이도를 선택 시, 등급의 불이익을 받을 수 있음을 알려드립니다.

희망 등급	난이도
IL	**난이도 1** 나는 10단어 이하의 단어로 말할 수 있습니다. **난이도 2** 나는 기본적인 물건, 색깔, 요일, 음식, 의류, 숫자 등을 말할 수 있습니다. 나는 항상 완벽한 문장을 구사하지 못하고 간단한 질문도 하기 어렵습니다.
IM1	**난이도 3** 나는 나 자신, 직장, 친한 사람과 장소, 일상에 대한 기본적인 정보를 간단한 문장으로 전달할 수 있습니다. 간단한 질문을 할 수 있습니다.
IM2	**난이도 4** 나는 나 자신, 일상, 일/학교와 취미에 대해 간단한 대화를 할 수 있습니다. 나는 이 친근한 주제와 일상에 대해 쉽게 간단한 문장들을 만들 수 있습니다. 나는 또한 내가 원하는 질문도 할 수 있습니다.
IM3 – AL	**난이도 5** 나는 친근한 주제와 가정, 일 학교, 개인과 사회적 관심사에 대해 자신 있게 대화할 수 있습니다. 나는 일어난 일과 일어나고 있는 일, 일어날 일에 대해 합리적으로 자신 있게 말할 수 있습니다. 필요한 경우 설명도 할 수 있습니다. 일상 생활에서 예기치 못한 상황이 발생하더라도 임기응변으로 대처할 수 있습니다. **난이도 6** 나는 개인적, 사회적 또는 전문적 주제에 나의 의견을 제시하여 토론할 수 있습니다. 나는 다양하고 어려운 주제에 대해 정확하고 다양한 어휘를 사용하여 자세히 설명할 수 있습니다.

OPIc 시험 화면

OPIc은 질문을 듣고, 답변을 녹음하는 스피킹 시험입니다. 시험 화면과 익숙해져야 실전에서 당황하지 않습니다. **진짜녀석들 OPIc**은 시험 화면과 흡사한 이미지를 지속적으로 보여주며 시험에 익숙하도록 도와줍니다.

① 총 문항 수를 표시해주며, 응시자가 몇 번 문제를 풀고 있는지 확인 할 수 있습니다.

② 각 문항마다 'Play' 버튼을 눌러 질문을 들을 수 있으며, 질문은 두 번 들을 수 있습니다.

③ 시험 화면 오른쪽 상단에 'Recording' 표시로 녹음이 되고 있음을 알 수 있습니다.

④ 'Next' 버튼을 클릭하여, 답변을 종료하며 자동으로 다음 문제로 넘어갑니다.

유형별 문제 설명

OPIc은 난이도 설정에 따라 Background Survey에서 응시자가 선택한 주제 및 선택하지 않아도 나오는 '돌발 주제'가 Random으로 12-15개의 문제가 출제됩니다. 각 주제는 콤보(2-3문제)로 출제되며, 콤보의 유형을 미리 파악하는 것이 중요합니다. **진짜녀석들 OPIc**은 난이도 설정에 따른 콤보 유형을 파악하고 답변 준비를 보다 더 효율적으로 할 수 있는 방법을 제공합니다. 유형은 크게 3가지로 묘사, 경험, 롤플레이 유형으로 나누어져 있습니다.

묘사 유형

일반 묘사

장소, 사람, 사물, 일상, 업무 등 콤보 문제의 첫 문제에 해당!
[현재 시제 사용!]

세부 묘사

앞의 묘사 문제의 세부적인 질문!
[루틴, 비교, 장단점, 전과 후, 이슈 등]

경험 유형

일반 경험

최근, 최초, 인상 깊었던 경험은 일반 경험으로 정리!
[무조건 과거 시제 사용!]

문제 해결 경험

해결점을 필히 제시해줘야 하는 경험!
[정확한 스토리 전개와 본인 감정 이입 필수]

롤플레이 유형

정보 요청

특정 상황 제시 후 추가 정보를 묻는 문제!
[인사말 ➡ 질문 1~3 ➡ 마무리 Format 사용]

문제 해결

특정 상황 제시 후 대안을 제시하는 문제!
[상황설명 ➡ 대안 1~3 ➡ 마무리 Format 사용]

단순 질문

면접관 'Eva' 에게 3~4개 질문하는 문제!
[인사말 ➡ 질문 1~3 ➡ 마무리 Format 사용]

난이도 1 & 2 선택 시 콤보 유형

난이도 3 & 4 선택 시 콤보 유형

난이도 5 & 6 선택 시 콤보 유형

OPIc 기출 문제 샘플

난이도 5 선택 시, 아래와 같은 유형으로 총 5개 주제(Background Survey에서 선택한 주제, 돌발 주제)로 출제됩니다. 어떤 주제가 출제되는지 미리 알 순 없지만, 질문 순서 별 유형은 정해져 있습니다.

1번: 자기소개
Let's start the interview now. Please tell me a little bit about yourself.

주제 1

2번: 묘사 – 술집/바 묘사
You indicated in the survey that you go to bars. Describe one of your favorite bars that you usually visit. What does it look like? Why do you like to visit that place? Please tell me everything about that place in detail.

3번: 세부묘사 – 술집/바에서 주로 하는 일
I would like to know what you usually do when you go to bars. Who do you usually go with? When do you go to bars? What do you usually do at the bars?

4번: 경험 – 술집/바에서 있었던 인상 깊었던 경험
Please tell me about a memorable incident that happened at a bar. When was it and who were you with? What happened there? And why was it so special? Please tell me everything from the beginning to the end.

주제 2

5번: 묘사 – 사람들이 인터넷으로 하는 활동 묘사
What do people normally do on the Internet? Do they play games, listen to music, or watch movies? Please tell me about the things people do online.

6번: 경험 – 처음 접한 인터넷 사이트 경험
Please tell me about your first experience of surfing the Internet. What was the name of that website? What did you do? How has Internet usage changed over the years?

7번: 경험 – 인터넷 사용 시, 기억에 남는 경험
I would like to ask you one of the unforgettable experiences you had while using the Internet. When was it and why was it so unforgettable? Please tell me all the stories from the beginning to the end.

주제 3

8번: 묘사 – 국내 여행지 묘사
You indicated in the survey that you go on domestic trips. I would like you to describe one of the cities you usually visit. Where do you usually go and what does the place look like? Why do you like to visit there? Please tell me in detail.

9번: 경험 – 어렸을 적 갔었던 국내 여행지 경험
Please tell me about the trip you went on when you were young. Where did you go? Who did you go there with? Why was it so special? Please tell me the story from the beginning to the end.

10번: 경험 – 가장 인상 깊었던 국내 여행의 경험
Please tell me your most memorable experience during your trip. Maybe something funny or unexpected happened. Where did you go and who were you with? Was there some special events going on or an unexpected thing happened? Please tell me the story from the beginning to the end.

주제 4

11번: 정보요청 롤플레이 – 호텔 예약 질문
I'm going to give you a situation and ask you to act it out. You would like to book a hotel for your trip. Call a hotel and ask three or four questions to make a reservation.

12번: 문제해결 롤플레이 – 체크 인 후, 청소가 되지 않은 상황 대안 제시
I'm sorry, but there is a problem that needs to be resolved. You have checked in, but the room is not cleaned up properly. Call the front desk, explain the situation, and offer two to three options to resolve this matter.

13번: 문제해결 경험 – 여행지에서 생긴 문제와 해결 경험
That's the end of the situation. Please talk about an unexpected incident that you have experienced during your trip. What happened? How did you handle the situation? Please tell me everything about that experience in detail.

주제 5

14번: 세부묘사 – 가수 혹은 작곡가 비교
Please pick two different types of music or composers that you are interested in. What is so special about each type of music? What are some similarities and differences between the two? Please give me all the details.

15번: 세부묘사 – 자주 사용하는 음악 장비
I would like to ask you about some gadgets or equipment that people in your country are interested in when they listen to music. Why do people use them and what do people like about them?

교재 구성

진짜녀석들 OPIc IM3-AL은 보다 더 효과적으로 학습할 수 있도록 교재의 구성 및 학습 순서에 대해 알려드립니다.

1. 유형별 답변 Format 숙지

OPIc은 면접에 의거한 스피킹 시험으로 각 유형별 필요 Format이 존재합니다.

단순 서론, 본론, 결론의 Format이 아닌, 유형별로 필요한 구조가 필요합니다.

답변 Format만 제대로 숙지한 후, 답변하신다면 답변의 길이가 길지 않아도 학습자의 생각이 명확히 전달됩니다.

진짜녀석들 OPIc IM3-AL을 통해서 3가지 유형(묘사, 경험, 롤플레이)의 답변 Format을 먼저 익히길 바랍니다.

2. 유형별 핵심 문장 암기

OPIc은 다양한 주제의 질문들에 맞는 답변을 준비해야 하는 스피킹 시험입니다.

문장의 난이도(Text Type)를 높여 주기 위해서 여러 문법과 어휘가 포함된 핵심 문장의 암기는 필수입니다.

다만 모든 주제의 답변에 필요한 많은 양의 암기가 아닌, 필요한 만큼의 암기만으로도 충분합니다.

진짜녀석들 OPIc IM3-AL의 핵심 문장으로 어떤 주제의 질문에도 답변이 가능하도록 암기하시기 바랍니다.

교재 구성

진짜녀석들 OPIc IM3-AL은 보다 더 효과적으로 학습할 수 있도록 교재의 구성 및 학습 순서에 대해 알려 드립니다.

3. 유형별 암기문장 활용법

OPIc은 여러 문제의 답변을 위해서 필수적으로 암기해야하는 문장이 존재합니다.

하지만 단순히 암기를 한다면 자신의 문장이 아니기 때문에 시험 도중 생각이 나지 않을 수가 있습니다.

또한, 해당 암기문장의 활용법을 모른다면 어떻게 사용해야 하는지도 몰라 답변을 못하는 경우가 발생합니다.

진짜녀석들 OPIc IM3-AL에서 암기한 문장들의 활용법을 배워 보다더 자연스럽게 암기를 합니다.

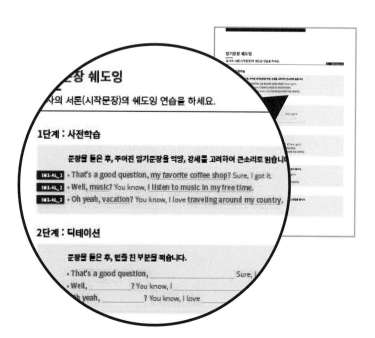

묘사의 암기　전치사

묘사 암기문장의 문법을 정확히 배우고 응용해 보세요.

You know, I think it's about 200m from my place.

· [전치사] about : 대략

01.　'about'은 '~에 대하여'란 의미를 가진 전치사로 있지만 시간, 거리, 수치 등에
02.　수치를 나타내는 표현 앞에 위치
03.　동일한 표현으로도는 like, around, approximately, almost 등

사용 방법

about + 시간, 거리, 수치

~und, approximately, almost

4. 유형별 암기문장 쉐도잉

OPIc은 원어민스러운 답변을 해야 보다 더 점수 획득에 도움을 받습니다.

채점자가 원어민이기에 무작정 암기한 문장만 나열한다면 답변의 전달이 안 될 염려가 있습니다.

그다지 발음이 좋지않아도 실제로 나의 답변처럼 말하는 방법을 배워야 합니다.

진짜녀석들 OPIc IM3-AL의 암기문장 쉐도잉으로 보다 더 자연스럽게 스피킹하는 방법을 획득하시기 바랍니다.

장 쉐도잉

사의 서론(시작문장)의 쉐도잉 연습을 하세요.

1단계 : 사전학습

문장을 들은 후, 주어진 암기문장을 억양, 강세를 고려하여 큰소리로 읽습니다

- IM3-AL_1 · That's a good question, my favorite coffee shop? Sure, I got it.
- IM3-AL_2 · Well, music? You know, I listen to music in my free time.
- IM3-AL_3 · Oh yeah, vacation? You know, I love traveling around my country.

2단계 : 딕테이션

문장을 들은 후, 민줄 친 부분을 적습니다.

- That's a good question, ＿＿＿＿＿＿＿＿＿ Sure, I
- Well, ＿＿＿＿＿＿ ? You know, I
- h yeah, ＿＿＿＿＿ ? You know, I love ＿＿＿＿

교재 구성

진짜녀석들 OPIc IM3-AL은 보다 더 효과적으로 학습할 수 있도록 교재의 구성 및 학습 순서에 대해 알려 드립니다.

5. 유형별 질문 리스닝 훈련

OPIc은 지문이 나오지 않기 때문에 질문을 알아듣지 못하면 답변을 할 수 없는 시험입니다.

리스닝 실력 향상에는 클래식한 방법이 정답입니다. 많이 듣고, 따라 읽는 것이 가장 직접적이면서 가시적인 효과가 있습니다.

다만, 무수히 많은 주제의 질문들을 기점으로 듣기 훈련을 하신다면 너무 긴 시간이 걸릴 것입니다.

따라서 **진짜녀석들 OPIc IM3-AL**을 통해서 3가지 유형(묘사, 경험, 롤플레이)의 질문을 듣고 키워드 캐치 능력을 키우시기 바랍니다.

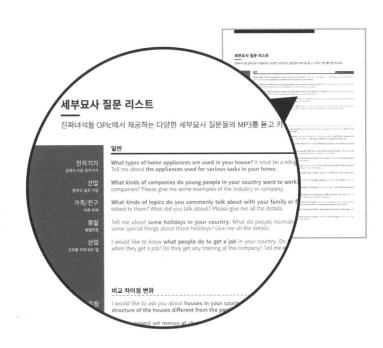

6. 유형별 답변 훈련

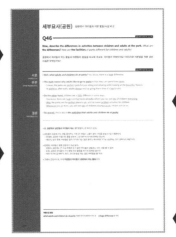

유형별 질문을 듣고 키워드를 캐치합니다.

답변의 한글 해석 또한 단락별로 나누어 제공하므로 보다 더 답변 Format에 익숙해질 수 있습니다.

답변 Format에 의거하여 핵심 문장과 본인 실력 문장을 사용하여 답변 훈련을 생성합니다.

유형별 핵심 암기 문장, 강조해야 할 키워드, 즉흥적으로 생성 가능한 문장들을 매 답변마다 제공합니다.

면접의 답변처럼 명확한 의미 전달에 중점을 두어 답변 훈련을 합니다.

추가로 학습 가능한 어휘 및 표현을 제공합니다.

교재 구성

진짜녀석들 OPIc IM3-AL은 보다 더 효과적으로 학습할 수 있도록 교재의 구성 및 학습 순서에 대해 알려 드립니다.

7. 유형별 모의고사

유형별 실제 시험에서 출제되는 질문 순서의 화면으로 시험에 익숙해집니다.
질문의 순서에 맞춰 실제 답변을 연습한 후, 모의 답변으로 자신의 실력을 확인합니다.

8. APPENDIX

MP3 질문 리스트 : 유형별 질문들로 다양한 방법으로 훈련을 할 수 있습니다.
핵심 암기 문장 리스트 : 유형별 암기해야 할 문장들을 모아둔 자료를 제공합니다.
어휘 및 표현 리스트 : 추가 학습 가능한 어휘 및 표현 리스트를 취합하여 제공합니다.

학습 가이드

진짜녀석들 OPIc IM3-AL 교재 + 온라인 강의 시청 의 학습 가이드를 제공합니다.

1강 이론	**유형1_묘사: 이론** 묘사 유형 이론 파악 묘사 암기문장(56줄) 암기
2강 이론	**유형 1_묘사: 암기문장 활용** 묘사 암기문장별 문법 이해 묘사 암기문장 활용법 학습
3강 훈련	**유형 1_묘사: 암기문장 쉐도잉** 묘사 암기문장 끊어 읽기 방법 묘사 암기문장 발음,억양 연습
4강 훈련	**유형 1_묘사: 리스닝 훈련** 묘사 유형 질문 키워드 캐치 훈련 묘사 유형 답변 준비 연습
5강 훈련	**유형 1_묘사(장소): 스크립트 훈련1** 묘사 유형(장소) 예시 스크립트 제공 나만의 문장 추가 요령
6강 훈련	**유형 1_묘사(일반): 스크립트 훈련2** 묘사 유형(일반) 예시 스크립트 제공 나만의 문장 추가 요령
7강 이론	**유형2_세부묘사: 이론** 세부묘사 유형 이론 파악 세부묘사 암기문장(10줄) 암기
8강 이론	**유형 2_세부묘사: 암기문장 활용** 세부묘사 암기문장별 문법 이해 세부묘사 암기문장 활용법 학습
9강 훈련	**유형 2_세부묘사: 암기문장 쉐도잉** 세부묘사 암기문장 끊어 읽기 방법 세부묘사 암기문장 발음,억양 연습
10강 훈련	**유형 2_세부묘사: 리스닝 훈련** 세부묘사 유형 질문 키워드 캐치 훈련 세부묘사 유형 답변 준비 연습
11강 훈련	**유형 2_세부묘사: 스크립트 훈련1** 세부묘사 유형 예시 스크립트 제공 나만의 문장 추가 요령
12강 훈련	**유형 2_세부묘사: 스크립트 훈련2** 세부묘사 유형 예시 스크립트 제공 나만의 문장 추가 요령
13강 훈련	**유형 2_세부묘사: 스크립트 훈련3** 세부묘사 유형 예시 스크립트 제공 나만의 문장 추가 요령
14강 훈련	**유형1,2_묘사, 세부묘사: 모의고사** 묘사, 세부묘사 질문 및 답변 (총 6개 질문)
15강 이론	**유형3_경험: 이론** 경험 유형 이론 파악 경험 암기문장(43줄) 암기
16강 이론	**유형 3_경험: 암기문장 활용** 경험 암기문장별 문법 이해 경험 암기문장 활용법 학습
17강 훈련	**유형 3_경험: 암기문장 쉐도잉** 경험 암기문장 끊어 읽기 방법 경험 암기문장 발음,억양 연습
18강 훈련	**유형 3_경험: 리스닝 훈련** 경험 유형 질문 키워드 캐치 훈련 경험 유형 답변 준비 연습
19강 훈련	**유형 3_경험(어릴적/최근): 스크립트 훈련1** 경험 유형(어릴적/최근) 예시 스크립트 제공 나만의 문장 추가 요청
20강 훈련	**유형 3_경험(인상/문제): 스크립트 훈련2** 경험 유형(인상/문제) 예시 스크립트 제공 나만의 문장 추가 요령
21강 훈련	**유형3_묘사,세부묘사,경험: 모의고사** 묘사/세부묘사/경험 질문 및 답변 (총 13개 질문)
22강 이론	**유형4_롤플레이: 이론** 롤플레이 유형 이론 파악 롤플레이 암기문장(11줄) 암기
23강 이론	**유형4_롤플레이: 암기문장 활용** 롤플레이 암기문장별 문법 이해 롤플레이 암기문장 활용법 학습
24강 훈련	**유형4_롤플레이: 암기문장 쉐도잉** 롤플레이 암기문장 끊어 읽기 방법 롤플레이 암기문장 발음,억양 연습
25강 훈련	**유형4_롤플레이: 리스닝 훈련** 롤플레이 유형 질문 키워드 캐치 훈련 롤플레이 유형 답변 준비 연습
26강 훈련	**유형4_롤플레이: 스크립트 훈련1** 정보요청 롤플레이 유형 예시 스크립트 제공 나만의 문장 추가 요령
27강 훈련	**유형4_롤플레이: 스크립트 훈련2** 문제해결 롤플레이 유형 예시 스크립트 제공 나만의 문장 추가 요령
28강 훈련	**유형4_롤플레이: 스크립트 훈련3** 문제해결 경험 유형 예시 스크립트 제공 나만의 문장 추가 요령
29강 훈련	**유형4_롤플레이: 모의고사** 롤플레이 질문 및 답변 (총 15개 질문)
30강 이론	**시험 전 정리** Background Survey / Self Assessment 15개 문제 준비

학습 완료 시

시험 응시를 준비합니다.

추가 학습 플랜

MP3 질문 듣기

유형별, MP3를 들으시며 질문의 키워드 캐치에 집중합니다.
(MP3 질문은 학습하시는 내내(이동 시, 업무 중, 자기 전) 들어야 익숙해집니다.)

유형별 답변 스피킹 훈련

4가지 유형의 답변을 지속적으로 훈련하여 보다 더 자연스러운 답변을 구사합니다.

본인 실력 문장 추가

보다 더 풍부한 답변을 만들기 위하여 본인 실력 문장을 추가하는 훈련을 합니다.

시험 신청

준비가 되었다고 생각하시기 2 – 3일 전에 시험 신청을 합니다.

시험 신청	시험 신청은 OPIc 홈페이지(www.opic.or.kr)에서 할 수 있습니다. OPIc은 연중 상시 시행 시험입니다. (일부 공휴일 제외) 다만 지역/센터별로 차이가 있을 수 있습니다. 신분증(주민등록증, 운전면허증, 공무원증, 기간만료 전 여권)을 필히 지참해야 합니다.
시험 재 응시 규정	시험 응시 후 재 응시 규정은 최소 25일 이후에 가능합니다. 다만 'Waiver' 제도를 사용하여 재 응시 규정을 무시하고 1번의 시험을 추가 응시 할 수 있습니다. 'Waiver' 제도는 150일에 한 번씩 사용이 가능합니다.
시험 결과	시험 결과는 응시일로부터 일주일 후 OPIc 홈페이지에서 성적 확인이 가능합니다. (일반적으로 오후 1시 발표) 취업 시즌 등의 경우 학습자 편의를 위해 성적 조기 발표(시험일로부터 3~5일)를 시행합니다.

OPIc IM3-AL

1강

유형 01 (묘사)

이론

묘사의 이해

OPIc 질문들은 콤보 형태로 나온다고 했죠?
난이도에 따라 질문의 유형도 달라진다고 했습니다.(OPIc 이해 – 유형별 문제 설명 p13 참조)
각 콤보 문제의 첫 질문은 대부분 묘사로 시작합니다.
묘사는 흔히 장소, 사람, 사물, 일상, 업무 등을 묘사하게 됩니다.

묘사가 나오는 질문 번호를 외우세요!

묘사가 나오는 질문 번호를 외우세요!
IM3 – AL등급 목표 시, 난이도 5으로 설정하시면, 묘사는 총 3문제 출제!

1	2	3	4	5	6	7	8	9	10	11	12	13	14	15
자기소개	묘사	세부묘사	경험	묘사	경험	경험	묘사	경험	경험	정보요청	문제해결	문제해결경험	세부묘사	세부묘사

묘사의 종류

Background Survey에서 선택한 모든 주제 & 모든 출제 가능한 돌발 주제의 묘사를 모두 암기하는 것은 불가능합니다. 따라서 **진짜녀석들 OPIc**은 3가지 묘사 종류로 분류합니다.

개방 공간 묘사	➡	밖을 묘사(평화롭고 조용하고 아름다운 풍경 표현)
독립 공간 묘사	➡	안을 묘사(5층 건물로 각 층의 묘사 표현)
일반적 묘사	➡	밖 & 안을 제외한 모든 주제 묘사

 문제를 집중하여 듣고, 키워드를 캐치한 후, 3가지 묘사 종류 중 택일!

묘사의 답변 Format

묘사는 정확한 '팩트 전달'이 중요한 질문으로 체계적인 답변 Format이 필요합니다.

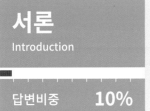

서론 Introduction 답변비중 10%

시작 문장
- 질문에서 물어본 부분(키워드 포함)의 포괄적인 답변 2 – 3줄!
- 면접관에게 답변을 시작한단 느낌을 전달!

본론 Body 답변비중 80%

단락 별 핵심 문장
- 질문에 부합하는 진짜녀석들 OPIc 묘사 암기문장 (4-5문장)
- 암기문장 뒷받침 하는 본인 실력 문장 (4-5문장)
- 질문의 '키워드' 필수 포함

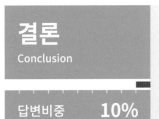

결론 Conclusion 답변비중 10%

마무리 문장
- 질문의 키워드를 필히 포함하여 깔끔하게 한 줄!
- 면접관에게 답변을 끝낸다는 느낌을 전달!

묘사의 암기문장 – 서론 & 결론

정확한 묘사의 답변을 위하여 서론과 결론에 필요한 암기문장을 제공합니다.

서론 - 시작문장

- 좋은 질문이야, <u>내가 좋아하는 커피숍</u>? 그래 알겠어.
  That's a good question, <u>my favorite coffee shop</u>? Sure, I got it.

- 음, 음악? 있잖아, <u>난 음악 듣는 걸 좋아해 쉬는 시간에</u>.
  Well, <u>music</u>? You know, <u>I listen to music in my free time</u>.

- 오 예, <u>휴가</u>? 있잖아, 난 좋아해 <u>우리나라 여행하는 것을</u>.
  Oh yeah, <u>vacation</u>? You know, I love <u>traveling around my country</u>.

결론 - 마무리문장

- 알겠어 에바, 이 정도면 <u>내가 좋아하는 해변</u>에 대한 이야기로 될 것 같아. 고마워.
  Alright Eva, this is all I can say about <u>my favorite beach</u>. Thank you.

- 음, 오케이 에바, 이 정도면 충분한 것 같아.
  Well, okay Eva, this is pretty much about it.

- 그래서 정리하자면, 이게 <u>내가 좋아하는 공원</u>이야.
  So overall, this is about <u>my favorite park</u>.

 암기문장 중, 밑줄 표시가 되어있는 부분은 주제별, 상황별로 학습자가 자유롭게 변형가능한 부분입니다.

묘사의 암기문장 – 본론(단락 별 핵심 암기 문장)

정확한 묘사의 답변을 위하여 본론에 필요한 암기문장을 제공합니다.

본론 - 단락 별 핵심 문장 (개방공간 묘사)

MP3 IM3-AL_7~26

개방공간의 일반 장소 문장

- 내가 좋아하는 커피숍에 대해서 말한다면, 2km 정도야 우리 집에서.
  When it comes to my favorite coffee shop, it's like 2km from where I live.
- 음, 난 확신해 공원은 대략 20분 정도인 걸 우리 집에서.
  Well, I'm pretty sure that the park is around 20-minutes away from my place.
- 해변에 대해 말해본다면, 완벽한 장소야 그냥 앉아서 쉬기 예쁜 꽃들을 보면서.
  Speaking of the beach, it's a perfect spot for just sitting and relaxing while looking at the beautiful flowers.
- 또한, 큰 러닝트랙이 있어 네가 볼 수 있는 많은 사람들을 운동하는.
  Also, there is a huge running track where you can see lots of people exercising.
- 내 말은, 큰 공원이 있어 다양한 영역으로 된, 축구를 하는, 크리켓을 하는 그리고 등등.
  I mean, there is a huge park with many different areas where people play soccer, cricket and so on.
- 추가로, 아름다운 옛날 집이 있어 지금은 카페로 바뀐 네가 따뜻한 차를 즐길 수 있는.
  In addition, there is a beautiful old house which is now a café where you can have afternoon tea.
- 사실상, 해변은 엄청 아름다워, 그리고 물은 수정같이 맑아.
  Actually, the beach is undeniably beautiful, and the water is crystal clear.
- 오! 이 말은 꼭 해야 해 일몰을 보는 것은 꽤 로맨틱해 그리고 그게 왜 그 장소가 유명한 이유야 커플들에게.
  Oh! I must say that watching the sunset is kinda romantic and that's why the place is famous for couples.
- 글쎄, 여름은 완벽한 타이밍이야 공원을 가기 그리고 야외활동을 하기.
  Well, summer is the perfect time to go to the park and do some outdoor activities.
- 내 생각엔, 자연으로 돌아가서, 밖에서 편히 쉬는 것은 꼭 필요한 것 같아 사람들에게.
  In my opinion, getting back to nature, just relaxing outside is essential for human beings.

사람들의 세부 행동 문장

- 솔직히, 난 선호해 그곳에 가는 걸 밤에 왜냐하면 난 즐길 수 있거든 평화로움과 조용함을.
  Seriously, I prefer to go there at night since I can enjoy the peace and quiet.
- 있잖아, 난 아마 그곳을 가는 편이야 한 달에 몇 번쯤.
  You know, I suppose I tend to visit there a few times a month.
- 항상 내가 그곳에 방문할 땐, 난 많은 사람들을 볼 수 있어 대화하고 쉬는.
  Whenever I visit there, I can see bunch of people talking and relaxing.
- 사실상, 난 항상 살아왔어 굉장히 조용한 곳에, 그래서 난 노력해 방문하는 것을 새로운.
  In fact, I've always lived in very quiet areas, so I'm trying to visit places that are new to me.
- 있잖아, 사람들은 많은 것들을 해 운동을 하거나, 음악을 듣거나, 그런 것들을.
  You know, people do many kinds of things such as playing sports, listening to music and stuff like that.
- 어쨌든, 많은 다른 것들을 할 수 있어 책을 읽거나, 그냥 쉬거나.
  However, there are many other things you can do such as reading books or just relaxing.
- 글쎄, 내 생각엔 대부분의 사람들은 그곳에 가 걷기 위해서/뛰기 위해서/수영하러.
  Well, I guess most people go there to walk/run and to swim.
- 중요한 점은 쇼핑몰은 항상 붐벼 많은 사람들로.
  All you need to know is that the shopping mall is always packed with lots of people.
- 언제나 내가 그곳에 갈 때면, 난 기분이 너무 좋아 그리고 참 큰 의미가 있어.
  Whenever I go there, it makes me feel so great and it means a lot to me.
- 추가로, 난 항상 결국 그곳에 가곤 해 왜냐하면 무료거든 입장이.
  In addition, I always end up going there since it's free to visit.

 암기문장 중, 밑줄 표시가 되어있는 부분은 주제별, 상황별로 학습자가 자유롭게 변형가능한 부분입니다.

묘사의 암기문장 – 본론(단락 별 핵심 암기 문장)

정확한 묘사의 답변을 위하여 본론에 필요한 암기문장을 제공합니다.

본론 - 단락 별 핵심 문장 (독립공간 묘사)

🎧 MP3 IM3-AL_27~46

독립공간의 전체적 장소문장

- 첫 번째로, 건물은 **5층**이고 옥상에 **테라스 가든**이 있어.
  First of all, the building has **5** floors and **a terrace garden**.
- 첫 번째로, 쇼핑몰은 **10층** 건물이야 그래서 확실히 눈에 띄어.
  Firstly, **the shopping mall** is a **10**-story building, so it definitely stands out.
- 있잖아, 이 말은 꼭 해야 해 가장 큰 건물이라고 도심에서 그리고 **ABC 타워**라고 불려.
  You know, I must say that it's the tallest building in the city and it's called **the ABC tower**.
- 사실상, 가장 유명한 **쇼핑센터**야 **도심 중앙**에 위치해 있는.
  In fact, it's the most famous **shopping center** which is located **in the middle of the town**.
- 네가 상상하듯, 1층에는, **리셉션 데스크**가 있어 그리고 넌 필요해 **ID 카드**가 들어가기 위해서.
  As you can imagine, on the first floor, there is **a reception desk** and you need **an ID card** to get in.
- 또한, 2층부터 4층에는, 많은 **명품 가게들**이 있어.
  Also, on the second to fourth floors, there are lots of **luxury stores**.
- 추가로, 9층에는, **헬스장**이 있어 내가 **운동하는**.
  Plus, on the ninth floor, there is **a gym** where I **work out**.
- 네가 예상하듯, 마지막 층에는, **커피숍**과 **아늑한 바**가 있어 네가 **쉴 수 있는**.
  As you can expect, on the top floor, there is **a coffee shop** and **a cozy bar** where you can **chill**.
- 우리 집에 대해서 말한다면, 우리 집엔 **안방**, **3**개의 방, 그리고 **2**개의 화장실이 있어.
  When it comes to my house, our place has **a master bedroom**, three bedrooms, and **two** baths.
- 네가 그곳에 가면, 통틀어, 넌 찾을 수 있어 **50**개가 넘는 **ATM 기계들**을.
  When you go there, in total, you can find more than **50 ATMs**.

독립공간의 세부공간 및 기능문장

- 첫 번째로 내가 보는 것은 **평면 TV**와 **아늑한 소파**야.
  The first thing I can see is **a flat screen TV** and **a cozy couch**.
- 가장 흥미로운 부분은 **이 지역**에 대해서, 모든 것들은 자동화되어 있어.
  The most interesting thing about **this place** is that every single thing is automated.
- 있잖아, **스마트 도어락**이 있어서 엄청 편해.
  You know, it has **a smart door lock** so it's handy.
- 일반적으로, 중앙난방과 에어컨 시스템이 있어 그래서 여름에 시원하고 겨울에 따뜻해.
  Generally, it has central heating and air-conditioning, so it's cool during summer and warm during winter.
- 당연하지만, 사람들은 쉽게 **엔지니어**를 부를 수 있어 만약 **엘리베이터**가 작동을 안 한다면.
  Obviously, people can easily call **the engineer** if **the elevator** is not working.
- 내 말은, **객실**은 엄청 깨끗해, 그리고 사람들은 엄청 친절해 그게 **내가 그곳에 가는** 이유야.
  I mean, **the room** is extremely clean, and the people are so friendly and that's why I love **to go there**.
- 하지만 있잖아, 항상 가득 차 있어 사람들로, 그래서 난 선호해 가는 것을 **아침 일찍**.
  But you know, it is always filled with lots of people, so I prefer going there **early in the morning**.
- 들어가면, 넌 아마 볼 거야 **내 동생**을 소파에만 누워있는.
  As you walk in, you will probably see **my brother** being a couch potato.
- 글쎄, 난 항상 주문해 **라테**를 **아침**에 하지만 가끔은 난 기다려야 해 긴 줄을.
  Well, I always order **Latte in the morning** but sometimes I need to stand in a long line.
- 살을 빼기 위해서, 난 **뛰어 러닝머신**을 매일.
  In order to lose weight, I **run on a treadmill** every day.

 암기문장 중, 밑줄 표시가 되어있는 부분은 주제별, 상황별로 학습자가 자유롭게 변형가능한 부분입니다.

묘사의 암기문장 – 본론(단락 별 핵심 암기 문장)

정확한 묘사의 답변을 위하여 본론에 필요한 암기문장을 제공합니다.

본론 - 단락 별 핵심 문장 (일반적 묘사)

🎧 MP3 IM3-AL_47~56

일반적 사람들의 행동문장

- 내 친구에 대해서 말한다면, 난 많은 시간을 보내 <u>John</u>과 그리고 난 <u>그</u>를 알아 <u>10살</u>부터.
  When it comes to my friend, I spend lots of time with <u>John</u> and I've known <u>him</u> since I was <u>10</u>.
- 사실, <u>그</u>는 많이 알아 <u>음악</u>에 대해서, 그래서 그는 <u>좋은 사람</u>이야 같이 가기.
  Actually, <u>he</u> knows a lot about <u>music</u>, so he is <u>a great person</u> to go with.
- 여름을 준비하기 위해서, 난 많은 시간을 보내 <u>헬스장</u>에서 왜냐하면 난 <u>살을 빼야 해</u>.
  In order to prepare for summer, I spend lots of time <u>at the gym</u> because I need to <u>lose weight</u>.
- 게다가, 난 정말 즐겨 모든 종류의 <u>영화를 보는 것</u>을 왜냐하면 스트레스를 풀 수 있거든.
  Moreover, I really enjoy <u>watching</u> all kinds of <u>movies</u> because it helps me release stress.
- 있잖아, 난 확실해 할인을 받을 수 있는 것을 왜냐하면 난 <u>멤버십 카드</u>가 있거든.
  You know, I'm pretty sure that I can get a discount since I got <u>a membership card</u>.
- 네가 예상하듯, <u>재활용</u>은 <u>필수</u>야 한국에선 그리고 사람들은 재활용을 해 종이, 유리, 금속 등등을.
  As you can imagine, <u>recycling</u> is <u>mandatory</u> in Korea and people recycle trash such as paper, glass, metal and etcetera.
- 내가 어렸을 때, 난 하곤 했어 <u>입는 것을 캐주얼 한 옷</u>을, 근데 지금은 난 <u>정장을 입어</u>.
  When I was young, I used to <u>wear something casual</u>, but now, I <u>wear something formal</u>.
- 내가 왜 집에 있는 가장 큰 이유는 난 <u>혼자 시간을 보낼 수 있거든</u>.
  The main reason why I like to stay at home is that I can <u>spend time alone</u>.
- 솔직히 말해서, 나도 잘 몰라, 근데 난 <u>술 마시는 것</u>을 하고 싶어.
  To be honest, I don't know why, but I kinda feel like <u>drinking</u>.
- 내 말은, 대부분의 <u>한국사람</u>은 사용해 왜냐하면 엄청나게 유명해지고 있거든.
  I mean, most <u>Koreans</u> are using it since it's getting increasingly popular.

 암기문장 중, 밑줄 표시가 되어있는 부분은 주제별, 상황별로 학습자가 자유롭게 변형가능한 부분입니다.

묘사 답변 준비 – 시험화면

난이도 5 설정 시, 묘사가 나오는 번호를 실제 시험화면으로 익숙해져야 합니다.

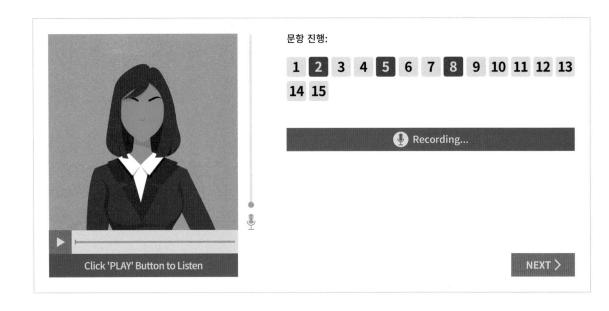

난이도 5 설정 시, 묘사 질문은 총 3문제(2, 5, 8번)가 출제됩니다.

1. 묘사 질문의 'Play' 버튼 클릭 전, 묘사임을 인지합니다.

2. 진짜녀석들 OPIc 묘사 종류(개방, 독립, 일반)을 생각합니다.

3. 'Play' 버튼 클릭 후, 첫 번째 문제에서 묘사의 키워드를 집중해서 듣습니다.

4. 'Replay' 버튼 클릭 후, 두 번째 문제는 듣지 않고 사용할 묘사 문장을 생각합니다.

5. 오른쪽 상단의 'Recording' 버튼 생성 시, '묘사 답변 Format' 대로 답변합니다.

 문제를 집중하여 듣고, 키워드를 캐치한 후, 3가지 묘사 종류 중 택일!

묘사 질문 파악 전략 - 예시

질문 듣기 전, 이미 유형을 알기에 키워드 캐치에 집중 하셔야 합니다.

예시 질문 - 바, 지리, 여가

• You indicated in the survey that you go to **bars.** Describe one of your favorite bars that you usually visit.
What does it look like? Why do you like to visit that place? Please tell me everything about that place in detail.

① bar 키워드 캐치 → ② 묘사 종류 선택 → ③ 답변 Format 준비 → ④ 답변

• I would like you to describe **the geography of your country.** Are there mountains, lakes or rivers?
Please describe the geographical features of your country in as much detail as possible.

① geography 키워드 캐치 → ② 묘사 종류 선택 → ③ 답변 Format 준비 → ④ 답변

• I would like to ask you about your **free time.** How much free time do you have?
Who do you usually meet and what do you usually do in your free time? Please tell me in detail.

① free time 키워드 캐치 → ② 묘사 종류 선택 → ③ 답변 Format 준비 → ④ 답변

정확한 키워드 캐치를 위한 리스닝 방법을 훈련합니다.

ⓐ **첫 번째 문제에서 무조건 키워드 캐치**
이미 묘사 유형임을 알고 있기에 키워드 단어에만 집중합니다.

ⓑ **묘사 종류 선택**
알맞은 진짜녀석들 OPIc의 3가지 묘사 종류 중 하나를 선택합니다.

ⓒ **두 번째 문제 'Replay' 하며 답변 준비**
두 번째 문제는 듣지 않고, 묘사 답변 Format에 맞추어 답변을 준비합니다.

묘사 답변 전략 – 예시

OPIc은 면접과 흡사한 시험으로 서론, 본론, 결론을 명확하게 지키며 답변합니다.

Q

You indicated in the survey that you go to **bars**. Describe one of your favorite bars that you usually visit. What does it look like? Why do you like to visit that place? Please tell me everything about that place in detail.

당신은 바에 간다고 했습니다. 당신이 종종 방문하는 바 중 한 곳을 묘사해주세요. 어떻게 생겼나요? 왜 그곳을 방문하죠? 그 장소에 대해 자세히 말해주세요.

예시 답변 - 바 묘사

서론
시작문장/10%

- That's a good question, *my favorite bar?* Sure, I got it. Well, I usually go to ABC lounge bar near my town.

본론
단락별 핵심문장/80%

- When it comes to ABC lounge bar, it's like 5km from where I live.
- So, I tend to visit there quite often after work.

- First of all, the bar has 5 floors and a terrace garden.
- Yeah, it's the most famous bar in town.
- And also, the bar is extremely clean, and the people are so friendly and that's why I love to go there.

- Moreover, they have all kinds of drinks and I like to drink scotch the most.
- Whenever I visit there, I can see bunch of people talking and relaxing.
- So, it is a great place to visit after a stressful day at work.

결론
마무리문장/10%

- So overall, this is about *my favorite bar that I usually visit.*

묘사 답변의 고득점을 향한 스피킹 방법을 훈련합니다.

ⓐ **부사 사용(녹색 색상 단어 참고)** 단락의 시작은 항상 부사(접속부사, 부사절 등) 및 추임새를 사용하여 간결함과 연결성을 전달해줍니다.	First of all, the bar has 5 floors and a terrace garden.
ⓑ **암기 문장(파란 색상 문장 참고)** 진짜녀석들 OPIc에서 제공하는 핵심 암기 문장을 사용하여 높은 점수를 받을 수 있는 표현들을 사용합니다.	When it comes to ABC lounge bar, it's like 5km from where I live.
ⓒ **본인 실력 문장(빨간 색상 문장 참고)** 핵심 암기 문장의 추가 설명으로 풍부한 답변이 되도록 본인 실력문장을 더해줍니다. (문법적인 오류가 있어도 자신 실력 문장이 추가되어야 실제 본인 답변처럼 들립니다.) 제공하는 핵심 암기문장을 자신의 실력을 추가하여 변형하기도 합니다.	Moreover, they have all kinds of drinks and I like to drink scotch the most.
ⓓ **강세 전달(밑줄 단어 참고)** 영어 말하기에서 강세는 의미를 전달하는 핵심 역할이므로 보다 더 자연스러운 답변을 위하여 강세 전달을 합니다.	So, it is a great place to visit after a stressful day at work.
ⓔ **답변 키워드 강조(기울어진 단어 참고)** 답변의 키워드(ex. beach)는 강조하여 읽어줍니다.	So overall, this is about my favorite bar that I usually visit.

2강

유형 01 (묘사)

암기문장 활용

전치사

동명사

관계부사

부사

동명사 주어

to부정사

I prefer~

현재완료

수동태

사역동사

복합형용사

주어/동사 수 일치

In order to~

feel like~

묘사의 암기   전치사

묘사 암기문장의 문법을 정확히 배우고 응용해 보세요.

You know, I think it's about 200m from my place.

• [전치사] about : 대략

01.　'about'은 '~에 대하여'란 의미를 가진 전치사도 있지만 **시간, 거리, 수치** 등을 대략적으로 나타낼 때도 사용

02.　수치를 나타내는 표현 앞에 위치

03.　동일한 표현으로는 like, around, approximately, almost 등

사용 방법

about + 시간, 거리, 수치

= like, around, approximately, almost

활용 및 응용

• I think it's about 200m from my place.

• It's like 20 minutes walking distance.

• It takes about 2 hours by bus.

MEMO

묘사의 암기 동명사

묘사 암기문장의 문법을 정확히 배우고 응용해 보세요.

Speaking of the beach, it's a perfect spot for just sitting and relaxing while looking at the beautiful flowers.

• [동명사] 동사+ing : ~하는 것

01. 동명사는 동사 뒤에 '–ing를 추가'하여 '명사' 형태로 만들어 주는 것
02. '명사' 위치에 올 수 있으며 '~하는 것' 으로 해석
03. 동일한 형태의 '분사' 형태와 헷갈리지 않는 것이 중요

사용 방법

동사 + ing

= 명사의 역할

활용 및 응용

• It's a perfect spot for just sitting and relaxing while looking at the beautiful flowers.

• People do many kinds of things such as playing sports, listening to music and stuff like that.

• There are many other things you can do such as reading books or just relaxing.

MEMO

묘사의 암기　관계부사

묘사 암기문장의 문법을 정확히 배우고 응용해 보세요.

I mean, there is a huge park with many different areas where people play soccer, cricket and so on.

• [관계부사] : 장소, 시간, 이유 등을 설명하는 관계대명사

01. **'관계부사'**는 문장과 문장을 이어주는 **'접속사'**의 역할을 하면서 선행사에 따라 장소, 시간, 이유, 방법 등의 내용을 뒤에 덧붙임
    a. 선행사가 장소일 때: where
    b. 선행사가 시간일 때: when
    c. 선행사가 이유일 때: why
    d. 선행사가 방법일 때: how
02. 문장과 문장을 이어주므로 관계부사 뒤에는 반드시 **주어+동사**

사용 방법

선행사 **+ 관계부사 +** 주어 + 동사

* 선행사: 장소 (where), 시간 (when), 이유 (why), 방법 (how)

활용 및 응용

• There is a huge park with many different areas where people play soccer, cricket and so on.

• There is a beautiful old house which is now a café where you can have afternoon tea.

• That is the reason why I love going to the beach at night.

MEMO

묘사의 암기　부사

묘사 암기문장의 문법을 정확히 배우고 응용해 보세요.

Actually, the beach is undeniably beautiful, and the water is crystal clear.

• [부사] undeniably : 명백하게, 틀림없이

01.　부사는 **동사, 형용사, 문장 전체** 및 **다른 부사**를 <u>수식</u>
02.　**형용사+ly** 형태가 보편적이나, 불규칙적인 표현도 다양
03.　**'~하게', '~히'** 등으로 해석
04.　부사의 위치는 자유롭게!

사용 방법

형용사+ly 형태

= 불규칙 형태도 다양하니 해석에 주의

활용 및 응용

• The beach is undeniably beautiful.

• The room is extremely clean, and the people are so friendly and that's why I love to go there.

• Most Koreans are using it since it's getting increasingly popular.

MEMO

묘사의 암기 　동명사 주어

묘사 암기문장의 문법을 정확히 배우고 응용해 보세요.

Oh! I must say that watching the sunset is kinda romantic and that's why the place is famous for couples.

• [동명사 주어] watching : ~보는 것은

01. 　문장의 주어 자리에는 보통 명사를 취급하므로, 동명사도 가능
02. 　**'~하는 것은'**으로 해석
03. 　단, 동명사는 항상 **'단수'** 취급
04. 　동명사 주어의 경우 일반동사는 3인칭 단수 형태로 변형

사용 방법

동명사 주어 + 동사 (3인칭 단수 취급)

활용 및 응용

• Watching the sunset is kinda romantic.

• Getting back to nature, just relaxing outside is essential for human beings.

• Working out helps me stay healthy and release stress.

MEMO

묘사의 암기　to부정사

묘사 암기문장의 문법을 정확히 배우고 응용해 보세요.

Well, summer is the perfect time **to go** to the park and do some outdoor activities.

• [to 부정사] to go : ~가기에

01.　**to 부정사**는 **'to + 동사원형'** 형태로 각 용법에 따라 의미가 달라짐

02.　여기서는 **'형용사'**적 용법으로 앞에 나온 '명사'를 수식해주는 의미로 사용되어 **'~할'**, **'~하는'**, **'~하기에'**로 해석

03.　간혹 동사와 함께 쓰이는 전치사가 올 경우 **to + 동사원형 + 전치사** 형태를 그대로 유지

　　(I live in a house > I have a house to live in)

사용 방법

명사 **+ to +** 동사원형

* 동사와 함께 쓰이는 전치사의 경우 to부정사 뒤에 위치

활용 및 응용

• Summer is the perfect **time to go** to the park.

• I guess most people go **there to walk/run** and **to swim.**

• You know, working out is the best **way to stay** healthy.

MEMO

묘사의 암기   I prefer~

묘사 암기문장의 문법을 정확히 배우고 응용해 보세요.

Seriously, I prefer to go there at night since I can enjoy the peace and quiet.

• [I prefer ~] : 나는 ~ 을/를 (더) 선호한다

01.   'prefer'은 보통 **두 가지의 대상 중 한 가지를 선택**할 때 사용
02.   '**더 좋아하다**', '**더 선호하다**'라는 의미를 전달
03.   'prefer'다음에 목적어는 명사로 동명사, to부정사 모두 사용 가능!
04.   단, 비교 대상의 형태는 항상 통일 (동명사 to 동명사, to부정사 to to부정사)
05.   이 때 **비교 대상**을 나타낼 때는 **전치사 'to'**를 사용

   Ex. prefer coffee to tea : 차보다 커피를 선호하다

사용 방법

prefer + 명사/동명사/to부정사 **to** + 명사/동명사/to부정사

활용 및 응용

• I prefer to go there at night since I can enjoy the peace and quiet.

• They prefer taking the bus to (taking) the subway.

• She prefers vegetables to meat.

MEMO

42

묘사의 암기　현재완료

묘사 암기문장의 문법을 정확히 배우고 응용해 보세요.

In fact, I've always lived in very quiet areas, so I'm trying to visit places that are new to me.

___

• [현재완료] I've lived : 나는 ~ 살아왔었다

01.　'현재완료'는 과거의 어느 시점부터 현재까지 영향을 미치는 동작이나 행동에 대해 표현할 때 사용되는 형식

02.　'have + 과거분사' 형태로 구성되어 흔히 '완료', '계속', '경험', '결과'와 같은 용법으로 사용

03.　과거의 특정한 시점에 대한 내용이 아니기에 과거 시점을 특정 짓는 표현이 함께 쓰일 수 없으니 주의!

　　　Ex. yesterday, 2 days ago, last year

사용 방법

have + 과거분사

* 과거 시점을 특정 짓는 표현과 함께 사용 X

활용 및 응용

• I've always lived in very quiet areas.

• When it comes to my friend, I spend lots of time with John and I've known him since I was 10.

• Actually, it was the best customer service I've ever had.

MEMO

묘사의 암기   수동태

묘사 암기문장의 문법을 정확히 배우고 응용해 보세요.

All you need to know is that the shopping mall is always packed with lots of people.

• [수동태] is ~ packed : ~ 로 가득 차 있다

01.   **'수동태'**는 be동사 + 과거분사 형태로 **'~되어지다'**로 해석

02.   다른 무언 가에 의해 상태나 동작이 **'당해 짐'**을 의미

03.   **전치사 'by'** 다음에는 명사로 **'행위자'**를 나타내지만 때에 따라 생략

04.   불규칙 과거분사에 주의하여 사용

사용 방법

be동사 + 과거분사 (+by)

활용 및 응용

• The shopping mall is always packed with lots of people.

• It is always filled with lots of people, so I prefer going there early in the morning.

• All the seats are taken by the new customers.

MEMO

44

묘사의 암기　사역동사

묘사 암기문장의 문법을 정확히 배우고 응용해 보세요.

Whenever I go there, it makes me feel so great and it means a lot to me.

• [사역동사] make : ~하게 만들다

01.　'사역동사'란 '~하도록 하다', '~하게 시키다' 로 해석되며 보통 5형식의 형태로 문장을 완성
　　　(주어+동사+목적어+목적격보어 (동사원형))
02.　대표적인 사역동사 : 'make', 'let', 'have'
03.　'~하도록 만들다'로 해석되는 탓에 목적격보어 자리에 'to부정사'가 온다고 헷갈리는 경우가 많으니 이 점 주의!
04.　단, 'help'는 준사역동사로 '동사원형', 'to부정사' 모두 사용 가능

사용 방법

사역동사 (make, let, have) + 목적어 + 동사원형

활용 및 응용

• It makes me feel so great and it means a lot to me.

• Moreover, I really enjoy watching all kinds of movies because it helps me release stress.

• I'm gonna have my brother pick me up from the airport.

MEMO

묘사의 암기　복합형용사

묘사 암기문장의 문법을 정확히 배우고 응용해 보세요.

Firstly, the shopping mall is a **10-story** building, so it definitely stands out.

• [복합형용사] 10-story : 10층짜리의

01.　**'복합형용사'**란 **두 개 이상의 단어가 하나로 결합**하여 형용사의 역할

02.　이 때 반드시 단어 사이에 **하이픈 (-)** 필요

03.　앞에 숫자가 나온 복합형용사의 경우, 하이픈 뒤에 나오는 '명사'는 반드시 원형 취급

　　　Ex. 2-story house, 7-year-old girl, 100-dollar bill

04.　앞에 숫자가 나오는 경우 보통 **'~짜리의'**라고 해석

사용 방법

두 개 이상의 단어를 하이픈 (-) 결합

= 숫자의 경우 뒤에 나오는 명사는 반드시 원형 취급

활용 및 응용

• The shopping mall is a **10-story** building, so it definitely stands out.

• But now, people have become a lot more **health-conscious** than in the past.

• It's my lucky day! I found a **100-dollar** bill on the floor!

MEMO

묘사의 암기　주어, 동사 수 일치

묘사 암기문장의 문법을 정확히 배우고 응용해 보세요.

When it comes to my house, our place has a master bedroom, three bedrooms, and two baths.

• [주어 동사 수일치] has : ~가지고 있다 (3인칭 단수형)

01.　영어 문법에서 가장 실수가 많은 부분 중 하나!

02.　현재시제에서 주어 뒤에 **일반동사**는 주어에 따라 변형될 수 있음

03.　**주어가 3인칭 단수**일 경우 동사는 반드시 **동사-s(es)** 형태

04.　단, 불규칙으로 변형하는 동사에 주의! (have > has)

　　a. 자음+y로 끝나는 동사 : y > i + es (cry > cries, try > tries)

　　b. 자음+y로 끝나는 동사 : y + s (pay > pays, say > says)

사용 방법

현재시제 3인칭 단수 주어 + 동사s (es)

* 불규칙 형태에 주의

활용 및 응용

• Our place has a master bedroom, three bedrooms, and two baths.

• He knows a lot about music, so he is a great person to go with.

• One of my friends goes to Hawaii every summer.

MEMO

묘사의 암기   In order to~

묘사 암기문장의 문법을 정확히 배우고 응용해 보세요.

In order to lose weight, I run on a treadmill every day.

• [숙어] in order to : ~하기 위해서

01.   'in order to'는 '~하기 위해서'로 해석되어 어떤 일의 목적을 표현

02.   'in order to' 다음에는 반드시 **동사 원형**

03.   숙어에 사용된 전치사를 헷갈리지 않도록 주의!

04.   '~하지 않기 위해서'처럼 **부정문**으로 만들 때는 '**in order not to**'

사용 방법

in order to + 동사원형

* **부정문: in order not to** + 동사원형

활용 및 응용

• In order to lose weight, I run on a treadmill every day.

• In order to prepare for summer, I spend lots of time at the gym because I need to lose weight.

• In order not to lose my phone, I always put it in my bag.

MEMO

묘사의 암기   feel like~

묘사 암기문장의 문법을 정확히 배우고 응용해 보세요.

To be honest, I don't know why, but I kinda feel like drinking.

• [feel like + 명사/동명사] : ~하고싶다

01.   '~하고싶다'를 의미하는 가장 대표적인 표현은 'I want to~'가 있지만 평소 회화체에서 'feel like~'도 자주 사용

02.   'feel like' 다음에는 반드시 **명사 혹은 동명사** 형태를 취급

사용 방법

feel like + 명사/동명사

활용 및 응용

• To be honest, I don't know why, but I kinda feel like drinking.

• As you can expect, I lost my wallet. Oh my god, I felt like a homeless person.

• Hey, I'm too bored. I feel like hitting the gym later.

MEMO

3강

유형 01 (묘사)

암기문장 쉐도잉

1단계 : 사전학습

2단계 : 딕테이션

3단계 : 문장 끊어 읽기

4단계 : 전체 문장 읽기

5단계 : 반복 학습

암기문장 쉐도잉

암기문장 쉐도잉은 총 5단계로 나누어져 있습니다.
진짜녀석들 OPIc의 암기문장을 반복듣기 하면서 쉐도잉을 진행합니다.

1단계 **사전학습**	문장을 들은 후, 주어진 암기문장을 억양, 강세를 고려하여 큰소리로 읽습니다. ex.) Actually, **It** is incredibly **beautiful** and **peaceful.**

2단계 **딕테이션**	문장을 들은 후, 밑줄 친 부분을 적습니다. ex.) Actually, ____ is incredibly _____ and _____.

3단계 **문장 끊어 읽기**	문장을 들은 후, 청크 단위로 끊어 읽어 봅니다. ex.) Actually, / **It** is incredibly **beautiful** / and **peaceful.**

4단계 **전체 문장 읽기**	문장을 들은 후, 3단계를 여러 번 반복한 후, 전체 문장을 한숨에 읽어 봅니다. ex.) Actually, **It** is incredibly **beautiful** and **peaceful.**

5단계 **반복학습**	위 단계를 반복하여, 영어의 어순으로 된 한글 해석을 보며, 쉐도잉 연습을 합니다. ex.) 사실, 그 곳은 숨막히게 아름다워 그리고 평화로워.

암기문장 쉐도잉

묘사의 서론(시작문장)의 쉐도잉 연습을 하세요.

🎧 MP3 IM3-AL_1~3

1단계 : 사전학습

문장을 들은 후, 주어진 암기문장을 억양, 강세를 고려하여 큰소리로 읽습니다.

IM3-AL_1 • That's a good question, <u>my favorite coffee shop</u>? Sure, I got it.

IM3-AL_2 • Well, <u>music</u>? You know, <u>I listen to music in my free time</u>.

IM3-AL_3 • Oh yeah, <u>vacation</u>? You know, I love <u>traveling around my country</u>.

2단계 : 딕테이션

문장을 들은 후, 밑줄 친 부분을 적습니다.

• That's a good question, _____ Sure, I got it.

• Well, _____? You know, I _____.

• Oh yeah, _____? You know, I love _____.

3단계 : 문장 끊어 읽기

문장을 들은 후, 청크 단위로 끊어 읽어 봅니다.

• That's a good question, / <u>my favorite coffee shop</u>? / Sure, I got it.

• Well, <u>music</u>? / You know, <u>I listen to music</u> / <u>in my free time</u>.

• Oh yeah, <u>vacation</u>? / You know, I love <u>traveling</u> / <u>around my country</u>.

4단계 : 전체 문장 읽기

문장을 들은 후, 3단계를 여러 번 반복한 후, 전체 문장을 한숨에 읽어 봅니다.

• That's a good question, <u>my favorite coffee shop</u>? Sure, I got it.

• Well, <u>music</u>? You know, I <u>listen to music in my free time</u>.

• Oh yeah, <u>vacation</u>? You know, I love <u>traveling around my country</u>.

5단계 : 반복 학습

위 단계를 반복하여, 영어의 어순으로 된 한글 해석을 보며, 쉐도잉 연습을 합니다.

• 좋은 질문이야, <u>내가 좋아하는 커피숍</u>? 그래 알겠어.

• 음, 음악? 있잖아, <u>난 음악 듣는 걸 좋아해 쉬는 시간에</u>.

• 오 예, <u>휴가</u>? 있잖아, 난 좋아해 <u>우리나라 여행하는 것을</u>.

암기문장 쉐도잉

묘사의 결론(마무리문장)의 쉐도잉 연습을 하세요.

🎧 **MP3 IM3-AL_4~6**

1단계 : 사전학습

문장을 들은 후, 주어진 암기문장을 억양, 강세를 고려하여 큰소리로 읽습니다.

IM3-AL_4 • Alright Eva, this is all I can say about <u>my favorite beach.</u> Thank you.

IM3-AL_5 • Well, okay Eva, this is pretty much about it.

IM3-AL_6 • So overall, this is about <u>my favorite park.</u>

2단계 : 딕테이션

문장을 들은 후, 밑줄 친 부분을 적습니다.

• Alright Eva, this is all I can say about _____. Thank you.

• Well, okay Eva, this is pretty much about it.

• So overall, this is about _____.

3단계 : 문장 끊어 읽기

문장을 들은 후, 청크 단위로 끊어 읽어 봅니다.

• Alright Eva, / this is all I can say about / <u>my favorite beach.</u> / Thank you.

• Well, okay Eva, / this is pretty much about it.

• So overall, / this is about / <u>my favorite park.</u>

4단계 : 전체 문장 읽기

문장을 들은 후, 3단계를 여러 번 반복한 후, 전체 문장을 한숨에 읽어 봅니다.

• Alright Eva, this is all I can say about <u>my favorite beach.</u> Thank you.

• Well, okay Eva, this is pretty much about it.

• So overall, this is about <u>my favorite park.</u>

5단계 : 반복 학습

위 단계를 반복하여, 영어의 어순으로 된 한글 해석을 보며, 쉐도잉 연습을 합니다.

• 알겠어 에바, 이 정도면 <u>내가 좋아하는 해변</u>에 대한 이야기로 될 것 같아. 고마워.

• 음, 오케이 에바, 이 정도면 충분한 것 같아.

• 그래서 정리하자면, 이게 <u>내가 좋아하는 공원</u>이야.

암기문장 쉐도잉

묘사의 본론(장소 묘사 문장 : **개방공간**)의 쉐도잉 연습을 하세요.

🎧 MP3 IM3-AL_7~26

1단계 : 사전학습

문장을 들은 후, 주어진 암기문장을 억양, 강세를 고려하여 큰소리로 읽습니다.

IM3-AL_7	• When it comes to <u>my favorite coffee shop</u>, it's like <u>2km</u> from <u>where I live</u>.
IM3-AL_8	• Well, I'm pretty sure that <u>the park</u> is around <u>20-minutes away</u> from <u>my place</u>.
IM3-AL_9	• Speaking of <u>the beach</u>, it's a perfect spot for just <u>sitting and relaxing</u> while looking at <u>the beautiful flowers</u>.
IM3-AL_10	• Also, there is <u>a huge running track</u> where you can see lots of people <u>exercising</u>.
IM3-AL_11	• I mean, there is <u>a huge park</u> with many different areas where people <u>play soccer</u>, <u>cricket</u> and so on.
IM3-AL_12	• In addition, there is <u>a beautiful old house</u> which is now <u>a café</u> where you can have <u>afternoon tea</u>.
IM3-AL_13	• Actually, <u>the beach</u> is undeniably beautiful, and the water is crystal clear.
IM3-AL_14	• Oh! I must say that <u>watching the sunset</u> is kinda romantic and that's why <u>the place</u> is famous for <u>couples</u>.
IM3-AL_15	• Well, <u>summer</u> is the perfect time to go to <u>the park</u> and do <u>some outdoor activities</u>.
IM3-AL_16	• In my opinion, getting back to nature, just relaxing outside is essential for human beings.
IM3-AL_17	• Seriously, I prefer to go <u>there at night</u> since I can enjoy <u>the peace and quiet</u>.
IM3-AL_18	• You know, I suppose I tend to <u>visit there a few times a month</u>.
IM3-AL_19	• Whenever I visit <u>there</u>, I can see bunch of people <u>talking and relaxing</u>.
IM3-AL_20	• In fact, I've always lived in <u>very quiet areas</u>, so I'm trying to visit places <u>that are new to me</u>.
IM3-AL_21	• You know, people do many kinds of things such as <u>playing sports</u>, <u>listening to music</u> and stuff like that.
IM3-AL_22	• However, there are many other things you can do such as <u>reading books</u> or <u>just relaxing</u>.
IM3-AL_23	• Well, I guess most people go there to walk/run and to swim.
IM3-AL_24	• All you need to know is that <u>the shopping mall</u> is always packed with lots of people.
IM3-AL_25	• Whenever I go <u>there</u>, it makes me feel so great and it means a lot to me.
IM3-AL_26	• In addition, I always end up <u>going there</u> since it's free to visit.

2단계 : 딕테이션

문장을 들은 후, 밑줄 친 부분을 적습니다.

- When it comes to _____, it's like ____ from _____.
- Well, I'm pretty sure that _____ is around _____ from _____.
- Speaking of _____, it's a perfect spot for just _____ while looking at _____.
- Also, there is _____ where you can see lots of people _____.
- I mean, there is _____ with many different areas where people _____, _____ and so on.
- In addition, there is _____ which is now _____ where you can have _____.
- Actually, _____ is undeniably beautiful, and the water is crystal clear.
- Oh! I must say that _____ is kinda romantic and that's why _____ is famous for _____.
- Well, _____ is the perfect time to go to _____ and do _____.
- In my opinion, getting back to nature, just relaxing outside is essential for human beings.
- Seriously, I prefer to go _____ since I can enjoy _____.
- You know, I suppose I tend to _____.
- Whenever I visit _____, I can see bunch of people _____.
- In fact, I've always lived in _____, so I'm trying to visit places _____.
- You know, people do many kinds of things such as _____, _____ and stuff like that.
- However, there are many other things you can do such as _____ or _____.
- Well, I guess most people go there to walk/run and to swim.
- All you need to know is that _____ is always packed with lots of people.
- Whenever I go _____, it makes me feel so great and it means a lot to me.
- In addition, I always end up _____ since it's free to visit.

암기문장 쉐도잉

묘사의 본론(장소 묘사 문장 : **개방공간**)의 쉐도잉 연습을 하세요.

3단계 : 문장 끊어 읽기

문장을 들은 후, 청크 단위로 끊어 읽어 봅니다.

- When it comes to <u>my</u> / <u>favorite coffee shop</u>, / it's like <u>2km</u> from / <u>where I live</u>.
- Well, I'm pretty sure that <u>the park</u> is / around <u>20-minutes away</u> / from <u>my place</u>.
- Speaking of <u>the beach</u>, / it's a perfect spot for just / <u>sitting and relaxing</u> while looking at <u>the</u> / <u>beautiful flowers</u>.
- Also, / there is <u>a huge running track</u> where you can see / lots of people <u>exercising</u>.
- I mean, / there is <u>a huge park</u> with / many different areas where people <u>play</u> / <u>soccer</u>, <u>cricket</u> and so on.
- In addition, / there is <u>a beautiful old house</u> which is / now <u>a café</u> where you can have / <u>afternoon tea</u>.
- Actually, / <u>the beach</u> is undeniably beautiful, and / the water is crystal clear.
- Oh! I must say that <u>watching the sunset</u> is kinda / romantic and that's why <u>the place</u> is / famous for <u>couples</u>.
- Well, <u>summer</u> is the perfect time to / go to <u>the park</u> and do <u>some</u> / <u>outdoor activities</u>.
- In my opinion, / getting back to nature, / just relaxing outside is essential / for human beings.
- Seriously, / I prefer to go <u>there at night</u> since I can / enjoy <u>the peace and quiet</u>.
- You know, / I suppose I tend to <u>visit there</u> / <u>a few times a month</u>.
- Whenever I visit <u>there,</u> / I can see bunch of people <u>talking</u> / <u>and relaxing</u>.
- In fact, / I've always lived in <u>very quiet areas</u>, so / I'm trying to visit places / <u>that are new to me</u>.
- You know, / people do many kinds of things such as / <u>playing sports</u>, <u>listening to music</u> and / stuff like that.
- However, / there are many other things you can do such as / <u>reading books</u> or <u>just relaxing</u>.
- Well, / I guess most people go there to / walk/run and to swim.
- All you need to know is that / <u>the shopping mall</u> is always packed with / lots of people.
- Whenever I go <u>there,</u> / it makes me feel so great and / it means a lot to me.
- In addition, / I always end up <u>going there</u> since it's / free to visit.

4단계 : 전체 문장 읽기

문장을 들은 후, 3단계를 여러 번 반복한 후, 전체 문장을 한숨에 읽어 봅니다.

- When it comes to <u>my favorite coffee shop</u>, it's like <u>2km</u> from <u>where I live</u>.
- Well, I'm pretty sure that <u>the park</u> is around <u>20-minutes away</u> from <u>my place</u>.
- Speaking of <u>the beach</u>, it's a perfect spot for just <u>sitting and relaxing</u> while looking at <u>the beautiful flowers</u>.
- Also, there is <u>a huge running track</u> where you can see lots of people <u>exercising</u>.
- I mean, there is <u>a huge park</u> with many different areas where people <u>play soccer</u>, <u>cricket</u> and so on.
- In addition, there is <u>a beautiful old house</u> which is now <u>a café</u> where you can have <u>afternoon tea</u>.
- Actually, <u>the beach</u> is undeniably beautiful, and the water is crystal clear.
- Oh! I must say that <u>watching the sunset</u> is kinda romantic and that's why <u>the place</u> is famous for <u>couples</u>.
- Well, <u>summer</u> is the perfect time to go to <u>the park</u> and do <u>some outdoor activities</u>.
- In my opinion, getting back to nature, just relaxing outside is essential for human beings.
- Seriously, I prefer to go <u>there at night</u> since I can enjoy <u>the peace and quiet</u>.
- You know, I suppose I tend to <u>visit there a few times a month</u>.
- Whenever I visit <u>there,</u> I can see bunch of people <u>talking and relaxing</u>.
- In fact, I've always lived in <u>very quiet areas</u>, so I'm trying to visit places <u>that are new to me</u>.
- You know, people do many kinds of things such as <u>playing sports</u>, <u>listening to music</u> and stuff like that.
- However, there are many other things you can do such as <u>reading books</u> or <u>just relaxing</u>.
- Well, I guess most people go there to walk/run and to swim.
- All you need to know is that <u>the shopping mall</u> is always packed with lots of people.
- Whenever I go <u>there,</u> it makes me feel so great and it means a lot to me.
- In addition, I always end up <u>going there</u> since it's free to visit.

암기문장 쉐도잉

묘사의 본론(장소 묘사 문장 : **개방공간**)의 쉐도잉 연습을 하세요.

🎧 MP3 IM3-AL_7~26

5단계 : 반복 학습

위 단계를 반복하여, 영어의 어순으로 된 한글 해석을 보며, 쉐도잉 연습을 합니다.

- 내가 좋아하는 커피숍에 대해서 말한다면, **2km** 정도야 **우리 집**에서.
- 음, 난 확신해 공원은 대략 **20분** 정도인 걸 **우리 집**에서.
- 해변에 대해 말해본다면, 완벽한 장소야 그냥 **앉아서 쉬기** 예쁜 꽃들을 보면서.
- 또한, **큰 러닝트랙**이 있어 네가 볼 수 있는 많은 사람들을 **운동하는**.
- 내 말은, **큰 공원**이 있어 다양한 영역으로 된, **축구를 하는, 크리켓을 하는** 그리고 등등.
- 추가로, **아름다운 옛날 집**이 있어 지금은 **카페**로 바뀐 네가 **따뜻한 차**를 즐길 수 있는.
- 사실상, **해변**은 엄청 아름다워, 그리고 물은 수정같이 맑아.
- 오! 이 말은 꼭 해야 해 **일몰을 보는 것**은 꽤 로맨틱해 그리고 그게 왜 **그 장소**가 유명한 이유야 **커플들**에게.
- 글쎄, **여름**은 완벽한 타이밍이야 **공원**을 가기 그리고 **야외활동**을 하기.
- 내 생각엔, 자연으로 돌아가서, 밖에서 편히 쉬는 것은 꼭 필요한 것 같아 사람들에게.
- 솔직히, 난 선호해 **그곳**에 가는 걸 **밤**에 왜냐하면 난 즐길 수 있거든 **평화로움과 조용함**을.
- 있잖아, 난 아마 **그곳**을 **가는** 편이야 **한 달에 몇 번쯤**.
- 항상 내가 **그곳**에 방문할 땐, 난 많은 사람들을 볼 수 있어 **대화하고 쉬는**.
- 사실상, 난 항상 살아왔어 **굉장히 조용한 곳**에, 그래서 난 노력해 방문하는 것을 **새로운**.
- 있잖아, 사람들은 많은 것들을 해 **운동을 하거나, 음악을 듣거나**, 그런 것들을.
- 어쨌든, 많은 다른 것들을 할 수 있어 **책을 읽거나, 그냥 쉬거나**.
- 글쎄, 내 생각엔 대부분의 사람들은 그곳에 가 걷기 위해서/뛰기 위해서/수영하러.
- 중요한 점은 쇼핑몰은 항상 붐벼 많은 사람들로.
- 언제나 내가 **그곳**에 갈 때면, 난 기분이 너무 좋아 그리고 참 큰 의미가 있어.
- 추가로, 난 항상 결국 **그곳에 가곤 해** 왜냐하면 무료거든 입장이.

암기문장 쉐도잉

묘사의 본론(장소 묘사 문장 : **독립공간**)의 쉐도잉 연습을 하세요.

MP3 IM3-AL_27~46

1단계 : 사전학습

문장을 들은 후, 주어진 암기문장을 억양, 강세를 고려하여 큰소리로 읽습니다.

IM3-AL_27 • First of all, the building has **5** floors and **a terrace garden**.

IM3-AL_28 • Firstly, **the shopping mall** is a **10**-story building, so it definitely stands out.

IM3-AL_29 • You know, I must say that it's the tallest building in the city and it's called **the ABC tower**.

IM3-AL_30 • In fact, it's the most famous **shopping center** which is located **in the middle of the town**.

IM3-AL_31 • As you can imagine, on the first floor, there is **a reception desk** and you need **an ID card** to get in.

IM3-AL_32 • Also, on the second to fourth floors, there are lots of **luxury stores**.

IM3-AL_33 • Plus, on the ninth floor, there is **a gym** where I **work out**.

IM3-AL_34 • As you can expect, on the top floor, there is **a coffee shop** and **a cozy bar** where you can **chill**.

IM3-AL_35 • When it comes to my house, our place has **a master bedroom**, three bedrooms, and **two** baths.

IM3-AL_36 • When you go there, in total, you can find more than **50 ATMs**.

IM3-AL_37 • The first thing I can see is **a flat screen TV** and **a cozy couch**.

IM3-AL_38 • The most interesting thing about **this place** is that every single thing is automated.

IM3-AL_39 • You know, it has **a smart door lock** so it's handy.

IM3-AL_40 • Generally, it has central heating and air-conditioning, so it's cool during summer and warm during winter.

IM3-AL_41 • Obviously, people can easily call **the engineer** if **the elevator** is not working.

IM3-AL_42 • I mean, **the room** is extremely clean, and the people are so friendly and that's why I love **to go there**.

IM3-AL_43 • But you know, it is always filled with lots of people, so I prefer going there **early in the morning**.

IM3-AL_44 • As you walk in, you will probably see **my brother** being a couch potato.

IM3-AL_45 • Well, I always order **Latte in the morning** but sometimes I need to stand in a long line.

IM3-AL_46 • In order to lose weight, I **run on a treadmill** every day.

2단계 : 딕테이션

문장을 들은 후, 밑줄 친 부분을 적습니다.

• First of all, the building has **5** floors and _____.

• Firstly, _____ is a ___-story building, so it definitely stands out.

• You know, I must say that it's the tallest building in the city and it's called _____.

• In fact, it's the most famous _____ which is located _____.

• As you can imagine, on the first floor, there is _____ and you need _____ to get in.

• Also, on the second to fourth floors, there are lots of _____.

• Plus, on the ninth floor, there is _____ where I _____.

• As you can expect, on the top floor, there is _____ and _____ where you can _____.

• When it comes to my house, our place has _____, three bedrooms, and _____ baths.

• When you go there, in total, you can find more than _____.

• The first thing I can see is _____ and _____.

• The most interesting thing about _____ is that every single thing is automated.

• You know, it has _____ so it's handy.

• Generally, it has central heating and air-conditioning, so it's cool during summer and warm during winter.

• Obviously, people can easily call _____ if _____ is not working.

• I mean, _____ is extremely clean, and the people are so friendly and that's why I love _____.

• But you know, it is always filled with lots of people, so I prefer going there _____.

• As you walk in, you will probably see _____ being a couch potato.

• Well, I always order _____ but sometimes I need to stand in a long line.

• In order to lose weight, I _____ every day.

암기문장 쉐도잉

묘사의 본론(장소 묘사 문장 : **독립공간**)의 쉐도잉 연습을 하세요.

🎧 **MP3 IM3-AL_27~46**

3단계 : 문장 끊어 읽기

문장을 들은 후, 청크 단위로 끊어 읽어 봅니다.

• First of all, / the building has <u>5</u> floors and / <u>a terrace garden</u>.
• Firstly, / <u>the shopping mall</u> is a <u>10</u>-story building, so / it definitely stands out.
• You know, / I must say that it's / the tallest building in the city and / it's called <u>the ABC tower</u>.
• In fact, / it's the most famous <u>shopping center</u> which is / located <u>in the middle of the town</u>.
• As you can imagine, on the first floor, / there is <u>a reception desk</u> and you need / <u>an ID card</u> to get in.
• Also, on the second to fourth floors, / there are lots of <u>luxury stores</u>.
• Plus, on the ninth floor, / there is <u>a gym</u> where I / <u>work out</u>.
• As you can expect, on the top floor, / there is <u>a coffee shop</u> and / <u>a cozy bar</u> where you can <u>chill</u>.
• When it comes to my house, / our place has <u>a master bedroom</u>, three bedrooms, and / <u>two</u> baths.
• When you go there, in total, / you can find more than <u>50 ATMs</u>.
• The first thing I can see is <u>a</u> / <u>flat screen TV</u> and / <u>a cozy couch</u>.
• The most interesting thing about <u>this place</u> is that / every single thing is automated.
• You know, it has a <u>a</u> / <u>smart door lock</u> so it's handy.
• Generally, / it has central heating and / air-conditioning, so it's cool during summer and / warm during winter.
• Obviously, / people can easily call <u>the engineer</u> if / <u>the elevator</u> is not working.
• I mean, / <u>the room</u> is extremely clean, and / the people are so friendly and that's why / I love <u>to go there</u>.
• But you know, / it is always filled with lots of people, so I / prefer going there <u>early in the morning</u>.
• As you walk in, / you will probably see <u>my brother</u> / being a couch potato.
• Well, / I always order <u>Latte in the morning</u> but sometimes / I need to stand in a long line.
• In order to lose weight, / I <u>run on a treadmill</u> every day.

4단계 : 전체 문장 읽기

문장을 들은 후, 3단계를 여러 번 반복한 후, 전체 문장을 한숨에 읽어 봅니다.

• When it comes to <u>my favorite coffee shop</u>, it's like <u>2km</u> from <u>where I live</u>.
• Well, I'm pretty sure that <u>the park</u> is around <u>20-minutes away</u> from <u>my place</u>.
• Speaking of <u>the beach,</u> it's a perfect spot for just <u>sitting and relaxing</u> while looking at <u>the beautiful flowers</u>.
• Also, there is <u>a huge running track</u> where you can see lots of people <u>exercising</u>.
• I mean, there is <u>a huge park</u> with many different areas where people <u>play soccer, cricket</u> and so on.
• In addition, there is <u>a beautiful old house</u> which is now <u>a café</u> where you can have <u>afternoon tea</u>.
• Actually, <u>the beach</u> is undeniably beautiful, and the water is crystal clear.
• Oh! I must say that <u>watching the sunset</u> is kinda romantic and that's why <u>the place</u> is famous for <u>couples</u>.
• Well, <u>summer</u> is the perfect time to go to <u>the park</u> and do <u>some outdoor activities</u>.
• In my opinion, getting back to nature, just relaxing outside is essential for human beings.
• Seriously, I prefer to go <u>there at night</u> since I can enjoy <u>the peace and quiet</u>.
• You know, I suppose I tend to <u>visit there a few times a month</u>.
• Whenever I visit <u>there</u>, I can see bunch of people <u>talking and relaxing</u>.
• In fact, I've always lived in <u>very quiet areas</u>, so I'm trying to visit places <u>that are new to me</u>.
• You know, people do many kinds of things such as <u>playing sports, listening to music</u> and stuff like that.
• However, there are many other things you can do such as <u>reading books</u> or <u>just relaxing</u>.
• Well, I guess most people go there to walk/run and to swim.
• All you need to know is that <u>the shopping mall</u> is always packed with lots of people.
• Whenever I go <u>there</u>, it makes me feel so great and it means a lot to me.
• In addition, I always end up <u>going there</u> since it's free to visit.

암기문장 쉐도잉

묘사의 본론(장소 묘사 문장 : **독립공간**)의 쉐도잉 연습을 하세요.

🎧 MP3 IM3-AL_27~46

5단계 : 반복 학습

위 단계를 반복하여, 영어의 어순으로 된 한글 해석을 보며, 쉐도잉 연습을 합니다.

- 첫 번째로, 건물은 **5**층이고 옥상에 <u>테라스 가든</u>이 있어.
- 첫 번째로, <u>쇼핑몰</u>은 **10**층 건물이야 그래서 확실히 눈에 띄어.
- 있잖아, 이 말은 꼭 해야 해 가장 큰 건물이라고 도심에서 그리고 <u>ABC 타워</u>라고 불려.
- 사실상, 가장 유명한 <u>쇼핑센터</u>야 <u>도심 중앙</u>에 위치해 있어.
- 네가 상상하듯, 1층에는, <u>리셉션 데스크</u>가 있어 그리고 넌 필요해 <u>ID 카드</u>가 들어가기 위해서.
- 또한, 2층부터 4층에는, 많은 <u>명품 가게들</u>이 있어.
- 추가로, 9층에는, 헬스장이 있어 내가 <u>운동하는</u>.
- 네가 예상하듯, 마지막 층에는, <u>커피숍</u>과 <u>아늑한 바</u>가 있어 네가 <u>쉴 수 있는</u>.
- 우리 집에 대해서 말한다면, 우리 집엔 <u>안방</u>, 3개의 방, 그리고 **2**개의 화장실이 있어.
- 네가 그곳에 가면, 통틀어, 넌 찾을 수 있어 **50**개가 넘는 <u>ATM 기계들</u>을.
- 첫 번째로 내가 보는 것은 <u>평면 TV</u>와 <u>아늑한 소파</u>야.
- 가장 흥미로운 부분은 <u>이 지역</u>에 대해서, 모든 것들은 자동화되어 있어.
- 있잖아, <u>스마트 도어락</u>이 있어서 엄청 편해.
- 일반적으로, 중앙난방과 에어컨 시스템이 있어 그래서 여름에 시원하고 겨울에 따뜻해.
- 당연하지만, 사람들은 쉽게 <u>엔지니어</u>를 부를 수 있어 만약 <u>엘리베이터</u>가 작동을 안 한다면.
- 내 말은, 객실은 엄청 깨끗해, 그리고 사람들은 엄청 친절해 그게 <u>내가 그곳에 가는</u> 이유야.
- 하지만 있잖아, 항상 가득 차 있어 사람들로, 그래서 난 선호해 가는 것을 <u>아침 일찍</u>.
- 들어가면, 넌 아마 볼 거야 <u>내 동생</u>을 소파에만 누워있는.
- 글쎄, 난 항상 주문해 <u>라테</u>를 <u>아침</u>에 하지만 가끔은 난 기다려야 해 긴 줄을.
- 살을 빼기 위해서, 난 <u>뛰어 러닝머신</u>을 매일.

암기문장 쉐도잉

묘사의 본론(**일반적 묘사 문장**)의 쉐도잉 연습을 하세요.

🎧 MP3 IM3-AL_47~56

1단계 : 사전학습

문장을 들은 후, 주어진 암기문장을 억양, 강세를 고려하여 큰소리로 읽습니다.

- **IM3-AL_47** • When it comes to my friend, I spend lots of time with <u>John</u> and I've known <u>him</u> since I was <u>10</u>.
- **IM3-AL_48** • Actually, <u>he</u> knows a lot about <u>music</u>, so he is <u>a great person</u> to go with.
- **IM3-AL_49** • In order to prepare for summer, I spend lots of time <u>at the gym</u> because I need to <u>lose weight</u>.
- **IM3-AL_50** • Moreover, I really enjoy <u>watching</u> all kinds of <u>movies</u> because it helps me release stress.
- **IM3-AL_51** • You know, I'm pretty sure that I can get a discount since I got <u>a membership card</u>.
- **IM3-AL_52** • As you can imagine, <u>recycling</u> is <u>mandatory</u> in Korea and people recycle trash such as paper, glass, metal and etcetera.
- **IM3-AL_53** • When I was young, I used to <u>wear something casual,</u> but now, I <u>wear something formal</u>.
- **IM3-AL_54** • The main reason why I like to stay at home is that I can <u>spend time alone</u>.
- **IM3-AL_55** • To be honest, I don't know why, but I kinda feel like <u>drinking</u>.
- **IM3-AL_56** • I mean, most <u>Koreans</u> are using it since it's getting increasingly popular.

2단계 : 딕테이션

문장을 들은 후, 밑줄 친 부분을 적습니다.

- **When it comes to my friend,** I spend lots of time with _____ and I've known _____ since I was _____.
- **Actually,** ___ knows a lot about _____, so he is _____ to go with.
- **In order to prepare for summer,** I spend lots of time _____ because I need to _____.
- **Moreover,** I really enjoy _____ all kinds of _____ because it helps me release stress.
- **You know,** I'm pretty sure that I can get a discount since I got _____.
- **As you can imagine,** _____ is _____ in Korea and people recycle trash such as paper, glass, metal and etcetera.
- **When I was young,** I used to _____, but now, I _____.
- **The main reason why I like to stay at home** is that I can _____.
- **To be honest,** I don't know why, but I kinda feel like _____.
- **I mean,** most _____ are using it since it's getting increasingly popular.

3단계 : 문장 끊어 읽기

문장을 들은 후, 청크 단위로 끊어 읽어 봅니다.

- **When it comes to my friend,** / I spend lots of time with <u>John</u> and / I've known <u>him</u> since I was <u>10</u>.
- **Actually,** / <u>he</u> knows a lot about <u>music,</u> so / he is <u>a great person</u> to go with.
- **In order to prepare for summer,** / I spend lots of time <u>at the gym</u> because / I need to <u>lose weight</u>.
- **Moreover,** / I really enjoy <u>watching</u> all kinds of <u>movies</u> because / it helps me release stress.
- **You know,** / I'm pretty sure that / I can get a discount since / I got <u>a membership card</u>.
- **As you can imagine,** / <u>recycling</u> is <u>mandatory</u> in Korea and / people recycle trash such as / paper, glass, metal and etcetera.
- **When I was young,** / I used to <u>wear something casual,</u> but now, / I <u>wear something formal</u>.
- **The main reason why I** / like to stay at home is that I can / <u>spend time alone</u>.
- **To be honest,** / I don't know why, but I kinda feel like / <u>drinking</u>.
- **I mean,** / most <u>Koreans</u> are using it since it's getting / increasingly popular.

암기문장 쉐도잉

묘사의 본론(**일반적 묘사 문장**)의 쉐도잉 연습을 하세요.

🎧 **MP3 IM3-AL_47~56**

4단계 : 전체 문장 읽기

문장을 들은 후, 3단계를 여러 번 반복한 후, 전체 문장을 한숨에 읽어 봅니다.

- When it comes to my friend, I spend lots of time with <u>John</u> and I've known <u>him</u> since I was <u>10</u>.
- Actually, <u>he</u> knows a lot about <u>music</u>, so he is <u>a great person</u> to go with.
- In order to prepare for summer, I spend lots of time <u>at the gym</u> because I need to <u>lose weight</u>.
- Moreover, I really enjoy <u>watching</u> all kinds of <u>movies</u> because it helps me release stress.
- You know, I'm pretty sure that I can get a discount since I got <u>a membership card</u>.
- As you can imagine, <u>recycling</u> is <u>mandatory</u> in Korea and people recycle trash such as paper, glass, metal and etcetera.
- When I was young, I used to <u>wear something casual</u>, but now, I <u>wear something formal</u>.
- The main reason why I like to stay at home is that I can <u>spend time alone</u>.
- To be honest, I don't know why, but I kinda feel like <u>drinking</u>.
- I mean, most <u>Koreans</u> are using it since it's getting increasingly popular.

5단계 : 반복 학습

위 단계를 반복하여, 영어의 어순으로 된 한글 해석을 보며, 쉐도잉 연습을 합니다.

- 내 친구에 대해서 말한다면, 난 많은 시간을 보내 <u>John</u>과 그리고 난 <u>그</u>를 알아 <u>10살</u>부터.
- 사실, <u>그</u>는 많이 알아 <u>음악</u>에 대해서, 그래서 그는 <u>좋은 사람</u>이야 같이 가기.
- 여름을 준비하기 위해서, 난 많은 시간을 보내 <u>헬스장</u>에서 왜냐하면 난 <u>살을 빼야 해</u>.
- 게다가, 난 정말 즐겨 모든 종류의 <u>영화를 보는 것</u>을 왜냐하면 스트레스를 풀 수 있거든.
- 있잖아, 난 확실해 할인을 받을 수 있는 것을 왜냐하면 난 <u>멤버십 카드</u>가 있거든.
- 네가 예상하듯, <u>재활용</u>은 <u>필수</u>야 한국에선 그리고 사람들은 재활용을 해 종이, 유리, 금속 등등을.
- 내가 어렸을 때, 난 하곤 했었어 <u>입는 것</u>을 캐주얼 한 옷을, 근데 지금은 난 <u>정장을 입어</u>.
- 내가 왜 집에 있는 가장 큰 이유는 난 <u>혼자 시간을 보낼 수 있거든</u>.
- 솔직히 말해서, 나도 잘 몰라, 근데 난 <u>술 마시는 것</u>을 하고 싶어.
- 내 말은, 대부분의 <u>한국사람</u>은 사용해 왜냐하면 엄청나게 유명해지고 있거든.

4강

유형 01 (묘사)

리스닝 훈련

묘사 질문 리스트

진짜녀석들 OPIc의 3가지 묘사(장소, 일반적 묘사) 질문들의 MP3를 듣고 키워드 캐치를 훈련하세요.

개방공간

You indicated in the survey that you like to go to **the beach.** Describe your favorite beach for me. Where is it? What does it look like? How often do you visit that beach? Please tell me in detail.

You indicated in the survey that you go on **international trips.** I would like you to describe one of the countries or cities you usually visit. What does the place look like? Why do you like to visit there? How are the people like there? Please tell me in detail.

You indicated in the survey that you go to **the parks** with your friends. Please tell me about one of the parks that you usually visit. Where is it located? What does it look like? Please describe your favorite park in detail.

I would like you to describe **the geography of your country.** Are there mountains, lakes or rivers? Please describe the geographical features of your country in as much detail as possible.

I would like to ask you about **a country that is nearby your country.** What is the name of that country? What is special about that country? How are the people there? Please give me all the details.

독립공간

You indicated in the survey that you go to cafes or coffee shops. What cafes or coffee shops are there in your neighborhood? Which café do you like to go to and why? Please describe one of your favorite cafes in detail.

I would like to ask you about your **favorite shopping mall.** Where is it located and what does it look like? Describe one of your favorite shopping malls in as much detail as possible.

A lot of people like to eat out during the weekends. I would like to know **one of your favorite restaurants** in your area. Where is it located? What does it look like? Also, what kind of food do they serve and why do you like to visit there? Please tell me in detail.

I would like to ask you where you live. Please describe your **house** in detail. What does it look like? How many rooms are there? Also, which room is your favorite room and why?

I would like to ask you about **the banks** in your country. What do they typically look like? Where are they usually located? Please tell me about the banks in your country.

일반적 묘사

What do people normally **do on the Internet?** Do they play games, listen to music, or watch movies? Please tell me about the things people do online.

I would like to know **what you like most about your cell phone.** Maybe you like the camera or other functions. Tell me why you like these kinds of features.

I would like to ask you about **how recycling is practiced** in your country. What do people especially do? Please tell me about all the different kinds of items that you recycle.

How do people in your country move around? **What types of transportation** do people usually use? Why do they use those types of transportation? Please tell me how people move around.

Please tell me about **some holidays in your country.** What do people in your country do to celebrate these holidays? Please tell me about some holidays in your country.

I would like you to **describe one of your family members or friends.** What is he or she like? What is special about that person?

I'd like you to describe **a healthy person you know of.** Who is he or she? What makes that person healthy? Why do you think that way? Please tell me everything about the things that make that person healthy.

I would like to ask you about **how people in your country dress.** What kind of clothes do they wear? Tell me about fashion styles in your country in as much detail as possible.

Please tell me about **the weather and seasons in your country.** What is the weather like in each season? Which season do you like? Please tell me in detail.

장소 묘사 - 개방공간

진짜녀석들 OPIc의 3가지 묘사(장소, 일반적 묘사) 질문들의 MP3를 듣고 키워드 캐치를 훈련하세요.

서베이 / 해변

🎧 MP3 IM3-AL_Q_1

자주가는 해변 묘사

You indicated in the survey that you like to go to the beach. Describe your favorite beach for me. Where is it? What does it look like? How often do you visit that beach? Please tell me in detail.

/ KEYWORD

서베이 / 여행

🎧 MP3 IM3-AL_Q_2

자주가는 해외여행지 묘사

You indicated in the survey that you go on international trips. I would like you to describe one of the countries or cities you usually visit. What does the place look like? Why do you like to visit there? How are the people like there? Please tell me in detail.

/ KEYWORD

서베이 / 공원

🎧 MP3 IM3-AL_Q_3

자주가는 공원 묘사

You indicated in the survey that you go to the parks with your friends. Please tell me about one of the parks that you usually visit. Where is it located? What does it look like? Please describe your favorite park in detail.

/ KEYWORD

돌발 / 지리

🎧 MP3 IM3-AL_Q_4

우리나라의 지리적 특징 묘사

I would like you to describe the geography of your country. Are there mountains, lakes or rivers? Please describe the geographical features of your country in as much detail as possible.

/ KEYWORD

돌발 / 이웃국가

🎧 MP3 IM3-AL_Q_5

이웃 국가 묘사

I would like to ask you about a country that is nearby your country. What is the name of that country? What is special about that country? How are the people there? Please give me all the details.

/ KEYWORD

장소 묘사 - 독립공간

진짜녀석들 OPIc의 3가지 묘사(장소, 일반적 묘사) 질문들의 MP3를 듣고 키워드 캐치를 훈련하세요.

MP3 IM3-AL_Q_6

서베이 / 커피숍

커피숍 묘사

You indicated in the survey that you go to cafes or coffee shops. What cafes or coffee shops are there in your neighborhood? Which café do you like to go to and why? Please describe one of your favorite cafes in detail.

/ KEYWORD

MP3 IM3-AL_Q_7

서베이 / 쇼핑

쇼핑몰 묘사

I would like to ask you about your favorite shopping mall. Where is it located and what does it look like? Describe one of your favorite shopping malls in as much detail as possible.

/ KEYWORD

MP3 IM3-AL_Q_8

돌발 / 레스토랑

레스토랑 묘사

A lot of people like to eat out during the weekends. I would like to know one of your favorite restaurants in your area. Where is it located? What does it look like? Also, what kind of food do they serve and why do you like to visit there? Please tell me in detail.

/ KEYWORD

MP3 IM3-AL_Q_9

서베이 / 집

집 묘사

I would like to ask you where you live. Please describe your house in detail. What does it look like? How many rooms are there? Also, which room is your favorite room and why?

/ KEYWORD

MP3 IM3-AL_Q_10

돌발 / 은행

은행 묘사

I would like to ask you about the banks in your country. What do they typically look like? Where are they usually located? Please tell me about the banks in your country.

/ KEYWORD

일반적 묘사

진짜녀석들 OPIc의 3가지 묘사(장소, 일반적 묘사) 질문들의 MP3를 듣고 키워드 캐치를 훈련하세요.

| 돌발 / 인터넷 | **MP3 IM3-AL_Q_11** |

인터넷 활동 묘사

What do people normally do on the Internet? Do they play games, listen to music, or watch movies? Please tell me about the things people do online.

/ KEYWORD

| 돌발 / 전화기 | **MP3 IM3-AL_Q_12** |

전화기 묘사

I would like to know what you like most about your cell phone. Maybe you like the camera or other functions. Tell me why you like these kinds of features.

/ KEYWORD

| 돌발 / 재활용 | **MP3 IM3-AL_Q_13** |

재활용 묘사

I would like to ask you about how recycling is practiced in your country. What do people especially do? Please tell me about all the different kinds of items that you recycle.

/ KEYWORD

| 돌발 / 교통 | **MP3 IM3-AL_Q_14** |

교통수단 묘사

How do people in your country move around? What types of transportation do people usually use? Why do they use those types of transportation? Please tell me how people move around.

/ KEYWORD

| 돌발 / 휴일 | **MP3 IM3-AL_Q_15** |

휴일 활동 묘사

Please tell me about some holidays in your country. What do people in your country do to celebrate these holidays? Please tell me about some holidays in your country.

/ KEYWORD

일반적 묘사

진짜녀석들 OPIc의 3가지 묘사(장소, 일반적 묘사) 질문들의 MP3를 듣고 키워드 캐치를 훈련하세요.

🎧 MP3 IM3-AL_Q_16

돌발 / 가족,친구

가족 혹은 친구 묘사

I would like you to describe one of your family members or friends. What is he or she like? What is special about that person?

/ KEYWORD

🎧 MP3 IM3-AL_Q_17

돌발 / 건강

건강한 사람 묘사

I'd like you to describe a healthy person you know of. Who is he or she? What makes that person healthy? Why do you think that way? Please tell me everything about the things that make that person healthy.

/ KEYWORD

🎧 MP3 IM3-AL_Q_18

돌발 / 패션

우리나라 패션 묘사

I would like to ask you about how people in your country dress. What kind of clothes do they wear? Tell me about fashion styles in your country in as much detail as possible.

/ KEYWORD

🎧 MP3 IM3-AL_Q_19

돌발 / 날씨

우리나라 날씨 묘사

Please tell me about the weather and seasons in your country. What is the weather like in each season? Which season do you like? Please tell me in detail.

/ KEYWORD

5강

유형 01 (묘사)

스크립트 훈련1

2번

5번

8번

개방공간 묘사 자주 가는 해변 묘사

Q1 ———— 🎧 MP3 IM3-AL_Q_1

You indicated in the survey that you like to go to **the beach.** Describe your favorite beach for me. Where is it? What does it look like? How often do you visit that beach? Please tell me in detail.

당신은 해변에 가는 것을 좋아한다고 했습니다. 당신이 자주 방문하는 해변을 묘사해주세요. 어디에 있죠? 어떻게 생겼습니까? 그 해변에 얼마나 자주 방문하죠? 상세히 말해주세요.

————————————————————————————— 🎧 MP3 IM3-AL_A_1

서론 / 시작문장/10%

- <u>That's</u> a good question, *my favorite <u>beach</u>?* Sure, I <u>usually</u> visit ABC beach with my friends.

본론 / 단락별 핵심문장/80%

- **When it comes to** my <u>favorite</u> beach, it has to be <u>ABC</u> beach and it's like <u>2</u>km from where I live.
  - <u>Actually</u>, ABC beach is undeniably <u>beautiful</u>, and as you can <u>expect</u>, the water is crystal clear.

- Well, night is the <u>perfect</u> time to visit the beach.
  - <u>Oh</u>! I must say that the night beach is kinda <u>romantic</u> and that's why the place is famous for <u>couples</u>.
  - So, I suppose I tend to visit there a <u>few</u> times a month.

- **Lastly,** the beach is a <u>perfect</u> spot for just sitting and <u>relaxing</u>.
  - So I <u>strongly</u> recommend you visit there with your boyfriend, Eva.

결론 / 마무리문장/10%

- **So overall,** this is about *my <u>favorite</u> beach.*

- 좋은 질문이야, **내가 좋아하는 해변?** 물론이지, 난 내 친구들과 함께 ABC 공원에 보통 가.

- 내가 좋아하는 해변에 대해서 말한다면, ABC 해변임에 틀림없어. 그리고 내가 사는 곳에서 2km 정도 떨어져 있어.
  - 사실, ABC 해변은 정말 아름다워, 그리고 네가 예상했듯이, 물은 크리스탈처럼 맑아.

- 음, 밤은 해변을 가기에 완벽한 때야.
  - 오! 밤에 해변은 로맨틱하다는 것을 말해야 되는데, 이게 커플들에게 그 장소가 인기 있는 이유야.
  - 그래서 나는 한 달에 몇 번씩 거기에 가곤 해.

- 마지막으로, 해변은 그냥 앉아서 쉬기에 완벽한 장소야.
  - 그래서 나는 네가 남자친구와 거기에 방문하기를 강력하게 추천해, 에바야.

- 그래서 전반적으로, 이게 **내가 좋아하는 해변**에 대한 이야기야.

어휘 및 표현

my favorite beach 내가 좋아하는 해변   **When it comes to** ~에 대해서 말한다면   **it has to be ~** ~이어야만 해   **undeniably** 명백하게
as you can expect 네가 예상하듯   **tend to** ~하는 경향이 있다   **I strongly recommend you visit there** 그곳을 방문할 것을 강력히 추천해

개방공간 묘사 자주 가는 해외여행지 묘사

Q2 ─────────────────────────────── 🎧 MP3 IM3-AL_Q_2

You indicated in the survey that you go on **international trips.** I would like you to describe one of the countries or cities you usually visit. What does the place look like? Why do you like to visit there? How are the people like there? Please tell me in detail.

당신은 해외여행 가는 것을 좋아한다고 했습니다. 당신이 자주 방문하는 나라 혹은 도시 중 한 곳을 묘사해주세요. 어떻게 생겼습니까? 왜 그 곳을 방문하는 것을 좋아하세요? 그곳의 사람들은 어떤가요? 상세히 말해주세요.

🎧 MP3 IM3-AL_A_2

서론
시작문장/10%

본론
단락별 핵심문장/80%

• Well, *international trips?* You know, I like to visit <u>Hawaii</u> since it's a <u>beautiful</u> place.

• **Speaking of Hawaii,** it's a <u>perfect</u> spot for vacations.
  - So, I <u>suppose</u> I tend to visit there once or twice a year.
  - <u>Actually,</u> the beaches in <u>Hawaii</u> are undeniably <u>beautiful</u>, and the water is crystal clear.

• **Whenever I visit there,** I can see bunch of <u>people</u> swimming and <u>tanning</u> at the beach.
  - Not only <u>that</u>, I can see <u>lots</u> of people do <u>many</u> kinds of things such as playing <u>sports</u>, listening to <u>music</u> and stuff like that.

• The <u>main</u> reason why I like to visit Hawaii is that I can spend time <u>alone</u>.
  - <u>Seriously,</u> I prefer to go to the beach in Hawaii at <u>night</u> since I can enjoy the <u>peace</u> and quiet.

결론
마무리문장/10%

• Alright Eva, this is <u>all</u> I can say about *the <u>country</u> that I <u>usually</u> visit.* Thank you.

• 음, **해외여행?** 있잖아, 난 하와이에 방문하는 것을 좋아하는데 아름다운 장소이기 때문이야.

• 하와이에 대해 말해본다면, 거기는 휴가를 보내기에 완벽한 장소야.
  - 그래서, 나는 일 년에 한두 번씩은 거기에 가곤 해.
  - 사실, 하와이에 있는 해변들은 정말 아름답고, 물은 크리스탈처럼 깨끗해.

• 내가 거기에 갈 때마다, 해변에서 수영하고 태닝하는 많은 사람들을 볼 수 있어.
  - 그뿐만 아니라, 나는 많은 사람들이 스포츠, 음악 듣기와 같은 많은 종류의 활동을 하고 있는 것을 볼 수 있어.

• 내가 하와이를 방문하는 가장 큰 이유는 혼자 시간을 보낼 수 있기 때문이야.
  - 진짜 나는 하와이 해변을 밤에 가는 것을 좋아해 왜냐하면 평화로움과 조용함을 즐길 수 있거든.

• 그래. 에바, 이게 **내가 보통 방문하는 나라**에 대한 전부야. 고마워.

어휘 및 표현
international trips 해외여행   once or twice a year 일년에 1-2번   swimming and tanning at the beach. 해변에서 수영하고 태닝하는 것
Not only that ~뿐만 아니라

개방공간 묘사 자주 가는 공원 묘사

Q3

🎧 MP3 IM3-AL_Q_3

You indicated in the survey that you go to **the parks** with your friends. Please tell me about one of the parks that you usually visit. Where is it located? What does it look like? Please describe your favorite park in detail.

당신은 공원 가는 것을 좋아한다고 했습니다. 당신이 자주 방문하는 공원에 대해 말해주세요. 어디에 있나요? 어떻게 생겼습니까? 좋아하는 공원에 대해 자세히 묘사해주세요.

🎧 MP3 IM3-AL_A_3

서론
시작문장/10%

- Oh yeah, *my favorite park?* You know, I <u>usually</u> visit the park in my <u>neighborhood</u>.

본론
단락별 핵심문장/80%

- Well, I'm <u>pretty</u> sure that the park is around <u>20</u>-minutes away from my place.
  - So, I suppose I tend to visit there <u>three</u> to four times a week.
  - <u>Seriously</u>, I <u>prefer</u> to go to the park at night since I can <u>enjoy</u> the peace and <u>quiet</u>.

- <u>Also,</u> there is a <u>huge</u> running track where you can see <u>lots</u> of people exercising.
  - So, when I'm stressed <u>out</u>, I go and run with them.
  - I guess it's the <u>perfect</u> way to release stress.

- In fact, I've <u>always</u> lived in a very quiet area, so that's <u>why</u> I love to spend time at the park.
  - In my <u>opinion</u>, getting back to nature, just relaxing outside is <u>essential</u> for human beings.

결론
마무리문장/10%

- Well, okay Eva, this is <u>pretty</u> much about *my favorite park.*

- -

- 오 예, 내가 제일 좋아하는 **공원?** 있잖아, 난 동네에 있는 공원에 보통 가.

- 음, 공원은 우리 집에서 대략 20분 정도에 있어.
  - 그래서, 일주일에 3-4번 거기에 방문하곤 해.
  - 솔직히, 나는 밤에 공원 가는 것 좋아하는데 왜냐하면 평화로움과 조용함을 즐길 수 있거든.

- 또한, 큰 러닝트랙이 있어서 많은 사람들이 운동하는 것을 볼 수 있어.
  - 그래서 내가 스트레스 받을 때, 나는 가서 사람들과 함께 뛰어.
  - 난 그게 스트레스를 해소할 수 있는 최선의 방법인 것 같아.

- 사실, 난 항상 조용한 곳에서 살아왔어 그래서 내가 공원에서 시간을 보내는 것을 좋아하는 이유야
  - 내 의견으로는, 자연으로 돌아가는 것과 밖에서 쉬는 것은 사람들에게 필수적이야.

- 음, 오케이 에바야, 이게 **내가 좋아하는 공원**이야.

어휘 및 표현
around 20-minutes away from my place 우리 집에서 약 20분 거리   three to four times a week 한 주에 3-4번   when I'm stressed out 내가 스트레스 받을 때   it's the perfect way to release stress 스트레스 풀기 가장 좋은 방법이야   is essential for ~에 필수적이다

개방공간 묘사 우리나라의 지리적 특징 묘사

Q4 ────────────────── 🎧 MP3 IM3-AL_Q_4

I would like you to describe **the geography of your country.** Are there mountains, lakes or rivers? Please describe the geographical features of your country in as much detail as possible.

나는 당신이 당신 나라의 지리에 대해 묘사하길 원합니다. 산, 호수, 강이 있나요? 당신 나라의 지리적 특징을 가능한 상세히 묘사해주세요.

🎧 MP3 IM3-AL_A_4

서론
시작문장/10%

- Oh yeah, *the geography of my country?*
  - You know, Korea is a peninsula, so it is surrounded by water to the south, east and west.

본론
단락별 핵심문장/80%

- As I just mentioned before, Korea is a peninsula and that means there are lots of beaches in Korea.
  - You know, the beaches in Korea are undeniably beautiful, and the water is crystal clear.
  - Well, summer is the perfect time to go to the beaches since you can do many things.

- Secondly, there are lots of mountains since Korea is a mountainous country.
  - Seriously, people prefer to go to the mountains since they can enjoy the peace and quiet.

- Also, there are lots of parks in Korea.
  - Speaking of parks, they are perfect spots for just sitting and relaxing.
  - Well, I guess most people go there to walk or run.

결론
마무리문장/10%

- Well, okay Eva, this is pretty much about *the geography of my country.*

- -

- 오 예, **우리나라의 지리?**
  - 있잖아, 한국은 반도이고, 그래서 남쪽, 동쪽 그리고 서쪽은 바다로 둘러싸여 있어.

- 내가 전에도 언급했듯이, 한국은 반도이고 그것은 한국에는 해변이 많다는 것을 의미해.
  - 있잖아, 한국에 있는 해변은 정말 아름답고 물은 크리스탈처럼 맑아.
  - 음. 여름은 해변에 가기에 완벽한 때야 왜냐하면 내가 거기에 가서 많은 것들을 할 수 있기 때문이야.

- 두 번째로, 한국은 산이 많은 나라야.
  - 솔직히, 사람들은 평화로움과 조용함을 즐기기 때문에 산에 가는 것을 좋아해.

- 또한, 한국에는 많은 공원들이 있어.
  - 공원에 대해 말해본다면, 공원은 그냥 앉아서 쉬기에 완벽한 장소야.
  - 음, 대부분의 사람들이 걷거나 뛰기 위해 공원에 가.

- 음, 오케이 에바, 이 정도면 **우리나라의 지리**에 대해 꽤 많이 말한 것 같아.

어휘 및 표현
the geography of my country 우리나라 지리   **Korea is a peninsula** 한국은 반도야   **is surrounded by water** 바다로 둘러싸여 있어
Korea is a mountainous country 한국은 산이 많은 나라야

개방공간 묘사 이웃 국가 묘사

Q5 ———

🎧 MP3 IM3-AL_Q_5

I would like to ask you about **a country that is nearby your country.** What is the name of that country? What is special about that country? How are the people there? Please give me all the details.

당신 나라와 가까운 나라에 대해 말해봅시다. 그 나라의 이름은 무엇인가요? 그 나라에 대해 특별한 점은 무엇인가요? 그 나라 사람들은 어떤 가요? 상세히 말해주세요.

🎧 MP3 IM3-AL_A_5

서론
시작문장/10%

- That's a good question, *a country that is nearby my country?* Sure, it's gotta be Thailand.

본론
단락별 핵심문장/80%

- When it comes to Thailand, it's like 600km away from Korea.
  - Well, I guess summer is the perfect time to visit Thailand and do some outdoor activities.
  - You know, people do many kinds of things in Thailand such as playing sports, swimming and stuff like that.

- Also, the shopping malls in Thailand are very famous for the tourists since it's very cheap.
  - However, all you need to know is that the shopping malls are always packed with lots of people.

- Speaking of the beach in Thailand, it's a perfect spot for just relaxing while looking at the beautiful beach view.
  - Whenever I go there, it makes me feel so great and it means a lot to me.

결론
마무리문장/10%

- So overall, this is about *a country that is nearby my country.*

- -

- 좋은 질문이야, **우리나라와 가까운 나라?** 물론, 그건 태국이야.

- 태국에 대해서 말한다면, 한국에서 600km 떨어져 있어.
  - 음, 여름은 태국을 방문하기에 완벽한 때이고 야외 활동을 할 수 있어.
  - 있잖아, 사람들은 태국에서 많은 것들을 해 예를 들어 운동, 수영과 같은 것들이 있어.

- 또한, 태국에 있는 쇼핑몰은 여행자들한테 매우 유명한데, 거기는 매우 싸기 때문이야.
  - 하지만, 중요한 점은 쇼핑몰이 많은 사람들로 항상 가득 차 있다는 거야.

- 태국 해변에 대해 말해본다면, 아름다운 해변 풍경을 보면서 그냥 쉬기에 완벽한 장소라는 거야.
  - 내가 거기에 갈 때마다, 난 기분이 정말 좋아지고, 그것은 나에게 많은 의미가 있어.

- 그래서 전반적으로, 이 정도가 **우리나라와 가까운 나라**에 대한 거야.

어휘 및 표현

a country that is nearby my country 우리나라와 가까운 나라   **it's gotta be Thailand** 태국이어야만 해

it's like 600km away 대략 600km 정도야   **since it's very cheap** 엄청 저렴하기 때문에   **beautiful beach view** 아름다운 해변 경치

독립공간 묘사 커피숍 묘사

Q6 ────────── 🎧 MP3 IM3-AL_Q_6

You indicated in the survey that you go to **cafes or coffee shops.** What cafes or coffee shops are there in your neighborhood? Which café do you like to go to and why? Please describe one of your favorite cafes in detail.

당신은 카페 혹은 커피숍에 간다고 했습니다. 당신 동네에 어떤 카페 혹은 커피숍이 있나요? 어떤 커피숍을 좋아하며 이유는 무엇인가요? 당신이 좋아하는 카페 중 한 곳을 묘사해주세요.

🎧 MP3 IM3-AL_A_6

서론
시작문장/10%

• Oh yeah, *my favorite coffee shop?* You know, it's gotta be Starbucks in my neighborhood.

본론
단락별 핵심문장/80%

• First of all, this Starbucks has 7 floors and a terrace garden.
  - I mean, it is unlike any other Starbucks in the world as it has 7 floors.
  - Well, I always order Latte in the morning but sometimes I need to stand in a long line.

• As you can expect, on the top floor, there is a terrace garden where you can chill.
  - I mean, the terrace garden is extremely clean, and the staff there are so friendly and that's why I love to go there.
  - Plus, I must say that the garden is such a romantic spot and that's why the place is famous for couples.

• In my opinion, people go to coffee shops to get rid of stress.
  - I mean, they can talk, laugh and enjoy their coffee after doing a stressful day at work.

결론
마무리문장/10%

• Well, okay Eva, this is pretty much about *my favorite coffee shop.*

• 오 예, **내가 제일 좋아하는 커피숍?** 있잖아, 그건 우리 동네에 있는 스타벅스야.

• 첫 번째로, 이 스타벅스는 7개의 층과 테라스 정원이 있어.
  - 내 말은, 7개 층이 있기 때문에 전 세계에 있는 다른 스타벅스와는 달라.
  - 음, 난 아침에 항상 라테를 주문해 하지만 가끔 긴 줄을 서야 할 필요가 있긴 해.

• 네가 예상했듯이, 꼭대기 층에는 네가 바람을 쐴 수 있는 테라스 정원이 있어.
  - 내 말은, 테라스 공원은 정말 깨끗하고 거기에 있는 스텝들은 정말 친절하고 그게 내가 거기에 가는 것을 좋아하는 이유야.
  - 추가로, 정원은 정말 로맨틱한 장소라고 말할 수 있어 그리고 그곳이 커플들한테 유명한 이유야.

• 내 생각은, 사람들은 스트레스를 없애기 위해 커피숍을 가.
  - 내 말은, 사람들은 업무에 지친 스트레스 받는 날에 와서 이야기하고 웃고 커피를 즐길 수 있어.

• 음, 오케이 에바, 이게 **내가 좋아하는 커피숍**에 대한 이야기야.

어휘 및 표현
in my neighborhood 우리 동네에 있는   it's unlike any other Starbucks 다른 스타벅스와는 다르게   as it has 7 floors 7층으로 되어있기 때문에
romantic spot 로맨틱한 장소   get rid of stress 스트레스를 없애다   after a stressful day at work 업무로부터 힘들었던 하루 끝에

독립공간 묘사 쇼핑몰 묘사

Q7

🎧 MP3 IM3-AL_Q_7

I would like to ask you about your **favorite shopping mall.** Where is it located and what does it look like? Describe one of your favorite shopping malls in as much detail as possible.

당신이 좋아하는 쇼핑몰에 대해 묻고 싶습니다. 어디에 있나요? 어떻게 생겼나요? 당신이 좋아하는 쇼핑몰 중 한 곳에 대해 상세히 설명해주세요.

🎧 MP3 IM3-AL_A_7

서론
시작문장/10%

본론
단락별 핵심문장/80%

결론
마무리문장/10%

- Well, *my favorite shopping mall?* You know, let me say, I'm a shopaholic.

- When it comes to my favorite shopping mall, it's like 10km from where I live.
  - You know, I must say that it's the tallest building in the city and it's called the ABC shopping mall.
  - Whenever I go there, it makes me feel so great and can't stop spending money at that mall.

- As you can imagine, on the first floor, you can find lots of cosmetics and perfumes.
  - Obviously, the cosmetic shops are always filled with lots of people since wearing makeup is common in Korea.
  - Also, second to fourth floors, there are lots of luxury stores.

- As you can expect, on the top floor, there is a coffee shop and a cozy bar where you can chill.
  - So, I sometimes visit there after shopping.

- Alright Eva, this is all I can say about *my favorite shopping mall.* Thank you.

- -

- **음, 내가 제일 좋아하는 쇼핑몰?** 있잖아, 내가 말해볼게, 난 거의 쇼핑중독자야.

- 내가 가장 좋아하는 쇼핑몰에 대해서 말한다면, 내가 사는 곳에서 10km 정도에 있어.
  - 있잖아, 이건 도시에서 가장 큰 건물이고 ABC 쇼핑몰이라고 해.
  - 내가 거기에 갈 때마다, 난 기분이 너무 좋고 쇼핑몰에서 돈 쓰는 것을 멈출 수 없어.

- 네가 상상할 수 있듯이, 1층에는, 많은 화장품과 향수가게를 볼 수 있어.
  - 명백히, 화장품 가게는 많은 사람들로 항상 가득 차 있어 왜냐하면 메이크업을 하는 것은 한국에서 흔하거든.
  - 또한, 2층부터 4층까지는, 많은 명품숍들이 있어.

- 네가 예상했듯이, 꼭대기 층에는, 네가 쉴 수 있는 바람을 쐴 수 있는 커피숍과 안락한 바가 있어.
  - 그래서, 난 쇼핑 후에 때때로 거기에 방문해.

- 그래 에바, 이게 **내가 좋아하는 쇼핑몰**에 대해 모두 말한 거야. 고마워.

어휘 및 표현

shopaholic 쇼핑중독   **can't stop spending money at that mall** 쇼핑몰에서 돈 쓰는 것을 멈출 수 없어   **lots of cosmetics and perfumes**
많은 화장품과 향수들   **wearing a makeup is common in Korea** 메이크업을 하는 것은 한국에서 흔해   **after shopping** 쇼핑 후에

독립공간 묘사 레스토랑 묘사

Q8 ———————————————————————— 🎧 MP3 IM3-AL_Q_8

A lot of people like to eat out during the weekends. I would like to know **one of your favorite restaurants** in your area. Where is it located? What does it look like? Also, what kind of food do they serve and why do you like to visit there? Please tell me in detail.

많은 사람들은 주말에 외식을 합니다. 당신이 좋아하는 레스토랑 중 한 곳을 알고 싶습니다. 어디에 있나요? 어떻게 생겼나요? 또한, 어떤 음식을 팔며, 그곳에 가는 이유는 무엇입니까? 상세히 설명해주세요.

🎧 MP3 IM3-AL_A_8

서론
시작문장/10%
본론
단락별 핵심문장/80%

- **Oh yeah,** *one of my favorite <u>restaurants</u>?* You know, it's gotta be ABC Korean <u>BBQ</u> restaurant.

- **Well,** I'm <u>pretty</u> sure that the restaurant is around <u>10</u>-minutes away from my <u>work</u>.
  - And <u>that</u> means, I go there quite <u>often</u> with my friends.
  - You know, they serve <u>good</u> food, and the price is quite <u>affordable</u>.

- **The <u>main</u> reason why I like visit that restaurant** is that I can get a <u>discount</u> since I'm a <u>regular</u>.
  - Whenever I go there after <u>work</u>, I <u>really</u> enjoy drinking beers because it helps me <u>release</u> stress.

- **In my <u>opinion</u>,** ABC Korean BBQ restaurant is a perfect spot for <u>family</u> dinner.
  - Oh my god! I don't know why, but I <u>kinda</u> feel like drinking.

결론
마무리문장/10%

- **Well, okay Eva,** this is <u>pretty</u> much about *ABC <u>Korean</u> BBQ restaurant.*

- -

- 오 예, **내가 제일 좋아하는 레스토랑 중 한 곳?** 있잖아, 그건 ABC 한국식 BBQ 레스토랑이야.

- 음, 내가 일하는 곳에서 그 레스토랑은 약 10분 정도 거리야.
  - 난 거기에 친구와 함께 종종 가.
  - 있잖아, 거기는 좋은 음식을 제공하고 가격이 꽤 합리적이거든.

- 내가 그 레스토랑에 방문하는 것을 좋아하는 가장 큰 이유는 단골이기 때문에 할인을 받을 수 있기 때문이야.
  - 내가 업무 끝나고 거기에 갈 때마다, 난 맥주 마시는 것을 정말 좋아해 왜냐하면 그건 스트레스 푸는 데 도움이 되기 때문이지.

- 내 생각은, ABC 한국식 BBQ 레스토랑은 가족 저녁식사를 하기에 완벽한 장소야.
  - 이럴 수가! 난 이유를 모르겠지만 지금 술을 먹고 싶어.

- 음, 오케이 에바, 이게 **ABC 한국식 BBQ 레스토랑**에 대한 것이야.

어휘 및 표현
from my work 내가 일하는 곳에서   **And that means~** 그 말은   **quite often** 꽤 종종   **they serve good food** 좋은 음식을 제공해
the price is quite affordable 가격이 꽤 합리적이야   **I'm a regular** 난 단골이야   **after work** 일이 끝나고   **family dinner** 가족 식사

독립공간 묘사 집 묘사

Q9 ───────────────────────

I would like to ask you where you live. Please **describe your house** in detail. What does it look like? How many rooms are there? Also, which room is your favorite room and why?

당신이 사는 곳에 대하여 알고 싶습니다. 집에 대하여 자세하게 묘사해 주세요. 어떻게 생겼나요? 방이 몇 개 있나요? 또한 가장 좋아하는 방은 어디이며 이유는 무엇인가요?

서론
시작문장/10%

본론
단락별 핵심문장/80%

결론
마무리문장/10%

- <u>That's</u> a good question, *where I <u>live</u>?* Sure, let me tell you about my <u>house</u>.

- **You know,** I must say that my <u>apartment</u> is the <u>tallest</u> building in the city.
  - When it comes to my <u>house</u>, our place has <u>five</u> bedrooms, and <u>three</u> baths.
  - Well, I'm <u>pretty</u> sure that my <u>apartment</u> is around <u>5</u>-minutes away from the <u>Seoul</u> station.

- **When you enter the <u>house</u>,** the <u>first</u> thing you can see is a <u>flat</u> screen TV and a <u>cozy</u> couch.
  - As you walk <u>in</u>, you will <u>probably</u> see my sister being a <u>couch</u> potato.

- <u>Speaking</u> of my favorite room, it <u>has</u> to be my bedroom.
  - You know, I <u>recently</u> bought a new bed and it's a <u>perfect</u> spot for just relaxing.

- So <u>overall</u>, this is about *my house.*

- 좋은 질문이야, **내가 사는 곳?** 물론이지, 난 우리 집에 대해 말해줄게.

- 있잖아, 우리 아파트는 도시에서 가장 높은 건물이야.
  - 우리 집에 대해서 말한다면, 5개의 침실과 3개의 화장실이 있어.
  - 음, 우리 아파트는 서울역에서 약 5분 거리야.

- 집에 들어갈 때, 제일 처음 보이는 것은 평면 TV와 안락한 소파야.
  - 네가 걸어 들어오면, 종일 소파에서 TV만 보고 있는 내 여동생을 아마 볼 수 있을 거야.

- 내가 제일 좋아하는 방에 대해 말해본다면, 내 방이지.
  - 있잖아, 난 최근에 새 침대를 샀고 이건 그냥 앉아서 쉬기에 완벽한 장소야.

- 그래서 전반적으로, 이게 **우리 집**에 대한 거야.

어휘 및 표현
where I live 내가 사는 곳   **As you walk in** 네가 걸어 들어오면   **couch potato** 하루 종일 TV만 보는 사람
I recently bought a new bed 난 최근에 새 침대를 샀어

독립공간 묘사 은행 묘사

Q10 ─────────
🎧 MP3 IM3-AL_Q_10

I would like to ask you about **the banks in your country**. What do they typically look like? Where are they usually located? Please tell me about the banks in your country.

당신 나라의 은행에 대해 묻고 싶습니다. 일반적으로 어떻게 생겼나요? 어디에 주로 위치해 있나요? 당신 나라 은행에 대해 상세히 설명해주세요.

🎧 MP3 IM3-AL_A_10

서론
시작문장/10%

- Well, *the banks in my country?* You know, there are lots of banks in Korea.

본론
단락별 핵심문장/80%

- First of all, the banks in Korea normally have 4 floors.
  - As you can imagine, on the first floor, there are lots of ATMs.
  - When you go there, in total, you can find more than 30 ATMs.

- Also, on the second to fourth floors, there are lots of bank tellers.
  - You know, there are always so many people waiting in a long line.
  - So I prefer going to the VIP room where I need an ID card to get in.

- As you can imagine, there is a coffee shop on the top floor.
  - People usually visit there and have some coffee.

결론
마무리문장/10%

- Alright Eva, this is all I can say about *the banks in my country.* Thank you.

- 음, **우리나라에 있는 은행?** 있잖아, 난 한국에는 많은 은행이 있어.

- 첫 번째로, 한국에 있는 은행들은 보통 4층이야
  - 네가 예상했듯이, 첫 번째 층에는 많은 ATM기가 있어.
  - 거기에 가면, 총 30개 이상의 ATM기를 볼 수 있어.

- 또한, 2층부터 4층까지는, 많은 은행원들이 있어.
  - 있잖아, 항상 많은 사람들이 그 앞에 기다리고 있어.
  - 그래서, 난 들어가기 위해 신분증이 필요한 VIP 룸으로 들어가는 것을 선호해.

- 네가 상상할 수 있듯이, 마지막 층에는 커피숍이 있어.
  - 사람들은 거기에 가서, 커피를 마셔.

- 그래 에바, 이게 **우리나라에 있는 은행**에 대한 거야. 고마워.

어휘 및 표현
bank tellers 은행원   so many people waiting in a long line 긴 줄로 기다리고 있는 많은 사람들
VIP room where I need an ID card to get in 들어가기 위해 신분증이 필요한 VIP룸

6강

유형 01 (묘사)

스크립트 훈련2

일반적 묘사 인터넷 활동 묘사

Q11 ————————————————— 🎧 MP3 IM3-AL_Q_11

What do people normally **do on the Internet?** Do they play games, listen to music, or watch movies? Please tell me about the things people do online.

사람들은 인터넷으로 보통 어떤 것들을 하나요? 게임을 하나요? 음악을 듣나요? 혹은 영화를 보나요? 사람들이 인터넷으로 하는 것들에 대해 말해주세요.

🎧 MP3 IM3-AL_A_11

서론
시작문장/10%

- **That's** a good question, *people do <u>lots</u> of things on the Internet!*

본론
단락별 핵심문장/80%

- **Obviously,** <u>most</u> people in the world use the Internet <u>every</u> single day.
  - I mean, can you live <u>without</u> your cell phone for a <u>day</u>?

- **Think** about it. How do you <u>start</u> your day?
  - You know, <u>some</u> people start their day by reading a <u>newspaper</u> on their phone.
  - Or, <u>some</u> people listen to <u>music</u>.

- **Plus,** I <u>always</u> go to a coffee shop and order <u>Latte</u> in the morning but <u>sometimes</u> I need to stand in a <u>long</u> line.
  - So I use an <u>app</u> to order <u>online</u>.

결론
마무리문장/10%

- So <u>overall,</u> this is about *what people <u>normally</u> do on the Internet.*

- -

- 좋은 질문이야, **사람들은 인터넷으로 많은 것들을 해.**

- 명백히, 대부분의 사람들은 매일매일 인터넷을 사용해.
  - 내 말은, 핸드폰 없이 하루도 살 수 있겠어?

- 한번 생각해 봐. 어떻게 하루를 시작하겠어?
  - 있잖아, 몇몇 사람들은 신문을 읽으면서 하루를 시작해.
  - 또는, 몇몇은 음악을 들어.

- 추가로, 난 항상 커피숍에 가서 아침에 라테를 주문해 하지만 때때로 난 긴 줄을 설 필요가 있어.
  - 그래서, 난 온라인으로 주문하기 위해 앱을 사용해.

- 그래서 전반적으로, 이게 **사람들이 보통 인터넷으로 하는 거야.**

어휘 및 표현
do lots of things on the Internet 인터넷으로 많은 것들을 한다   every single day 매일   for a day 하루동안   Think about it 생각해봐
How do you start your day? 하루를 어떻게 시작하나요?   on their phone 핸드폰으로   I use an app to order online
난 온라인으로 주문하기 위해 앱을 사용해   what people normally do on the Internet 사람들이 보통 인터넷으로 하는 것

일반적 묘사 전화기 묘사

Q12 ───────────────────── 🎧 MP3 IM3-AL_Q_12

I would like to know **what you like most about your cell phone.** Maybe you like the camera or other functions. Tell me why you like these kinds of features.

당신의 핸드폰에서 가장 좋아하는 것에 대해 묻고 싶습니다. 아마 카메라 또는 다른 기능들을 좋아하겠지요. 왜 당신이 이러한 종류의 기능들을 좋아하는지 말해 주세요.

─────────────────────────────── 🎧 MP3 IM3-AL_A_12

서론
시작문장/10%

- Well, *what I like <u>most</u> about my cell phone?* You know, I <u>cannot</u> live without my cell phone.

본론
단락별 핵심문장/80%

- **The <u>main</u> reason why I love my phone** is that I can <u>enjoy</u> listening to music <u>anywhere</u>.
  - Speaking of music, I <u>really</u> enjoy listening to <u>all</u> kinds of music because it helps me <u>release</u> stress.

- **However,** there are <u>many</u> other things I can do using a <u>cell</u> phone.
  - You know, I <u>always</u> order Latte in the morning, but the <u>coffee</u> shops are <u>always</u> filled with lots of people in the morning.
  - So, I use my <u>cell</u> phone to order <u>online</u>.

- **Moreover,** I love shopping, but the <u>shopping</u> malls are <u>always</u> packed on the <u>weekends</u>.
  - So I started to shop <u>online</u> using my phone.

결론
마무리문장/10%

- <u>Alright</u> Eva, this is <u>all</u> I can say about *what <u>I</u> like most about my cell phone.* <u>Thank</u> you.

- **음, 내가 핸드폰에서 가장 좋아하는 것?** 있잖아, 난 핸드폰 없이 살 수가 없어.

- 내가 핸드폰을 사랑하는 가장 큰 이유는 어디서든지 음악을 들을 수 있기 때문이야.
  - 음악에 대해 말해본다면, 난 모든 종류의 음악을 듣는 것을 좋아해 왜냐하면 그건 스트레스를 해소하는 데 도움이 되거든.

- 하지만, 내가 핸드폰을 사용해서 할 수 있는 많은 다른 것들이 있어.
  - 있잖아, 난 항상 아침에 라테를 주문하지만 커피숍은 아침에 많은 사람들이 항상 붐비거든.
  - 그래서, 나는 온라인으로 주문하려고 핸드폰을 사용해.

- 게다가, 난 쇼핑을 좋아하지만, 쇼핑몰은 항상 주말에 붐벼.
  - 그래서 난 핸드폰을 사용해서 온라인 쇼핑을 하기 시작했어.

- 그래 에바, 이게 **내가 핸드폰에서 가장 좋아하는 것**에 대해 말한 거야. 고마워.

어휘 및 표현

what I like most about my cell phone 내가 핸드폰에서 가장 좋아하는 것   **using a cell phone** 핸드폰을 사용하면서
order online 온라인으로 주문하다   **on the weekends** 주말에   **I started to shop online** 난 온라인으로 쇼핑하는 것을 시작했어

일반적 묘사 재활용 묘사

Q13 ————————————————————— 🎧 MP3 IM3-AL_Q_13

I would like to ask you about **how recycling is practiced** in your country. What do people especially do? Please tell me about all the different kinds of items that you recycle.

당신 나라의 재활용은 어떠한 식으로 되어있는지 알고 싶습니다. 사람들은 어떻게 재활용을 하나요? 사람들이 재활용하는 모든 품목에 대해 말해주세요.

🎧 MP3 IM3-AL_A_13

서론
시작문장/10%
본론
단락별 핵심문장/80%

결론
마무리문장/10%

- Oh yeah, _recycling?_ You know, most Koreans recycle like 2 to 3 times a week.

- When it comes to recycling, it is mandatory in Korea and people normally recycle 3 times a week.
  - In Korea, there are many recycling centers which are normally located in the middle of the town.

- As you can imagine, people recycle trash in the recycling centers such as paper, glass, metal and etcetera.
  - You know what? We need to separate the trash carefully otherwise we could be fined.

- Well, okay Eva, this is pretty much about _how recycling is **practiced** in my country._

- -

- 오 예, **재활용?** 있잖아, 대부분의 한국인들은 한 주에 2-3번씩 재활용을 해.

- 재활용에 대해서 말한다면, 한국에서는 재활용이 의무사항이고 1주에 보통 3번 재활용을 해.
  - 한국에서는, 시내 중심에 보통 위치해 있는 많은 재활용센터들이 있어.

- 네가 상상할 수 있듯이, 사람들은 재활용센터에서 종이, 유리, 고철류 등을 재활용해.
  - 그거 알아? 우리는 벌금을 내지 않으려면 주의 깊게 쓰레기 분리수거를 할 필요가 있어.

- 음, 오케이 에바, 이게 우리 **동네에서 재활용을 하는 방식**이야.

어휘 및 표현
recycle like 2 to 3 times a week 일주에 2-3번 재활용을 해   **3 times a week** 일주에 3번   **recycling center** 재활용 센터
We need to separate the trash carefully 주의 깊게 분리수거 해야 해   **otherwise** 그렇지 않으면   **we could be fined** 우리는 벌금을 낼 수 있어

일반적 묘사 교통수단 묘사

Q14 ───────────

How do people in your country move around? **What types of transportation** do people usually use? Why do they use those types of transportation? Please tell me how people move around.

당신 나라에 있는 사람들은 어떻게 이동하나요? 사람들은 보통 어떤 교통 수단을 사용하나요? 사람들은 왜 이러한 교통 수단을 사용하나요? 사람들이 이동하는 수단에 대해서 말해주세요.

🎧 MP3 IM3-AL_A_14

서론
시작문장/10%

본론
단락별 핵심문장/80%

- That's a good question, *types of transportation do people use?* Sure, I got it.

- When it comes to transportation, most Koreans use public transportation.
  - The main reason why people like to use public transportation is that it's cheaper and reliable.

- However, public transportation is always packed with lots of people.
  - So, people prefer taking cabs since it's fast and convenient.

- Lastly, riding bikes is another idea in Korea since the traffic is congested.
  - Also, people love riding bikes because they can lose weight.

결론
마무리문장/10%

- So overall, this is about *different types of transportation people use in Korea.*

- 좋은 질문이야, **사람들이 사용하는 교통수단?** 물론이지, 알았어.

- 교통수단에 대해서 말한다면, 대부분의 사람들은 대중교통을 이용해.
  - 사람들이 대중교통을 이용하는 가장 큰 이유는 싸고 믿을 만해서야.

- 하지만, 대중교통은 항상 많은 사람들로 가득 차 있어.
  - 그래서, 사람들은 택시 타는 것을 선호해 왜냐하면 빠르고 편하기 때문이야.

- 마지막으로, 자전거를 타는 것은 교통이 막힐 때 한국에서 다른 대안이야.
  - 또한, 사람들은 자전거를 타는 것을 좋아해 왜냐하면 살을 뺄 수 있기 때문이지.

- 그래서 전반적으로, 이게 **한국에서 사람들이 사용하는 다른 종류의 교통수단**이야.

어휘 및 표현
what I like most about my cell phone 내가 핸드폰에서 가장 좋아하는 것   using a cell phone 핸드폰을 사용하면서
order online 온라인으로 주문하다   on the weekends 주말에   I started to shop online 난 온라인으로 쇼핑하는 것을 시작했어

일반적 묘사 휴일 활동 묘사

Q15 ———

Please tell me about **some holidays in your country.** What do people in your country do to celebrate these holidays? Please tell me about some holidays in your country.

당신 나라의 휴일에 대해 말해주세요. 당신 나라 사람들은 휴일을 어떻게 보내나요? 당신 나라의 휴일들에 대해 말해주세요.

서론
시작문장/10%

본론
단락별 핵심문장/80%

결론
마무리문장/10%

- Oh yeah, *some holidays in my country?* It must be New year's Eve and Thanksgiving Day.

- Speaking of holidays in Korea, people usually go to the parks or the beaches with their family.
  - Well, holidays in Korea are the perfect time to go to the park and do some outdoor activities.
  - I mean, there are many huge parks in Korea with many different areas where people play soccer, cricket and so on.
  - So, lots of families come out to play sports or listen to music together.

- In addition, people prefer going to the beaches on holidays since people can enjoy the peace and quiet.
  - Also, I guess most people go there to swim.

- Plus, people usually grab a beer with their family.
  - I mean, most Koreans love going to bars and drink.

- Well, okay Eva, this is pretty much about *some holidays in my country.*

- -

- 오 예, **우리나라 휴일?** 그건 새해 전날과 추석이야.

- 한국 휴일에 대해 말해본다면, 사람들은 보통 가족과 함께 공원이나 해변에 가.
  - 음, 한국 휴일은 공원에 가고 몇몇 야외활동을 하기에 완벽한 때야.
  - 내 말은, 사람들이 축구, 크리켓 등을 할 수 있는 곳을 가진 큰 공원들이 한국에는 많아.
  - 그래서, 많은 가족들이 나와서 운동을 하거나 함께 음악을 들어.

- 게다가, 사람들은 휴일에 해변에 가는 것을 좋아해 왜냐하면 사람들은 평화로움과 조용함을 즐길 수 있기 때문이야.
  - 또한, 난 대부분의 사람들이 수영을 하러 거기에 간다고 생각해.

- 추가로, 사람들은 가족과 함께 보통 맥주를 마셔.
  - 내 말은, 대부분은 한국인들은 바에 가서 술을 마시는 것을 좋아해.

- 음 오케이 에바, 이게 **우리나라 휴일**이야.

어휘 및 표현
some holidays in my country 우리나라 휴일　　New year's Eve 새해 전날　　Thanksgiving Day 추석
lots of families come out to play sports 많은 가족들이 나와서 운동을 해　　love going to bars and drink 바에 가서 술 마시는 것을 즐겨

일반적 묘사 가족 혹은 친구 묘사

Q16 ──────────────── 🎧 MP3 IM3-AL_Q_16

I would like you to **describe one of your family members or friends.** What is he or she like? What is special about that person?

당신의 가족 이나 친구 중 한 명에 대해서 묘사하고 싶습니다. 그 또는 그녀는 어떻게 생겼나요? 그 사람에 대해 특별한 점이 무엇인가요?

──────────────── 🎧 MP3 IM3-AL_A_16

서론
시작문장/10%

• <u>That's</u> a good question, *let me tell you one of my <u>friends</u> and his name is <u>Ryan</u>.*

본론
단락별 핵심문장/80%

• When it <u>comes</u> to my friend Ryan, I spend <u>lots</u> of time with him and I've known him since I was <u>24</u>.
  - Well, he is <u>tall</u> and a <u>good</u>-looking guy.

• <u>Actually,</u> he knows a <u>lot</u> about music, so whenever I go to <u>concerts</u>, I take him with me.
  - You know, he <u>really</u> enjoys listening <u>all</u> kinds of music, so he is a <u>great</u> person to go with.

• <u>Moreover,</u> he just became a <u>personal</u> trainer.
  - So we hit the gym and work out <u>together</u>.

결론
마무리문장/10%

• So <u>overall,</u> this is about *my friend <u>Ryan</u>.*

- -

• 좋은 질문이야, **내 친구 중에 한 명에 대해 말해줄게** 그의 이름은 Ryan이야.

• 내 친구 Ryan에 대해서 말한다면, 난 많은 시간을 그와 함께 보내고 나는 24살 때부터 그를 알았어.
  - 음, 그는 키가 크고 잘생긴 사람 중에 한 명이야.

• 사실, 그는 음악에 대해 많이 알고 있고, 그래서 내가 콘서트에 갈 때마다 난 그를 데려가.
  - 있잖아, 난 모든 종류의 음악을 듣는 것을 좋아하고 그는 같이 가기에 정말 좋은 사람이야.

• 게다가, 그는 막 트레이너가 됐어.
  - 그래서 우리는 헬스장에 가서 같이 운동을 해.

• 그래서 전반적으로, 이게 **내 친구 Ryan**에 대한 거야.

어휘 및 표현
one of my friends 내 친구 중 한 명   spend lots of time with~ ~와 많은 시간을 보내다   good-looking 잘생긴
whenever I go to concerts 콘서트를 갈 때면   I take him with me 그를 데려가   he just became a personal trainer 이제 막 트레이너가 되었어
hit the gym and work out together 헬스장에 가서 같이 운동을 해

일반적 묘사 건강한 사람 묘사

Q17

🎧 MP3 IM3-AL_Q_17

I'd like you to describe **a healthy person you know of.** Who is he or she? What makes that person healthy? Why do you think that way? Please tell me everything about the things that make that person healthy.

당신이 알고 있는 건강한 사람을 묘사해주세요. 누구입니까? 무엇이 그 사람을 건강하게 만들죠? 왜 그렇게 생각하나요? 그 사람을 건강하게 만드는 모든 것들에 대해 모두 말해주세요.

🎧 MP3 IM3-AL_A_17

서론
시작문장/10%

- Well, *a healthy person I know?* You know, It must be my brother <u>Danny</u>.

본론
단락별 핵심문장/80%

- <u>Speaking of Danny,</u> he is <u>physically</u>, mentally and socially well <u>balanced</u>.
  - In <u>order</u> to stay healthy, he spends <u>lots</u> of time at the gym because working out is very <u>important</u> for a healthy life.

- <u>Moreover,</u> he is an <u>outgoing</u> person and likes <u>socializing</u>.
  - So, he usually has social <u>gatherings</u> in his <u>free</u> time.
  - I mean, talking and laughing with <u>people</u> helps him stay <u>healthy</u>.

- <u>Lastly,</u> he really <u>enjoys</u> watching <u>all</u> kinds of movies because it helps him <u>release</u> stress.
  - In <u>order</u> to stay healthy, I'm <u>going</u> to do the <u>same</u> things that he does.

결론
마무리문장/10%

- <u>Alright Eva,</u> this is <u>all</u> I can say about *a <u>healthy</u> person I know of.* Thank you.

- 음, 내가 아는 건강한 사람? 있잖아, 바로 내 남동생 Danny야.

- Danny에 대해 말해본다면, 그는 신체적으로, 정신적으로, 사회적으로 잘 균형 잡힌 사람이야.
  - 건강하게 유지하기 위해, 그는 헬스장에서 많은 시간을 보내 왜냐하면 운동하는 것은 건강한 삶에 있어 정말 중요하거든.

- 게다가, 그는 활발하고 사람 만나는 것을 좋아해.
  - 그래서, 그는 여가 시간에 사람들과 모임을 가져.
  - 내 말은, 사람들과 이야기하고 웃는 것은 그가 건강하게 유지하도록 해.

- 마지막으로, 그는 모든 종류의 영화를 보는 것을 정말 좋아해 왜냐하면 그가 스트레스를 해소하는 데 도움이 되기 때문이야.
  - 건강을 유지하기 위해, 나는 그가 했던 같은 걸 할 거야.

- 그래 에바, 이게 내가 아는 건강한 사람이야. 고마워.

어휘 및 표현

a healthy person I know 내가 아는 건강한 사람   It must be~ ~이어야만 해   physically, mentally and socially well balanced 신체적으로, 정신적으로, 사회적으로 잘 균형 잡힌   In order to stay healthy 건강하게 유지하기 위해   working out is very important for a healthy life 운동하는 것은 건강한 삶에 있어 정말 중요해   he is an outgoing person and likes socializing 그는 활발하고 사람 만나는 것을 좋아해   social gatherings 모임   talking and laughing with people helps him stay healthy 사람들과 대화하고 웃는 것이 그를 건강하게 해   do the same things 같은 것을 하다

일반적 묘사 우리나라 패션 묘사

Q18 ━━━━━━━━━━━━━━━━━━━━━━━━━━━ 🎧 MP3 IM3-AL_Q_18

I would like to ask you about **how people in your country dress.** What kind of clothes do they wear? Tell me about fashion styles in your country in as much detail as possible.

당신 나라 사람들이 옷을 어떻게 입는지 묻고 싶습니다. 어떤 옷들을 입나요? 당신 나라 사람들의 패션 스타일에 대해 자세히 말해주세요.

━━━ 🎧 MP3 IM3-AL_A_18

서론
시작문장/10%

- Oh yeah, *how <u>people</u> in my country <u>dress</u>?* You know, Koreans wear something <u>casual</u>.

본론
단락별 핵심문장/80%

- As I mentioned <u>before,</u> there are <u>lots</u> of parks in Korea and people enjoy their <u>free</u> time at the parks.
  - I mean, you will see people do <u>many</u> kinds of things such as playing <u>sports</u>, listening to <u>music</u> and stuff like that.
  - So <u>most</u> Koreans wear something <u>casual</u> when they go to parks.

- In <u>addition,</u> <u>most</u> Koreans are <u>concerned</u> about their health.
  - So, people spend <u>lots</u> of time at the gym because they like to stay <u>healthy</u>.
  - Which means, they <u>usually</u> wear gym clothes.

결론
마무리문장/10%

- Well, <u>okay</u> Eva, this is <u>pretty</u> much about **how people dress in <u>Korea.</u>**

- -

- 오 예, **우리나라 사람들이 옷을 어떻게 입는지?** 있잖아, 한국인들은 캐주얼한 옷을 입어.

- 내가 전에도 언급했듯, 한국에는 많은 공원이 있고 사람들은 공원에서 여가 시간을 보내는 것을 좋아해.
  - 내 말은, 너는 사람들이 운동, 음악 감상과 같은 많은 종류의 것들을 하는 것을 볼 거야.
  - 그래서 대부분의 한국인들은 공원에 갈 때 캐주얼한 옷을 입어.

- 게다가, 대부분의 한국인들은 건강에 관심이 많아.
  - 그래서, 사람들은 많은 시간을 헬스장에서 보내 왜냐하면 그들은 건강함을 유지하고 싶기 때문이야.
  - 그 말은, 그들은 주로 운동복을 입어.

- 음, 오케이 에바. 이게 **한국에서 사람들이 옷을 입는 방식**이야.

어휘 및 표현
how people in my country dress 우리나라 사람들이 옷 입는 법   people enjoy their free time at the parks
사람들은 공원에서 여가 시간을 보내는 것을 좋아해   most Koreans are concerned about their health 대부분의 한국사람들은 건강을 걱정해
they like to stay healthy 그들은 건강을 유지하고 싶어해   gym clothes 운동복

일반적 묘사 우리나라 날씨 묘사

Q19

Please tell me about **the weather and seasons in your country.** What is the weather like in each season? Which season do you like? Please tell me in detail.

당신 나라의 날씨 및 계절에 대해 말해주세요. 각 계절마다의 날씨는 어떤가요? 당신은 어느 계절을 좋아하나요? 상세히 말해주세요.

🎧 MP3 IM3-AL_A_19

서론
시작문장/10%

- That's a good question, *the weather and seasons in my country?* Sure, I got it.

본론
단락별 핵심문장/80%

- As you may know, there are 4 distinct seasons in Korea.
  - Obviously, it is scorching hot during summer and freezing cold during winter.

- Speaking of my favorite season, I must say, it's summer since I love going to the beach.
  - Well, summer is the perfect time to go to the beach and do some outdoor activities.
  - The main reason why I like summer is to watch the sunset at the beach. It is kinda romantic.
  - Whenever I go there, it makes me feel so great and it means a lot to me.

결론
마무리문장/10%

- So overall, this is about *the weather and seasons in my country.*

- -

- 좋은 질문이야, **우리나라 날씨와 계절?** 물론, 알겠어.

- 네가 알다시피, 한국에는 뚜렷한 4계절이 있어.
  - 명백하게, 여름에는 타는 듯이 덥고 겨울에는 정말 추워.

- 내가 제일 좋아하는 계절에 대해 말해본다면, 난 해변에 가는 것을 좋아하기 때문에 여름이야.
  - 음, 여름은 해변에 가고 몇몇 실외활동을 하기에 완벽한 시기야.
  - 내가 여름을 좋아하는 가장 큰 이유는 해변에서 노을을 보는 것은 정말 로맨틱하기 때문이야.
  - 내가 거기에 갈 때마다, 난 기분이 정말 좋아지고 그건 많은 의미가 있어.

- 그래서 전반적으로, 이게 **우리나라의 날씨와 계절**이야.

어휘 및 표현

the weather and seasons in my country 우리나라 날씨와 계절   **As you may know** 네가 알다시피
there are 4 distinct seasons in Korea 한국에는 뚜렷한 4계절이 있어   **it's scorching hot** 타는 듯이 더워   **freezing cold** 얼도록 추운

7강

유형 02 (세부묘사)

이론

세부묘사의 이해

OPIc 질문들은 콤보 형태로 나온다고 했죠?
난이도에 따라 질문의 유형도 달라진다고 했습니다.(OPIc의 이해 – 유형별 문제 설명 p13 참조)
세부묘사는 묘사 질문 뒤에 출제되며 난이도 5 or 6 선택 시, 3번, 14번, 15번에 출제됩니다.
난이도 5-6수준의 세부묘사 질문 종류는 비교, 이슈에 집중이 되어 있습니다.

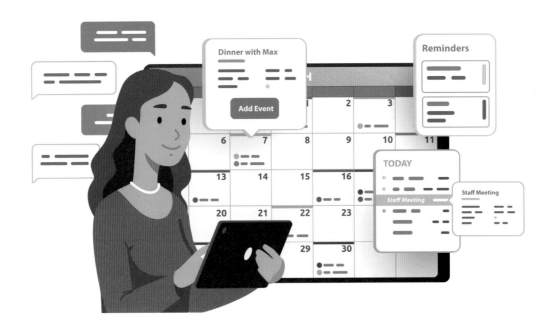

세부묘사가 나오는 질문 번호를 외우세요!

세부묘사가 나오는 질문 번호를 외우세요!
IM3-AL등급 목표 시, 난이도 5로 설정하시면, 세부묘사는 총 3문제 출제!

1	2	3	4	5	6	7	8	9	10	11	12	13	14	15
자기소개	묘사	세부묘사	경험	묘사	경험	경험	묘사	경험	경험	정보요청	문제해결	문제해결경험	세부묘사	세부묘사

세부묘사의 종류

세부묘사는 바로 앞에 출제된 '묘사' 질문의 세부적인 질문입니다.
자주 출제되는 세부 묘사 질문의 종류는 아래와 같습니다.

일반	➡	앞의 묘사 문제에서 조금 더 Detail한 질문 (6하 원칙으로 질문)
루틴	➡	공원, 헬스장, 여행 등 해당 장소에서 하는 행동의 순서 설명
비교	➡	토픽(ex. 음악 등)의 전과 후 행동 및 취향 변화 설명
시작 계기	➡	토픽(ex. 조깅, 걷기 등)을 시작하게 된 계기에 대한 설명
준비물	➡	토픽(ex. 여행, 운동 등)을 시작하기 전의 준비 단계 및 준비물에 대한 설명
장단점	➡	토픽(ex. 기기사용 등)을 사용함에 있어 장점과 단점에 대한 설명
이슈, 뉴스	➡	토픽(ex. 산업, 전자기기기 등)의 현재 이슈 혹은 뉴스 관련 설명

 문제를 집중하여 듣고, 키워드를 캐치한 후, 배운 묘사 문장을 최대한 활용!

세부묘사의 답변 Format

세부묘사는 앞의 '묘사' 질문에 대한 세부적인 설명으로 간략하지만 앞의 '묘사' 답변과 연결성 있는 체계적인 답변 Format이 필요합니다.

서론 Introduction 답변비중 **10%**	**시작 문장** • 질문에서 물어본 부분(키워드 포함)의 포괄적인 답변 1 – 2줄! • 면접관에게 답변을 시작한단 느낌을 전달!
본론 Body 답변비중 **80%**	**단락 별 핵심 문장** • 질문에 부합하는 진짜녀석들 OPIc 묘사 암기문장 (4-5문장) • 암기문장 뒷받침 하는 본인 실력 문장 (4-5문장) • 질문의 '키워드' 필수 포함
결론 Conclusion 답변비중 **10%**	**마무리 문장** • 질문의 키워드를 필히 포함하여 깔끔하게 한 줄! • 면접관에게 답변을 끝낸다는 느낌을 전달!

세부묘사의 암기문장 – 본론(단락 별 핵심 암기 문장)

정확한 세부묘사의 답변 제공을 위하여 본론에 필요한 암기문장을 제공합니다.

본론 - 단락별 핵심　　　　　　　　　　　　　　　　　　　　🎧 **MP3 IM3-AL_57~66**

- 내가 어렸을 땐, 난 하곤 했어 **원룸에 사는 것**을, 하지만 지금은 난 **3층 집에 살아**.
  When I was little, I used to **live in a studio apartment,** but now I **live in a 3-story house**.

- 예전에는, **핸드폰**은 오직 사용되었어 **전화하는 것**으로만. 하지만 지금은 **핸드폰은** 많은 기능이 있어 **사진을 찍거나**, **게임을 하거나**.
  In the past, **the cell phones** were only used to **make calls**. However, **the cell phones** today have **various functions** such as **taking pictures** or **playing games**.

- 가전제품에 대해서 말한다면, 내 생각엔 **진공청소기**가 가장 큰 변화를 가져다주었어 우리의 삶에.
  When it comes to the home appliances, I guess **the vacuum** is the biggest change in our lives.

- 어쨌든, **입맛**은 많이 변했어 몇 년간.
  However, **taste buds** have changed a lot over the years.

- 하지만 지금은, 하루 일과가 되었어 사람들에게 익숙해진.
  But now, it has become a daily routine that people are very used to.

- 하지만 지금은, 사람들은 건강을 의식하게 되었어 과거보다.
  But now, people have become a lot more health-conscious than in the past.

- 다른 한편으로는, **그들**은 조금 달라 여러 가지 방면으로.
  On the other hand, **they** are a little different in some ways.

- 이슈에 대해서 말한다면, 사람들은 경험해 많은 문제들을 **주택임대**에 대해 대화할 때.
  Speaking of issues, people can experience various problems when they talk about **renting a house**.

- 어쨌든, **공원**에 관한 큰 이슈 중 하나는 **쓰레기 문제**야.
  However, one of the biggest issues about **parks** is **garbage problems**.

- 솔직히 말하자면, 그다지 이슈가 많지 않아 **재활용**에 대해서 말한다면.
  Frankly speaking, there are not many issues when it comes to **recycling**.

세부묘사 답변 준비 – 시험화면

난이도 5 설정 시, 묘사가 나오는 번호를 실제 시험화면으로 익숙해져야 합니다.

난이도 5 설정 시, 세부 묘사 질문은 총 3문제(3, 14, 15번)가 출제됩니다.

1. 3, 14, 15번의 세부묘사 질문 'Play' 버튼 클릭 전, 세부 묘사임을 인지합니다.

2. 배운 세부묘사 종류(ex. 비교, 이슈 등)를 생각 및 암기문장을 암기문장을 생각합니다.

3. 'Play' 버튼 클릭 후, 첫 번째 문제에서 세부묘사의 키워드를 집중해서 듣습니다.

4. 'Replay' 버튼 클릭 후, 두 번째 문제는 듣지 않고 사용할 세부묘사 문장을 생각합니다.

5. 오른쪽 상단의 'Recording' 버튼 생성 시, '세부묘사 답변 Format' 대로 답변합니다.

 문제를 집중하여 듣고, 키워드를 캐치한 후, 묘사,세부묘사 사용!

8강

암기문장 활용

used to

When it comes to~

Frankly speaking

be used to

연결어

세부묘사의 암기문장　used to

세부묘사의 문법을 정확히 배우고 응용해 보세요.

When I was little, I used to live in a studio apartment, but now I live in a 3-story house.

• [특수조동사] used to : ~하곤 했었다

01. 'used to'는 <u>과거시제</u>에만 사용되며, <u>과거의 상태나 습관</u>을 표현
02. '<u>~하곤 했었다</u>'로 해석되어 <u>과거에는 했지만 현재는 아닌 상태</u>
03. 'used to'다음에는 반드시 <u>동사원형</u>을 취급
04. 'be used to'와 헷갈리지 않도록 주의!

사용 방법

used to + 동사원형

* 부정문으로 만들 경우 형태 변화에 주의, didn't + use to + 동사원형

활용 및 응용

• I used to live in a studio apartment, but now I live in a 3-story house.

• When I was young, I used to wear something casual, but now, I wear something formal.

• Actually, I didn't use to run at the park. I ran on a treadmill.

MEMO

세부묘사의 암기문장　When it comes to~

세부묘사의 문법을 정확히 배우고 응용해 보세요.

When it comes to the home appliances, I guess the vacuum is the biggest change in our lives.

• [When it comes to + 명사] : ~에 대해 말하자면

01.　　답변 발화시 **'키워드'를 언급**하기 좋은 표현!

02.　　'When it comes to' 의 **'to'**는 <u>전치사</u>이므로 반드시 **명사나 동명사**만 취급

03.　　동일한 표현 : speaking of, in terms of, regarding 등

사용 방법

When it comes to + 명사/동명사

= speaking of, in terms of, regarding 등

활용 및 응용

• When it comes to the home appliances, I guess the vacuum is the biggest change in our lives.

• In terms of losing something, I remember when I lost my cell phone.

• Speaking of the health issue, I guess people talk about losing weight a lot.

MEMO

세부묘사의 암기문장　Frankly speaking

세부묘사의 문법을 정확히 배우고 응용해 보세요.

Frankly speaking, there are not many issues when it comes to recycling.

• [Frankly speaking] : 솔직히 말하자면

01.　한국어로 말을 할 때도 문장 전에 추임새처럼 나오는 표현이 있듯이 영어에서도 자연스럽게 나오는 표현 중 하나

02.　실제로 '솔직한' 내용을 전달할 때도 쓰이지만, 큰 의미 없이 문장 시작 전에 버릇처럼 사용하기도 함

03.　동일한 표현 : honestly, honestly speaking, actually, 등

사용 방법

본 문장 말하기 전에 추임새처럼 사용

= honestly, honestly speaking, actually 등

활용 및 응용

• Frankly speaking, there are not many issues when it comes to recycling.

• Actually, I love staying home and watching all kinds of movies.

• Honestly, I don't understand why people eat junk food.

MEMO

세부묘사의 암기문장　be used to

세부묘사의 문법을 정확히 배우고 응용해 보세요.

But now, it has become a daily routine that people are very used to.

• [be used to + 명사] : ~에 익숙해지다

01.　'used to'는 사용 형태나 상황에 따라 다르게 해석되기에 문맥에 맞춰 주의하여 사용하는 것이 중요!

02.　'used to'의 다양한 형태

    a.　주어 + used to + 동사원형 : ~하곤 했었다 (과거 습관)

    b.　주어 + be동사 + used to + 명사/동명사 : ~에 익숙해지다

    c.　주어 + be동사 + used to + 동사원형 : ~에 사용되다 (수동태)

사용 방법

명사 **+ to +** 동사원형

주어 + be동사 **+ used to +** 명사/동명사

활용 및 응용

• But now, it has become a daily routine that people are very used to.

• Actually, we are used to using smartphones on a daily basis.

• I bought a new car and finally, I am used to this new car.

MEMO

세부묘사의 암기문장　연결어

세부묘사의 문법을 정확히 배우고 응용해 보세요.

On the other hand, they are a little different in some ways.

• [연결어] On the other hand : 반면에

01. 고 등급 취득을 위해서는 자연스러운 답변 연결을 위한 **'연결어 (접속사/접속부사/부사절)'** 등의 사용이 매우 중요!

02. 'On the other hand'는 앞 내용과 뒤 내용의 대조가 있을 경우 사용하면 좋은 표현 > 형태 그대로 사용 하는 것이 중요!

03. 유사한 표현 : However, But, Whereas, In contrast 등

사용 방법

앞 내용과 뒤 내용이 대조될 때 뒤 문장 앞에서 사용

= However, But, Whereas, In contrast 등

활용 및 응용

• On the other hand, they are a little different in some ways.

• However, one of the biggest issues about parks is garbage problems.

• My brother is outgoing whereas my sister is quiet.

MEMO

9강

유형 02 (세부묘사)

암기문장 쉐도잉

암기문장 쉐도잉

암기문장 쉐도잉은 총 5단계로 나누어져 있습니다.
진짜녀석들 OPIc의 암기문장을 반복듣기 하면서 쉐도잉을 진행합니다.

1단계 사전학습	문장을 들은 후, 주어진 암기문장을 억양, 강세를 고려하여 큰소리로 읽습니다. ex.) Actually, **It** is incredibly **beautiful** and **peaceful.**
2단계 딕테이션	문장을 들은 후, 밑줄 친 부분을 적습니다. ex.) Actually, ____ is incredibly _____ and _____.
3단계 문장 끊어 읽기	문장을 들은 후, 청크 단위로 끊어 읽어 봅니다. ex.) Actually, / **It** is incredibly **beautiful** / and **peaceful.**
4단계 전체 문장 읽기	문장을 들은 후, 3단계를 여러 번 반복한 후, 전체 문장을 한숨에 읽어 봅니다. ex.) Actually, **It** is incredibly **beautiful** and **peaceful.**
5단계 반복학습	위 단계를 반복하여, 영어의 어순으로 된 한글 해석을 보며, 쉐도잉 연습을 합니다. ex.) 사실, <u>그 곳은</u> 숨막히게 <u>아름다워</u> 그리고 <u>평화로워.</u>

암기문장 쉐도잉

세부묘사 문장의 쉐도잉 연습을 하세요.

1단계 : 사전학습

문장을 들은 후, 주어진 암기문장을 억양, 강세를 고려하여 큰소리로 읽습니다.

IM3-AL_57	• When I was little, I used to <u>live in a studio apartment</u>, but now I <u>live in a 3-story house</u>.
IM3-AL_58	• In the past, <u>the cell phones</u> were only used to <u>make calls</u>. However, <u>the cell phones</u> today have <u>various functions</u> such as <u>taking pictures</u> or <u>playing games</u>.
IM3-AL_59	• When it comes to the home appliances, I guess <u>the vacuum</u> is the biggest change in our lives.
IM3-AL_60	• However, <u>taste buds</u> have changed a lot over the years.
IM3-AL_61	• But now, it has become a daily routine that people are very used to.
IM3-AL_62	• But now, people have become a lot more health-conscious than in the past.
IM3-AL_63	• On the other hand, <u>they</u> are a little different in some ways.
IM3-AL_64	• Speaking of issues, people can experience various problems when they talk about <u>renting a house</u>.
IM3-AL_65	• However, one of the biggest issues about <u>parks</u> is <u>garbage problems</u>.
IM3-AL_66	• Frankly speaking, there are not many issues when it comes to <u>recycling</u>.

2단계 : 딕테이션

문장을 들은 후, 밑줄 친 부분을 적습니다.

• When I was little, I used to _____, but now I _____.
• In the past, _____ were only used to _____. However, _____ today have _____ such as _____ or _____.
• When it comes to the home appliances, I guess _____ is the biggest change in our lives.
• However, _____ have changed a lot over the years.
• But now, it has become a daily routine that people are very used to.
• But now, people have become a lot more health-conscious than in the past.
• On the other hand, _____ are a little different in some ways.
• Speaking of issues, people can experience various problems when they talk about _____.
• However, one of the biggest issues about _____ is _____.
• Frankly speaking, there are not many issues when it comes to _____.

3단계 : 문장 끊어 읽기

문장을 들은 후, 청크 단위로 끊어 읽어 봅니다.

• When I was little, / I used to <u>live in a studio apartment</u>, but now / I <u>live in a 3-story house</u>.
• In the past, / <u>the cell phones</u> were only / used to <u>make calls</u>. / However, <u>the cell phones</u> today have / <u>various functions</u> such as / <u>taking pictures</u> or <u>playing games</u>.
• When it comes to the home appliances, / I guess <u>the vacuum</u> is the biggest change / in our lives.
• However, / <u>taste buds</u> have changed a lot / over the years.
• But now, / it has become a daily routine that / people are very used to.
• But now, / people have become a lot more health-conscious than / in the past.
• On the other hand, / <u>they</u> are a little different in some ways.
• Speaking of issues, / people can experience various problems when they / talk about <u>renting a house</u>.
• However, / one of the biggest issues about <u>parks</u> is / <u>garbage problems</u>.
• Frankly speaking, / there are not many issues when it comes to / <u>recycling</u>.

암기문장 쉐도잉

세부묘사 문장의 쉐도잉 연습을 하세요.

🎧 **MP3 IM3-AL_57~66**

4단계 : 전체 문장 읽기

문장을 들은 후, 3단계를 여러 번 반복한 후, 전체 문장을 한숨에 읽어 봅니다.

- When I was little, I used to <u>live in a studio apartment</u>, but now I <u>live in a 3-story house</u>.
- In the past, <u>the cell phones</u> were only used to <u>make calls</u>. However, <u>the cell phones</u> today have <u>various functions</u> such as <u>taking pictures</u> or <u>playing games</u>.
- When it comes to the home appliances, I guess <u>the vacuum</u> is the biggest change in our lives.
- However, <u>taste buds</u> have changed a lot over the years.
- But now, it has become a daily routine that people are very used to.
- But now, people have become a lot more health-conscious than in the past.
- On the other hand, <u>they</u> are a little different in some ways.
- Speaking of issues, people can experience various problems when they talk about <u>renting a house</u>.
- However, one of the biggest issues about <u>parks</u> is <u>garbage problems</u>.
- Frankly speaking, there are not many issues when it comes to <u>recycling.</u>

5단계 : 반복 학습

위 단계를 반복하여, 영어의 어순으로 된 한글 해석을 보며, 쉐도잉 연습을 합니다.

- 내가 어렸을 땐, 난 하곤 했어 <u>원룸에 사는 것</u>을, 하지만 지금은 난 <u>3층 집에 살아</u>.
- 예전에는, <u>핸드폰</u>은 오직 사용되었어 <u>전화하는 것</u>으로만. 하지만 지금은 <u>핸드폰</u>은 많은 기능이 있어 <u>사진을 찍거나</u>, <u>게임을 하거나</u>.
- 가전제품에 대해서 말한다면, 내 생각엔 <u>진공청소기</u>가 가장 큰 변화를 가져다주었어 우리의 삶에.
- 어쨌든, <u>입맛</u>은 많이 변했어 몇 년간.
- 하지만 지금은, 하루 일과가 되었어 사람들에게 익숙해진.
- 하지만 지금은, 사람들은 건강을 의식하게 되었어 과거보다.
- 다른 한편으로는, <u>그들</u>은 조금 달라 여러 가지 방면으로.
- 이슈에 대해서 말한다면, 사람들은 경험해 많은 문제들을 <u>주택임대</u>에 대해 대화할 때.
- 어쨌든, <u>공원</u>에 관한 큰 이슈 중 하나는 <u>쓰레기 문제</u>야.
- 솔직히 말하자면, 그다지 이슈가 많지 않아 <u>재활용</u>에 대해서 말한다면.

10강

유형 02 (세부묘사)

리스닝 훈련

세부묘사 질문 리스트

세부묘사

세부묘사 질문 리스트

진짜녀석들 OPIc에서 제공하는 다양한 세부묘사 질문들의 MP3를 듣고 키워드 캐치를 훈련하세요.

일반

🎧 MP3 IM3-AL_Q_20~47

전자기기
집에서 사용 전자기기

What types of home appliances are used in your house? It must be a refrigerator, a microwave, or a dishwasher. Tell me about **the appliances used for various tasks in your home.**

산업
일하고 싶은 기업

What kinds of companies do young people in your country want to work? Why do they want to work at those companies? Please give me some examples of the industry or company.

가족/친구
대화 주제

What kinds of topics do you commonly talk about with your family or friends? When was the last time you talked to them? What did you talk about? Please give me all the details.

휴일
특별한점

Tell me about **some holidays in your country.** What do people normally do during those holidays? What are some special things about those holidays? Give me all the details.

산업
진로를 위해 하는 일

I would like to know **what people do to get a job** in your country. Do they go to school? And what do they do when they get a job? Do they get any training at the company? Tell me everything they do to get a job.

비교 차이점 변화

하우징
과거현재 비교

I would like to ask you about **houses in your country.** Perhaps houses have changed over the years. **How is the structure of the houses different from the past?**

레스토랑
음식점 비교

You can expect set menus at chain restaurants such as Outback. On the other hand, **small local restaurants** have their own menus, and you may not know what to expect. **Talk about difference between those two.**

전화기
예전지금 전화기 비교

Do you remember the phone you used for the first time? What is **the difference between the phone you used back then and the phone you use now?**

재활용
과거현재 비교

How is recycling you practiced when you were young different from what you do today? What are **the differences** and **similarities?** Please tell me about how recycling has changed over the years.

공원
어른,아이들
공원활동 시설비교

Now, describe the differences in activities between children and adults at the park. What are **the differences?** How are **the facilities** at parks different for children and adults?

모임
과거-현재 모임 차이

Let's talk about the ways of gatherings. It has changed over the years. **How was it in the past? How is it now?** What are **the differences and the similarities?** Please give me all the details.

건강
유지방법 차이

In the past, tell me **how your parents' generation kept their health. How is it different from what your generation does?** Give me all the details.

인터넷
연령별 인터넷 이용 차이

How is Internet usage different among generations? What do **younger people** commonly **do online?** What do **older people do online?** Please give me all the details.

가족/친구
두명 유사점/차이점

Now, I would like you to pick two of your family members or friends and tell me about **their differences and similarities.** Please give me all details.

전자기기
우리 삶의 변화

Home appliances have changed our lives. **How was life before the appliances different from life now?** Tell me the biggest change that has had an impact on our lives. Please give me specific details.

레스토랑
건강식 메뉴 변화 추세

People have become a lot more health-conscious than in the past. So, lots of restaurants are changing their menus for those customers. Talk about **the changes you notice about a restaurant related to this trend.**

식품
식품 구매 방식 변화

How has the way people bought food changed over the years? Where did people buy food in the past, and where do they **buy it now?**

지형/이웃국가
국가 변화 추세

Tell me about a country that is **a geographically similar to your country.** What are **the changes** that the country has gone through in recent years? Please give me all the details.

세부묘사 질문 리스트

진짜녀석들 OPIc에서 제공하는 다양한 세부묘사 질문들의 MP3를 듣고 키워드 캐치를 훈련하세요.

뉴스기사

🎧 MP3 IM3-AL_Q_20~47

식품
식품 오염 뉴스

Food can become contaminated because of bacteria. It can cause consumer illness. **I would like you to tell me about an incident you heard on the news** regarding food contamination. What was **the problem?** How was it **dealt with?**

재활용
최근 재활용 뉴스

Let's talk about **one of the recycling issues** that you heard in the news recently. **What was the news about?** What is being done to **solve the issue?** Please give me all the details about that issue on recycling.

지형/이웃국가
이웃국가 정치경제 기사

I would like to ask you about **an article** you read about **the country you have mentioned before.** What was the issue about? Also, how was it **related to the politics or the economy of that country?**

이슈 어려움

건강
최근 언급 건강관련 이슈

There must be some issues related to our health in the news these days. Do people in your country talk about that topic a lot? Please **describe common health-related concerns people have.**

공원
관련 이슈 및 해결책

I would like to ask you about **one of the issues about parks in your country.** What are some challenges public parks are faced with these days? Discuss what has caused these concerns. **What steps do we take in order to solve this problem?**

인터넷
이슈,보안문제

Let's talk about some issues that people talk about regarding the Internet. What are their concerns, and Why are those concerns a problem? Are there any security problems? If so, talk about the issue.

전화기
사회적 문제

Now, **let's talk about some issues related to cell phones. Why** do people talk about that topic? Why is it **a problem?** Please give me all the details.

하우징
임대 어려움

There must be **a problem when people rent a house.** Why do you think those problems occur? How do people in your country **solve those problems?**

모임
계획과정 어려운 점

It is not easy to make plans for gatherings. **What are some issues related to making plans for gathering?** How do people **deal with those problems?**

휴일
휴일관련 걱정거리

Let's talk about some issues or concerns that people in your country have regarding holidays. What steps do people need to take in order to **solve this problem?**

세부묘사 질문 리스트 14,15 SET별

세트별의 질문들을 mp3 제목으로 검색하여 연습하세요.

🎧 MP3 IM3-AL_Q_20~47

전자기기
집에서 사용 전자기기

전자기기 --

What types of home appliances are used in your house? It must be a refrigerator, a microwave, or a dishwasher. Tell me about **the appliances used for various tasks in your home.**

전자기기
우리 삶의 변화

Home appliances have changed our lives. **How was life before the appliances different from life now?** Tell me the biggest change that has had an impact on our lives. Please give me specific details.

산업
일하고 싶은 기업

산업 --

What kinds of companies do young people in your country want to work? Why do they want to work at those companies? Please give me some examples of the industry or company.

산업
진로를 위해 하는 일

I would like to know **what people do to get a job in your country.** Do they go to school? And what do they do when they get a job? Do they get any training at the company? Tell me everything they do to get a job.

가족/친구
두 명 유사점/차이점

가족 --

Now, **I would like you to pick two of your family members or friends** and tell me about **their differences and similarities.** Please give me all details.

가족/친구
대화 주제

What kinds of topics do you commonly talk about with your family or friends? When was the last time you talked to them? What did you talk about? Please give me all the details.

전화기
예전,지금 전화기 비교

전화기 --

Do you remember the phone you used for the first time? What is **the difference between the phone you used back then and the phone you use now?**

전화기
사회적 문제

Now, **let's talk about some issues related to cell phones. Why** do people talk about that topic? Why is it **a problem?** Please give me all the details.

건강
유지방법 차이

건강 --

In the past, tell me **how your parents' generation kept their health. How is it different from what your generation does?** Give me all the details.

건강
최근 언급 건강관련 이슈

There must be some issues related to our health in the news these days. Do people in your country talk about that topic a lot? Please **describe common health-related concerns people have.**

하우징
과거현재 비교

하우징 --

I would like to ask you about **houses in your country.** Perhaps houses have changed over the years. **How is the structure of the houses different from the past?**

하우징
임대 어려움

There must be **a problem when people rent a house. Why do you think those problems occur?** How do people in your country solve those problems?

인터넷
연령별(세대별) 인터넷
이용 차이점

인터넷 --

How is Internet usage different among generations? What do **younger people** commonly **do online?** What do **older people do online?** Please give me all the details.

인터넷
이슈,보안문제

Let's talk about some issues that people talk about regarding the Internet. What are their concerns, and why are those concerns a problem? Are there any security problems? If so, talk about the issue.

레스토랑
음식점 비교

레스토랑 --

You can expect set menus at chain restaurants such as Outback. On the other hand, **small local restaurants** have their own menus, and you may not know what to expect. **Talk about difference between those two.**

레스토랑
건강식 메뉴 변화 추세

People have become a lot more health-conscious than in the past. So, lots of restaurants are changing their menus for those customers. Talk about **the changes you notice about a restaurant related to this trend.**

세부묘사 질문 리스트 14,15 SET별

세트별의 질문들을 mp3 제목으로 검색하여 연습하세요.

MP3 IM3-AL_Q_20~47

식품 --

식품
식품 구매 방식 변화

How has the way people bought food changed over the years? Where did people buy food in the past, and where do they buy it now?

식품
식품 오염 뉴스

Food can become contaminated because of bacteria. It can cause consumer illness. I would like you to tell me about an incident you heard on the news regarding food contamination. What was the problem? How was it dealt with?

모임 --

모임
과거·현재 모임 차이

Let's talk about the ways of gatherings. It has changed over the years. How was it in the past? How is it now? What are the differences and the similarities? Please give me all the details.

모임
계획과정 어려운 점

It is not easy to make plans for gatherings. What are some issues related to making plans for gathering? How do people deal with those problems?

지형/이웃국가 --

지형/이웃국가
국가 변화 추세

Tell me about a country that is a geographically similar to your country. What are the changes that the country has gone through in recent years? Please give me all the details.

지형/이웃국가
이웃국가 정치경제 기사

I would like to ask you about an article you read about the country you have mentioned before. What was the issue about? Also, how was it related to the politics or the economy of that country?

휴일 --

휴일
특별한점

Tell me about some holidays in your country. What do people normally do during those holidays? What are some special things about those holidays? Give me all the details.

휴일
휴일관련 걱정거리

Let's talk about some issues or concerns that people in your country have regarding holidays. What steps do people need to take in order to solve this problem?

재활용 --

재활용
과거현재 비교

How is recycling you practiced when you were young different from what you do today? What are the differences and similarities? Please tell me about how recycling has changed over the years.

재활용
최근 재활용 뉴스

Let's talk about one of the recycling issues that you heard in the news recently. What was the news about? What is being done to solve the issue? Please give me all the details about that issue on recycling.

공원 --

공원
어른,아이들
공원활동시설비교

Now, describe the differences in activities between children and adults at the park. What are the differences? How are the facilities at parks different for children and adults?

공원
관련 이슈 및 해결책

I would like to ask you about one of the issues about parks in your country. What are some challenges public parks are faced with these days? Discuss what has caused these concerns. What steps do we take in order to solve this problem?

세부묘사

진짜녀석들 OPIc에서 제공하는 다양한 세부묘사 질문들의 MP3를 듣고 키워드 캐치를 훈련하세요.

🎧 MP3 IM3-AL_Q_20-21

돌발 / 전자기기

집에서 사용하는 전자기기

What types of home appliances are used in your house? It must be a refrigerator, a microwave, or a dishwasher. Tell me about the appliances used for various tasks in your home.

/ KEYWORD

가전제품이 가져다 준 삶의 변화

Home appliances have changed our lives. How was life before the appliances different from life now? Tell me the biggest change that has had an impact on our lives. Please give me specific details.

/ KEYWORD

🎧 MP3 IM3-AL_Q_22-23

돌발 / 산업

일하고 싶은 기업

What kinds of companies do young people in your country want to work? Why do they want to work at those companies? Please give me some examples of the industry or company.

/ KEYWORD

진로를 위해 하는 일

I would like to know what people do to get a job in your country. Do they go to school? And what do they do when they get a job? Do they get any training at the company? Tell me everything they do to get a job.

/ KEYWORD

🎧 MP3 IM3-AL_Q_24-25

돌발 / 가족,친구

두 명 유사점/차이점

Now, I would like you to pick two of your family members or friends and tell me about their differences and similarities. Please give me all details.

/ KEYWORD

대화주제

What kinds of topics do you commonly talk about with your family or friends? When was the last time you talked to them? What did you talk about? Please give me all the details.

/ KEYWORD

세부묘사

진짜녀석들 OPIc에서 제공하는 다양한 세부묘사 질문들의 MP3를 듣고 키워드 캐치를 훈련하세요.

MP3 IM3-AL_Q_26-27

돌발 / 전화기

예전과 지금의 전화기 비교

Do you remember the phone you used for the first time? What is the difference between the phone you used back then and the phone you use now?

/ KEYWORD

핸드폰의 사회적 문제

Now, let's talk about some issues related to cell phones. Why do people talk about that topic? Why is it a problem? Please give me all the details.

/ KEYWORD

MP3 IM3-AL_Q_28-29

돌발 / 건강

유지 방법 차이

In the past, tell me how your parents' generation kept their health. How is it different from what your generation does? Give me all the details.

/ KEYWORD

최근 언급된 건강 관련 이슈

There must be some issues related to our health in the news these days. Do people in your country talk about that topic a lot? Please describe common health-related concerns people have.

/ KEYWORD

MP3 IM3-AL_Q_30-31

돌발 / 하우징

과거, 현재 비교

I would like to ask you about houses in your country. Perhaps houses have changed over the years. How is the structure of the houses different from the past?

/ KEYWORD

임대 어려움

There must be a problem when people rent a house. Why do you think those problems occur? How do people in your country solve those problems?

/ KEYWORD

세부묘사

진짜녀석들 OPIc에서 제공하는 다양한 세부묘사 질문들의 MP3를 듣고 키워드 캐치를 훈련하세요.

🎧 MP3 IM3-AL_Q_32-33

돌발 / 인터넷

연령별(세대별) 인터넷 이용 차이점

How is Internet usage different among generations? What do younger people commonly do online? What do older people do online? Please give me all the details.

/ KEYWORD

이슈, 보안 문제

Let's talk about some issues that people talk about regarding the Internet. What are their concerns, and why are those concerns a problem? Are there any security problems? If so, talk about the issue.

/ KEYWORD

🎧 MP3 IM3-AL_Q_34-35

돌발 / 레스토랑

음식점 비교

You can expect set menus at chain restaurants such as Outback. On the other hand, small local restaurants have their own menus, and you may not know what to expect. Talk about the difference between those two.

/ KEYWORD

건강식 메뉴 변화 추세

People have become a lot more health-conscious than in the past. So, lots of restaurants are changing their menus for those customers. Talk about the changes you notice about a restaurant related to this trend.

/ KEYWORD

🎧 MP3 IM3-AL_Q_36-37

돌발 / 식품

식품 구매 방식 변화

How has the way people bought food changed over the years? Where did people buy food in the past, and where do they buy it now?

/ KEYWORD

식품 오염 뉴스

Food can become contaminated because of bacteria. It can cause consumer illness. I would like you to tell me about an incident you heard on the news regarding food contamination. What was the problem? How was it dealt with?

/ KEYWORD

세부묘사

진짜녀석들 OPIc에서 제공하는 다양한 세부묘사 질문들의 MP3를 듣고 키워드 캐치를 훈련하세요.

돌발 / 모임

🎧 MP3 IM3-AL_Q_38-39

과거, 현재의 모임 차이

Let's talk about the ways of gatherings. It has changed over the years. How was it in the past? How is it now? What are the differences and the similarities? Please give me all the details.

/ KEYWORD

계획 과정 어려운 점

It is not easy to make plans for gatherings. What are some issues related to making plans for gathering? How do people deal with those problems?

/ KEYWORD

돌발 / 지형, 이웃국가

🎧 MP3 IM3-AL_Q_40-41

이웃 국가 변화 추세

Tell me about a country that is a geographically similar to your country. What are the changes that the country has gone through in recent years? Please give me all the details.

/ KEYWORD

이웃 국가 정치, 경제 기사

I would like to ask you about an article you read about the country you have mentioned before. What was the issue about? Also, how was it related to the politics or the economy of that country?

/ KEYWORD

돌발 / 휴일

🎧 MP3 IM3-AL_Q_42-43

우리나라 휴일의 특별한 점

Tell me about some holidays in your country. What do people normally do during those holidays? What are some special things about those holidays? Give me all the details.

/ KEYWORD

휴일 관련 걱정거리

Let's talk about some issues or concerns that people in your country have regarding holidays. What steps do people need to take in order to solve this problem?

/ KEYWORD

세부묘사

진짜녀석들 OPIc에서 제공하는 다양한 세부묘사 질문들의 MP3를 듣고 키워드 캐치를 훈련하세요.

🎧 MP3 IM3-AL_Q_44-45

돌발 / 재활용

재활용 과거, 현재 비교

How is recycling you practiced when you were young different from what you do today? What are the differences and similarities? Please tell me about how recycling has changed over the years.

/ KEYWORD

최근 재활용 뉴스

Let's talk about one of the recycling issues that you heard in the news recently. What was the news about? What is being done to solve the issue? Please give me all the details about that issue on recycling.

/ KEYWORD

🎧 MP3 IM3-AL_Q_46-47

서베이 / 공원

어른, 아이들 공원활동 및 시설 비교

Now, describe the differences in activities between children and adults at the park. What are the differences? How are the facilities at parks different for children and adults?

/ KEYWORD

공원 관련 이슈 및 해결책

I would like to ask you about one of the issues about parks in your country. What are some challenges public parks are faced with these days? Discuss what has caused these concerns. What steps do we take in order to solve this problem?

/ KEYWORD

11 강   유형 02 (세부묘사)

스크립트 훈련1

세부묘사(전자기기) 집에서 사용하는 가전제품

Q20 ———

🎧 MP3 IM3-AL_Q_20

What types of home appliances are used in your house? It must be a refrigerator, a microwave, or a dishwasher. Tell me about **the appliances used for various tasks in your home.**

당신의 집에서 어떤 가전제품을 사용하나요? 아마 냉장고, 전자레인지 또는 식기세척기 일 것입니다. 당신의 집에서 다양한 목적으로 사용되는 가전제품에 대하여 말해 주세요.

🎧 MP3 IM3-AL_A_20

서론
시작문장/10%

- Well, *the types of home <u>appliances</u> that are used in my <u>house?</u>* You know, I <u>cannot</u> live without a TV.

본론
단락별 핵심문장/80%

- When it comes to a home <u>appliance,</u> it <u>has</u> to be my <u>TV.</u>
  - I mean, when you visit my <u>place</u>, the <u>first</u> thing you can see is a <u>flat</u> screen TV and a <u>cozy</u> couch.
  - As you walk <u>in</u>, you will <u>probably</u> see me being a <u>couch</u> potato.

- The <u>most</u> interesting thing about my TV is that it has <u>powerful</u> speakers.
  - So, I do <u>many</u> kinds of things such as listening to <u>music</u>, watching <u>movies</u> and stuff like that.
  - You know, the <u>main</u> reason why I like to stay at home is that I can spend time <u>alone</u> watching TV.

- <u>Speaking</u> of watching TV, I think it is one of the most <u>efficient</u> ways to release stress.
  - So, <u>most</u> Koreans are watching TV these days.

결론
마무리문장/10%

- <u>Alright</u> Eva, this is <u>all</u> I can say about *the types of home <u>appliances</u> that are used in my <u>house.</u>* Thank you.

- -

- 음, **우리 집에서 사용하는 가전제품?** 있잖아, 난 TV 없이 살 수 없어.

- 가전제품에 대해서 말한다면, 바로 내 TV 지.
  - 내 말은, 내가 우리 집을 가면 처음 보이는 것은 평면 TV와 안락한 소파야.
  - 더 걸어 들어가면, 너는 카우치 포테이토가 되어있는 날 볼 수 있을 거야.

- TV에서 가장 흥미로운 것은 강력한 스피커가 있다는 거야.
  - 그래서, 나는 음악을 듣고, 영화를 보는 등의 많은 것들을 해.
  - 있잖아, 내가 집에 있는 것을 좋아하는 가장 큰 이유는 TV를 보면서 혼자 시간을 보낼 수 있기 때문이야.

- TV 보는 것에 대해 말해본다면, 스트레스를 해소하는 가장 효율적인 방법 중 하나라고 생각해.
  - 그래서, 대부분의 한국인들은 요즘 TV를 봐.

- 그래 에바, 이게 우리 **집에서 사용하는 가전제품**이야. 고마워.

어휘 및 표현

the types of appliances that are used in my house 우리 집에서 사용하는 가전제품 종류   **it has to be my TV** 내 TV 이어야만 해
when you visit my place 우리 집을 방문하면   **it has powerful speakers** 강력한 스피커가 있어
one of the most efficient ways to release stress 스트레스를 해소하는 가장 효율적인 방법 중 하나

세부묘사(전자기기) 가전제품이 가져다 준 삶의 변화

Q21 ━━━━━━━━━━━━━━━━━━━━━━━━━━━ 🎧 MP3 IM3-AL_Q_21

Home appliances have changed our lives. **How was life before the appliances different from life now?** Tell me the biggest change that has had an impact on our lives. Please give me specific details.

가전제품은 우리 삶의 변화를 주었습니다. 가전제품이 없던 전의 삶과 현재 삶은 어떻게 다른가요? 우리 삶에 영향을 주었던 가장 큰 변화는 무엇인가요? 상세히 알려주세요.

━━━━━━━━━━━━━━━━━━━━━━━━━━━━━━━━━━━━━━ 🎧 MP3 IM3-AL_A_21

서론
시작문장/10%

• <u>That's</u> a good question, *How have <u>home</u> appliances changed our <u>lives</u>?* Sure, I got it.

본론
단락별 핵심문장/80%

• **When it <u>comes</u> to the home appliances,** I guess the <u>coffee</u> maker is the <u>biggest</u> change in our lives.
  - I mean, <u>most</u> Koreans are using it since it's getting <u>increasingly</u> popular.

• **In the <u>past</u>,** people could <u>only</u> get their coffee at <u>coffee</u> shops.
  - But you know, the coffee shops were <u>always</u> filled with <u>lots</u> of people.
  - So, people had to stand in a <u>long</u> line.

• **However, <u>these</u> days,** we can make our <u>own</u> coffee at home.
  - Well, using a coffee maker is very <u>convenient</u>.
  - I mean, you <u>don't</u> have to get dressed up to get a bit of <u>caffeine</u>.

결론
마무리문장/10%

• Well, okay Eva, this is <u>pretty</u> much about *how the <u>coffee</u> makers have changed our lives.*

- -

• 좋은 질문이야, **가전제품이 가져다준 삶의 변화?** 물론이지, 알겠어.

• 가전제품에 대해서 말한다면, 커피 메이커가 우리 삶에 가져다준 가장 큰 변화라고 생각해.
  - 내 말은, 대부분의 한국인들이 그걸 사용해 왜냐하면 점점 인기 있어지고 있거든.

• 과거에는, 사람들은 커피를 사려면 커피숍에 가야 했어.
  - 그런데, 커피숍은 항상 많은 사람들로 가득 차 있었어.
  - 그래서 사람들은 긴 줄을 서야만 했었어.

• 하지만, 요즘은 집에서 커피를 만들 수 있어.
  - 음, 커피 메이커를 사용하는 것은 매우 편해.
  - 내 말은, 넌 카페인 조금을 얻기 위해 옷을 차려입을 필요가 없어.

• 음 오케이 에바, 이게 **커피 메이커가 우리 삶에 준 변화**야.

어휘 및 표현
home appliances 가전제품   **people could only get their coffee at coffee shops** 커피숍에서만 커피를 마실 수 있었어
we can make our own coffee at home 집에서 커피를 만들 수 있어   **very convenient** 매우 편리해
you don't have to get dressed up 차려 입지 않아도 돼   **a bit of caffeine** 카페인

세부묘사(산업) 우리나라 젊은 사람들이 일하고 싶은 회사

Q22

🎧 MP3 IM3-AL_Q_22

What kinds of companies do young people in your country want to work? Why do they want to work at those companies? Please give me some examples of the industry or company.

당신 나라에 있는 젊은이들은 어떤 회사에서 일하길 원하나요? 왜 그들은 그 회사에서 일하길 원하죠? 산업 혹은 회사에 관한 예를 들어주세요.

🎧 MP3 IM3-AL_A_22

서론
시작문장/10%

- Oh yeah, *the companies that <u>young</u> people want to work?* You know, I got <u>two</u> kinds of companies to <u>talk</u> about.

본론
단락별 핵심문장/80%

- Speaking of <u>young</u> people, they want to work in the <u>cell</u> phone industry.
  - <u>First</u> of all, it is one of the <u>rising</u> industries in Korea.
  - And the cell phone has <u>various</u> functions such as taking <u>pictures</u>, listening to <u>music</u> or playing <u>games</u>.
  - And as you may know, the <u>cell</u> phones in Korea are getting <u>increasingly</u> popular.

- <u>Plus,</u> young people also want to work in the <u>coffee</u> industry.
  - When it comes to <u>coffee</u>, Koreans <u>normally</u> take one to <u>three</u> cups of coffee a day.

결론
마무리문장/10%

- Well, okay Eva, this is <u>pretty</u> much about *the <u>companies</u> that young people want to work.*

- -

- 오 예, **젊은 사람들이 일하고 싶어 하는 회사?** 있잖아, 난 이야기하고 싶은 게 2가지 종류의 회사가 있어.

- 젊은 사람들에 대해 말해본다면, 그들은 핸드폰 사업에서 일하고 싶어 해.
  - 첫 번째로, 한국에서 그건 뜨고 있는 산업 중에 하나야.
  - 그리고, 핸드폰은 사진 찍기, 음악 듣기, 게임하기와 같은 다양한 기능이 있어.
  - 그리고 너도 알다시피, 한국에서 핸드폰은 점점 인기 있어지고 있어.

- 추가로, 젊은 사람들은 커피 산업에서 일하고 싶어 해.
  - 커피에 대해서 말한다면, 한국인들은 하루에 1~3잔씩 보통 커피를 마시거든.
  - 나는 항상 아침에 라테를 마시고 항상 긴 줄을 서야 돼.

- 음, 오케이 에바, 이게 **젊은 사람들이 일하고 싶어 하는 회사야.**

어휘 및 표현

the companies that young people want to work 젊은 사람들이 일하고 싶어하는 회사   two kinds of companies to talk about
말하고 싶은 2가지 종류의 회사   cell phone industry 핸드폰 산업   one of the rising industries in Korea 한국에서 그건 뜨고 있는 산업 중에 하나
Koreans normally take one to three coffees a day 한국인들은 하루에 1~3잔씩 보통 커피를 마셔

세부묘사(산업) 우리나라 사람들이 진로를 위해 하는 일

Q23 ──────────────────────────────── 🎧 MP3 IM3-AL_Q_23

I would like to know **what people do to get a job** in your country. Do they go to school? And what do they do when they get a job? Do they get any training at the company? Tell me everything they do to get a job.

당신 나라 사람들이 직업을 얻기 위해 무엇을 하는 지 알고 싶습니다. 학교에 진학하나요? 직업을 구할 때 무엇을 하나요? 회사에서 교육을 받나요? 그들이 직업을 얻기 위해 하는 모든 것들에 대해 말해주세요.

──────────────────────────────── 🎧 MP3 IM3-AL_A_23

서론
시작문장/10%

본론
단락별 핵심문장/80%

• Oh yeah, *what <u>people</u> do to get a <u>job?</u>* You know, they study about the <u>industries</u> that they are interested in.

• **When it comes to <u>people</u> who are interested in the <u>music</u> industry,** they study <u>music</u>.
  - I mean, in <u>order</u> to study the music <u>industry</u>, they try to listen to <u>all</u> kinds of <u>music</u>.
  - <u>Moreover</u>, they attend K-POP <u>concerts</u> since it's getting <u>increasingly</u> popular.

• **Speaking of the <u>coffee</u> industry,** people visit <u>lots</u> of coffee shops.
  - I mean, they see if the coffee shops are <u>extremely</u> clean, and the people are <u>friendly</u> or not.
  - Also, they stand in a <u>long</u> line to order their coffee to <u>taste</u> them.

• <u>Lastly</u>, I think people need to experience <u>various</u> industries in order to get a <u>job</u>.

결론
마무리문장/10%

• Well, <u>okay</u> Eva, this is <u>pretty</u> much about *what people do to get a job.*

- -

• **오 예, 사람들이 직업을 구하기 위해 하는 것?** 있잖아, 그들이 관심 있는 산업들에 대해서 공부해.

• 음악 산업에 관심 있는 사람들에 대해서 말한다면, 그들은 음악을 공부해.
  - 내 말은, 음악산업을 공부하기 위해서는 모든 종류의 음악을 들으려고 해야 돼.
  - 게다가, 그들은 K-pop 콘서트에 가 왜냐하면 그건 점점 인기 있어지고 있거든.

• 커피 산업에 대해 말해본다면, 사람들은 많은 커피숍에 방문해.
  - 내 말은, 그들은 커피숍이 깨끗한지 사람들이 친절한지 아닌지에 대해서 봐.
  - 또한, 커피를 주문하기 위하여 긴 줄을 서야 돼.

• 마지막으로, 직업을 얻기 위해서는 다양한 산업의 경험을 필요로 해.

• 음, 오케이 에바, 이게 **사람들이 직업을 얻기 위해 하는 것이야.**

어휘 및 표현
what people do to get a job 사람들이 직업을 갖기 위해 하는 것   the industries that they are interested in 그들이 관심 있는 산업들
people who are interested in the music industry 음악 산업에 관심 있는 사람들   they attend K-POP concerts 케이팝 콘서트에 가
taste them 맛을 봐.

세부묘사(가족/친구) 가족 혹은 친구 중 두 명 유사점 & 차이점

Q24 ──────────────────────────────── 🎧 MP3 IM3-AL_Q_24

Now, I would like you to pick **two of your family members or friends** and tell me about **their differences and similarities.** Please give me all details.

당신의 가족이나 친구 중에 2명을 골라보세요. 그리고 차이점과 유사점에 대해 말해주세요. 상세히 말해 주세요.

──────────────────────────────────── 🎧 MP3 IM3-AL_A_24

서론
시작문장/10%

본론
단락별 핵심문장/80%

- Oh yeah, _differences_ and _similarities_ _about my friends?_ You know, let me tell you about my old school buddies.

- **When it comes to my friends,** it has to be Ryan and John.
  - Actually, I spend lots of time with them and I've known them since I was 15.

- **Speaking of Ryan,** he is a personal trainer.
  - When I'm with him, I can do many kinds of things such as playing sports, going to the gym and stuff like that.

- **When it comes to John,** he is a musician.
  - Which means, he knows a lot about music.
  - So, whenever I go to concerts, he is a great person to go with.

- **Frankly speaking,** both of them love to drink.
  - So we usually drink beers like there's no tomorrow.

결론
마무리문장/10%

- **Alright Eva,** this is all I can say about _the differences_ and _similarities_ _about my friends._ Thank you.

- -

- 오 예, **내 친구의 차이점과 유사점?** 있잖아, 내 오래된 친구들에 대해 너에게 이야기해줄게.

- 내 친구에 대해서 말한다면, Ryan과 John이야.
  - 실제로, 난 그들과 많은 시간을 보내고 15살 때부터 그들을 알아왔어.

- Ryan에 대해 말해본다면, 그는 개인 트레이너야.
  - 내가 그와 함께 있을 때, 나는 운동, 헬스장 가는 것과 같은 많은 것들을 할 수 있어.

- John에 대해서 말한다면, 그는 뮤지션이야.
  - 이것은 그가 음악에 대해 많이 안다는 것을 의미해.
  - 그래서 내가 콘서트에 갈 때마다, 그는 같이 가기에 좋은 사람이야.

- 솔직히 말하면, 둘 다 술 마시는 것을 좋아해.
  - 그래서 우리는 내일이 없는 것처럼 보통 술을 마셔.

- 그래 에바, 이게 **내 친구의 차이점과 공통점**이야. 고마워.

어휘 및 표현

differences and similarities 차이점과 유사점   old school buddies 오래된 친구   When I'm with him 내가 그와 함께 있을 때
both of them love to drink 둘 다 술 마시는 것을 좋아해   drink beers like there's no tomorrow 내일이 없는 것처럼 술을 마셔

세부묘사(가족/친구) 가족/친구와 주로 하는 대화

Q25 ━━━━━━━━━━━━━━━━━━━━━━━━━━━━ 🎧 MP3 IM3-AL_Q_25

What kinds of topics do you commonly talk about with your family or friends? When was the last time you talked to them? What did you talk about? Please give me all the details.

당신이 가족과 또는 친구와 주로 어떤 주제에 대해 이야기를 나누시나요? 가장 최근에 그들과 대화한 적은 언제인가요? 어떤 주제에 대해 대화했나요? 상세히 말해주세요.

━━ 🎧 MP3 IM3-AL_A_25

서론
시작문장/10%

본론
단락별 핵심문장/80%

결론
마무리문장/10%

• <u>That's</u> a good question, *what I talk about with my <u>friends</u>?* Sure, I got it.

• **When it comes to the <u>topic</u>,** it is about how to lose <u>weight</u>.
  - You know, in <u>order</u> to prepare for summer, I must spend <u>lots</u> of time at the gym because I need to lose <u>weight</u>.
  - And I <u>always</u> talk to my friend Rachel about losing <u>weight</u> because she is a <u>personal</u> trainer.

• In <u>addition</u>, we <u>talk</u> about going to the gym to run on a <u>treadmill</u>.
  - But I <u>always</u> end up going to the <u>park</u> to run since it's free to <u>visit</u>.
  - <u>Also</u>, there is a <u>huge</u> running track where you can see <u>lots</u> of people exercising.

• So <u>overall</u>, this is about *what I talk about with my <u>friends</u>.*

- -

• 좋은 질문이야, **친구들과 이야기하는 것?** 물론이지, 알겠어.

• 내가 이야기하는 토픽에 대해서 말한다면, 살을 빼는 법에 관해서야.
  - 있잖아, 여름을 준비하기 위해 난 헬스장에서 많은 시간을 보내야만 해. 왜냐하면 난 살을 뺄 필요가 있거든.
  - 그리고 난 항상 내 친구 Rachel과 살 빼는 것에 대해 이야기해. 왜냐하면 그녀는 개인 트레이너거든.

• 게다가, 러닝머신을 하기 위해 헬스장에 가는 것에 대해 말해.
  - 그러나, 난 결국은 뛰기 위해 공원으로 가는 것으로 끝나 왜냐하면 공원은 공짜잖아.
  - 또한, 많은 사람들이 운동하고 있는 것을 볼 수 있는 큰 러닝트랙이 있어.

• 그래서 전반적으로, 이게 **내 친구들과 이야기하는 것**이야.

어휘 및 표현
what I talk about with my friends 친구들과 하는 대화   **how to lose weight** 살을 빼는 방법   **going to the gym** 헬스장에 가는 것
end up ~ing ~로 결국 끝나다

세부묘사(전화기) 예전/지금 전화기 비교

Q26 ───────────────

Do you remember the phone you used for the first time? What is **the difference between the phone you used back then and the phone you use now?**

당신이 사용했던 첫 번째 핸드폰에 대해 기억이 나시나요? 예전에 사용했던 핸드폰과 지금 사용하는 핸드폰의 차이는 무엇인가요?

서론
시작문장/10%

본론
단락별 핵심문장/80%

- Oh yeah, *the difference between the phone I used back then and now?* Perfect!

- **When I was little,** I used to use a flip phone.
  - I mean, in the past, the cell phones were only used to make calls.

- **However,** the cell phones today have various functions such as taking pictures or playing games.
  - The most interesting thing about the cell phones today is the voice recognition.
  - In order to use that feature, you just talk to the phone.
  - Then, the phone will dial or text to people you want to.

결론
마무리문장/10%

- Alright Eva, this is all I can say about *the difference between the phone I used back then and now.*
  - Thank you.

- -

- 오 예, 예전에 사용했던 핸드폰과 지금 사용하는 핸드폰의 차이? 완벽해!

- 내가 어렸을 때, 난 폴더폰을 쓰곤 했어.
  - 내 말은, 과거에는 핸드폰들은 오직 전화를 거는 데만 사용되었어.

- 하지만, 오늘날 휴대폰은 사진 찍기 게임하기 등과 같이 다양한 기능이 있어.
  - 오늘날 핸드폰에서 가장 흥미로운 점은 음성인식 기능이야.
  - 이 기능을 사용하기 위해서는 그냥 핸드폰에 대고 말하면 돼.
  - 그러면, 핸드폰은 네가 원하는 사람들에게 전화를 걸거나 문자를 할 거야.

- 그래 에바, 이게 **내가 이전에 사용했던 핸드폰과 지금 사용하는 핸드폰의 차이야.** 고마워.

어휘 및 표현
the phone I used back then and now 예전과 지금 사용하는 핸드폰   a flip phone 폴더폰   the cell phones were only used to make calls
핸드폰들은 오직 전화를 거는 데만 사용되었어   the voice recognition 음성인식   feature 기능
the phone will dial or text to people 핸드폰이 사람에게 전화를 걸거나 문자를 해줘

세부묘사(전화기) 핸드폰 사회적 문제

Q27 ──────────────── 🎧 MP3 IM3-AL_Q_27

Now, **let's talk about some issues related to cell phones. Why** do people talk about that topic? Why is it **a problem?** Please give me all the details.

사람들이 핸드폰에 관하여 이야기하는 몇몇 문제들을 이야기 해주세요. 사람들은 그 주제에 관하여 왜 이야기 하나요? 왜 그게 문제인가요? 상세히 말해주세요.

──────────────── 🎧 MP3 IM3-AL_A_27

서론
시작문장/10%

본론
단락별 핵심문장/80%

- Oh yeah, *some issues people talk about related to cell phones?* People cannot live without a cell phone.

- Speaking of issues, people become a phone addict.
  - In the past, people used to meet up for social gatherings in their free time.
  - Also, they did many kinds of things such as playing sports, listening to music and stuff like that.

- However, people are so addicted to their phones these days.
  - I mean, it is one of the biggest issues related to cell phones.

- In order to solve this problem, people need to have lots of social gatherings with their family or friends.
  - Because they are missing out on so many things.

결론
마무리문장/10%

- Alright Eva, this is all I can say about *some issues people talk about related to cell phones.* Thank you.

- -

- 오 예, 사람들이 **핸드폰에 관하여 이야기하는 몇몇 문제들?** 사람들은 핸드폰 없이 살 수가 없어.

- 문제들에 대해 말해본다면, 사람들은 핸드폰 중독자가 되고 있어.
  - 과거에는, 사람들은 여가시간에 사회적인 모임을 위해 만나곤 했어.
  - 그래서, 그들은 운동을 하고, 음악을 듣는 등과 같은 많은 종류의 것들을 했어.

- 하지만, 사람들은 요즘 핸드폰에 점점 중독이 되어 가고 있어.
  - 내 말은, 그것은 핸드폰과 관련된 가장 큰 문제들 중에 하나야.

- 이 문제를 해결하기 위하여, 사람들은 가족 또는 친구들과 많은 사회적인 모임을 할 필요가 있어.
  - 왜냐하면 그들은 많은 것들을 놓치고 있기 때문이야.

- 그래 에바, 이게 **핸드폰에 관하여 이야기하는 몇몇 문제들**이야. 고마워.

어휘 및 표현
some issues people talk about related to cell phones 사람들이 말하는 핸드폰 관련 이슈   **people became a phone addict**
핸드폰 중독자가 되었어   **people are so addicted to their phones** 사람들은 핸드폰에 너무 중독이 되었어
they are missing out on so many things 많은 것들을 놓친다

12강

유형 02 (세부묘사)

스크립트 훈련2

3번

14번

15번

세부묘사(건강) 세대별 건강 유지 방법 차이

Q28

🎧 MP3 IM3-AL_Q_28

In the past, tell me **how your parents' generation kept their health. How is it different from what your generation does?** Give me all the details.

당신의 부모세대가 과거에 어떻게 건강을 유지했는지에 대해 말해주세요. 당신 세대와는 어떻게 다른가요? 세부적으로 말해주세요.

🎧 MP3 IM3-AL_A_28

서론
시작문장/10%

본론
단락별 핵심문장/80%

결론
마무리문장/10%

- <u>That's</u> a good question, *how to maintain their <u>health</u>?* Sure, I got it.

- In the <u>past,</u> they used to go to <u>parks</u> to exercise.
  - Because there were <u>running</u> tracks at the parks.
  - <u>Also,</u> at parks, there were <u>many</u> different areas where people play <u>soccer</u>, cricket and so on.

- <u>Frankly</u> speaking, there aren't <u>many</u> differences when it comes to <u>our</u> generation.
  - I mean, people have become a <u>lot</u> more <u>health</u>-conscious than in the past.
  - So people spend <u>lots</u> of time at the gym in <u>order</u> to lose weight.
  - You know, going to the <u>gym</u> has become a <u>daily</u> routine.

- Well, <u>okay</u> Eva, this is <u>pretty</u> much about *how people maintain their <u>health</u>.*

- -

- 좋은 질문이야, **그들의 건강을 유지하는 법?** 물론이지, 알겠어.

- 과거에는, 사람들이 운동하기 위해 공원에 가곤 했어.
  - 왜냐하면 공원에는 러닝트랙이 있었거든.
  - 그래서, 공원에서는 사람들이 축구, 크리켓 등을 할 수 있는 많은 다른 장소가 있었어.

- 솔직히 말하면, 우리 세대에 관해서는 많은 차이점이 있진 않아.
  - 내 말은, 사람들은 과거보다 더 많이 건강을 신경 쓰게 되었어.
  - 그래서 사람들은 살을 빼기 위해 헬스장에서 많은 시간을 보내.
  - 있잖아, 헬스장에 가는 것은 일상생활이 되었어.

- 음, 오케이 에바, 이게 **사람들이 건강을 유지하는 법이야.**

어휘 및 표현
how to maintain their health 그들의 건강을 유지하는 법   **our generation** 우리 세대   **going to the gym** 헬스장에 가는 것

세부묘사(건강) 최근 언급된 건강 관련 이슈

Q29 ────────── 🎧 MP3 IM3-AL_Q_29

There must be some issues related to our health in the news these days. Do people in your country talk about that topic a lot? Please **describe common health-related concerns people have.**

요즘 뉴스에서 건강과 관련된 이슈들이 많이 나오고 있습니다. 당신 나라 사람들은 그 주제에 대해 많이 이야기 하나요? 사람들이 가지고 있는 흔한 건강 관련 걱정들에 대하여 설명해 주세요.

────────── 🎧 MP3 IM3-AL_A_29

서론
시작문장/10%

• Oh yeah, *some issues related to our health?* You know, many Koreans work late in the office.

본론
단락별 핵심문장/80%

• When it comes to health, people have become a lot more health-conscious than in the past.
  - However, many people don't have time to workout.

• In order to solve this problem, Koreans are trying to work out a lot.
  - So, lots of people go to parks to exercise because there are huge running tracks at the parks.
  - Also, you can find many different areas where people play soccer, cricket and so on.
  - When they are busy or too cold to run, they hit the gym.
  - As you can imagine, people run on treadmills every day.

결론
마무리문장/10%

• Alright Eva, this is all I can say about *one of the issues related to our health.* Thank you.

- -

• 오 예, **우리 건강과 관련된 몇몇 이슈?** 있잖아, 한국인들은 회사에서 늦은 시간까지 일을 많이 해.

• 건강에 대해서 말한다면, 사람들은 과거보다 더 많이 건강을 신경 쓰고 있어.
  - 하지만, 많은 사람들은 운동을 할 수 있는 시간이 없어.

• 이 문제를 해결하기 위해서, 한국 사람들은 운동을 많이 하려고 노력해.
  - 그래서 많은 사람들은 공원에 가서 운동을 해. 왜냐하면 공원에는 큰 러닝트랙이 있거든.
  - 추가로, 공원에서는 사람들이 축구, 크리켓 등을 하는 많은 다른 지역들이 있어.
  - 그들이 바쁘거나 뛰기에 너무 추울 때, 그들은 헬스장에 가.
  - 네가 상상하듯이, 사람들은 매일 러닝머신을 해.

• 그래 에바, 이게 **우리 건강과 관련된 이슈들 중에 하나야.** 고마워.

어휘 및 표현
some issues related to our health 건강 관련 이슈   **Koreans work late in the office** 한국사람들은 늦게까지 일을 한다
When they are busy or too cold to run 그들이 바쁘거나 뛰기에 너무 추울 때   **hit the gym** 헬스장에 가다

세부묘사(하우징) 거주지 과거/현재 비교

Q30 ──────────

I would like to ask you about **houses in your country.** Perhaps houses have changed over the years. **How is the structure of the houses different from the past?**

당신 나라에 있는 집에 관하여 당신에게 물어보고 싶습니다. 아마 집은 몇 년에 걸쳐 변했겠죠. 예전에 비해 집 구조의 차이가 어떻게 달라졌나요?

🎧 MP3 IM3-AL_A_30

서론
시작문장/10%

본론
단락별 핵심문장/80%

- That's a good question, *the structure of the houses?* This is pretty interesting.

- **In the past,** houses in Korea were so small.
  - Basically, there was 1 bedroom with a small living room, kitchen and a bathroom.

- **But now,** most houses have 5 floors and a terrace garden.
  - When it comes to my house, our place has four bedrooms, two baths and a huge garden on the top floor.
  - The most interesting thing about houses today is that every single thing is automated.

- **Generally,** it has central heating and air-conditioning, so it's cool during summer and warm during winter.
  - As you can imagine, yeah, the structure of the houses in Korea has changed a lot over the years.

결론
마무리문장/10%

- Well, okay Eva, this is pretty much about *the structure of the houses.*

- -

- 좋은 질문이야, **집의 구조?** 꽤 흥미롭네.

- 과거에는, 한국 집은 매우 작았어.
  - 기본적으로, 작은 거실에 하나의 침실, 부엌, 화장실이 있었어.

- 그러나 지금은, 대부분의 집은 5층까지 있고 테라스 정원이 있어.
  - 우리 집에 대해서 말한다면, 4개의 침실, 2개의 화장실, 꼭대기 층에는 큰 정원이 있어.
  - 우리 집에서 가장 흥미로운 점은 모든 것들이 자동화되어 있다는 거야.

- 일반적으로는, 중앙난방과 에어컨이 있어 그래서 여름에는 시원하고 겨울에는 따뜻해.
  - 네가 상상할 수 있듯이, 한국 집의 구조는 몇 년 동안 많이 바뀌었어.

- 음, 오케이 에바, 이게 **집의 구조**에 관한 거야.

어휘 및 표현

the structure of the houses 집의 구조   This is pretty interesting 매우 흥미롭네요   Basically 기본적으로   houses today 오늘날의 집들

136

세부묘사(하우징) 집 임대 시, 사람들이 겪는 어려움

Q31 ─────────────────────────── 🎧 MP3 IM3-AL_Q_31

There must be **a problem when people rent a house. Why do you think those problems occur? How do people in your country solve those problems?**

사람들이 집을 렌트 할 때 문제가 있을 것입니다. 왜 당신은 그러한 문제들이 발생한다고 생각하나요? 당신 나라에 있는 사람들은 그러한 문제들을 어떻게 해결하나요?

─────────────────────────── 🎧 MP3 IM3-AL_A_31

서론
시작문장/10%

본론
단락별 핵심문장/80%

- <u>That's</u> a good question, *a __problem__ when people rent a __house__?* Sure, I got it.

- **Speaking of issues,** people can experience <u>various</u> problems when they <u>talk</u> about renting a <u>house</u>.
  - One of the <u>biggest</u> issues about renting a house is the <u>high</u> cost.
  - When it <u>comes</u> to <u>normal</u> Korean family, most Koreans have a <u>big</u> family.
  - As you can <u>imagine</u>, people need a <u>huge</u> house for <u>everyone</u> to live in.

- **In order to <u>solve</u> this problem,** <u>lots</u> of Koreans are moving to <u>rural</u> areas since the houses are <u>cheaper</u> and reliable.
  - <u>Plus</u>, in rural areas, there are <u>many</u> different areas where people play <u>soccer</u>, cricket and so on.
  - In my <u>opinion</u>, getting back to nature, just relaxing outside is <u>essential</u> for human beings.

결론
마무리문장/10%

- **Well, <u>okay</u> Eva,** this is <u>pretty</u> much about *a __problem__ when people rent a __house__.*
  ··

- -

- 좋은 질문이야, **사람들이 집을 렌트할 때 문제?** 물론이지, 알겠어.

- 문제들에 대해 말해본다면, 사람들은 집을 렌트하는 것에 대한 이야기할 때 다양한 문제를 겪고 있어.
  - 집을 렌트하는 것에서 가장 큰 문제 중의 하나는 높은 비용이야.
  - 일반적인 한국 가족에 대해서 말한다면 대부분의 한국인들은 큰 가족이야.
  - 네가 상상할 수 있듯이, 사람들은 모든 가족들이 살 수 있을 정도로 큰 집을 필요로 해.

- 이러한 문제를 해결하기 위하여, 많은 한국인들은 지방으로 이사를 가 왜냐하면 집들이 더 싸고 합리적이기 때문이야.
  - 추가로, 지방에서는 사람들이 축구, 크리켓 등을 할 수 있는 장소들이 많이 있어.
  - 내 생각으로는 자연으로 돌아가서 밖에서 쉬는 것은 인간에게 필수적이야.

- 음, 오케이 에바, 이게 **사람들이 집을 렌트할 때 문제**야.

어휘 및 표현

a problem when people rent a house 집 렌트 시 겪는 문제 high cost 높은 비용 most Koreans have a big family 대부분의 한국인들은 대 가족이야
a huge house for everyone to live in 모든 사람들이 살기에 큰 집 lots of Koreans are moving to rural areas 많은 한국사람들은 지방으로 이사를 가
the houses are cheaper and reliable 집들은 저렴하고 믿을만 해

세부묘사(인터넷) 연령별(세대별) 인터넷 이용 차이점

Q32

🎧 MP3 IM3-AL_Q_32

How is Internet usage different among generations? What do **younger people** commonly **do online?** What do **older people do online?** Please give me all the details.

세대 간 인터넷 사용은 어떻게 다른가요? 젊은 사람들은 보통 온라인으로 무엇을 하나요 그리고 나이 든 사람들은 온라인으로 무엇을 하나요?

🎧 MP3 IM3-AL_A_32

서론
시작문장/10%

- Well, *different Internet usage among generations?*

본론
단락별 핵심문장/80%

- For younger people, they use the Internet for lots of things.
  - For instance, they shop many things online.
  - there are many other things you can do such as reading books or ordering coffee online.

- On the other hand, the older people are a little different in some ways.
  - When they use the Internet, they normally listen to music or watch movies.
  - And also, rather than using a cell phone, they prefer their PCs when they use the Internet.

결론
마무리문장/10%

- So overall, this is about *different Internet usage among generations.*

- -

- 음, 세대 간 다른 인터넷 사용?

- 젊은 사람들은, 많은 것을 위하여 인터넷을 사용해.
  - 예를 들어, 그들은 온라인으로 많은 것들을 해.
  - 독서 또는 온라인 커피 주문과 같은 할 수 있는 것들이 많이 있어.

- 반면에, 나이 든 사람들은 조금 달라.
  - 인터넷을 사용할 때, 보통 음악을 듣거나 영화를 봐.
  - 그리고 또한, 핸드폰을 사용하는 것보다 인터넷을 할 때 컴퓨터를 사용하는 것을 선호해.

- 그래서 전반적으로, 이게 **세대 간 다른 인터넷 사용**에 대한 거야.

어휘 및 표현

different Internet usage among generations 세대 간 다른 인터넷 사용 　**For younger people** 젊은 사람들은 　**For instance** 예를 들어
they shop many things online 온라인으로 쇼핑을 많이 해 　**ordering coffee online** 온라인으로 커피를 주문하는 것
rather than using a cell phone 핸드폰을 사용하는 것보다 　**they prefer their PCs** PC사용을 선호해

세부묘사(인터넷) 인터넷 보안 관련 이슈

Q33 ————— 🎧 MP3 IM3-AL_Q_33

Let's talk about some issues that people talk about regarding the Internet. What are their concerns, and why are those concerns a problem? Are there any security problems? If so, talk about the issue.

사람들이 인터넷에 관하여 말하는 몇 가지 이슈들에 대해서 말해봅시다. 그들의 걱정은 무엇이죠, 그리고 왜 그들은 그 문제를 걱정하죠? 보안 문제가 있나요? 그렇다면, 그 문제에 대해서 말해 주세요.

🎧 MP3 IM3-AL_A_33

서론
시작문장/10%

본론
단락별 핵심문장/80%

결론
마무리문장/10%

• Well, *some issues people talk about regarding the Internet?*

• **Speaking of issues,** people can experience various problems when they talk about security on the Internet.
  - I mean, there are lots of hackers who are trying to steal people's personal information.

• **In order to protect our personal information,** we need to create strong and unique passwords for our online accounts.
  - And plus, it is better to change our passwords every 3 months.

• **All we need to know is that** filling out our social media profile is not a good idea.
  - Lastly, we need to back-up our data at all time.

• So overall, this is about *one of the biggest issues people talk about regarding the Internet.*

- -

• 음, 사람들이 인터넷에 관해 이야기하는 몇몇 문제들?

• 문제들에 대해 말해본다면, 사람들은 인터넷 보안에 대해 말할 때 다양한 문제들을 경험할 수 있어.
  - 내 말은, 사람들의 개인 정보를 훔치려고 하는 해커들이 많아.

• 우리 개인정보를 보호하기 위해, 우리는 온라인 계정에 대한 비밀번호를 강력하고 독특한 비밀번호로 만들 필요가 있어.
  - 그리고 추가로, 비밀번호를 3개월마다 바꾸는 게 좋아.

• 우리가 알 필요가 있는 모든 것은 소셜미디어 프로필을 가득 채우는 것은 좋은 생각은 아니라는 거야.
  - 마지막으로, 우리는 항상 데이터를 백업할 필요가 있어.

• 그래서 전반적으로, 이게 **사람들이 인터넷에 관해 이야기하는 몇몇 문제들 중 하나야.**

어휘 및 표현
some issues people talk about regarding the Internet 사람들이 얘기하는 인터넷 관련 이슈   regarding ~에 관하여   security 보안
there are lots of hackers 해커가 많다   steal people's personal information 개인 정보를 훔치다   create strong and unique passwords
강력하고 독특한 비밀번호   it is better to change 바꾸는 것이 좋다   every 3 months 3개월마다   filling out our social media profile
소셜미디어 프로필 작성   we need to back-up our data 데이터 백업을 해야 해

세부묘사(레스토랑) 프렌차이즈 음식점과 일반 음식점 메뉴

Q34 ———————————————————————————————— 🎧 MP3 IM3-AL_Q_34

You can expect set menus at chain restaurants such as Outback. On the other hand, **small local restaurants** have their own menus, and you may not know what to expect. **Talk about the difference between those two.**

아웃백과 같은 체인레스토랑은 당신이 예상하는 세트 메뉴가 있습니다. 반면에, 작은 로컬레스토랑은 그들의 메뉴가 있고 당신은 아마 예상하기 힘들 수도 있습니다. 그 둘의 차이점에 대해 말해주세요.

—— 🎧 MP3 IM3-AL_A_34

서론
시작문장/10%

• Well, *the difference between* _chain_ *restaurants and* _small_ *local restaurants?* I got it.

본론
단락별 핵심문장/80%

• When it comes to _chain_ restaurants, they have _set_ menus.
  - The _main_ reason why people like to go there is that the restaurants are _extremely_ clean, and the people are _so_ friendly.
  - But you know, the restaurants are _always_ filled with _lots_ of people.

• On the _other_ hand, small local restaurants are a _little_ different in some ways.
  - I mean, they can _easily_ adapt their menus for _customers_.
  - Because people have become a _lot_ more health-conscious than in the past.

결론
마무리문장/10%

• So _overall_, this is about *the difference between* _chain_ *restaurants and* _small_ *local restaurants.*

- -

• 음, 체인 레스토랑과 작은 로컬 식당의 차이점? 알겠어.

• 체인 레스토랑에 대해서 말한다면, 미리 만들어진 메뉴들이 있어.
  - 사람들이 거기에 가는 주요한 이유는 레스토랑이 깨끗하고 친절하기 때문이야.
  - 하지만 있잖아, 레스토랑은 항상 많은 사람들로 가득 차 있어.

• 반면에, 작은 현지 식당은 몇몇 관점에서 조금 달라.
  - 내 말은, 그들은 고객들을 위해 메뉴를 쉽게 조정할 수 있어.
  - 왜냐하면 사람들은 과거보다 더 많이 건강에 신경을 쓰고 있기 때문이야.

• 그래서 전반적으로, 이게 **체인 레스토랑과 작은 현지 식당의 차이**야.

———

어휘 및 표현
they have set menus 세트메뉴가 있어   **pre-built** 미리 만들어진   **On the other hand** 반면에   **easily adapt their menus** 메뉴를 쉽게 조정하다
health-conscious 건강에 신경을 쓰는

세부묘사(레스토랑) 레스토랑의 건강식 메뉴 변화 추세

Q35 ———————————————— 🎧 MP3 IM3-AL_Q_35

People have become a lot more health-conscious than in the past. So, lots of restaurants are changing their menus for those customers. Talk about **the changes you notice about a restaurant related to this trend.**

사람들은 예전보다 더 건강에 신경을 쓰고 있습니다. 따라서, 많은 레스토랑들은 메뉴를 바꾸고 있습니다. 이러한 트렌드와 관련하여 당신 나라에서 당신이 알아차릴 수 있는 식당의 변화들에 대하여 말해 주세요.

———————————————————————————————————— 🎧 MP3 IM3-AL_A_35

서론
시작문장/10%

- Well, *changing their menus?* You know, I got a <u>lot</u> to tell you.

본론
단락별 핵심문장/80%

- As you can **expect,** there are <u>lots</u> of restaurants in Korea since Koreans love <u>all</u> kinds of food.
  - But <u>many</u> restaurants are changing their menus for <u>customers</u>.
  - Because <u>most</u> Koreans are gaining <u>too</u> much weight and it is one of the <u>biggest</u> issues in Korea.

- As you can **imagine,** people have become a <u>lot</u> more health-<u>conscious</u> than in the past.
  - So, <u>lots</u> of restaurants are making <u>healthy</u> menus such as <u>avocado</u> sandwiches or <u>spinach</u> salad.

- In <u>order</u> to lose weight, <u>most</u> Koreans run on the treadmill <u>every</u> day.
  - In my <u>opinion</u>, I guess it is <u>important</u> to eat low-calorie foods for our <u>health</u>.

결론
마무리문장/10%

- So <u>overall</u>, this is about *what <u>restaurants</u> are doing for customers.*

- -

- 음, **메뉴에서 변화?** 있잖아, 난 너에게 말할게 많아.

- 네가 예상했듯이, 한국인들은 모든 종류의 음식을 좋아하기 때문에 한국에는 많은 식당이 있어.
  - 그러나, 많은 식당들은 고객을 위해 메뉴를 변화시키고 있어.
  - 왜냐하면 대부분의 한국인들은 살이 많이 찌고 있고 한국에서 가장 큰 이슈 중에 하나야.

- 네가 예상했듯이, 사람들은 과거에 비해 더 건강에 신경을 쓰고 있어.
  - 그래서, 많은 식당들은 아보카도 샌드위치 또는 시금치 샐러드와 같이 건강한 메뉴를 만들고 있어.

- 살을 빼기 위하여 대부분의 한국인들은 매일 러닝머신에서 뛰어.
  - 내 생각으로는, 저칼로리 음식을 먹는 게 건강에 좋을 것 같아.

- 그래서 전반적으로, 이게 **식당들에서 고객들을 위해 하는** 거야.

어휘 및 표현
changing their menus 메뉴를 바꾸는 것   **gain too much weight** 살이 많이 찌다
it is important to eat low-calorie foods 낮은 칼로리 음식을 먹는 것이 중요하다

13강

유형 02 (세부묘사)

스크립트 훈련3

3번

14번

15번

세부묘사(식품) 식품 구매 방식의 변화

Q36 🎧 MP3 IM3-AL_Q_36

How has the way people bought food changed over the years? Where did people buy food in the past, and where do they buy it now?

사람들이 음식을 사는 법은 몇 년 동안 어떻게 변했나요? 사람들은 과거에 어디서 음식을 샀나요? 그리고 그들은 지금 어디서 음식을 사나요?

🎧 MP3 IM3-AL_A_36

서론 시작문장/10%

- Oh yeah, *How has the way people buy food changed over the years?*

본론 단락별 핵심문장/80%

- **In the past,** I suppose people tend to visit the grocery stores once or twice a month.
  - All you need to know is that the grocery stores were always packed with lots of people.

- **But now,** most Koreans go to the huge malls to buy food.
  - In fact, there are lots of famous food malls in town.
  - You know, the malls are normally 10-story buildings, so it definitely stands out.
  - And also, people prefer going there because there are many other things people can do.
  - After shopping, people can have some coffee or watch movies at the mall.

결론 마무리문장/10%

- **Alright Eva,** this is all I can say about *where people buy food in the past and now.* Thank you.

- 오 예, **사람들이 몇 년 동안 음식을 사는 방식이 어떻게 변했는지?**

- 과거에는, 사람들은 한 달에 한두 번씩 식료품점에 가곤 했어.
  - 중요한 점은 식료품점이 항상 많은 사람들로 가득 차 있었다는 거야.

- 그러나 지금, 대부분의 한국인들은 음식을 사기 위해 큰 몰에 가.
  - 사실은, 시내에 유명한 몰들이 많이 있어.
  - 있잖아, 몰들은 보통 10층짜리 건물이고 그래서 눈에 잘 띄어.
  - 그리고 또한, 사람들은 거기에 가는 것을 좋아해 왜냐하면 사람들이 할 수 있는 게 많기 때문이야.
  - 쇼핑 후에, 사람들은 커피를 마실 수 있고 몰에서 영화를 볼 수 있어.

- 그래 에바, 이게 **사람들이 과거와 현재에 음식을 사는 장소야.** 고마워.

어휘 및 표현

the way people buy food 사람들이 음식을 사는 방법   the grocery stores 식료품점   once or twice a month 한 달에 한 두 번

세부묘사(식품) 식품 오염 뉴스

Q37 ── 🎧 MP3 IM3-AL_Q_37

Food can become contaminated because of bacteria. It can cause consumer illness. **I would like you to tell me about an incident you heard on the news** regarding food contamination. What was **the problem?** How was it **dealt with?**

음식은 세균 때문에 오염될 수 있습니다. 그것을 소비자들이 병에 걸리는 것을 유발할 수 있습니다. 식품 오염에 대해서 뉴스를 들었던 사건에 대해서 말해 주세요. 문제는 무엇이었나요? 그것을 어떻게 처리했나요?

🎧 MP3 IM3-AL_A_37

서론
시작문장/10%

• Well, *food **contamination**?* You know, let me tell you the news I heard last summer.

본론
단락별 핵심문장/80%

• **According to the news,** something was wrong with the food at food court.
  - You know, I must say that the food court was in the tallest building in the city.

• **As you may know,** there are 4 distinct seasons in Korea.
  - And obviously, it is scorching hot during summer in Korea.

• **So,** by that reason, the food was contaminated by bacteria.
  - In result, lots of people had to stay in the hospital for a few days.

결론
마무리문장/10%

• **Alright Eva,** this is all I can say about **the news.** Thank you.

- -

• 음, **식품 오염?** 있잖아, 지난여름에 들었던 뉴스에 대해서 말해 줄게.

• 뉴스에 따르면, 푸드코트에 있는 음식은 상했어.
  - 있잖아, 푸드코트는 도시에 있는 가장 큰 건물에 있었어.

• 너도 알다시피, 한국은 뚜렷한 사계절이 있어.
  - 그리고 명백하게, 한국 여름은 정말 뜨거워.

• 그래서, 이러한 이유로, 음식은 박테리아에 의해 오염되었어.
  - 결과적으로, 많은 사람들은 며칠 동안 병원에 입원해야만 했어.

• 그래 에바, 이게 **그 뉴스**에 관한 거야. 고마워.

어휘 및 표현

food contamination 식품 오염   **the news I heard last summer** 작년 여름에 들었던 뉴스   **something was wrong with the food** 음식에 문제가 있었어   **by that reason** 이러한 이유로   **the food was contaminated by bacteria** 음식은 박테리아로 오염되었어
In result 결과적으로   **for a few days** 며칠 동안

세부묘사(모임) 과거/현재 모임 차이

Q38 ──────────────────────────── 🎧 MP3 IM3-AL_Q_38

Let's talk about the ways of gatherings. It has changed over the years. **How was it in the past? How is it now?** What are **the differences and the similarities?** Please give me all the details.

모임의 방식에 대해 말해봅시다. 모임의 방식은 몇 년 동안 변화하고 있습니다. 과거에는 어땠나요? 그리고 지금은 어떤 가요? 차이점과 공통점은 무엇인가요? 자세하게 말해 주세요.

🎧 MP3 IM3-AL_A_38

서론
시작문장/10%

• Oh yeah, *the ways of gatherings?* You know, it has changed a lot over the years.

본론
단락별 핵심문장/80%

• In the past, we normally went to the beaches for gatherings.
  - Because the beaches were perfect spots for playing sports and having parties.
  - And also, watching the sunset was kinda romantic and that's why the beaches were famous for gatherings.
  - You know, people could do many kinds of things such as playing sports, listening to music and stuff like that.

• However, the ways of gatherings have changed a lot over the years.
  - Now, people normally go to the coffee shops for gatherings.
  - Whenever I visit there, I can see bunch of people talking and relaxing.
  - And also, there are many other things you can do such as reading books or just relaxing.

• Overall, people really enjoy meeting people because it helps them release stress.
  - Plus, it is one of the best ways to make friends.

결론
마무리문장/10%

• Alright Eva, this is all I can say about *the ways of gatherings in the past and now.* Thank you.

- -

• 오 예, **모임의 방식?** 있잖아, 그건 몇 년에 걸쳐 많이 바뀌어 왔어.

• 과거에는, 모임을 위해 보통 해변에 갔어.
  - 왜냐하면 해변은 운동을 하고 파티를 하기에 가장 완벽한 장소야.
  - 그리고 또한, 선셋을 보는 것은 로맨틱하고 이게 해변이 모임 하기에 유명한 이유야.
  - 있잖아, 사람들은 운동, 음악 듣기와 같은 많은 종류의 것들을 할 수 있어.

• 하지만, 모임 하는 방식은 몇 년에 걸쳐 변해왔어.
  - 지금, 사람들은 주로 모임을 하기 위해 커피숍에 가.
  - 내가 거기에 갈 때마다, 난 많은 사람들이 이야기하고 쉬는 것을 볼 수 있어.
  - 그리고 또한 독서, 휴식과 같이 할 수 있는 많은 다른 것들이 있어.

• 전반적으로, 사람들은 스트레스 해소에 도움이 되기 때문에 사람들 만나는 것을 좋아해.
  - 추가로, 친구들을 사귈 수 있는 가장 좋은 방법 중 하나야.

• 그래 에바, 이게 **과거와 현재에 모임을 하는 방식**이야. 고마워.

어휘 및 표현
the ways of gatherings 모임의 방식   that's why~ ~하는 이유야   the beaches were famous for gatherings 해변이 모임 하기에 유명하다
one of the best ways to make friends 친구들을 사귀는 가장 좋은 방법 중 하나

세부묘사(모임) 모임 계획 시 겪는 어려운 점

Q39 ──────────────────── 🎧 MP3 IM3-AL_Q_39

It is not easy to make plans for gatherings. **What are some issues related to making plans for gathering?** How do people **deal with those problems?**

모임을 위해 계획을 세우는 과정은 쉽지 않습니다. 모임을 위해 계획을 세우는 것과 관련하여 문제가 무엇인가요? 사람들은 그러한 문제들을 어떻게 해결하죠?

🎧 MP3 IM3-AL_A_39

서론
시작문장/10%

본론
단락별 핵심문장/80%

- Well, *some issues related to making plans for gathering?* This is quite an interesting question.

- Frankly speaking, there aren't many issues when it comes to making plans for gathering.
  - But if I had to choose one, it's that people find it difficult to decide where to meet.

- In the past, people used to meet up at parks for gatherings.
  - Because, the parks were the perfect places to talk and do some outdoor activities.

- However, younger people prefer going to coffee shops for gatherings.
  - But most Koreans like to drink, play sports, listen to music and do some outdoor activities.
  - So, in order to solve this problem, it might be a good idea to have gatherings at coffee shops during winter and at parks during summer.

결론
마무리문장/10%

- So overall, this is about *some issues related to making plans for gathering.*

- -

- 음, **모임을 위해 계획을 세우는 것과 관련된 문제?** 꽤 재미있는 질문이야.

- 솔직히 말하면, 모임을 위해 계획을 세우는 것에 관하여 많은 문제는 없어.
  - 그러나 하나를 골라야만 한다면, 사람들이 만나는 장소를 결정하기 어려운 것을 찾을 수 있어.

- 과거에는, 사람들은 모임을 위해 공원에서 만나곤 했어.
  - 왜냐하면, 공원들은 이야기하고 몇몇 야외 활동을 하기에 완벽한 장소였어.

- 하지만, 어린 사람들은 모임을 위해 커피숍을 가는 것을 좋아해.
  - 그러나 대부분의 한국인들은 술 마시는 것을 좋아하고, 운동하는 것을 좋아하고, 음악을 듣고 몇몇 야외활동을 하는 것을 좋아해.
  - 그래서 이 문제를 해결하기 위해, 여름에는 공원, 겨울에는 커피숍에서 모임을 하는 것이 좋은 생각일 수 있어.

- 그래서 전반적으로, 이게 모임을 위해 **계획을 세우는 것과 관련된 몇몇 문제**에 대한 거야.

어휘 및 표현
some issues related to making plans for gathering 모임 계획에 관련된 이슈   **people find it difficult to decide where to meet**
어디서 만날지 정하는 것을 어려워 해   **in order to solve this problem** 이 문제를 풀기 위해서

세부묘사(지형/이웃국가) 지형적으로 유사한 이웃국가의 변화 추세

Q40

Tell me about a country that is **a geographically similar to your country.** What are **the changes** that the country has gone through in recent years? Please give me all the details.

당신 나라에서 지리적으로 비슷한 나라에 대해 말해 주세요. 최근에 그 나라에서 변화를 겪은 것은 무엇인가요? 상세히 말해주세요.

서론 시작문장/10%
본론 단락별 핵심문장/80%
결론 마무리문장/10%

- That's a good question, *a geographically similar to my country?* Sure, it has to be Thailand.

- **When it comes to Thailand,** there are lots of mountains and beaches just like Korea.
  - Speaking of the beaches in Thailand, they are perfect spots for just sitting and relaxing.
  - Moreover, the beaches are undeniably beautiful, and the water is crystal clear.
  - Oh! I must say that watching the sunset is kinda romantic and that's why the place is famous for tourists.

- **However,** one of the biggest issues about Thailand is that too many people are visiting.
  - As you can imagine, the beaches are always filled with lots of tourists.
  - So, people prefer going to other countries for their vacations.

- Well, okay Eva, this is pretty much about *a country that is a geographically similar to my country.*

- 좋은 질문이야, **우리나라와 지리적으로 비슷한 나라?** 물론이지, 그건 태국이야.

- 태국에 대해서 말한다면, 한국과 같은 많은 산과 해변들이 있어.
  - 태국의 해변들에 대해 말해본다면, 앉아서 쉬기에 완벽한 장소야.
  - 게다가, 해변들은 정말 아름답고 물은 크리스탈처럼 맑아.
  - 오! 노을을 보는 건 로맨틱하고 이 장소가 여행객들에게 유명한 이유야.

- 하지만, 태국에서 가장 큰 문제 중 하나는 너무 많은 사람들이 방문한다는 거야.
  - 너도 상상하듯이, 해변은 항상 많은 관광객들로 가득 차 있어.
  - 그래서 사람들은 다른 나라로 휴가를 가는 것을 선호해.

- 음, 오케이 에바, 이게 **우리나라와 지리적으로 비슷한 나라**에 대한 거야.

어휘 및 표현

a geographically similar to my country 우리나라와 지리적으로 비슷한 나라   **for tourists** 관광객에게
too many people are visiting 너무 많은 사람들이 방문해

세부묘사(지형/이웃국가) 이웃 국가의 정치/경제 기사

Q41 🎧 MP3 IM3-AL_Q_41

I would like to ask you about **an article** you read about **the country you have mentioned before.** What was the issue about? Also, how was it **related to the politics or the economy of that country?**

당신이 전에 언급했던 나라에 대해 읽었던 기사에 대해 물어보고 싶습니다. 어떤 문제였나요? 또한, 그 나라의 정치 또는 경제에 어떻게 관련이 있었나요?

🎧 MP3 IM3-AL_A_41

서론
시작문장/10%

본론
단락별 핵심문장/80%

결론
마무리문장/10%

- <u>That's</u> a good question, *an <u>article</u>* related to the <u>economy</u> of that country? Sure, I got it.

- As you can imagine, <u>Thailand</u> is <u>very</u> famous country for its <u>beautiful</u> beaches and other <u>tourism</u> places.
  - However, the country is <u>always</u> filled with <u>lots</u> of tourists and they throw <u>trash</u> on the streets.

- The <u>main</u> reason why people like to visit <u>Thailand</u> is that they can <u>enjoy</u> the peace and quiet.
  - But <u>unfortunately</u>, the country is getting <u>dirtier</u> and <u>losing</u> the number of tourists.
  - Because <u>lots</u> of tourists prefer going to <u>other</u> countries for their vacations.

- **Alright Eva,** this is <u>all</u> I can say about *an article I read.* Thank you.

- -

- 좋은 질문이야, **그 나라의 경제에 관련된 기사?** 물론이지, 알겠어.

- 너도 알다시피, 태국은 아름다운 해변과 다른 관광 명소에 대해 매우 유명한 나라야.
  - 하지만, 나라는 항상 많은 여행객들로 가득 차 있고 사람들은 길거리에 쓰레기를 버려.

- 사람들이 태국을 방문하는 것을 좋아하는 가장 큰 이유는 평화로움과 조용함을 즐길 수 있기 때문이야.
  - 그러나 불행히도, 나라는 점점 더러워지고, 관광객들을 잃고 있어.
  - 왜냐하면 많은 여행객들은 휴가를 위해 다른 나라에 가는 것을 선호하게 되었기 때문이야.

- 그래 에바, 이게 **내가 읽었던 기사**야. 고마워.

어휘 및 표현

an article related to~ ~에 관련된 기사   **tourism places** 관광 명소   **throw trash** 쓰레기를 버리다   **unfortunately** 불행히도
the country is getting dirtier 나라가 점점 더러워지다   **the country is losing the number of tourists** 관광객 수가 줄어든다

세부묘사(휴일) 우리나라 휴일의 특별한 점

Q42 ────────────────── 🎧 MP3 IM3-AL_Q_42

Tell me about **some holidays in your country.** What do people normally do during those holidays? What are some special things about those holidays? Give me all the details.

당신 나라의 휴일에 대해 말해주세요. 사람들은 휴일 동안 무엇을 하나요? 그 휴일에 대해 특별한 것은 무엇인가요? 상세히 말해주세요.

🎧 MP3 IM3-AL_A_42

서론
시작문장/10%
본론
단락별 핵심문장/80%

• Well, *some holidays in my country?* You know, I guess young people celebrate Christmas the most.

• When it comes to Christmas, most Koreans visit the beaches.
  - Speaking of going to the beach on Christmas, it's a perfect spot for just sitting and relaxing.
  - Whenever I visit there, I can see bunch of people talking and relaxing with their family or friends.

• In addition, there are many other things you can do at the beach such as reading books or listening to music.
  - Whenever I go there, it makes me feel so great and it means a lot to me.
  - So, I usually take my girlfriend since it's such a romantic place.

• Lastly, I must say that watching the sunset is kinda romantic and that's why the place is famous for couples.
  - Hey Eva! If there is any chance to visit Korea on Christmas, you should visit one of the beaches in Korea.

결론
마무리문장/10%

• Alright Eva, this is all I can say about *some holidays in my country.* Thank you.

- -

• 음, 우리나라 휴일? 있잖아, 난 젊은 사람들은 크리스마스를 가장 좋아한다고 생각해.

• 크리스마스에 대해서 말한다면, 대부분의 한국인들이 해변에 가.
  - 크리스마스 해변에 대해 말해본다면, 그냥 앉아서 쉬기에 완벽한 장소야.
  - 내가 거기에 방문할 때마다, 나는 가족들과 또는 친구들과 함께 이야기면서 쉬고 있는 많은 사람들을 볼 수 있어.

• 게다가, 독서, 음악 감상과 같이 해변에서 할 수 있는 많은 것들이 있어.
  - 내가 거기에 갈 때마다, 난 기분이 좋아지고 그건 나에게 많은 의미가 있어.
  - 그래서 난 보통 내 여자친구를 데리고 가 왜냐하면 거기는 로맨틱한 장소이거든.

• 마지막으로, 노을을 보는 것은 로맨틱하고 그곳이 커플들에게 유명한 이유야.
  - 헤이 에바! 크리스마스에 한국을 방문할 기회가 있다면, 너는 한국 해변 중 한곳을 반드시 방문해야 돼.

• 그래 에바, 이게 **우리나라 휴일**에 관해서 이야기한 거야.

어휘 및 표현

young people celebrate Christmas the most 젊은 사람들은 크리스마스를 가장 축하해 going to the beach on Christmas
크리스마스에 해변을 가는 것   I usually take my girlfriend 난 보통 여자친구를 데려간다   it's such a romantic place 로맨틱한 장소야
If there is any chance to visit Korea on Christmas 크리스마스에 한국을 방문할 기회가 있다면

세부묘사(휴일) 휴일 관련 걱정거리

Q43 ─────────────────────────────── 🎧 MP3 IM3-AL_Q_43

Let's talk about some issues or concerns that people in your country have regarding holidays. What steps do people need to take in order to solve this problem?

휴일과 관련하여 사람들이 가지고 있는 문제 혹은 걱정에 대해 말해봅시다. 사람들은 이러한 문제를 해결하기 위해 무엇을 할 필요가 있나요?

──────────────────────────────── 🎧 MP3 IM3-AL_A_43

서론
시작문장/10%
본론
단락별 핵심문장/80%

• Oh yeah, *some issues or <u>concerns</u> people have regarding <u>holidays</u>?*

• When it comes to <u>holidays,</u> <u>most</u> Koreans visit <u>shopping</u> malls.
  - You know, people do <u>many</u> kinds of things at shopping malls such as watching <u>movies</u>, <u>shopping</u> and stuff like that.
  - <u>However</u>, there is a <u>problem</u> at the shopping malls because it is <u>always</u> packed with <u>lots</u> of people.
  - You know, there are <u>many</u> restaurants and coffee shops but, we <u>always</u> need to stand in a <u>long</u> line.

• So <u>nowadays,</u> people prefer going to <u>parks</u> on their holidays since they can <u>enjoy</u> the peace and quiet.
  - In <u>addition</u>, people love going there since it's <u>free</u> to visit.

결론
마무리문장/10%

• <u>Alright</u> Eva, this is <u>all</u> I can say about **some *issues* or <u>concerns</u> people have regarding <u>holidays.</u>** Thank you.

- -

• 오 예, 사람들이 휴일과 관련되어 가지고 있는 몇몇 문제 혹은 걱정?

• 휴일에 대해서 말한다면, 대부분의 한국인들이 쇼핑몰을 방문해.
  - 있잖아, 사람들은 쇼핑몰에서 많은 것들을 하는데 예를 들어 영화 보기, 쇼핑 등과 같은 것들이 있어.
  - 하지만, 쇼핑몰은 문제가 있는데 왜냐하면 항상 많은 사람들로 가득 차 있기 때문이야.
  - 있잖아, 많은 레스토랑과 커피숍이 있지만 항상 긴 줄을 설 필요가 있어.

• 그래서 요즘 사람들은 휴일에 가는 것을 좋아해 왜냐하면 평화로움과 조용함을 즐길 수 있거든.
  - 게다가, 사람들은 방문하는 게 무료이기 때문에 거기에 가는 것을 좋아해.

• 그래 에바, 이게 **사람들이 휴가에 관련되어 가지고 있는 몇몇 문제 혹은 걱정**이야. 고마워.

어휘 및 표현
some issues or concerns people have regarding holidays 휴일 관련한 사람들의 이슈 및 걱정

세부묘사(재활용) 과거/현재 재활용 비교

Q44 ───────────────────────── 🎧 MP3 IM3-AL_Q_44

How is recycling you practiced when you were young different from what you do today? What are **the differences** and **similarities?** Please tell me about how recycling has changed over the years.

당신이 어렸을 때와 지금 재활용 하는 방식은 어떻게 다른가요? 차이점과 유사점은 무엇인가요? 재활용이 몇 년 동안 어떻게 변했는지 말해주세요.

🎧 MP3 IM3-AL_A_44

서론
시작문장/10%

• <u>That's</u> a good question, *how recycling has <u>changed</u>?* Sure, I got it.

본론
단락별 핵심문장/80%

• **When I was little,** people <u>only</u> recycled food waste.
  - <u>Frankly</u> speaking, there were <u>not</u> many issues when it came to <u>recycling</u>.

• **However,** one of the <u>biggest</u> issues about Korea is <u>garbage</u> problems.
  - So now, recycling is <u>mandatory</u> in Korea so people recycle trash such as <u>paper</u>, glass, metal and <u>etcetera</u>.
  - In <u>fact</u>, there are <u>lots</u> of recycling centers in town.
  - So, recycling has become a <u>daily</u> routine that people are <u>very</u> used to.

결론
마무리문장/10%

• Well, <u>okay</u> Eva, this is <u>pretty</u> much about *how recycling has <u>changed</u> over the years.*

- -

• 좋은 질문이야, **재활용이 어떻게 변했냐고?** 물론이지, 알겠어.

• 내가 어렸을 때, 사람들은 음식만 재활용 했어.
  - 솔직히 말하면, 재활용에 관해서는 많은 이슈들이 없었어.

• 하지만, 한국에서 가장 큰 이슈 중에 하나는 쓰레기 문제야.
  - 그래서 지금, 한국에서 재활용은 의무이고 사람들은 종이, 유리, 금속 등을 재활용해.
  - 사실, 시내에 많은 재활용 센터가 있어.
  - 그래서, 재활용은 사람들이 하곤 하는 일상생활이 되었어.

• 음, 오케이 에바, 이게 **재활용이 몇 년 동안 어떻게 변했는지**에 관한 거야.

어휘 및 표현

how recycling has changed 재활용이 변한 점   **people only recycled food waste** 음식물 쓰레기만 재활용했어

세부묘사(재활용) 최근 재활용 뉴스

Q45 ———— 🎧 MP3 IM3-AL_Q_45

Let's talk about one of **the recycling** issues that you heard in the news recently. What was **the news about?** What is being done to **solve the issue?** Please give me all the details about that issue on recycling.

최근에 뉴스에서 들었던 재활용 문제 중 하나에 대해 이야기 해봅시다. 그 뉴스는 무엇에 관한 내용이었나요? 그 문제를 해결하기 위해 어떤 것들을 하고 있나요? 재활용 문제에 대해서 자세하게 말해 주세요.

🎧 MP3 IM3-AL_A_45

서론
시작문장/10%

본론
단락별 핵심문장/80%

결론
마무리문장/10%

• Oh yeah, *one of the recycling issues?*

• **Frankly speaking,** there are <u>not</u> many issues when it comes to <u>recycling</u>.
  - But if I <u>had</u> to choose one, <u>lots</u> of people throw trash on the <u>streets</u>.
  - I mean, <u>people</u> keep throwing trash <u>anywhere</u>!

• **As you can imagine,** recycling is <u>mandatory</u> in Korea.
  - So, Korea is making <u>lots</u> of recycling centers in towns.
  - As you can <u>imagine</u>, on the first floor, there is a <u>reception</u> desk and you need an <u>ID</u> card to get in.
  - Also, on the <u>second</u> to fourth floors, people recycle <u>trash</u> such as paper, glass, metal and <u>etcetera</u>.
  - You know, <u>most</u> Koreans are going to recycling <u>centers</u> since the recycling policy is pretty <u>strict</u> in Korea.

• Well, <u>okay</u> Eva, this is <u>pretty</u> much about *the recycling issue in <u>Korea</u>.*

• 오 예, **재활용 문제 중에 하나?**

• 솔직히 말하면, 재활용에 관해 많은 이슈들이 없어.
  - 그러나 하나를 골라야만 한다면, 많은 사람들이 길거리에 쓰레기를 버렸다는 거야.
  - 내 말은, 사람들은 어디서나 쓰레기를 버리고 있어.

• 네가 상상할 수 있듯이, 한국에서는 재활용이 의무사항이야.
  - 그래서, 한국은 시내에 많은 재활용센터를 만들고 있어.
  - 네가 상상할 수 있듯이, 1층에는 안내 데스크가 있고 들어가려면 신분증이 필요해.
  - 또한 2층부터 4층까지는, 사람들은 종이, 유리, 고철류 등을 재활용해.
  - 있잖아, 대부분의 한국인 들은 재활용 센터에 가고 있어 왜냐하면 한국 재활용 정책은 꽤 엄격하거든.

• 음 오케이 에바, 이게 **한국의 재활용 문제**야.

어휘 및 표현
one of the recycling issues 재활용 이슈 중 하나 **if I had to choose one** 한 가지를 고른다면
throw trash on the streets 길거리에 쓰레기를 버리다 **recycling policy is pretty strict in Korea** 한국 재활용 정책은 엄격해

세부묘사(공원) 공원에서 아이들과 어른 활동/시설 비교

Q46 —————————————— 🎧 MP3 IM3-AL_Q_46

Now, describe the differences in activities between children and adults at the park. What are the differences? How are **the facilities** at parks different for children and adults?

공원에서 아이들이 하는 활동과 어른들이 활동을 비교해 주세요. 차이점이 무엇인가요? 어린이와 어른들을 위한 공원 시설은 무엇인가요?

🎧 MP3 IM3-AL_A_46

서론
시작문장/10%

• Well, *what adults and children do at parks?* You know, there is a huge difference.

본론
단락별 핵심문장/80%

• The main reason why adults like to go to parks is that they can spend time alone.
  - I mean, the parks are perfect spots for just sitting and relaxing while looking at the beautiful flowers.
  - In addition, after work, adults always end up going there since it's free to visit.

• On the other hand, children are a little different in some ways.
  - You know, there are huge running tracks at parks where you can see lots of children exercising.
  - Also, the parks are the perfect place to go, and do some outdoor activities for children.
  - Whenever you go there, you will see lots of children playing soccer, cricket and so on.

결론
마무리문장/10%

• So overall, this is about *the activities that adults and children do at parks.*

- -

• 음, 공원에서 성인들과 아이들이 하는 것? 있잖아, 큰 차이가 있어.

• 성인들이 공원에 가는 것을 좋아하는 가장 큰 이유는 그들이 혼자 시간을 보낼 수 있기 때문이야.
  - 내 말은, 공원은 아름다운 꽃을 보면서 그냥 앉아서 쉬기에 완벽한 장소야.
  - 게다가, 업무 후에, 어른들은 결국 거기에 가는 걸로 끝이나 왜냐하면 거기는 방문하는 것이 공짜이기 때문이야.

• 반면에, 아이들은 몇몇 관점에서 조금 달라.
  - 있잖아, 공원에는 큰 러닝 트랙이 있고 많은 아이들이 운동하고 있는 것을 볼 수 있어.
  - 또한, 공원은 아이들이 가서 몇몇 야외 활동을 하기에 완벽한 장소야.
  - 네가 거기에 갈 때마다, 축구, 크리켓 등을 하는 많은 아이들을 볼 거야.

• 그래서 전반적으로, 이게 **어른들과 아이들이 공원에서 하는 활동**이야.

어휘 및 표현
what adults and children do at parks 어른과 아이가 공원에서 하는 것   **a huge difference** 큰 차이

세부묘사(공원) 공원 관련 이슈 및 해결책

Q47 ─────────────────────── 🎧 MP3 IM3-AL_Q_47

I would like to ask you about **one of the issues about parks in your country.** What are some challenges public parks are faced with these days? Discuss what has caused these concerns. **What steps do we take in order to solve this problem?**

당신 나라 공원이 마주하고 있는 문제들 중의 하나에 대해 말해주세요. 요즘 공원들에서 마주하고 있는 도전은 무엇인가요? 이러한 문제들을 일으키는 것에 대해 말해주세요. 이러한 이슈를 해결하기 위하여 어떤 종류의 것을 할 필요가 있나요?

🎧 MP3 IM3-AL_A_47

서론
시작문장/10%

• That's a good question, *one of the issues about parks in Korea?* I guess I got something to tell you Eva.

본론
단락별 핵심문장/80%

• In the past, the parks were perfect spots for just sitting and relaxing while looking at the beautiful flowers.
  - Seriously, I preferred to go there at night since I could enjoy the peace and quiet.

• However, these days, there are too many people at the parks.
  - The biggest issue is that people cannot enjoy their time in the parks anymore.
  - I mean, all you need to know is that parks are always packed with lots of people.
  - I think lots of people are visiting parks since it's free to visit.

• In my opinion, we need to have more parks so people can spend their free time with their family or friends.
  - Because getting back to nature, just relaxing outside is essential for human beings.

결론
마무리문장/10%

• Well, okay Eva, this is pretty much about *the parks in Korea.*

- -

• 좋은 질문이야, **한국에서 공원에 대한 문제 중에 하나?** 말할 게 좀 있을 것 같아 에바.

• 과거에는, 공원들이 아름다운 꽃을 보면서 그냥 앉아서 쉬기에 완벽한 장소였어.
  - 솔직히, 난 거기에 밤에 가는 것을 좋아했고 내가 평화로움과 조용함을 즐길 수 있기 때문이었어.

• 하지만, 요즘에는 공원에 사람들이 너무 많아.
  - 가장 큰 문제는 사람들이 더 이상 공원에서 시간을 즐길 수 없다는 거야.
  - 내 말은, 중요한 점은 공원이 많은 사람들로 항상 가득 차 있다는 거야.
  - 내 생각엔 많은 사람들은 공원이 무료이기 때문에 방문하고 있어.

• 내 생각으로는, 우리는 사람들이 가족 또는 친구들과 여가시간을 보낼 수 있도록 더 많은 공원을 만들 필요가 있어.
  - 왜냐하면 자연으로 돌아가서 밖에 앉아 있는 것은 인간에게 필수적이기 때문이야.

• 음, 오케이 에바, 이게 **한국에서 공원에 대한 거야.**

어휘 및 표현
one of the issues about parks in Korea 한국 공원의 이슈 중 하나   these days 요즘   we need to have more parks 더 많은 공원이 필요하다

14강

유형 01 (묘사)
유형 02 (세부묘사)

모의고사

묘사 모의고사 준비

난이도 5 설정 시, 묘사 및 세부묘사 질문은 총 6문제(2, 3, 5, 8, 14, 15번)가 출제됩니다.

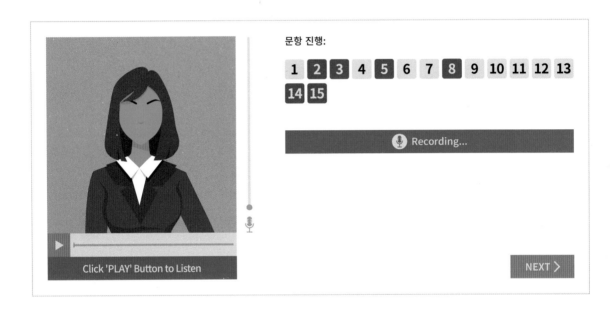

2 5 8 14	
유형	묘사 & 세부묘사
주제	<u>알 수 없음</u>
준비시간	20초
사용문장	묘사 & 세부묘사
집중내용	문장
	문제 키워드 캐치
	답변 Format 정리

3 15	
유형	세부묘사
주제	<u>알고 있음</u>
준비시간	20초
사용문장	묘사 & 세부묘사
집중내용	문장
	문제 키워드 캐치
	답변 Format 정리

묘사 모의고사

실제 시험처럼 각 문제의 MP3를 듣고, 훈련을 해보세요.

🎧 MP3 IM3-AL_Q_48~53

Q48
2번 – 집휴가 묘사

You indicated in the survey that **you take vacations at home.** Who do you normally meet and spend time during your vacations at home?

Q49
3번 – 집휴가 비교

What do people in your country normally do during vacations at home? **How has their ways of spending vacations changed over the years?** Please tell me in detail.

Q50
5번 – 걷는 장소 묘사

You indicated in the survey that you like to **take a walk.** Where do you normally take a walk? What does the place look like? And where is it located? Please describe the place you normally take a walk.

Q51
8번 – 콘서트 묘사

You indicated in the survey that **you often go to concerts.** What type of concerts do you enjoy going to? And why do you like going to concerts? Please tell me in detail.

Q52
14번 – 국내여행
(과거/현재 어려워진 점)

How is traveling today different from the past? What are some difficulties that people go through regarding going on domestic trips? Has traveling become more difficult in any way? If so, tell me why.

Q53
15번 – 국내여행
(여행객 우려/걱정)

What are **some issues people have related to traveling?** What do people need to do in order to solve those problems?

2번 집휴가 묘사

Q48

You indicated in the survey that **you take vacations at home.** Who do you normally meet and spend time during your vacations at home?

서베이에서 당신은 집에서 휴가를 보낸다고 선택하였습니다 . 당신은 누구와 주로 만나고 휴일 동안 집에서 시간을 보내나요?

서론
시작문장/10%

- <u>That's</u> a good question, *yes, I <u>usually</u>* take vacations at home and let me tell you about it.

본론
단락별 핵심문장/80%

- In <u>order</u> to take vacations at home, I <u>always</u> spend <u>lots</u> of time with one of my buddies named John.
  - You know, we do <u>many</u> kinds of things such as watching <u>movies</u>, listening to <u>music</u> and stuff like that.
  - <u>Actually</u>, he knows a <u>lot</u> about music and movies, so he is a <u>great</u> person to spend time with.

- As I mentioned <u>before,</u> I live in a <u>3</u>-story house and there's a terrace <u>garden</u> on the top floor.
  - Speaking of the garden, it's a <u>perfect</u> spot for just sitting and <u>relaxing</u> while looking at the <u>beautiful</u> flowers.
  - Whenever I spend time at <u>home</u>, I <u>always</u> end up going there since it makes me feel <u>so</u> great.

결론
마무리문장/10%

- Well, <u>okay</u> Eva, this is <u>pretty</u> much about *taking vacations at <u>home</u>.*

- -

- 좋은 질문이야, 응, 난 집에서 보통 휴가를 보내고 내가 너에게 그것에 대해 말해줄게.

- 집에서 휴가를 보내기 위해서, 내 친구들 중에 한 명인 John이라는 친구와 난 항상 많은 시간을 보내.
  - 있잖아, 우리는 영화 보기, 음악 듣기와 같은 많은 것들을 해.
  - 사실, 그는 음악과 영화에 대해 많이 알고, 그래서 시간을 함께 보내기 좋은 사람이야.

- 전에도 언급했듯이, 나는 3층 집에 살고 꼭대기 층에는 테라스 정원이 있어.
  - 정원에 대해 말해본다면, 아름다운 꽃들을 보면서 그냥 앉아서 쉬기에 완벽한 장소야.
  - 내가 집에 있을 때마다, 난 항상 거기에 가는 것으로 끝나는데 거기에 가면 기분이 정말 좋게 때문이야.

- 음, 오케이 에바, 이게 **집에서 보내는 휴가**야.

어휘 및 표현
I usually take vacations at home 난 종종 집에서 휴가를 보내   **one of oy buddies** 친구 중 한 명

3번 집휴가 비교

Q49 ━━━━━━━━━━━━━━━━━━━━━━━━━━━━━ 🎧 MP3 IM3-AL_Q_49

What do people in your country normally do during vacations at home? **How has their ways of spending vacations changed over the years?** Please tell me in detail.

당신 나라에 있는 사람들은 집에서 휴가 동안 무엇을 하나요? 휴가를 보내는 방법은 몇 년 동안 어떻게 변해왔나요? 자세히 말해주세요.

━━━━━━━━━━━━━━━━━━━━━━━━━━━━━━━━━━━━━━━ 🎧 MP3 IM3-AL_A_49

서론
시작문장/10%

- Well, *how has their ways of spending vacations <u>changed</u> over the years?*

본론
단락별 핵심문장/80%

- In the past, people <u>used</u> to spend time alone.
  - I mean, the <u>main</u> reason why people liked to stay at home is that people could spend time <u>alone</u>.
  - <u>Seriously</u>, people preferred to spend time alone since they can <u>enjoy</u> the peace and quiet.

- <u>However,</u> the <u>way</u> of spending their vacations have changed a <u>lot</u> over the years.
  - Well, I guess <u>most</u> people invite their friends to throw <u>parties</u>.
  - You know, people can do <u>many</u> kinds of things such as <u>drinking</u>, watching <u>movies</u> and listening to music together.

결론
마무리문장/10%

- So <u>overall</u>, this is about *how has their ways of spending <u>vacations</u> changed over the years.*

┄┄

- 음, 휴가를 보내는 방법은 몇 년 동안 어떻게 변해왔냐고?

- 과거에는, 사람들은 혼자 시간을 보내곤 했어.
  - 내 말은, 사람들이 집에 있는 것을 좋아했던 가장 큰 이유는 사람들이 혼자 시간을 보낼 수 있기 때문이었어.
  - 솔직히, 사람들은 평화로움과 조용함을 즐길 수 있기 때문에 혼자 시간을 보내는 것을 좋아했어.

- 하지만, 그들의 휴가를 보내는 방식은 몇 년 동안 많이 변해왔어.
  - 음, 대부분의 사람들은 파티를 열기 위해 친구들을 초대해.
  - 있잖아, 사람들은 술 마시기, 영화 보기, 함께 음악 듣기와 같이 많은 것들을 할 수 있어.

- 그래서 전반적으로, 이게 **몇 년 동안 휴가를 보내는 방식이 어떻게 변했는지** 야.

━━

어휘 및 표현
their ways of spending vacations 휴가를 보내는 그들의 방법   people preferred to spend time alone 혼자 시간을 보내는 것을 즐겼다
the way of spending their vacations 그들의 휴가를 보내는 방식   throw parties 파티를 열다

5번 걷는 장소 묘사

Q50

You indicated in the survey that you like to **take a walk.** Where do you normally take a walk? What does the place look like? And where is it located? Please describe the place you normally take a walk.

당신은 산책하는 것을 좋아한다고 했습니다. 어디서 주로 산책을 하나요? 그 장소는 어떻게 생겼나요? 그리고 어디에 있나요? 주로 산책하는 장소를 묘사해주세요.

MP3 IM3-AL_A_50

서론
시작문장/10%

- Well, *taking a walk?* You know, I <u>usually</u> take a walk at the park in my <u>neighborhood</u>.

본론
단락별 핵심문장/80%

- **Well,** there is a <u>huge</u> park with <u>many</u> different areas where people play <u>soccer</u>, cricket and so on.
  - <u>Also</u>, there is a <u>huge</u> running track where you can see <u>lots</u> of people exercising.
  - And that's where I take a <u>walk</u>.
  - Whenever I take a walk, it makes me feel <u>so</u> great and it means a <u>lot</u> to me.

- **Well,** I'm <u>pretty</u> sure that the park is around <u>20</u>-minutes away from my place.
  - You know, I <u>suppose</u> I tend to visit there a <u>few</u> times a month.
  - And I <u>really</u> enjoy taking a walk because it helps me <u>release</u> stress.

- **In** <u>addition,</u> in the park, there is a <u>beautiful</u> old house which is now a café where you can have afternoon tea.
  - <u>After</u> taking a walk, I <u>sometimes</u> visit there and have a <u>coffee</u>.

결론
마무리문장/10%

- <u>Alright</u> Eva, this is <u>all</u> I can say about *the place I take a **walk.*** Thank you.

- 음, **산책?** 있잖아, 난 보통 우리 동네에 있는 공원에서 산책을 해.

- 있잖아, 큰 공원에는 사람들이 축구, 크리켓 등을 하는 많은 다른 장소들이 있어.
  - 또한, 많은 사람들이 운동하는 것을 볼 수 있는 큰 러닝 트랙도 있어.
  - 그곳이 내가 산책하는 장소야.
  - 내가 산책할 때마다, 난 기분이 정말 좋고, 그것은 나에게 많은 의미가 있어.

- 음, 공원은 분명 우리 집에서 약 20분 정도 이거든.
  - 있잖아, 난 한 달에 몇 번씩 거기에 가는 경향이 있어.
  - 그리고 난 산책하는 것을 정말로 좋아해 왜냐하면 그건 스트레스 해소에 도움이 되기 때문이지.

- 게다가, 공원에는 네가 따뜻한 차를 마실 수 있는 지금 카페인 오래된 집이 있어.
  - 산책 후에는, 난 때때로 거기에 가서 커피를 먹어.

- 그래 에바, 이게 **내가 산책을 하는 곳에 대한 거**야. 고마워.

어휘 및 표현
that's where I take a walk 내가 산책하는 장소   **a few times a month** 한 달에 몇 번   **After taking a walk** 산책 후

8번 좋아하는 콘서트 묘사

Q51 ———

🎧 MP3 IM3-AL_Q_51

You indicated in the survey that **you often go to concerts.** What type of concerts do you enjoy going to? And why do you like going to concerts? Please tell me in detail.

당신은 종종 콘서트를 간다고 서베이에서 답변했습니다. 당신은 어떤 콘서트에 가는 것을 좋아하나요? 왜 콘서트에 가는 것을 좋아하나요? 상세히 말해 주세요.

🎧 MP3 IM3-AL_A_51

서론
시작문장/10%

• <u>That's</u> a good question, *type of <u>concerts</u> I enjoy going to?* Sure, I got it.

본론
단락별 핵심문장/80%

• **When it comes to <u>concerts</u>,** there is a <u>huge</u> concert hall like <u>2</u>km from where I live.
  - You know, I <u>really</u> enjoy <u>all</u> kinds of concerts but if I had to choose <u>one</u>, it must be <u>hip</u>-hop.
  - <u>All</u> you need to know is that the <u>concerts</u> are <u>always</u> packed with lots of people.

• **Whenever I go to a <u>concert</u>,** I <u>always</u> take one of my friends John since he knows a <u>lot</u> about music.
  - I <u>really</u> love going to concerts because it helps me <u>release</u> stress.
  - In <u>addition</u>, I'm <u>pretty</u> sure that I can get a discount since I got a <u>membership</u> card.

결론
마무리문장/10%

• Well, <u>okay</u> Eva, this is <u>pretty</u> much about *the <u>type</u> of concerts I <u>enjoy</u> going to.*

- -

• **좋은 질문이야,** 내가 어떤 콘서트에 가는 것을 좋아하냐고? 그래, 알겠어.

• 콘서트에 대해서 말한다면, 내가 사는 곳에서 2km 떨어진 곳에 큰 콘서트홀이 있어.
  - 있잖아, 난 모든 종류의 콘서트를 좋아하지만 하나만 골라야 한다면 그건 힙합이야.
  - 중요한 점은 콘서트가 항상 많은 사람들로 가득 차 있다는 거야.

• 내가 콘서트에 갈 때마다, 난 내 친구 중에 한 명인 John을 데려가는데 왜냐하면 그는 음악에 대해 많이 알기 때문이야.
  - 난 스트레스 해소하는 데 도움이 되기 때문에 콘서트 가는 것을 좋아해.
  - 게다가, 난 멤버십 카드가 있기 때문에 할인을 받을 수 있다는 것을 꽤 확신해.

• 음, 오케이 에바, 이게 **내가 어떤 콘서트에 가는 것을 좋아하는 지야.**

어휘 및 표현
type of concerts I enjoy going to 내가 자주 가는 콘서트 종류   **a huge concert hall** 큰 콘서트장

Q52

🎧 MP3 IM3-AL_Q_52

How is traveling today different from the past? What are **some difficulties** people go through regarding going on domestic trips? Has traveling become more difficult in any way? If so, tell me why.

여행은 과거에서 오늘날 어떻게 변했나요? 국내 여행과 관련하여 사람들이 어떤 어려운 점을 겪고 있나요? 어떤 점에서 여행은 더 어렵게 되었나요? 그렇다면, 이유를 말해주세요.

🎧 MP3 IM3-AL_A_52

서론
시작문장/10%

본론
단락별 핵심문장/80%

- Well, *How is traveling today different from the past?* You know, I guess I got something to tell you Eva.

- When it <u>comes</u> to trips, people <u>used</u> to visit <u>beautiful</u> beaches in Korea.
  - As you can <u>imagine</u>, Korea is <u>surrounded</u> by the oceans.
  - Speaking of the beach, they are <u>perfect</u> spots for just sitting and <u>relaxing</u>.

- However, one of the <u>biggest</u> issues about trips in <u>Korea</u> is that <u>too</u> many people are visiting beaches.
  - As you can <u>imagine</u>, the beaches are <u>always</u> filled with lots of <u>tourists</u>.
  - So, people prefer just staying at <u>home</u> or going to <u>other</u> countries for their vacations.

- In <u>order</u> to solve this problem, we need to make <u>more</u> places to entertain.
  - You know, there are <u>lots</u> of parks in Korea and <u>many</u> people go to parks on their <u>holidays</u>.

결론
마무리문장/10%

- So <u>overall,</u> this is about *how <u>traveling</u> today is different from the <u>past</u>.*

- -

- 음, **여행은 과거에서 오늘날 어떻게 변했냐고?** 있잖아, 난 너에게 말할 게 있어.

- 여행에 대해서 말한다면, 사람들은 한국에서 아름다운 해변을 방문하곤 했어.
  - 네가 상상하듯이, 한국은 바다로 둘러싸야 있어.
  - 해변에 대해 말해본다면, 그냥 앉아서 쉬기에 완벽한 장소야.

- 하지만, 한국 여행에 대한 가장 큰 이슈 중 하나는 너무 많은 사람들이 해변을 방문한다는 거야.
  - 네가 상상할 수 있듯이, 해변은 항상 많은 여행객들로 가득 차 있어.
  - 그래서, 사람들은 그냥 집에 있거나 휴가로 해외를 가는 것을 선호해.

- 이러한 문제를 해결하기 위해, 우리는 즐길 수 있는 더 많은 장소를 만들 필요가 있어.
  - 있잖아, 한국에는 많은 공원이 있고 많은 사람들이 휴일에 공원에 가.

- 그래서 전반적으로, 이게 **오늘날의 여행이 과거와 어떻게 다른 지**야.

어휘 및 표현
Korea is surrounded by the oceans 한국은 바다로 둘러싸여져 있다
we need to make more places to entertain 즐길 수 있는 장소를 더 만들 필요가 있어

15번 국내 여행객의 걱정/우려

Q53 ━━━━━━━━━━━━━━━━━━━━━━━ 🎧 MP3 IM3-AL_Q_53

What are **some issues people have related to traveling?** What do people need to do in order to solve those problems?

사람들은 여행과 관련하여 어떤 문제나 걱정이 있나요? 사람들은 이러한 문제나 걱정을 해결하기 위하여 어떤 것을 하나요?

━━━━━━━━━━━━━━━━━━━━━━━━━━━━ 🎧 MP3 IM3-AL_A_53

서론
시작문장/10%

- <u>That's</u> a good question, *some <u>issues</u> or concerns people have related to <u>traveling</u>?* Sure, I got it.

본론
단락별 핵심문장/80%

- **When it <u>comes</u> to issues related to traveling,** there are <u>too</u> many people in <u>high</u> peak seasons.
  - You know, <u>many</u> people visit beaches or mountains on their <u>vacations</u>.
  - But you need to know that it is <u>always</u> packed with <u>lots</u> of people.

- **In <u>order</u> to solve this problem,** <u>most</u> people just stay at <u>home</u> on their vacations.
  - You know, they <u>rather</u> go on trips in <u>low</u> peak seasons like in <u>October</u> or November.

결론
마무리문장/10%

- <u>Alright</u> Eva, this is <u>all</u> I can say about **the issue <u>people</u> have related to traveling.** Thank you.

- -

- 좋은 질문이야, **사람들이 여행과 관련하여 가지고 있는 문제?** 물론이지, 알겠어.

- 여행에 관한 문제에 대해서 말한다면, 성수기에는 사람들이 너무 많아.
  - 있잖아, 많은 사람들은 해변 또는 산을 휴가 때 방문해.
  - 그러나 항상 많은 사람들로 가득 차 있다는 것을 너도 알 필요가 있어.

- 이 문제를 해결하기 위해서, 대부분의 사람들은 휴가 때 집에 그냥 있어.
  - 있잖아, 그들은 차라리 10월이나 11월 같은 비수기에 여행을 가.

- 그래 에바, 이게 **사람들이 여행과 관련하여 가지고 있는 문제**에 대한 거야. 고마워.

어휘 및 표현
some issues or concerns people have related to traveling 여행 관련된 이슈 및 사람들의 걱정   in high peak seasons 성수기에
they rather go on trips in low peak seasons 차라리 비수기에 여행을 가

15강

유형 03 (경험)

이론

경험의 이해

OPIc 질문들 중 과거시제를 필히 사용해야 하는 경험 질문입니다.
난이도에 따라 경험 질문의 개수가 달라집니다.
각 콤보 문제에서 적게는 1문제, 많게는 2문제가 출제됩니다.
경험은 흔히 최초 경험, 최근 경험, 인상 깊었던 경험, 문제 해결 경험으로 나뉩니다.

경험이 나오는 질문 번호를 외우세요!

경험이 나오는 질문 번호를 외우세요!
IM3 – AL 등급 목표 시, 난이도 5으로 설정하시면, 경험은 총 6문제 출제!

1	2	3	4	5	6	7	8	9	10	11	12	13	14	15
자기소개	묘사	세부묘사	경험	묘사	경험	경험	묘사	경험	경험	정보요청	문제해결	문제해결경험	세부묘사	세부묘사

경험의 종류

Background Survey에서 선택한 모든 주제 & 모든 출제 가능한 돌발 주제의 경험을 모두 암기하는 것은 불가능합니다. 따라서 **진짜녀석들 OPIc**은 3가지 경험 종류로 분류합니다.

개방 공간 경험	➡	밖에서 일어난 경험
독립 공간 경험	➡	안에서 일어난 경험
문제 해결 경험	➡	문제 발생 및 해결점 제시하는 경험

 이미 문제 유형을 알기에, 문제를 듣기 전, 3가지 경험 종류 중 택일!

경험의 답변 Format

경험은 매끄러운 '스토리텔링' 이 필요하므로 체계적인 답변 Format이 필요합니다.

진짜녀석들 OPIc의 '스토리텔링'은 했던 일 – 반전 – 결과의 순서로 되어 있습니다.

했던 일은 묘사에서 암기한 문장을 시제를 바꾸어 작성합니다.

(IM3-AL목표의 OPIc 공부라고 해도 너무 많은 양의 경험 문장을 암기할 필요가 없기 때문입니다.)

서론
Introduction
답변비중 10%

시작 문장
- 경험 주제의 키워드를 필히 포함하여 자신감 있게 한 줄!
- 면접관에게 답변을 시작한단 느낌을 전달!

본론
Body
답변비중 80%

했던 일(40%) • 6하원칙을 사용하여 스토리 전개 생성 (묘사 암기 문장 활용)

반전(20%) • 진짜녀석들 OPIc 경험 암기문장 활용 (본인 실력 문장 포함)

결과(20%) • 진짜녀석들 OPIc 경험 암기문장 활용 (본인 실력 문장 포함)

결론
Conclusion
답변비중 10%

마무리 문장
- 경험 주제의 키워드를 필히 포함하여 깔끔하게 한 줄!
- 면접관에게 답변을 끝낸다는 느낌을 전달!

경험의 암기문장 – 서론 & 결론

정확한 경험의 답변을 위하여 서론과 결론에 필요한 암기문장을 제공합니다.

서론 - 시작문장

MP3 IM3-AL_67~69

- 알겠어 에바, <u>여행 관련 경험?</u>
  I got it Eva, <u>experience about my trip</u>?

- 좋아, <u>내 해변 경험?</u>
  Great, you mean **my beach experience**?

- 좋아, <u>내 첫 번째 콘서트 경험</u>을 말해 줄게.
  Alright! Let me tell you **my first concert experience**.

결론 - 마무리문장

MP3 IM3-AL_70~72

- 음 그래, 여기까지가 내가 기억하는 부분이야 에바. 고마워.
  Um yeah, this is all I remember Eva. Thank you.

- 오케이 에바, 이게 **내 공원의 경험**이야.
  Okay Eva, this is **my park experience**.

- 알겠어 에바, 내 생각에 이 정도면 될 것 같아.
  Alright Eva, I guess this is pretty much about it.

경험의 암기문장 – 본론(단락 별 핵심 암기 문장)

정확한 경험의 답변을 위하여 본론에 필요한 암기문장을 제공합니다.

본론 - 단락 별 핵심 문장

🎧 MP3 IM3-AL_73~75

개방공간 경험 1 – 어딘가에서 운동해서 살을 뺀 경험

반전

• 음, 아마 한 500미터 후쯤? 난 이미 숨이 차기 시작했어.
Well, after like 500 meters? I was already out of breath.

• 근데 한 2km 뛴 후에, 난 마침내 내 페이스를 찾았어. 그리고 맞아, 난 **칼로리를 많이 소모할 수 있었어.**
But after running about 2 km, I finally found my optimal pace. And yeah, I could **burn a lot of calories.**

결과

• 있잖아, 난 살을 많이 뺐고 너무 행복했어. 그래서 난 언제나 스트레스를 받으면, **나가서 뛰어.**
You know what, I could lose weight and I became super happy. So, whenever I'm under stress, I **go out and run.**

🎧 MP3 IM3-AL_76~78

개방공간 경험 2 – 어딘가에서 음악을 들으며 미친 듯 논 경험

반전

• 우리가 들어갔을 때, 내가 예상했듯, 엄청 많은 사람들이 **춤을 추고 있었어.**
When we got in, as I expected, there were full of people **dancing.**

• 한 20분 후, 우린 시간이 가는 것을 잊고, 춤추고, 뛰었어. 내 말은 우린 정말 미친 듯 놀았어.
After like 20 minutes? We totally lost track of time, we danced, jumped, I mean, we just went crazy.

결과

• 그리고 페스티벌 후에, 우린 **바에 가서 맥주를 마셨어.** 내 말은, 정말 좋은 방법이었어 하루를 마무리하기.
And after the festival, we went to **a bar and grabbed a beer.** I mean, it was a great way to wrap up all of the fun.

🎧 MP3 IM3-AL_79~81

개방공간 경험 3 – 어딘가에서 놀다가 비가 와서 망친 경험

반전

• 있잖아, **영화**는 훌륭했어, 그리고 진짜 즐거웠어.
You know, the **movie** was great, and we had so much fun.

• 근데 음, 우리가 **무언가를 먹으려고** 한순간, 비가 오기 시작했어. 내 말은, 날씨가 좋았는데 엄청 퍼부었어!
But um, when we were about to **eat something,** it started to rain. I mean, the weather was so sunny, but it poured!

결과

• 그래서 어떻게 되었냐고? 우린 흠뻑 젖었어. 글쎄, 우리가 뭘 할 수 있었겠어? 우린 그냥 **집에 돌아와 버렸어.**
Guess what! We were completely soaked. Well, what could we do? We ended up **going back home.**

🎧 MP3 IM3-AL_82~84

개방공간 경험 4 – 어딘가에서 술을 마시고 필름이 끊긴 경험

반전

• 한 30분 정도밖에 지나지 않았었는데, 난 너무 취했어.
After only being there for 30 minutes, I got so drunk.

• 내 말은, 난 내일이 없는 것처럼 술을 마셨어. 내가 오직 기억하는 한 가지는 난 계속 **춤을 추고 웃었어.**
I mean, I drank like there's no tomorrow. The only thing I remember is that I kept **dancing and laughing.**

결과

• 음, 그다음 날? 난 **하루 종일 침대에 누워 있었어.** 근데 있잖아, 진짜 재미있는 날이었고, 또 한잔이 하고 싶어.
Well, the next day? I ended up **staying in my bed all day.** But you know? It was kinda fun and I feel like drinking again.

 암기문장 중, 밑줄 표시가 되어있는 부분은 주제별, 상황별로 학습자가 자유롭게 변형가능한 부분입니다.

경험의 암기문장 – 본론(단락 별 핵심 암기 문장)

정확한 경험의 답변을 위하여 본론에 필요한 암기문장을 제공합니다.

본론 - 단락 별 핵심 문장

🎧 MP3 IM3-AL_85~87

독립공간 경험 1 – 어딘가에서 지갑을 잃어버린 경험

반전
- 쇼핑 후에, 난 결재를 하려 했는데, 난 큰일이 난 걸 알아차렸어.
  After shopping, I tried to pay, but I realized that I was in trouble.

- 네가 예상하듯, 난 <u>지갑</u>을 잃어버렸어. 맙소사, 난 진짜 노숙자가 된 기분이었어.
  As you can expect, I lost <u>my wallet</u>. Oh my god, I felt like a homeless person.

결과
- 윽, 난 진짜 짜증이 났어, 내 말은, 난 <u>모든 신용카드를 정지시켜야 했어</u>. 그거 알아? <u>지갑을 잃어버리는 건</u> 새로운 삶을 시작하는 것 같아.
  Ugh, I felt sick, I mean, I had to <u>cancel all my credit cards</u>. You know what? <u>Losing a wallet</u> is like starting a new life.

🎧 MP3 IM3-AL_88~90

독립공간 경험 2 – 어딘가에서 계단에서 넘어져 병원 간 경험

반전
- 한 3시간 후쯤, 난 마지막 <u>지하철을 놓칠 것</u>을 알아차렸어. 그래서 난 계단을 뛰어 내려갔지.
  After like 3 hours, I realized that <u>I'd miss the last train</u>, so I ran down the stairs.

- 이유는 모르겠는데, 난 균형을 잃고 넘어졌어.
  I don't know why, but I just lost balance and fell over.

결과
- 맙소사, 난 너무 아파서 울었어. 그래서 난 앰뷸런스를 불러서 병원에서 <u>2일</u> 동안 있었어.
  Oh my god, it was so painful, and I was crying. So, I called an ambulance and I stayed in the hospital for <u>2 days</u>.

🎧 MP3 IM3-AL_91~93

독립공간 경험 3 – 어딘가에서 너무 오래 기다려 캔슬 한 경험

반전
- 한 30분 정도가 지났는데도, 난 아직 주문을 못 받았고, 난 인내심을 잃기 시작했어
  After like 30 min, I still haven't received my order and I started to lose my patience.

- 우리의 기념일을 망치지 않기 위해, 난 그냥 <u>그곳을 나왔어</u>.
  In order not to ruin our anniversary, I just decided to <u>leave there</u>.

결과
- 있잖아, 모든 곳은 예약이 다 찼었어! 그래서 우린 그냥 <u>편의점</u>에 가서 <u>저녁</u>을 먹었어.
  You know what, everywhere was fully booked! So, we just went to <u>a convenience store</u> for <u>our dinner</u>.

🎧 MP3 IM3-AL_94~96

독립공간 경험 4 – 어딘가에서 갑자기 정전이 된 경험

반전
- 우리가 즐기고 있을 때, 갑자기, 정전이 되었고, 우린 너무 놀랐어.
  While we were having fun, all of a sudden, the power went out and we freaked out.

- 이 문제를 풀기 위해서, 난 재빨리 <u>초를 찾았고 초를 켰어</u>.
  In order to solve this problem, I quickly <u>found candles and lit them</u>.

결과
- 솔직히 말해서, 정말 기억에 남는 경험이었어. 그래서 우린 그 상황을 즐기며 <u>음식을 먹었어</u>.
  To be honest, it was such a memorable experience. So, we enjoyed being in that situation and <u>finished our meal</u>.

 암기문장 중, 밑줄 표시가 되어있는 부분은 주제별, 상황별로 학습자가 자유롭게 변형가능한 부분입니다.

경험의 암기문장 – 본론(단락 별 핵심 암기 문장)

정확한 경험의 답변을 위하여 본론에 필요한 암기문장을 제공합니다.

본론 - 단락 별 핵심 문장

🎧 MP3 IM3-AL_97~99

문제해결 경험 1 – 어딘가에서 짐을 놓고 갔다가 다시 찾은 경험

반전

- 우리가 체크아웃 했을 때, 우린 택시를 타고 **공항**으로 갔어.
  When we checked out, we grabbed a cab to go to **the airport**.

- 우리가 공항에 거의 도착했을 때, 난 알아차렸어 내가 **짐**을 **호텔**에 놓고 온 것을. 상상이 되니?
  When we were just about to arrive at the airport, I realized that I left **my luggage** at **the hotel**. Can you imagine that?

결과

- 그래서, 난 기사님에게 돌아가자 했어. 다행히 **호텔 직원**이 **2**시간 동안 노력해서 찾았어! 난 보답으로 **20**불을 줬어.
  So, I asked the driver to go back. Luckily, **the hotel staff** searched for my luggage for **2 hours** and found it! In return, I gave him **20 dollars**.

🎧 MP3 IM3-AL_100~103

문제해결 경험 2 – 어딘가에서 무엇이 고장이 나서 수리한 경험

반전

- 우리가 음악을 즐기고 있는 동안, 내 친구가 **내 노트북**에 **커피**를 흘렸어.
  While we were enjoying the music, my friend spilled **coffee** on **my laptop**.

- 맙소사, 처음엔 정말 화가 났는데, 난 괜찮은 척했어.
  Oh my god, it was annoying at first, but I pretended like it was ok.

- 그래서, 내 친구는 급하게 엔지니어를 불렀고 **그**는 한 **10**분 만에 왔어.
  So quickly, my friend called an engineer and **he** came in like **10**min.

결과

- 내 생각엔, 그는 대략 **1시간** 정도 걸려서 고쳤어. 그리고 있잖아, 난 **미화 천 불**을 냈어야 했어.
  I guess, he worked on it for about **an hour**. And you know, I ended up spending $**1,000 USD**.

🎧 MP3 IM3-AL_104~106

문제해결 경험 3 – 어딘가에서 무엇이 부서져 환불한 경험

반전

- 내 생일 선물로, 내 여자친구는 커피 메이커를 사줬어. 한 **10**일이 지나서, 난 **커피 메이커**를 받았는데 부서져있었어!
  For my birthday present, my girlfriend bought me **a coffee maker**. After like **10 days**, I got **the coffee maker**, but it was broken!

- 그래서, 난 상점에 전화를 했고 내 망가진 **커피 메이커**에 대해 얘기했어.
  So, I called **the store** and told them about my broken **coffee maker**.

결과

- 내가 엄청 화가 났기 때문에, 그들은 사과를 했고 난 교환을 제공받았어. 하지만 난 너무 화가 났고 난 강하게 환불을 요청했어.
  Because I was so mad, they apologized and offered an exchange. But I was very upset, so I strongly asked them for a refund.

🎧 MP3 IM3-AL_107~109

문제해결 경험 4 – 어딘가에 잘못 주문해 교환한 경험

반전

- 내가 영화관에 도착했을 때, 난 **티켓**을 잘못 구매한 것을 알아차렸어.
  When I arrived at the movie theater, I realized that I bought the wrong **ticket**.

- 그래서, 난 **티켓 오피스**에 가서 상황을 설명했어.
  So, I went to **the ticket booth** and explained the whole situation.

결과

- 고맙게도, 그들은 **다음 영화**로 바꾸어 주었어. 게다가 추가 금액은 없었어. 사실, 이건 내가 받아본 서비스 중 최고였어.
  Thankfully, they offered an exchange for **the next movie**. Moreover, there was no additional payment. Actually, it was the best customer service I've ever had.

📢 암기문장 중, 밑줄 표시가 되어있는 부분은 주제별, 상황별로 학습자가 자유롭게 변형가능한 부분입니다.

경험 답변 준비 – 시험화면

난이도 5 설정 시, 경험이 나오는 번호를 실제 시험화면으로 익숙해져야 합니다.

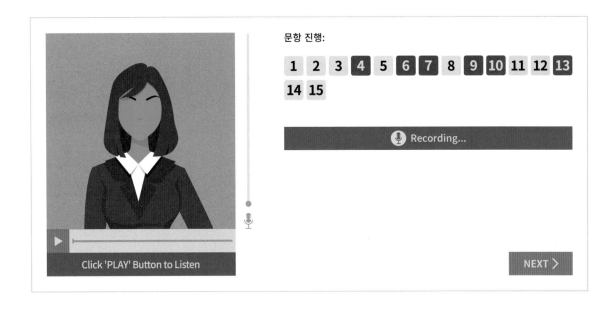

난이도 5 설정 시, 경험 질문은 총 6문제(4, 6, 7, 9, 10, 13번)가 출제됩니다.

1. 이미 유형을 알고 있기에 'Play' 버튼 클릭 전, 사용할 경험의 종류를 결정합니다.

2. 본론(했던 일 – 반전 – 결과)을 매끄러운 스토리텔링으로 답변 Format을 준비합니다.

3. 'Play' 버튼 클릭 후, 첫 번째 문제에서 경험 질문의 키워드를 집중해서 듣습니다.

4. 'Replay' 버튼 클릭 후, 두 번째 문제는 듣지 않고 답변 Format을 다시 준비합니다.

5. 오른쪽 상단의 'Recording' 버튼 생성 시, '경험 답변 Format' 대로 답변합니다.

 문제를 집중하여 듣고, 필히 과거시제를 사용하여 매끄러운 스토리텔링으로 답변!

경험 질문 파악 전략 – 예시

질문 듣기 전, 이미 유형을 알기에 매끄러운 '스토리텔링' 답변 Format 만들기에 집중 하셔야 합니다.

예시 질문 - 여가, 커피숍, 전자기기

• Think about the last time you had some free time when you were little. Did you spend the time with your parents or friends? **When** was it and **what** did you do? Did something **special** or unexpected happen? Please tell me from the beginning to the end.

① 했던 일(when, what) :   진짜녀석들 OPIc 묘사 문장을 과거 시제로 바꾸어 사용
② 반전(special) :   진짜녀석들 OPIc 경험 문장 사용
③ 결과(special) :   진짜녀석들 OPIc 경험 문장 사용

• Tell me about a memorable incident that happened at a coffee shop. **When** was it and **who** were you with? **What** exactly happened and what was it so **special**? Please tell all the stories from the beginning to the end.

① 했던 일(when, who) :   진짜녀석들 OPIc 묘사 문장을 과거 시제로 바꾸어 사용
② 반전(what, special) :   진짜녀석들 OPIc 경험 문장 사용
③ 결과(what, special) :   진짜녀석들 OPIc 경험 문장 사용

• That's the end of the situation. Have you every broken someone's mp3 player? **Whose** mp3 player was it? **Why** did you break it? **How** did you handle the situation? Please tell me everything about that experience in detail.

① 했던 일(whose, why) :   진짜녀석들 OPIc 묘사 문장을 과거 시제로 바꾸어 사용
② 반전(how) :   진짜녀석들 OPIc 경험 문장 사용
③ 결과(how) :   진짜녀석들 OPIc 경험 문장 사용

매끄러운 '스토리텔링' 을 위한 답변 Format 작성을 훈련합니다.

ⓐ **했던 일**
일반적인 6하 원칙(누가, 언제, 어디서 등)을 배운 진짜녀석들 OPIc 묘사 문장 및 본인 실력 문장을 포함합니다.

ⓑ **반전**
스릴러 영화의 반전이 아닌, 이야기 전개의 명분을 줄 수 있는 진짜녀석들 OPIc의 '반전' 문장을 사용합니다.

ⓒ **결과**
매끄러운 마무리를 위해 감정을 섞어 진짜녀석들 OPIc의 '결과' 문장을 사용합니다.

• 진짜녀석들 OPIc 묘사 답변 훈련과 같이 모든 단락에 <u>본인 실력 문장</u>을 필히 포함해 주시기 바랍니다.

경험 답변 전략 – 예시

OPIc은 면접과 흡사한 시험으로 서론, 본론, 결론을 명확하게 지키며 답변합니다.

Q

Tell me about a memorable day at the park. **Who** were you with? Was there **some special event going on?** Or **an unexpected thing happened? What made that day so memorable?** Please tell me all the stories from the beginning to the end.

공원에서 일어난 특별한 경험에 대해 말해주세요. 누구와 갔나요? 특별한 일이 있었나요? 혹은 예상하지 못했던 일이 발생했나요? 무엇이 그 날을 특별하게 만들었나요? 경험에 대해 처음부터 끝까지 상세히 말해주세요.

예시 답변 – 인상 깊었던 공원 경험

- Okay Eva, *experience about the park?* Yeah, I'm pretty sure that it was like 3 weeks ago.

- When I was 23, I used to visit this huge park in my neighborhood.
  - The main reason why I went there was that there were many other things I could do such as playing sports, listening to music and stuff like that.
  - Also, there was a huge running track where lots of people were exercising.
  - So, I took one of my buddies named Kevin since he was a personal trainer.
  - We started to run.

- Well, after like 500 meters? I was already out of breath.
  - But after running at about 3 km, luckily, I finally found my optimal pace.
  - And yeah, I could burn a lot of calories.

- You know what, I lost weight and I was super happy.
  - So, whenever I'm under stress, I go out and run.
  - Plus, whenever I run, it makes me feel so great and it means a lot to me.

- Um yeah, I think this is all I remember about *my park experience.* Thank you.

경험 답변의 고득점을 향한 스피킹 방법을 훈련합니다.

ⓐ 부사 사용(녹색 색상 단어 참고)
단락의 시작은 항상 부사(접속부사, 부사절 등) 및 추임새를 사용하여 간결함과 연결성을 전달해줍니다.

When I was 23, I used to visit this huge park in my neighborhood.

ⓑ 암기 문장(파란 색상 문장 참고)
진짜녀석들 OPIc에서 제공하는 핵심 암기 문장을 사용하여 높은 점수를 받을 수 있는 표현들을 사용합니다.

Well, after like 500 meters? I was already out of breath.

ⓒ 본인 실력 문장(빨간 색상 문장 참고)
핵심 암기 문장의 추가 설명으로 풍부한 답변이 되도록 본인 실력문장을 더해줍니다. (문법적인 오류가 있어도 자신 실력 문장이 추가되어야 실제 본인 답변처럼 들립니다.) 제공하는 핵심 암기문장을 자신의 실력을 추가하여 변형하기도 합니다.

So, I took one of my buddies named Kevin since he was a personal trainer.

ⓓ 강세 전달(밑줄 단어 참고)
영어 말하기에서 강세는 의미를 전달하는 핵심 역할이므로 보다 더 자연스러운 답변을 위하여 강세 전달을 합니다.

- Also, there was a huge running track where lots of people were exercising.

ⓔ 답변 키워드 강조(기울어진 단어 참고)
답변의 키워드(ex. park)는 강조하여 읽어줍니다.

Um yeah, I think this is all I remember about my park experience. Thank you.

16강

유형 03 (경험)

암기문장 활용

과거시제

접속사

등위접속사

be about to

과거 수동태

I ended up~

I realized that~

You know what?

과거진행

현재분사

경험의 암기문장　과거시제

경험의 문법을 정확히 배우고 응용해 보세요.

But after running about 2 km, I finally **found** my optimal pace. And yeah, I **could** burn a lot of calories.

• [과거시제] found : 찾았다

01.　영어의 모든 동사는 시제에 따라 형태가 변함

02.　규칙동사의 경우 동사형태 뒤에 **–ed / -d** 추가

03.　불규칙동사는 형태 자체가 변화하므로 주의해서 사용

04.　특히 경험은 '**과거시제**'가 중요한 유형인만큼 실수하지 않기!

사용 방법

규칙동사 과거시제 :　동사+d/ed

불규칙동사 과거시제 :　형태 변화에 주의!

(be-was/were, go-went, do-did, lose-lost, take-took, drink-drank)

활용 및 응용

• I finally **found** my optimal pace. And yeah, I **could** burn a lot of calories.

• After like 20 minutes? We totally **lost** track of time, we **danced**, **jumped**, I mean, we just **went** crazy.

• You know what, I **could** lose weight and I **became** super happy. So, whenever I'm under stress, I go out and run.

MEMO

경험의 암기문장　접속사

경험의 문법을 정확히 배우고 응용해 보세요.

When we got in, as I expected, there were full of people dancing.

• [접속사] as : ~처럼

01.　'as'는 여러 품사로 사용되지만 여기서는 접속사로 문장과 문장을 이어주는 역할

02.　이 땐 'as' 뒤에는 **주어+동사** 형태를 취급

03.　'as'는 여러 가지 의미가 있기에 문맥에 맞춰 해석하는 것이 중요

04.　**'~처럼'**, **'~때문에'**, **'~하면서'**

사용 방법

as + 주어 + 동사

활용 및 응용

• When we got in, as I expected, there were full of people dancing.

• As I mentioned before, I go to the park twice a week.

• I could see lots of people playing at the park as you said.

MEMO

경험의 암기문장 등위접속사

경험의 문법을 정확히 배우고 응용해 보세요.

And after the festival, we went to a bar **and** grabbed a beer. I mean, it was a great way to wrap up all of the fun.

• [등위접속사] and : 그리고

01. **'등위접속사'**는 단어와 단어, 문장과 문장을 연결해주는 **'접속사'**의 역할

02. 중요한 것은 앞 뒤 문장을 **'동일하게'** 이어주는 것

03. 따라서 앞 뒤 문장에서 사용된 명사나 동사의 형태를 반드시 통일 시켜주는 것이 중요!

04. '등위접속사'로는 and, but, or 등

사용 방법

문장과 문장 / 단어와 단어 사이에 and

* 반드시 등위접속사로 이어진 두 문장, 단어는 동사나 명사의 형태 통일!

활용 및 응용

• We went to a bar **and** grabbed a beer. I mean, it was a great way to wrap up all of the fun.

• So, I called the store **and** told them about my broken coffee maker.

• The only thing I remember is that I kept dancing **and** laughing.

MEMO

경험의 암기문장　be about to

경험의 문법을 정확히 배우고 응용해 보세요.

But um, when we were about to eat something, it started to rain. I mean, the weather was so sunny, but it poured!

• [be about to + 동사원형] : 막 ~하려고 하다

01.　과거 시점에서 **'막 ~하려고 하다'**로 해석되어 어떤 행동을 막 하려던 때를 특정해서 말할 때 자주 사용

02.　**'be + about to + 동사원형'** 형태를 유지하며 시제를 변형하려면 **be동사 시제만 변형**하고 to 다음 동사원형은 그대로 유지!

사용 방법

be동사 + about to + 동사원형

활용 및 응용

• When we were about to eat something, it started to rain. I mean, the weather was so sunny, but it poured!

• When we were just about to arrive at the airport, I realized that I left my luggage at the hotel.

• I am about to leave my house.

MEMO

경험의 암기문장 과거수동태

경험의 문법을 정확히 배우고 응용해 보세요.

Guess what! We **were** completely **soaked**. Well, what could we do? We ended up going back home.

• [과거 수동태] were soaked : 홀딱 젖게 되었다

01. 수동태를 **과거**의 시제로 사용할 때는 **be동사만 과거형**으로!
02. 주어에 따라 **was/were**로 **주어-동사 수일치**에 주의
03. 마찬가지로 불규칙 동사 과거분사 형태에 주의
04. 가끔 'get (got) + 과거분사' 형태로 수동태가 만들어지기도 함
05. 이 때는 그 '당시'의 상황/상태 보다는 그 상황/상태로 '되어지는' (become)의 의미가 더 강함

사용 방법

was/were + 과거분사

활용 및 응용

• We **were** completely **soaked**.

• Everywhere **was** fully **booked**! So, we just went to a convenience store for our dinner.

• After only being there for 30 minutes, I **got** so **drunk**.

MEMO

경험의 암기문장   I ended up~

경험의 문법을 정확히 배우고 응용해 보세요.

Well, the next day? I ended up staying in my bed all day. But you know? It was kinda fun and I feel like drinking again.

• [I ended up ~] : 나는 결국 ~하게 되었다

01.   영어 표현 중 어떤 상황의 결과를 말할 때 자주 사용 하는 구문

02.   'end up' 다음에는 다양한 형태가 오는데, 그 중 **'동명사 (동사+ing)'** 혹은 **'in+장소'** 형태가 종종 사용됨

03.   **'결국 ~하게 되었다'**로 해석되어 예상치 못한 상황이거나 원치 않았던 상황에 처했다는 뉘앙스로 표현

사용 방법

ended up + 동명사 / in + 장소

활용 및 응용

• I ended up staying in my bed all day. But you know? It was kinda fun and I feel like drinking again.

• I guess, he worked on it for about an hour. And you know, I ended up spending $1,000 USD.

• I ended up in the hospital. But it was fun.

MEMO

경험의 암기문장 I realized that~

경험의 문법을 정확히 배우고 응용해 보세요.

After shopping, I tried to pay, but I realized that I was in trouble.

• [I realized that 주어 + 동사] : 나는 ~라고 깨달았다

01. 영어 표현 중 **어떤 상황을 인지했다는 표현**을 할 때 자주 활용되는 표현으로 that 다음으로는 '**주어+동사**'형태의 절을 취급

02. 유사한 표현으로는
     a. I noticed that 주어 + 동사
     b. I found out that 주어 + 동사

사용 방법

I realized that + 주어 + 동사

활용 및 응용

• I tried to pay, but I realized that I was in trouble.

• After like 3 hours, I realized that I'd miss the last train, so I ran down the stairs.

• When I arrived at the movie theater, I found out that I bought the wrong ticket.

MEMO

경험의 암기문장   You know what?

경험의 문법을 정확히 배우고 응용해 보세요.

You know what? Losing a wallet is like starting a new life.

• [You know what?] : 그거 알아?

01.   **'경험'** 유형에는 생동감 있는 '스토리텔링'을 위해서 듣는 사람의 집중을 끌어올 수 있는 **'호응 요구'의** <u>filler</u> 사용이 매우 중요!

02.   또한, '경험'의 반전, 즉 해프닝에 대한 이야기를 하기 전에 집중을 끌 목적으로 사용하기에 좋은 표현!

03.   유사한 표현 : guess what? you know what happened? guess what happened? 등

사용 방법

상대의 집중을 끌어올 때 / 호응을 필요로 할 때 사용

활용 및 응용

• I mean, I had to cancel all my credit cards. You know what? Losing a wallet is like starting a new life.

• I went outside with my new dress but guess what happened? It rained so hard and I got soaked!

• We went shopping and guess what happened? We saw Beyonce at the shopping mall!

MEMO

경험의 암기문장　과거진행

경험의 문법을 정확히 배우고 응용해 보세요.

While we were having fun, all of a sudden, the power went out and we freaked out.

• [과거진행] was/were + 동사ing : ~하고 있었다

01.　과거의 어느 **특정 시점**에서 어떤 행동이나 동작을 하고 있던 상황에 대해 묘사할 때 쓰이는 문법

02.　be동사의 과거인 was/were 다음에 동사ing 형태로 사용

사용 방법

was/were + 동사 ing

활용 및 응용

• While we were having fun, all of a sudden, the power went out and we freaked out.

• While we were enjoying the music, my friend spilled coffee on my laptop.

• I was taking a shower when he called me last night.

MEMO

경험의 암기문장   현재분사

경험의 문법을 정확히 배우고 응용해 보세요.

Oh my god, it was annoying at first, but I pretended like it was ok.

• [현재분사] annoying : 짜증나는

01.   분사는 **'동사'**의 활용형으로 **'형용사'**의 역할을 하는 형태
a. 현재분사 : 동사 + ing '~하는' (능동의 의미)
b. 과거분사 : P.P. '~된' (수동의 의미)
02.   특히 감정을 나타내는 동사에서는 분사 형태에 따라 의미가 전혀 다르게 전달되니 주의해서 사용
a. I was annoying : 나는 짜증났다 ('나'가 짜증을 유발)
b. I was annoyed : 나는 짜증났다 ('나'가 짜증이란 감정을 느낌)

사용 방법

동사 + ing, 형용사의 역할

* 감정의 경우 현재분사는 해당 감정을 '유발'시키는 의미로 해석

활용 및 응용

• It was annoying at first, but I pretended like it was ok.

• This new advertisement was very interesting.

• Actually, walking at the park alone can be very boring.

MEMO

17강

유형 03 (경험)

암기문장 쉐도잉

1단계 : 사전학습

2단계 : 딕테이션

3단계 : 문장 끊어 읽기

4단계 : 전체 문장 읽기

5단계 : 반복 학습

암기문장 쉐도잉

암기문장 쉐도잉은 총 5단계로 나누어져 있습니다.

진짜녀석들 OPIc의 암기문장을 반복듣기 하면서 쉐도잉을 진행합니다.

1단계 **사전학습**	문장을 들은 후, 주어진 암기문장을 억양, 강세를 고려하여 큰소리로 읽습니다. ex.) Actually, **It** is incredibly **beautiful** and **peaceful.**
2단계 **딕테이션**	문장을 들은 후, 밑줄 친 부분을 적습니다. ex.) Actually, ____ is incredibly _____ and _____.
3단계 **문장 끊어 읽기**	문장을 들은 후, 청크 단위로 끊어 읽어 봅니다. ex.) Actually, / **It** is incredibly **beautiful** / and **peaceful.**
4단계 **전체 문장 읽기**	문장을 들은 후, 3단계를 여러 번 반복한 후, 전체 문장을 한숨에 읽어 봅니다. ex.) Actually, **It** is incredibly **beautiful** and **peaceful.**
5단계 **반복학습**	위 단계를 반복하여, 영어의 어순으로 된 한글 해석을 보며, 쉐도잉 연습을 합니다. ex.) 사실, **그 곳은** 숨막히게 **아름다워** 그리고 **평화로워.**

암기문장 쉐도잉

경험의 서론(시작문장)의 쉐도잉 연습을 하세요.

1단계 : 사전학습

문장을 들은 후, 주어진 암기문장을 억양, 강세를 고려하여 큰소리로 읽습니다.

IM3-AL_67 • I got it Eva, <u>experience about my trip</u>?
IM3-AL_68 • Great, you mean <u>my beach experience</u>?
IM3-AL_69 • Alright! Let me tell you <u>my first concert experience</u>.

2단계 : 딕테이션

문장을 들은 후, 밑줄 친 부분을 적습니다.

• I got it Eva, _____?
• Great, you mean _____?
• Alright! Let me tell you _____.

3단계 : 문장 끊어 읽기

문장을 들은 후, 청크 단위로 끊어 읽어 봅니다.

• I got it Eva, **/** <u>experience about my trip</u>?
• Great, **/** you mean <u>my beach experience</u>?
• Alright! **/** Let me tell you <u>my first concert experience</u>.

4단계 : 전체 문장 읽기

문장을 들은 후, 3단계를 여러 번 반복한 후, 전체 문장을 한숨에 읽어 봅니다.

• I got it Eva, <u>experience about my trip</u>?
• Great, you mean <u>my beach experience</u>?
• Alright! Let me tell you <u>my first concert experience</u>.

5단계 : 반복 학습

위 단계를 반복하여, 영어의 어순으로 된 한글 해석을 보며, 쉐도잉 연습을 합니다.

• 알겠어 에바, <u>여행 관련 경험?</u>
• 좋아, <u>내 해변 경험?</u>
• 좋아, <u>내 첫 번째 콘서트 경험</u>을 말해 줄게.

암기문장 쉐도잉

경험의 결론(마무리문장)의 쉐도잉 연습을 하세요.

🎧 MP3 IM3-AL_70~72

1단계 : 사전학습

문장을 들은 후, 주어진 암기문장을 억양, 강세를 고려하여 큰소리로 읽습니다.

IM3-AL_70 • **Um yeah,** this is all I remember Eva. Thank you.
IM3-AL_71 • **Okay Eva,** this is **my park experience**.
IM3-AL_72 • **Alright Eva,** I guess this is pretty much about it.

2단계 : 딕테이션

문장을 들은 후, 밑줄 친 부분을 적습니다.

• **Um yeah,** this is all I remember Eva. Thank you.
• **Okay Eva,** this is _____.
• **Alright Eva,** I guess this is pretty much about it.

3단계 : 문장 끊어 읽기

문장을 들은 후, 청크 단위로 끊어 읽어 봅니다.

• **Um yeah,** / this is all I remember Eva. Thank you.
• **Okay Eva,** / this is **my park experience**.
• **Alright Eva,** / I guess this is pretty much about it.

4단계 : 전체 문장 읽기

문장을 들은 후, 3단계를 여러 번 반복한 후, 전체 문장을 한숨에 읽어 봅니다.

• **Um yeah,** this is all I remember Eva. Thank you.
• **Okay Eva,** this is **my park experience**.
• **Alright Eva,** I guess this is pretty much about it.

5단계 : 반복 학습

위 단계를 반복하여, 영어의 어순으로 된 한글 해석을 보며, 쉐도잉 연습을 합니다.

• **음 그래,** 여기까지가 내가 기억하는 부분이야 에바. 고마워.
• **오케이 에바,** 이게 **내 공원의 경험**이야.
• **알겠어 에바,** 내 생각에 이 정도면 될 것 같아.

암기문장 쉐도잉

개방공간 경험 문장의 쉐도잉 연습을 하세요.

1단계 : 사전학습

문장을 들은 후, 주어진 암기문장을 억양, 강세를 고려하여 큰소리로 읽습니다.

IM3-AL_73	• Well, after like 500 meters? I was already out of breath.
IM3-AL_74	• But after running about 2 km, I finally found my optimal pace. And yeah, I could **burn a lot of calories**.
IM3-AL_75	• You know what, I could lose weight and I became super happy. So, whenever I'm under stress, I **go out and run**.

IM3-AL_76	• When we got in, as I expected, there were full of people **dancing**.
IM3-AL_77	• After like 20 minutes? We totally lost track of time, we danced, jumped, I mean, we just went crazy.
IM3-AL_78	• And after the festival, we went to **a bar and grabbed a beer**. I mean, it was a great way to wrap up all of the fun.

IM3-AL_79	• You know, the **movie** was great, and we had so much fun.
IM3-AL_80	• But um, when we were about to **eat something**, it started to rain. I mean, the weather was so sunny, but it poured!
IM3-AL_81	• Guess what! We were completely soaked. Well, what could we do? We ended up **going back home**.

IM3-AL_82	• After only being there for 30 minutes, I got so drunk.
IM3-AL_83	• I mean, I drank like there's no tomorrow. The only thing I remember is that I kept **dancing and laughing**.
IM3-AL_84	• Well, the next day? I ended up **staying in my bed all day**. But you know? It was kinda fun and I feel like drinking again.

2단계 : 딕테이션

문장을 들은 후, 밑줄 친 부분을 적습니다.

반전	• Well, after like 500 meters? I was already out of breath.
반전	• But after running about 2 km, I finally found my optimal pace. And yeah, I could _____.
결과	• You know what, I could lose weight and I became super happy. So, whenever I'm under stress, I _____.

반전	• When we got in, as I expected, there were full of people _____.
반전	• After like 20 minutes? We totally lost track of time, we danced, jumped, I mean, we just went crazy.
결과	• And after the festival, we went to _____. I mean, it was a great way to wrap up all of the fun.

반전	• You know, the _____ was great, and we had so much fun.
반전	• But um, when we were about to _____, it started to rain. I mean, the weather was so sunny, but it poured!
결과	• Guess what! We were completely soaked. Well, what could we do? We ended up _____.

반전	• After only being there for 30 minutes, I got so drunk.
반전	• I mean, I drank like there's no tomorrow. The only thing I remember is that I kept _____.
결과	• Well, the next day? I ended up _____. But you know? It was kinda fun and I feel like drinking again.

암기문장 쉐도잉

개방공간 경험 문장의 쉐도잉 연습을 하세요.

3단계 : 문장 끊어 읽기

문장을 들은 후, 청크 단위로 끊어 읽어 봅니다.

- **반전** • Well, after like 500 meters? **/** I was already out of breath.
- **반전** • But after running about 2 km, **/** I finally found my optimal pace. **/** And yeah, I could <u>burn</u> **/** <u>a lot of calories</u>.
- **결과** • You know what, **/** I could lose weight and **/** I became super happy. **/** So, whenever I'm under stress, **/** I <u>go out and run</u>.

- **반전** • When we got in, **/** as I expected, **/** there were full of people <u>dancing</u>.
- **반전** • After like 20 minutes? **/** We totally lost track of time, **/** we danced, jumped, I mean, **/** we just went crazy.
- **결과** • And after the festival, **/** we went to <u>a bar and</u> **/** <u>grabbed a beer</u>. **/** I mean, it was a great way to **/** <u>wrap up all of the fun</u>.

- **반전** • You know, **/** the <u>movie</u> was great, and **/** we had so much fun.
- **반전** • But um, **/** when we were about to <u>eat something,</u> **/** it started to rain. **/** I mean, the weather was so sunny, **/** but it poured!
- **결과** • Guess what! **/** We were completely soaked. **/** Well, what could we do? **/** We ended up <u>going back home</u>.

- **반전** • After only being there for 30 minutes, **/** I got so drunk.
- **반전** • I mean, **/** I drank like there's no tomorrow. **/** The only thing I remember is that I kept **/** <u>dancing and laughing</u>.
- **결과** • Well, the next day? **/** I ended up <u>staying in my bed all day</u>. **/** But you know? **/** It was kinda fun and I feel like **/** drinking again.

4단계 : 전체 문장 읽기

문장을 들은 후, 3단계를 여러 번 반복한 후, 전체 문장을 한숨에 읽어 봅니다.

- **반전** • Well, after like 500 meters? I was already out of breath.
- **반전** • But after running about 2 km, I finally found my optimal pace. And yeah, I could <u>burn a lot of calories</u>.
- **결과** • You know what, I could lose weight and I became super happy. So, whenever I'm under stress, I <u>go out and run</u>.

- **반전** • When we got in, as I expected, there were full of people <u>dancing</u>.
- **반전** • After like 20 minutes? We totally lost track of time, we danced, jumped, I mean, we just went crazy.
- **결과** • And after the festival, we went to <u>a bar and grabbed a beer</u>. I mean, it was a great way to wrap up all of the fun.

- **반전** • You know, the <u>movie</u> was great, and we had so much fun.
- **반전** • But um, when we were about to <u>eat something</u>, it started to rain. I mean, the weather was so sunny, but it poured!
- **결과** • Guess what! We were completely soaked. Well, what could we do? We ended up <u>going back home</u>.

- **반전** • After only being there for 30 minutes, I got so drunk.
- **반전** • I mean, I drank like there's no tomorrow. The only thing I remember is that I kept <u>dancing and laughing</u>.
- **결과** • Well, the next day? I ended up <u>staying in my bed all day</u>. But you know? It was kinda fun and I feel like drinking again.

암기문장 쉐도잉

개방공간 경험 문장의 쉐도잉 연습을 하세요.

MP3 IM3-AL_73~84

5단계 : 반복 학습

위 단계를 반복하여, 영어의 어순으로 된 한글 해석을 보며, 쉐도잉 연습을 합니다.

- 음, 아마 한 500미터 후쯤? 난 이미 숨이 차기 시작했어.
- 근데 한 2km 뛴 후에, 난 마침내 내 페이스를 찾았어. 그리고 맞아, 난 **칼로리를 많이 소모할 수 있었어.**
- 있잖아, 난 살을 많이 뺐고 너무 행복했어. 그래서 난 언제나 스트레스를 받으면, **나가서 뛰어.**
- -
- 우리가 들어갔을 때, 내가 예상했듯, 엄청 많은 사람들이 **춤을 추고 있었어.**
- 한 20분 후, 우린 시간이 가는 것을 잊고, 춤추고, 뛰었어. 내 말은 우린 완전 미친 듯 놀았어.
- 그리고 페스티벌 후에, 우린 **바에 가서 맥주를 마셨어.** 내 말은, 완전 좋은 방법이었어 하루를 마무리하기.
- -
- 있잖아, **영화**는 훌륭했어, 그리고 진짜 즐거웠어.
- 근데 음, 우리가 **무언가를 먹으려고** 한순간, 비가 오기 시작했어. 내 말은, 날씨가 좋았는데 엄청 퍼부었어!
- 그래서 어떻게 되었냐고? 우린 흠뻑 젖었어. 글쎄, 우리가 뭘 할 수 있었겠어? 우린 그냥 **집에 돌아와 버렸어.**
- -
- 한 30분 정도밖에 지나지 않았었는데, 난 너무 취했어.
- 내 말은, 난 내일이 없는 것처럼 술을 마셨어. 내가 오직 기억하는 한 가지는 난 계속 **춤을 추고 웃었어.**
- 음, 그다음 날? 난 **하루 종일 침대에 누워 있었어.** 근데 있잖아, 진짜 재미있는 날이었고, 또 한잔이 하고 싶어.

196

암기문장 쉐도잉

독립공간 경험 문장의 쉐도잉 연습을 하세요.

🎧 MP3 IM3-AL_85~96

1단계 : 사전학습

문장을 들은 후, 주어진 암기문장을 억양, 강세를 고려하여 큰소리로 읽습니다.

`IM3-AL_85` • After shopping, I tried to pay, but I realized that I was in trouble.

`IM3-AL_86` • As you can expect, I lost <u>my wallet</u>. Oh my god, I felt like a homeless person.

`IM3-AL_87` • Ugh, I felt sick, I mean, I had to <u>cancel all my credit cards</u>. You know what? <u>Losing a wallet</u> is like starting a new life.

- -

`IM3-AL_88` • After like 3 hours, I realized that <u>I'd miss the last train,</u> so I ran down the stairs.

`IM3-AL_89` • I don't know why, but I just lost balance and fell over.

`IM3-AL_90` • Oh my god, it was so painful, and I was crying. So, I called an ambulance and I stayed in the hospital for <u>2 days</u>.

- -

`IM3-AL_91` • After like 30 min, I still haven't received my order and I started to lose my patience.

`IM3-AL_92` • In order not to ruin our anniversary, I just decided to <u>leave there</u>.

`IM3-AL_93` • You know what, everywhere was fully booked! So, we just went to <u>a convenience store</u> for <u>our dinner</u>.

- -

`IM3-AL_94` • While we were having fun, all of a sudden, the power went out and we freaked out.

`IM3-AL_95` • In order to solve this problem, I quickly <u>found candles and lit them</u>.

`IM3-AL_96` • To be honest, it was such a memorable experience. So, we enjoyed being in that situation and <u>finished our meal</u>.

2단계 : 딕테이션

문장을 들은 후, 밑줄 친 부분을 적습니다.

`반전` • After shopping, I tried to pay, but I realized that I was in trouble.

`반전` • As you can expect, I lost _____. Oh my god, I felt like a homeless person.

`결과` • Ugh, I felt sick, I mean, I had to _____. You know what? _____ is like starting a new life.

- -

`반전` • After like 3 hours, I realized that _____, so I ran down the stairs.

`반전` • I don't know why, but I just lost balance and fell over.

`결과` • Oh my god, it was so painful, and I was crying. So, I called an ambulance and I stayed in the hospital for _____.

- -

`반전` • After like 30 min, I still haven't received my order and I started to lose my patience.

`반전` • In order not to ruin our anniversary, I just decided to _____.

`결과` • You know what, everywhere was fully booked! So, we just went to _____ for _____.

- -

`반전` • While we were having fun, all of a sudden, the power went out and we freaked out.

`반전` • In order to solve this problem, I quickly _____.

`결과` • To be honest, it was such a memorable experience. So, we enjoyed being in that situation and _____.

암기문장 쉐도잉

독립공간 경험 문장의 쉐도잉 연습을 하세요.

🎧 MP3 IM3-AL_85~96

3단계 : 문장 끊어 읽기

문장을 들은 후, 청크 단위로 끊어 읽어 봅니다.

- 반전 • **After shopping,** / I tried to pay, but I realized that / I was in trouble.
- 반전 • **As you can expect,** / I lost **my wallet.** / Oh my god, / I felt like a homeless person.
- 결과 • **Ugh, I felt sick,** / I mean, I had to **cancel all my credit cards.** / You know what? / **Losing a wallet** is like / starting a new life.

- -

- 반전 • **After like 3 hours,** / I realized that **I'd miss the last train,** so / I ran down the stairs.
- 반전 • **I don't know why,** but I just / lost balance and fell over.
- 결과 • **Oh my god,** / it was so painful, and I was crying. So, I / called an ambulance and / I stayed in the hospital for **2 days.**

- -

- 반전 • **After like 30 min,** / I still haven't received my order and / I started to lose my patience.
- 반전 • **In order not to ruin our anniversary,** / I just decided to **leave there.**
- 결과 • **You know what,** / everywhere was fully booked! So, / we just went to **a convenience store** / for **our dinner.**

- -

- 반전 • **While we were having fun, all of a sudden,** / the power went out and / we freaked out.
- 반전 • **In order to solve this problem,** / I quickly **found candles and lit them.**
- 결과 • **To be honest,** / it was such a memorable experience. / So, we enjoyed being in that situation and / **finished our meal.**

4단계 : 전체 문장 읽기

문장을 들은 후, 3단계를 여러 번 반복한 후, 전체 문장을 한숨에 읽어 봅니다.

- 반전 • **After shopping,** I tried to pay, but I realized that I was in trouble.
- 반전 • **As you can expect,** I lost **my wallet.** Oh my god, I felt like a homeless person.
- 결과 • **Ugh, I felt sick,** I mean, I had to **cancel all my credit cards.** You know what? **Losing a wallet** is like starting a new life.

- -

- 반전 • **After like 3 hours,** I realized that **I'd miss the last train,** so I ran down the stairs.
- 반전 • **I don't know why,** but I just lost balance and fell over.
- 결과 • **Oh my god,** it was so painful, and I was crying. So, I called an ambulance and I stayed in the hospital for **2 days.**

- -

- 반전 • **After like 30 min,** I still haven't received my order and I started to lose my patience.
- 반전 • **In order not to ruin our anniversary,** I just decided to **leave there.**
- 결과 • **You know what,** everywhere was fully booked! So, we just went to **a convenience store** for **our dinner.**

- -

- 반전 • **While we were having fun, all of a sudden,** the power went out and we freaked out.
- 반전 • **In order to solve this problem,** I quickly **found candles and lit them.**
- 결과 • **To be honest,** it was such a memorable experience. So, we enjoyed being in that situation and **finished our meal.**

암기문장 쉐도잉

독립공간 경험 문장의 쉐도잉 연습을 하세요.

MP3 IM3-AL_85~96

5단계 : 반복 학습

위 단계를 반복하여, 영어의 어순으로 된 한글 해석을 보며, 쉐도잉 연습을 합니다.

• **쇼핑 후에,** 난 결재를 하려 했는데, 난 큰일이 난 걸 알아차렸어.

• **네가 예상하듯,** 난 **지갑**을 잃어버렸어. 맙소사, 난 진짜 노숙자가 된 기분이었어.

• **윽, 난 진짜 짜증이 났어,** 내 말은, 난 **모든 신용카드를 정지시켜야 했어.** 그거 알아? **지갑을 잃어버리는 건** 새로운 삶을 시작하는 것 같아.

• **한 3시간 후쯤,** 난 마지막 **지하철을 놓칠 것**을 알아차렸어. 그래서 난 계단을 뛰어 내려갔지.

• **이유는 모르겠는데,** 난 균형을 잃고 넘어졌어.

• **맙소사,** 난 너무 아파서 울었어. 그래서 난 앰불런스를 불러서 병원에서 **2일**동안 있었어.

• **한 30분 정도가 지났는데도,** 난 아직 주문을 못 받았고, 난 인내심을 잃기 시작했어

• **우리의 기념일을 망치지 않기 위해,** 난 그냥 **그곳을 나왔어.**

• **있잖아,** 모든 곳은 예약이 다 찼었어! 그래서 우린 그냥 **편의점**에 가서 **저녁**을 먹었어.

• **우리가 즐기고 있을 때,** 갑자기, 정전이 되었고, 우린 너무 놀랐어.

• **이 문제를 풀기 위해서,** 난 재빨리 **초를 찾았고 초를 켰어.**

• **솔직히 말해서,** 정말 기억에 남는 경험이었어. 그래서 우린 그 상황을 즐기며 **음식을 먹었어.**

암기문장 쉐도잉

문제해결 경험 문장의 쉐도잉 연습을 하세요.

1단계 : 사전학습

문장을 들은 후, 주어진 암기문장을 억양, 강세를 고려하여 큰소리로 읽습니다.

IM3-AL_97 • **When we checked out,** we grabbed a cab to go to <u>the airport</u>.

IM3-AL_98 • **When we were just about to arrive at the airport,** I realized that I left <u>**my luggage**</u> at <u>the hotel</u>. Can you imagine that?

IM3-AL_99 • **So,** I asked the driver to go back. Luckily, <u>**the hotel staff**</u> searched for my luggage for <u>**2 hours**</u> and found it! In return, I gave him <u>**20 dollars**</u>.

- -

IM3-AL_100 • **While we were enjoying the music,** my friend spilled <u>coffee</u> on <u>my laptop</u>.

IM3-AL_101 • **Oh my god,** it was annoying at first, but I pretended like it was ok.

IM3-AL_102 • **So quickly,** my friend called an engineer and <u>he</u> came in like <u>10</u>min.

IM3-AL_103 • **I guess,** he worked on it for about <u>an hour</u>. And you know, I ended up spending <u>**$1,000 USD**</u>.

- -

IM3-AL_104 • **For my birthday present,** <u>**my girlfriend**</u> bought me <u>**a coffee maker**</u>. After like <u>10 days</u>, I got <u>the coffee maker</u>, but it was broken!

IM3-AL_105 • **So,** I called <u>the store</u> and told them about my broken <u>**coffee maker**</u>.

IM3-AL_106 • **Because I was so mad,** they apologized and offered an exchange. But I was very upset, so I strongly asked them for a refund.

- -

IM3-AL_107 • **When I arrived at the movie theater,** I realized that I bought the wrong <u>ticket</u>.

IM3-AL_108 • **So,** I went to <u>**the ticket booth**</u> and explained the whole situation.

IM3-AL_109 • **Thankfully,** they offered an exchange for <u>**the next movie**</u>. Moreover, there was no additional payment. Actually, it was the best customer service I've ever had.

2단계 : 딕테이션

문장을 들은 후, 밑줄 친 부분을 적습니다.

반전 • **When we checked out,** we grabbed a cab to go to _____.

반전 • **When we were just about to arrive at the airport,** I realized that I left _____ at _____. Can you imagine that?

결과 • **So,** I asked the driver to go back. Luckily, _____ searched for my luggage for _____ and found it! In return, I gave him _____.

- -

반전 • **While we were enjoying the music,** my friend spilled _____ on _____.

반전 • **Oh my god,** it was annoying at first, but I pretended like it was ok.

반전 • **So quickly,** my friend called an engineer and ____ came in like _____min.

결과 • **I guess,** he worked on it for about _____. And you know, I ended up spending $_____.

- -

반전 • **For my birthday present,** _____ bought me _____. After like _____, I got _____, but it was broken!

반전 • **So,** I called _____ and told them about my broken _____.

결과 • **Because I was so mad,** they apologized and offered an exchange. But I was very upset, so I strongly asked them for a refund.

- -

반전 • **When I arrived at the movie theater,** I realized that I bought the wrong _____.

반전 • **So,** I went to _____ and explained the whole situation.

결과 • **Thankfully,** they offered an exchange for _____. Moreover, there was no additional payment. Actually, it was the best customer service I've ever had.

암기문장 쉐도잉

문제해결 경험 문장의 쉐도잉 연습을 하세요.

🎧 MP3 IM3-AL_97~109

3단계 : 문장 끊어 읽기

문장을 들은 후, 청크 단위로 끊어 읽어 봅니다.

- 반전 • When we checked out, / we grabbed a cab to / go to <u>the airport</u>.
- 반전 • When we were just about to arrive at the airport, / I realized that / I left <u>my luggage</u> at <u>the hotel</u>. / Can you imagine that?
- 결과 • So, I asked the driver to go back. / Luckily, <u>the hotel staff</u> searched for my luggage for / <u>2 hours</u> and found it! / In return, I gave him <u>20 dollars</u>.

- -

- 반전 • While we were enjoying the music, / my friend spilled <u>coffee</u> / on <u>my laptop</u>.
- 반전 • Oh my god, / it was annoying at first, but / I pretended like it was ok.
- 반전 • So quickly, / my friend called an engineer and / <u>he</u> came in like <u>10</u>min.
- 결과 • I guess, / he worked on it for about <u>an hour</u>. / And you know, I ended up spending / <u>$1,000 USD</u>.

- -

- 반전 • For my birthday present, / <u>my girlfriend</u> bought me <u>a coffee maker</u>. / After like <u>10 days</u>, / I got <u>the coffee maker</u>, but it was broken!
- 반전 • So, I called <u>the store</u> and told them / about my broken <u>coffee maker</u>.
- 결과 • Because I was so mad, / they apologized and offered an exchange. / But I was very upset, so / I strongly asked them for a refund.

- -

- 반전 • When I arrived at the movie theater, / I realized that I bought the wrong <u>ticket</u>.
- 반전 • So, I went to <u>the ticket booth</u> and / explained the whole situation.
- 결과 • Thankfully, / they offered an exchange for <u>the next movie</u>. / Moreover, there was no additional payment. / Actually, it was the best customer service I've ever had.

4단계 : 전체 문장 읽기

문장을 들은 후, 3단계를 여러 번 반복한 후, 전체 문장을 한숨에 읽어 봅니다.

- 반전 • When we checked out, we grabbed a cab to go to <u>the airport</u>.
- 반전 • When we were just about to arrive at the airport, I realized that I left <u>my luggage</u> at <u>the hotel</u>. Can you imagine that?
- 결과 • So, I asked the driver to go back. Luckily, <u>the hotel staff</u> searched for my luggage for <u>2 hours</u> and found it! In return, I gave him <u>20 dollars</u>.

- -

- 반전 • While we were enjoying the music, my friend spilled <u>coffee</u> on <u>my laptop</u>.
- 반전 • Oh my god, it was annoying at first, but I pretended like it was ok.
- 반전 • So quickly, my friend called an engineer and <u>he</u> came in like <u>10</u>min.
- 결과 • I guess, he worked on it for about <u>an hour</u>. And you know, I ended up spending <u>$1,000 USD</u>.

- -

- 반전 • For my birthday present, <u>my girlfriend</u> bought me <u>a coffee maker</u>. After like <u>10 days</u>, I got <u>the coffee maker</u>, but it was broken!
- 반전 • So, I called <u>the store</u> and told them about my broken <u>coffee maker</u>.
- 결과 • Because I was so mad, they apologized and offered an exchange. But I was very upset, so I strongly asked them for a refund.

- -

- 반전 • When I arrived at the movie theater, I realized that I bought the wrong <u>ticket</u>.
- 반전 • So, I went to <u>the ticket booth</u> and explained the whole situation.
- 결과 • Thankfully, they offered an exchange for <u>the next movie</u>. Moreover, there was no additional payment. Actually, it was the best customer service I've ever had.

암기문장 쉐도잉

문제해결 경험 문장의 쉐도잉 연습을 하세요.

🎧 MP3 IM3-AL_97~109

5단계 : 반복 학습

위 단계를 반복하여, 영어의 어순으로 된 한글 해석을 보며, 쉐도잉 연습을 합니다.

- **우리가 체크아웃 했을 때,** 우린 택시를 타고 **공항**으로 갔어.
- **우리가 공항에 거의 도착했을 때,** 난 알아차렸어 내가 **짐**을 **호텔**에 놓고 온 것을. 상상이 되니?
- **그래서,** 난 기사님에게 돌아가자 했어. 다행히 **호텔 직원**이 **2**시간 동안 노력해서 찾았어! 난 보답으로 **20**불을 줬어.

- **우리가 음악을 즐기고 있은 동안,** 내 친구가 **내 노트북**에 **커피**를 흘렸어.
- **맙소사,** 처음엔 정말 화가 났었는데, 난 괜찮은 척했어.
- **그래서,** 내 친구는 급하게 엔지니어를 불렀고 **그**는 한 **10**분 만에 왔어.
- **내 생각엔,** 그는 대략 **1**시간 정도 걸려서 고쳤어. 그리고 있잖아, 난 **미화 천불**을 냈어야 했어.

- **내 생일 선물로, 내 여자친구**는 **커피 메이커**를 사줬어. 한 **10**일이 지나서, 난 **커피 메이커**를 받았는데 부서져있었어!
- **그래서,** 난 상점에 전화를 하고 내 망가진 **커피 메이커**에 대해 얘기했어.
- **내가 엄청 화가 났었기 때문에,** 그들은 사과를 했고 난 교환을 제공받았어. 하지만 난 너무 화가 났었고 난 강하게 환불을 요청했어.

- **내가 영화관에 도착했을 때,** 난 **티켓**을 잘못 구매한 것을 알아차렸어.
- **그래서,** 난 **티켓 오피스**에 가서 상황을 설명했어.
- **고맙게도,** 그들은 **다음 영화**로 바꾸어 주었어. 게다가 추가 금액은 없었어. 사실, 이건 내가 받아본 서비스 중 최고였어.

18강

유형 03 (경험)

리스닝 훈련

경험 질문 리스트

어릴적 경험

최근 경험

인상 깊었던 경험

문제 해결 경험

경험 질문 리스트

진짜녀석들 OPIc의 다양한 경험 질문들의 MP3를 듣고 키워드 캐치를 훈련하세요.

어릴적 경험

I would like to ask you about a restaurant you used to go when you were a child. **Who** did you go there with? **What** was the **place like?** What did you **eat?** **What** do you remember most about that restaurant? Tell me about that experience in as much detail as possible.

Now, think about what you did during your **free time as a child.** You may have spent time with your parents or with your friends. I would like you to tell me about **how** you mostly **spent** your free time when you were a child.

Please tell me about a visit to a friend or one of your relatives in your childhood. **Who** did you visit? **Where** did you go and **whom** did you go there with? **What** did you do there? Why was it so special?

I would like to talk about a holiday from your childhood. **What** did you do? **Who** did you spend time with? What was **so special** about that holiday? Tell me everything about that holiday in detail.

Think about a trip you went on when you were little. **Where** did you go, and **whom** did you go there with? What made that trip **memorable?** Tell me everything you remember about that trip in detail.

- -

최근 경험

When was the last time you went for shopping? Tell about a time you went to buy **some clothes. Where** did you go, and **whom** did you go there with? **What** did you buy? What was **so special** about that shopping experience?

I would like to ask you about the most recent holiday you celebrated. **When** was it, and **who** were you with? **How** did you celebrate that holiday? Why was that holiday **memorable?** Tell me why that holiday was particularly unforgettable?

Tell me about a time you ate out at recently. **What kind of restaurant** did you go to? What did you **eat? When** was it and **whom** did you go with? Did you like **the food** there? Tell me everything about that experience in detail.

I would like to ask you about **a take-out or delivery restaurant** you got food from recently. **What** kind of restaurant was it and what was their **menu?** What did you **order?** Did you like **the food** there? Tell me everything in detail.

Let's talk about a recent phone call you remember. **Whom** did you talk to, and **what kind of topic** did you talk about? What made that phone call **so special?** Please tell me about that phone call in as much detail as possible.

Think about the last time you had some free time. **When** was it? **Who** were you with? **Where** did you go? **What** did you do? How did you **feel** on that day? Tell me everything you did on that day in detail.

Do you remember what you did on the Internet yesterday? **Which website** did you visit? **Why** did you visit that website? Please tell me about the things you did on that website yesterday.

경험 질문 리스트

진짜녀석들 OPIc의 다양한 경험 질문들의 MP3를 듣고 키워드 캐치를 훈련하세요.

🎧 MP3 IM3-AL_Q_66~78

인상깊었던 경험

Tell me about a memorable trip to the beach. **When** was it, and **who** were you with? **Which beach** were you at? **What** did you do there? What made this trip to the beach **so special?** Please tell me everything you did at the beach from the moment you arrived there.

Tell me about the most memorable video that you have watched on the Internet. Maybe the video was **something funny,** or **something related to work, school,** or **leisure.** Tell me everything about that video in as much detail as possible.

Tell me your most memorable experience while traveling overseas. Maybe **something funny** or **unexpected happened. Where** did you go and **who** were you with? Please tell me the story from the beginning to the end.

Have you ever had a special experience at a park? **When** was it and **what** happened? **Who** were you with? Why is it **so special?** Please tell me about that story from the beginning to the end.

Think about a memorable hotel you stayed at. **Where** was it located? **Who** did you go there with? **What made you visit** to that hotel? Was there **something interesting** happened? Please tell me about that story from the beginning to the end.

In the past, **how** did you use the Internet to get your project done at school? **When** was it? **What** was the project about? **Was it useful** to use the Internet? Please give me all the details.

Think about a time when you visited one of your friends or relatives. **When** was it? **What** did you do when you visited them? Why was it **so special?** Please tell me everything from the beginning to the end.

Think about a memorable experience you had while eating something at home. **What** did you eat? Did you **like the food?** Why was it **so memorable?** Please tell me everything about that story from the beginning to the end.

문제해결 경험

Pick one of the problems you have experienced at home. **What** exactly **happened?** Please tell me how the problem **started** and how it **ended.** Please tell me how you **solved** that problem in detail.

Tell me about **some difficulties or challenges** that industry had before. What were the **challenges** that industry **dealt with?** How did they **solve** that problem? Please tell me about that story from the beginning to the end.

Have you ever experienced **any problems when you were using the Internet?** Perhaps a website that you wanted to open suddenly stopped working. **What exactly happened?** How did you **solve the situation?** Please tell me about the story from the beginning to the end.

Think about a time when you had trouble while using public transportation. **When** was it and **who** were you with? **What exactly happened?** How did you **deal with the situation?** Please give me all the details.

I would like to ask you about an unexpected incident regarding recycling. **When** was it? **Who** were you with? **What exactly happened?** How did you **solve the situation?** Tell me everything about that day from the beginning to the end.

어릴적 경험

진짜녀석들 OPIc의 다양한 경험 질문들의 MP3를 듣고 키워드 캐치를 훈련하세요.

MP3 IM3-AL_Q_54

돌발 / 레스토랑

어릴 적 갔던 레스토랑 경험

I would like to ask you about a restaurant you used to go when you were a child. Who did you go there with? What was the place like? What did you eat? What do you remember most about that restaurant? Tell me about that experience in as much detail as possible.

/ KEYWORD

MP3 IM3-AL_Q_55

돌발 / 자유시간

어렸을 적 가졌던 자유시간 경험

Now, think about what you did during your free time as a child. You may have spent time with your parents or with your friends. I would like you to tell me about how you mostly spent your free time when you were a child.

/ KEYWORD

MP3 IM3-AL_Q_56

돌발 / 가족,친구

어렸을 적 가족/친구 집 방문한 경험

Please tell me about a visit to a friend or one of your relatives in your childhood. Who did you visit? Where did you go and whom did you go there with? What did you do there? Why was it so special?

/ KEYWORD

MP3 IM3-AL_Q_57

돌발 / 휴일

어렸을 적 휴일에 있었던 경험

I would like to talk about a holiday from your childhood. What did you do? Who did you spend time with? What was so special about that holiday? Tell me everything about that holiday in detail.

/ KEYWORD

MP3 IM3-AL_Q_58

서베이 / 여행

어렸을 적 갔었던 여행 경험

Think about a trip you went on when you were little. Where did you go, and whom did you go there with? What made that trip memorable? Tell me everything you remember about that trip in detail.

/ KEYWORD

최근 경험

진짜녀석들 OPIc의 다양한 경험 질문들의 MP3를 듣고 키워드 캐치를 훈련하세요.

서베이 / 쇼핑

🎧 MP3 IM3-AL_Q_59

최근에 옷을 사러 간 경험

When was the last time you went for shopping? Tell about a time you went to buy some clothes. Where did you go, and whom did you go there with? What did you buy? What was so special about that shopping experience?

/ KEYWORD

돌발 / 휴일

🎧 MP3 IM3-AL_Q_60

최근 휴일에 있었던 경험

I would like to ask you about the most recent holiday you celebrated. When was it, and who were you with? How did you celebrate that holiday? Why was that holiday memorable? Tell me why that holiday was particularly unforgettable?

/ KEYWORD

돌발 / 레스토랑

🎧 MP3 IM3-AL_Q_61

최근에 방문한 레스토랑의 경험

Tell me about a time you ate out at recently. What kind of restaurant did you go to? What did you eat? When was it and whom did you go with? Did you like the food there? Tell me everything about that experience in detail.

/ KEYWORD

돌발 / 레스토랑

🎧 MP3 IM3-AL_Q_62

최근에 테이크아웃/배달음식점에 음식 주문한 경험

I would like to ask you about a take-out or delivery restaurant you got food from recently. What kind of restaurant was it and what was their menu? What did you order? Did you like the food there? Tell me everything in detail.

/ KEYWORD

돌발 / 전화통화

🎧 MP3 IM3-AL_Q_63

최근에 한 기억에 남는 전화통화 경험

Let's talk about a recent phone call you remember. Whom did you talk to, and what kind of topic did you talk about? What made that phone call so special? Please tell me about that phone call in as much detail as possible.

/ KEYWORD

최근 경험

진짜녀석들 OPIc의 다양한 경험 질문들의 MP3를 듣고 키워드 캐치를 훈련하세요.

MP3 IM3-AL_Q_64

돌발 / 자유시간

최근 자유시간을 즐긴 경험

Think about the last time you had some free time. When was it? Who were you with? Where did you go? What did you do? How did you feel on that day? Tell me everything you did on that day in detail.

/ KEYWORD

MP3 IM3-AL_Q_65

돌발 / 인터넷

어제 인터넷으로 방문한 웹사이트 경험

Do you remember what you did on the Internet yesterday? Which website did you visit? Why did you visit that website? Please tell me about the things you did on that website yesterday.

/ KEYWORD

인상 깊었던 경험

진짜녀석들 OPIc의 다양한 경험 질문들의 MP3를 듣고 키워드 캐치를 훈련하세요.

서베이 / 해변

🎧 MP3 IM3-AL_Q_66

기억에 남는 해변 경험

Tell me about a memorable trip to the beach. When was it, and who were you with? Which beach were you at? What did you do there? What made this trip to the beach so special? Please tell me everything you did at the beach from the moment you arrived there.

/ KEYWORD

돌발 / 인터넷

🎧 MP3 IM3-AL_Q_67

인터넷에서 본 가장 기억에 남는 동영상

Tell me about the most memorable video that you have watched on the Internet. Maybe the video was something funny, or something related to work, school, or leisure. Tell me everything about that video in as much detail as possible.

/ KEYWORD

서베이 / 여행

🎧 MP3 IM3-AL_Q_68

기억에 남는 해외여행 경험

Tell me your most memorable experience while traveling overseas. Maybe something funny or unexpected happened. Where did you go and who were you with? Please tell me the story from the beginning to the end.

/ KEYWORD

서베이 / 공원

🎧 MP3 IM3-AL_Q_69

공원에서 있었던 기억에 남는 경험

Have you ever had a special experience at a park? When was it and what happened? Who were you with? Why is it so special? Please tell me about that story from the beginning to the end.

/ KEYWORD

돌발 / 호텔

🎧 MP3 IM3-AL_Q_70

머물었던 호텔에서 가장 기억에 남는 경험

Think about a memorable hotel you stayed at. Where was it located? Who did you go there with? What made you visit to that hotel? Was there something interesting happened? Please tell me about that story from the beginning to the end.

/ KEYWORD

인상 깊었던 경험

진짜녀석들 OPIc의 다양한 경험 질문들의 MP3를 듣고 키워드 캐치를 훈련하세요.

🎧 MP3 IM3-AL_Q_71

돌발 / 인터넷

학창시절 인터넷을 이용해 수행한 프로젝트 경험

In the past, how did you use the Internet to get your project done at school? When was it? What was the project about? Was it useful to use the Internet? Please give me all the details.

/ KEYWORD

🎧 MP3 IM3-AL_Q_72

돌발 / 가족,친구

가족,친구 집에 방문했던 경험

Think about a time when you visited one of your friends or relatives. When was it? What did you do when you visited them? Why was it so special? Please tell me everything from the beginning to the end.

/ KEYWORD

🎧 MP3 IM3-AL_Q_73

돌발 / 음식

집에서 먹은 요리 중 기억에 남는 경험

Think about a memorable experience you had while eating something at home. What did you eat? Did you like the food? Why was it so memorable? Please tell me everything about that story from the beginning to the end.

/ KEYWORD

문제 해결 경험

진짜녀석들 OPIc의 다양한 경험 질문들의 MP3를 듣고 키워드 캐치를 훈련하세요.

서베이 / 거주지

🎧 MP3 IM3-AL_Q_74

집에서 일어난 문제를 해결한 경험

Pick one of the problems you have experienced at home. What exactly happened? Please tell me how the problem started and how it ended. Please tell me how you solved that problem in detail.

/ KEYWORD

돌발 / 산업

🎧 MP3 IM3-AL_Q_75

그 산업에 직면한 문제를 해결한 경험

Tell me about some difficulties or challenges that industry had before. What were the challenges that industry dealt with? How did they solve that problem? Please tell me about that story from the beginning to the end.

/ KEYWORD

돌발 / 인터넷

🎧 MP3 IM3-AL_Q_76

인터넷을 사용하며 발생한 문제의 해결 경험

Have you ever experienced any problems when you were using the Internet? Perhaps a website that you wanted to open suddenly stopped working. What exactly happened? How did you solve the situation? Please tell me about the story from the beginning to the end.

/ KEYWORD

돌발 / 대중교통

🎧 MP3 IM3-AL_Q_77

대중교통 이용 시, 발생한 문제의 해결 경험

Think about a time when you had trouble while using public transportation. When was it and who were you with? What exactly happened? How did you deal with the situation? Please give me all the details.

돌발 / 재활용

🎧 MP3 IM3-AL_Q_78

재활용 관련 기억에 남는 에피소드

I would like to ask you about an unexpected incident regarding recycling. When was it? Who were you with? What exactly happened? How did you solve the situation? Tell me everything about that day from the beginning to the end.

/ KEYWORD

19강

유형 03 (경험)

스크립트 훈련1

어릴 적 경험 어릴 적 갔던 레스토랑 경험

Q54 ──────────────────────────────── 🎧 MP3 IM3-AL_Q_54

I would like to ask you about a restaurant you used to go when you were a child. **Who** did you go there with? **What** was the **place like?** What did you **eat? What** do you remember most about that restaurant? Tell me about that experience in as much detail as possible.

당신이 어렸을 때 가곤 했던 레스토랑에 대해 물어보고 싶습니다. 누구와 함께 갔나요? 그 장소는 어떻게 생겼나요? 당신은 무엇을 먹었나요? 레스토랑에서 뭐가 제일 기억이 남나요? 최대한 상세히 경험에 대하여 말해 주세요.

🎧 MP3 IM3-AL_A_54

서론
시작문장/10%

• _Great,_ you mean *my experience about a restaurant I used to go when I was a child?*

본론
했던 일/40%

• When I was little, I used to go to this huge Chinese restaurant with my parents.
  - The main reason why I liked to visit that restaurant was due to amazing food.
  - And also, I must say that the restaurant was the tallest building in the city, and it had 5 floors.
  - I clearly remember that it was my parent's wedding anniversary.
  - So our family went to the restaurant to celebrate the anniversary.
  - You know, we ordered many kinds of Chinese food.

본론
반전/20%

• After like 30 min, I still haven't received my order and I started to lose my patience.
  - Well, all you need to know is that the restaurant was always packed with lots of people.
  - So I waited another 20min.
  - After 30min, I still haven't received my order.

본론
결과/20%

• But, in order not to ruin my parent's anniversary, we just decided to leave there.
  - You know what, everywhere was fully booked! So, we just went to a convenience store for our dinner.
  - After that day, I decided not to go to that restaurant again.

결론
마무리문장/10%

• Okay Eva, this is *my experience about a restaurant I used to go when I was a child.*

• 좋아, **내가 어렸을 때 가곤 했던 레스토랑에 대한 경험** 말이야?

• 내가 어렸을 때, 나는 부모님과 함께 큰 중식당에 가곤 했었어.
  - 내가 그 식당에 가는 것을 좋아했던 가장 큰 이유는 음식이 환상적이었기 때문이야.
  - 그리고 또한, 그 레스토랑은 도시에서 가장 큰 건물 안에 있었고 5층까지 있었어.
  - 난 우리 부모님의 결혼기념일이었다고 기억해.
  - 그래서 우리 가족은 기념일을 축하하기 위해 그 식당을 갔었어.
  - 있잖아, 우리는 많은 종류의 중식을 주문했어.

• 30분 후에도, 난 여전히 내 주문을 받지 못하였고 인내심을 잃기 시작했어.
  - 음, 중요한 점은 레스토랑이 항상 많은 사람들로 가득 차 있었다는 거야.
  - 그래서 난 20분을 추가로 기다렸어.
  - 30분 후에도, 난 여전히 주문을 받지 못하였어.

• 하지만, 부모님 기념일을 망치고 싶지 않아서, 우리는 그곳을 떠나기로 결정했어.
  - 근데 모든 장소는 예약이 꽉 차있었어! 그래서, 우리는 저녁을 위해 편의점에 갔었어.
  - 그 후에, 나는 다시 레스토랑에 가지 않기로 결정했어.

• 오케이 에바, 이게 **내가 어렸을 때 가곤 했던 레스토랑에 대한 경험**이야.

────────────────────────────────────

어휘 및 표현

when I was a child 내가 어렸을 때   due to amazing food 맛있는 음식 때문에   it was my parent's wedding anniversary 부모님 결혼기념일이었어
I waited another 20min 20분을 더 기다렸어   I decided not to go 안 가기로 결심했어

어릴 적 경험 어렸을 적 가졌던 자유시간 경험

Q55 ─────────────── 🎧 MP3 IM3-AL_Q_55

Now, think about what you did during your **free time as a child.** You may have spent time with your parents or with your friends. I would like you to tell me about **how** you mostly **spent** your free time when you were a child.

어린 아이였을 때 여가시간에 무엇을 했는지에 대해 생각해보세요. 당신은 아마 부모님 또는 친구들과 함께 시간을 보냈을 겁니다. 당신이 어렸을 때 여가시간을 어떻게 보냈는지에 대해 말해주세요.

🎧 MP3 IM3-AL_A_55

서론
시작문장/10%

본론
했던 일/40%

본론
반전/20%

본론
결과/20%

결론
마무리문장/10%

- **Alright!** Let me tell you *how I spent my <u>free</u> time when I was a <u>child</u>.*

- **When I was little,** I used to spend time at the <u>parks</u> with bunch of my <u>friends</u>.
  - I mean, there was a <u>huge</u> park with <u>many</u> different areas where people played <u>soccer</u>, cricket and so on.
  - As I <u>recall</u>, it was like <u>2</u>km from where I lived.
  - <u>Also</u>, there was a <u>huge</u> running track where you could see <u>lots</u> of people exercising.
  - I <u>usually</u> took my friend to run because he was good at <u>sports</u>.
  - And we decided to <u>run</u>.

- **Well, after like <u>500</u> meters?** it started to rain. I mean, the weather was <u>so</u> sunny, but it <u>poured</u>!
  - And you know, I was <u>already</u> out of breath.
  - But <u>after</u> running about <u>2</u> km, I <u>finally</u> found my optimal pace. And <u>yeah</u>, I could burn a <u>lot</u> of calories.

- **You know what,** I could lose <u>weight</u> and I became <u>super</u> happy.
  - Well, summer was the <u>perfect</u> time to visit the park to do some <u>outdoor</u> activities.
  - So, whenever I was under <u>stress</u>, I went out and <u>ran</u>.

- **<u>Alright</u> Eva,** I guess this is <u>pretty</u> much about *how I spent my <u>free</u> time when I was a <u>child</u>.*

- 그래, **내가 어렸을 때 어떻게 여가 시간을 보냈는지** 말해줄게.

- 내가 어렸을 때, 많은 친구들과 함께 공원에서 시간을 보내곤 했어.
  - 내 말은, 사람들이 축구, 크리켓 등을 했던 많은 장소를 가진 큰 공원이 있었어.
  - 내 기억으론, 내가 사는 곳에서 2km 정도 떨어져 있었어.
  - 또한 그곳엔 많은 사람들이 운동을 하는 큰 러닝트랙이 있었어.
  - 난 주로 친구를 데려가서 함께 뛰었는데 운동을 잘했기 때문에 데려갔었지.
  - 그리고 우리는 뛰었어.

- 음, 500m쯤 후에? 비가 내리기 시작했어. 내 말은, 날씨가 정말 화창했었거든, 그런데 비가 퍼부었어!
  - 그리고 있잖아, 난 이미 숨이 찼어.
  - 하지만 2km 달린 후에, 나는 마침내 내 최적의 페이스를 찾았어. 난 많은 칼로리를 태울 수 있었지.

- 있잖아, 난 살을 뺄 수 있었고 난 정말 행복했어.
  - 음, 여름은 야외 활동을 하기 위해 공원을 방문하기에 가장 완벽한 시간이었어.
  - 그래서 내가 스트레스를 받을 때마다, 난 가서 달렸어.

- 그래 에바, 이게 **내가 어렸을 때 여가시간을 어떻게 보냈는지**에 관한 거야.

어휘 및 표현
As I recall 내가 기억하기론   **he was good at sports** 그는 운동을 잘했어

어릴 적 경험 어렸을 적 가족/친구 집 방문한 경험

Q56 ━━━━━━━━━━━━━━━━━━━━━━━━━━━━━━━ 🎧 MP3 IM3-AL_Q_56

Please tell me about a visit to a friend or one of your relatives in your childhood. **Who** did you visit? **Where** did you go and **whom** did you go there with? **What** did you do there? Why was it so special?

어린 시절에 당신의 친척 또는 친구에게 방문한 경험에 대해 말해 주세요. 당신은 누구를 방문했나요? 언제 갔나요 그리고 거기에 누구와 갔나요? 거기에서 무엇을 했나요? 왜 그 경험이 특별했나요?

━━ 🎧 MP3 IM3-AL_A_56

서론
시작문장/10%

- Okay Eva, *experience the time I visited one of my <u>friend's</u> house when I was <u>little</u>?*

본론
했던 일/40%

- When it <u>comes</u> to my friend, I spent <u>lots</u> of time with John and I've known him since I was <u>5</u>.
  - As I <u>recall</u>, his father was <u>very</u> rich, so he lived in a <u>3</u>-story house.
  - The <u>first</u> thing I could see was a <u>flat</u> screen TV and a cozy <u>couch</u>.
  - We <u>really</u> enjoyed watching <u>all</u> kinds of movies.
  - And we <u>also</u> played soccer since there was a <u>huge</u> terrace on the <u>top</u> floor.
  - I think we played soccer for like <u>3</u> hours.

본론
반전/20%

- After like <u>3</u> hours, I <u>realized</u> that I'd miss the <u>last</u> train, so I <u>ran</u> down the stairs.
  - As I mentioned <u>before</u>, his house was a <u>3</u>-stories, <u>right</u>?
  - I <u>don't</u> know why, but I just lost <u>balance</u> and fell over.

본론
결과/20%

- Oh my god, it was <u>so</u> painful, and I was crying. So, I called an <u>ambulance</u> and I stayed in the hospital for <u>2</u> days.
  - But <u>come</u> to think of it, it was one of my <u>memorable</u> experiences in my life.

결론
마무리문장/10%

- Um <u>yeah</u>, I think this is <u>all</u> I remember about *an experience I visited my <u>friend's</u> house when I was <u>little</u>.*

- -

- 오케이 에바, **어렸을 때 친구 집에 방문했던 경험?**

- 내 친구에 대해서 말한다면, john과 함께 많은 시간을 보냈고 5살 때부터 그를 알고 지냈어.
  - 기억해 보면, 그의 아빠는 엄청난 부자였고 3층 집에 살았어.
  - 내가 처음 볼 수 있었던 것은 평면 TV와 안락한 소파 였어.
  - 우린 다양한 종류의 영화를 보는 것을 좋아했어.
  - 그리고 우리는 축구를 했는데 왜냐하면 꼭대기 층에 큰 테라스가 있었기 때문이야.
  - 아마 우리는 3시간 동안 축구를 했던 것 같아.

- 3시간 후쯤, 난 마지막 기차를 놓쳤다는 것을 깨달았어. 그래서 난 계단 밑으로 뛰어 내려갔어.
  - 내가 전에도 언급했듯이, 그의 집은 3층 집이었잖아, 맞지?
  - 왜인지는 잘 모르겠지만, 난 균형을 잃고 넘어졌어.

- 이럴 수가, 정말 아팠고, 난 울었어.
  - 그래서, 난 앰뷸런스를 불렀고 병원에 이틀 동안 입원했어.
  - 하지만 돌이켜 생각해보면, 내 인생에서 기억에 남을만한 경험 중 하나였어.

- 음 예, 이게 **내가 어렸을 때 내 친구 집에 방문했던 경험**이야.

어휘 및 표현
his father was very rich 그의 아버지는 엄청 부자였어   come to think of it 돌이켜 생각해보면

어릴 적 경험 어렸을 적 휴일에 있었던 경험

Q57 ───────────── 🎧 MP3 IM3-AL_Q_57

I would like to talk about a holiday from your childhood. **What** did you do? **Who** did you spend time with? What was **so special** about that holiday? Tell me everything about that holiday in detail.

어린 시절에 휴가 경험에 대해 물어보고 싶습니다. 당신은 무엇을 했나요? 누구와 함께 시간을 보냈나요? 그 휴일에서 무엇이 특별했나요? 휴가에 대해 세부적으로 모든 것을 말해 주세요.

─────────────────── 🎧 MP3 IM3-AL_A_57

서론
시작문장/10%

• <u>Great,</u> you mean *a holiday I spent when I was a <u>child</u>?*

본론
했던 일/40%

• <u>First of all,</u> it was my <u>birthday</u>.
  - So my parents took me to the <u>shopping</u> mall.
  - On the <u>second</u> floor, there were <u>lots</u> of furniture stores.
  - Actually I <u>really</u> wanted to buy a new <u>bed</u>.
  - I was <u>so</u> hyped to get a new bed and we got into the <u>store</u>.

본론
반전/20%

• **For my <u>birthday</u> present,** my mom bought me a <u>new</u> bed!
  - I was <u>super</u> happy.
  - After like <u>10</u> days, I got the bed but, it was <u>broken</u>!

본론
결과/20%

• **Can you <u>imagine</u> this Eva?** it was a <u>new</u> bed!
  - So, I <u>called</u> the store and told them about my <u>broken</u> bed.
  - Because I was <u>so</u> mad, they <u>apologized</u> and offered an <u>exchange</u>.
  - But I was <u>very</u> upset, so I <u>strongly</u> asked them for a <u>refund</u>.

결론
마무리문장/10%

• <u>Okay</u> Eva, this is my *<u>worst</u> holiday experience when I was a kid.*

- -

• **좋아, 어린 시절 보냈던 휴가** 말이지?

• 첫 번째로, 내 생일이었어.
  - 그래서 우리 부모님은 날 쇼핑몰에 데려가셨어.
  - 2층에는, 많은 가구 가게들이 있었어.
  - 사실, 난 새 침대를 정말 사고 싶었어.
  - 새 침대에 난 너무 흥분을 했고 우린 상점에 들어갔어.

• 내 생일 선물로, 우리 엄마는 새 침대를 내게 사줬어!
  - 난 정말 행복했어.
  - 10일 후에, 난 새 침대를 받았는데 부서져 있었어!

• 에바, 이게 상상이 가니? 그건 새 침대였어!
  - 그래서, 난 상점에 전화했고 그들에게 내 침대가 부서졌다고 말했어.
  - 내가 정말 화가 나 있었기 때문에, 그들은 사과했고 교환을 해줬어.
  - 난 정말 화가 났기 때문에 강하게 환불을 요청했어.

• 오케이 에바, 이게 **내가 어렸을 적 최악의 휴가 경험**이야.

어휘 및 표현
my parents took me to the shopping mall 부모님이 쇼핑몰에 데려가셨어   **I was so hyped** 엄청 흥분했어
we got into the store 상점으로 들어갔어

어릴 적 경험 어렸을 적 갔었던 여행 경험

Q58 ──────────────────────── 🎧 MP3 IM3-AL_Q_58

Think about a trip you went on when you were little. **Where** did you go, and **whom** did you go there with? What made that trip **memorable?** Tell me everything you remember about that trip in detail.

당신이 어렸을 때 갔던 여행에 대해 생각해 보세요. 어디에 갔고 누구와 거기에 갔나요? 무엇이 그 여행을 기억에 남게 했나요? 여행에 대해 기억하는 모든 점을 자세히 말해 주세요.

──────────────────────── 🎧 MP3 IM3-AL_A_58

서론
시작문장/10%

- Alright! Let me tell you *about the trip I went on when I was little.*

본론
했던.일/40%

- **When I was 15,** my family went to Thailand for our summer vacation.
  - Actually, the beach in Thailand was undeniably beautiful, and the water was crystal clear.
  - I think that was the main reason why my family went to Thailand.
  - Also, the hotel was amazing too.
  - In fact, it was the most famous hotel which was located in the middle of the town.
  - I mean, the room was extremely clean, and the people were so friendly.
  - You know, we really had a great time there.

본론
반전/20%

- The next day, when we checked out, we grabbed a cab to go to the airport.
  - Oh my god Eva, you are not going to believe what happened!
  - When we were just about to arrive at the airport, I realized that I left my luggage at the hotel. Can you imagine that?

본론
결과/20%

- So, I asked the driver to go back. Luckily, the hotel staff searched for my luggage for 2 hours and found it!
  - In return, I gave him 20 dollars.
  - As I mentioned before, the people were so friendly.
  - It was the best customer service I've ever had.

결론
마무리문장/10%

- Alright Eva, I guess this is pretty much about the *trip I went on when I was little.*

- -

- 그래! **내가 어렸을 때 갔던 여행**에 대해 말해줄게.

- 내가 15살 때, 우리 가족은 여름휴가로 태국에 갔어.
  - 사실, 태국에 있는 해변은 너무 아름다웠고 바다는 크리스탈처럼 깨끗했어.
  - 내 생각에 그게 우리 가족이 태국에 갔던 가장 큰 이유였어.
  - 또한, 호텔은 정말 좋았어.
  - 사실은, 시내 중앙에 위치했던 가장 유명한 호텔이었어.
  - 내 말은, 방은 정말 깨끗했고, 사람들은 정말 친절했어.
  - 있잖아, 우리는 거기서 정말 즐거운 시간을 보냈어.

- 다음날, 우리가 체크아웃을 했을 때, 공항에 가기 위해 택시를 잡았어.
  - 이럴 수가 에바야, 넌 일어난 일에 대해 믿지 못할 거야!
  - 우리가 공항에 막 도착했을 때, 난 내가 짐을 호텔에 놓고 왔다는 것을 깨달았어. 상상이 가니?

- 그래서, 난 운전기사에게 돌아가 달라고 요청했어. 다행히도, 호텔 직원이 2시간 동안 내 짐을 찾았고 그것을 찾았어!
  - 돌아와서, 난 그에게 20달러를 줬어.
  - 내가 이전에도 언급했듯이, 사람들은 정말 친절했어.
  - 내가 이때까지 겪었던 것 중 가장 좋았던 서비스였어.

- 그래 에바, 이게 **내가 어렸을 때 내가 갔던 여행**에 대한 거야.

───────────────────────────────────────

어휘 및 표현

my family went to Thailand for our summer vacation 우리 가족은 여름휴가로 태국에 갔어   the hotel was amazing too 호텔 또한 굉장했어
we really had a great time there 정말 즐거웠어   you are not going to believe what happened! 무슨 일이 있었는지 못 믿을거야

최근 경험 최근에 옷을 사러 간 경험

Q59 ────────────────────── 🎧 MP3 IM3-AL_Q_59

When was the last time you went for shopping? Tell about a time you went to buy **some clothes**. **Where** did you go, and **whom** did you go there with? **What** did you buy? What was so special about that shopping experience?

당신이 마지막으로 쇼핑했던 때는 언제인가요? 옷을 사기를 원했던 때에 대해 말해 주세요. 어디에 갔고, 누구와 거기에 갔나요? 무엇을 샀나요? 쇼핑 경험에 대해서 무엇이 특별했나요?

────────────────────── 🎧 MP3 IM3-AL_A_59

서론
시작문장/10%

- Okay Eva, *experience about the last time I went for shopping?* Yeah, I guess it was like 3 days ago.

본론
했던 일/40%

- **Let me say,** I'm a shopaholic.
  - You know, I suppose I tend to go shopping quite often.
  - So, I went shopping 3 days ago with my friend Susan.
  - You know, the shopping mall was a 10-story building and I must say that it was the tallest building in the city.
  - As I recall, there were lots of luxury stores on the second to fourth floors.
  - So, we spent lots of time collecting our favorite clothes.

본론
반전/20%

- **After** shopping, I tried to pay, but I realized that I was in trouble.
  - Oh my god Eva, you are not going to believe what happened!
  - As you can expect, I lost my wallet. Oh my god, I felt like a homeless person.

본론
결과/20%

- **Ugh, I felt sick,** I mean, I had to cancel all my credit cards.
  - So, we apologized and ended up going back home.
  - You know what? Losing a wallet is like starting a new life.

결론
마무리문장/10%

- **Um yeah,** I think this is all I remember about *the last time I went for shopping.*

- -

- 오케이 에바, **내가 마지막으로 쇼핑을 갔던 경험?** 응, 내 생각엔 3일 전쯤인 것 같아.

- 말해볼게, 난 쇼핑중독이야.
  - 있잖아, 난 꽤 자주 쇼핑을 가는 경향이 있는 것 같아.
  - 그래서 난 3일 전에 내 친구 Susan과 함께 쇼핑을 갔어.
  - 있잖아, 쇼핑몰은 10층짜리 건물이었고, 이건 그 도시에서 가장 큰 건물이었어.
  - 회상해 보면, 2층에서 4층까지는 많은 명품숍들이 있었어.
  - 그래서, 우리는 좋아하는 옷들을 고르는데 많은 시간을 보냈어.

- 쇼핑 후에, 난 계산을 하려고 했는데, 내가 곤경에 처했다는 것을 깨달았어.
  - 이럴 수가 에바야, 넌 어떤 일이 있어났는지 믿지 못할 거야!
  - 네가 예상하듯이 난 지갑을 잃어버렸어. 이럴 수가, 난 노숙자 같은 느낌이었어.

- 윽, 난 너무 짜증이 났어, 내 말은, 내 모든 신용카드를 취소해야 했어.
  - 그래서, 우리는 사과를 하고 결국 집으로 돌아왔어.
  - 그거 알아? 지갑을 잃어버린 것은 삶을 새롭게 시작하는 것과 같아.

- 음 예, 이게 **내가 마지막으로 쇼핑을 갔던 경험**이야.

───────────────────────────

어휘 및 표현
I guess it was like 3 days ago 한 3일 전쯤 인 것 같아   **I'm a shopaholic** 난 쇼핑중독이야
we spent lots of time collecting our favorite clothes 좋아하는 옷을 고르는데 시간을 소비했어

최근 경험 최근 휴일에 있었던 경험

Q60 ──────────────── 🎧 MP3 IM3-AL_Q_60

I would like to ask you about the most recent holiday you celebrated. **When** was it, and **who** were you with? **How** did you celebrate that holiday? Why was that holiday **memorable**? Tell me why that holiday was particularly unforgettable?

가장 최근 휴일 경험에 대해 물어보고 싶습니다. 언제 였나요 그리고 누구와 함께 갔나요? 당신은 그 휴일은 어떻게 축하했나요? 왜 그 휴일이 기억에 남았나요? 그 휴일이 특히 잊지 못할 경험인 이유에 대하여 말해 주세요.

🎧 MP3 IM3-AL_A_60

서론
시작문장/10%

· **Great,** you mean *the <u>most</u> recent holiday I celebrated?* Let me tell you when I went to <u>BUSAN</u>.

본론
했던 일/40%

· **When it comes to the <u>most</u> recent holiday,** I went to <u>HAEWOONDAE</u> beach with my <u>girlfriend</u>.
  - You know, it was <u>summer</u> because summer was the <u>perfect</u> time to visit there.
  - As you can <u>imagine</u>, the beach was undeniably <u>beautiful</u>.
  - Well, we just <u>sat</u> down and enjoyed the <u>peace</u> and quiet.
  - Yeah, it was a <u>perfect</u> spot for just sitting and <u>relaxing</u>.
  - In <u>addition</u>, the <u>main</u> reason why we like to visit there is that there <u>aren't</u> many people around that <u>beach</u>.
  - We listened to <u>music</u> and we even watched a <u>movie</u> using my laptop.

본론
반전/20%

· **You know,** the movie was <u>great</u>, and we had <u>so</u> much fun.
  - But um, it started to <u>rain</u>. I mean, the weather was <u>so</u> sunny, but it <u>poured</u>!
  - <u>Jesus</u> Christ! I was <u>so</u> disappointed.

본론
결과/20%

· **Guess what!** We were <u>completely</u> soaked.
  - Well, what could we do? We just <u>ended</u> up going back home.
  - But, <u>come</u> to think of it, it was <u>kinda</u> romantic.

결론
마무리문장/10%

· <u>Okay</u> Eva, this is *about the <u>most</u> recent holiday I celebrated.*

- -

· 좋아, **축하했던 가장 최근의 휴일?** 내가 부산에 갔던 때에 대해서 말해줄게.

· 가장 최근 휴일에 대해서 말한다면, 난 여자친구와 해운대에 갔어.
  - 있잖아, 여름이 그곳을 방문하기에 완벽한 때였기에 여름에 갔어.
  - 너도 상상할 수 있듯이, 해변은 정말 아름다웠어.
  - 음, 우리는 거기 앉아서 평화로움과 조용함을 즐겼어.
  - 그래, 그냥 앉아서 쉬기에 완벽한 장소였어.
  - 게다가, 우리가 거기에 가는 것을 좋아하는 가장 큰 이유는 해변 근처에 사람들이 많지 않다는 거야.
  - 우리는 음악을 들었고 노트북을 이용해서 영화를 보기도 했어.

· 있잖아, 영화는 재미있었고 우린 즐거운 시간을 보냈어.
  - 근데 음, 비가 내리기 시작했어. 내 말은, 날씨가 엄청 화창했었는데 갑자기 비가 퍼부었어.
  - 이럴 수가! 난 정말 실망했어.

· 그래서 어떻게 되었냐고? 우리는 완전히 젖었어.
  - 음, 우리는 무엇을 할 수 있었을까? 우리는 그냥 집에 가는 것으로 끝이 났어.
  - 근데 돌이켜 생각해 보면, 이건 꽤 로맨틱했어.

· 오케이 에바, 이게 **내가 축하했던 가장 최근의 휴일이야.**

어휘 및 표현
there aren't many people around that beach 해변 주위에 사람들이 많지 않아   **using my laptop** 노트북을 사용하며
I was so disappointed 난 너무 실망했어

최근 경험 최근에 방문한 레스토랑의 경험

Q61 ──────────────── 🎧 MP3 IM3-AL_Q_61

Tell me about a time you ate out at recently. **What kind of restaurant** did you go to? What did you **eat? When** was it and **whom** did you go with? Did you like **the food** there? Tell me everything about that experience in detail.

최근에 외식했던 경험에 대해 말해주세요. 당신은 어떤 종류의 식당에 갔나요? 무엇을 먹었나요? 그건 언제였고 누구와 같이 먹었나요? 거기 음식이 좋았나요? 그 경험에 대해 세부적으로 모든 것을 말해주세요.

──────────────── 🎧 MP3 IM3-AL_A_61

서론
시작문장/10%

본론
했던 일/40%

본론
반전/20%

본론
결과/20%

결론
마무리문장/10%

• <u>Alright</u>! Let me tell you *about a <u>restaurant</u> I've been to lately*.

• **When I was little,** I used to <u>only</u> eat Korean food.
  - However, my <u>taste</u> buds have <u>changed</u> a lot over the years.
  - Well, it was my <u>girlfriend's</u> birthday, so we went to a <u>fancy</u> Italian restaurant to celebrate.
  - You know, the restaurant was <u>extremely</u> clean, and the staffs were <u>so</u> friendly.
  - <u>Plus</u>, the <u>atmosphere</u> was excellent.
  - You know, the food was <u>great</u>, and we had <u>so</u> much fun.

• **While we were having fun,** <u>all</u> of a sudden, the <u>power</u> went out and we <u>freaked</u> out.
  - In <u>order</u> to solve this problem, I quickly found <u>candles</u> and lit them.

• <u>To</u> be honest, it was such a <u>memorable</u> experience.
  - Oh! I must say that the <u>atmosphere</u> was so <u>romantic</u>.
  - So, we <u>enjoyed</u> being in that situation and finished our <u>meal</u>.

• <u>Alright</u> Eva, I guess this is <u>pretty</u> much about *a restaurant I've been to <u>lately</u>*.

• **그래! 내가 최근에 갔던 레스토랑**에 대해 말해줄게.

• 내가 어렸을 때, 난 한식만 먹곤 했어.
  - 하지만, 내 먹는 습관은 몇 년에 걸쳐 많이 변했어.
  - 음, 내 여자친구의 생일이었는데, 난 근사한 이탈리안 레스토랑에 축하해 주기 위해 갔어.
  - 있잖아, 레스토랑은 정말 깨끗했고, 직원들도 친절했어.
  - 추가로, 분위기도 좋았어.
  - 있잖아, 음식은 정말 맛있었고, 우린 즐거웠어.

• 즐겁게 시간을 보내고 있었는데, 갑자기 정전이 됐고 우리는 당황했어.
  - 문제를 해결하기 위해, 난 빠르게 촛불을 찾아서 불을 붙였어.

• 솔직히 말하면, 그건 정말 기억에 남을만한 경험이었어.
  - 오! 분위기도 정말 로맨틱했어.
  - 그래서, 우리는 그 상황을 즐기며 음식을 먹었어.

• 그래 에바, 이게 **내가 최근에 갔던 레스토랑**에 대한 이야기야.

어휘 및 표현
a restaurant I've been to lately 최근에 간 레스토랑　　**I used to only eat Korean food** 난 한식만 먹곤 했어
we went to a fancy Italian restaurant 근사한 이탈리안 레스토랑에 갔어　　**the atmosphere was excellent** 분위기는 최고였어

최근 경험 최근에 테이크아웃/배달음식점에 음식 주문한 경험

Q62 — 🎧 MP3 IM3-AL_Q_62

I would like to ask you about **a take-out or delivery restaurant** you got food from recently. **What kind of restaurant was it and what was their menu?** What did you **order?** Did you like **the food there?** Tell me everything in detail.

최근에 음식을 샀던 포장 혹은 배달음식점에 대하여 물어보고 싶습니다. 어떤 종류의 레스토랑이었고 메뉴는 무엇이었나요? 무엇을 주문했나요? 거기 음식은 좋았나요? 세부적으로 모든 것에 대해 말해주세요.

🎧 MP3 IM3-AL_A_62

서론
시작문장/10%

본론
했던 일/40%

본론
반전/20%

본론
결과/20%

결론
마무리문장/10%

• <u>Okay</u> Eva, *the time I ordered food from a <u>take</u>-out or delivery <u>restaurant</u>?*

• In the <u>past,</u> I used to eat <u>Junk</u> food such as <u>hamburgers</u>, pizza and etcetera.
  - But now, I have become a <u>lot</u> more health-<u>conscious</u> than in the past.
  - So I went to this <u>sandwich</u> store and bought an <u>avocado</u> sandwich.
  - When I came <u>home</u>, I opened the box, and I just <u>freaked</u> out.

• As soon as I <u>opened</u> the box, I <u>realized</u> that I bought the <u>wrong</u> sandwich.
  - You know, I ordered an <u>avocado</u> sandwich, but it was a <u>tuna</u> sandwich.

• So, I called the <u>restaurant</u> and explained the <u>whole</u> situation.
  - <u>Thankfully</u>, they offered an <u>exchange</u> for an avocado sandwich.
  - <u>Moreover</u>, there was no <u>additional</u> payment.
  - But you know what? It felt like a <u>hassle</u> to go back. So I just had my <u>tuna</u> sandwich.
  - But it was the <u>best</u> customer service I've <u>ever</u> had.

• Um <u>yeah,</u> I think this is <u>all</u> I remember *about what I <u>ordered</u> at a take-out restaurant.*

• 오케이 에바, 내가 포장 혹은 배달음식점에서 음식을 주문했던 적?

• 과거에는, 난 햄버거, 피자 등과 같은 정크푸드를 먹곤 했어.
  - 하지만 지금은 난 과거보다 더 많이 건강에 신경 쓰고 있어.
  - 그래서 난 샌드위치 가게에 갔고, 아보카도 샌드위치를 사 왔어.
  - 내가 집에 왔을 때, 난 상자를 열어봤고 당황했어.

• 내가 상자를 열자마자, 난 잘못된 샌드위치를 사 왔다는 것을 깨달았어.
  - 있잖아, 난 아보카도 샌드위치를 주문했지만, 그건 참치 샌드위치였어.

• 그래서, 난 식당에 전화했고 전체 상황을 설명했어.
  - 고맙게도, 그들은 아보카도 샌드위치로 다시 교환해 주겠다 했어.
  - 게다가, 추가적인 지불도 필요 없었어.
  - 근데 그거 알아? 난 다시 돌아가는 게 귀찮게 느껴졌어. 그래서 난 그냥 참치 샌드위치를 먹었어.
  - 하지만 이건 내가 받았던 최고의 고객 서비스였어.

• 음 예, 이게 **내가 포장음식점에서 음식을 주문했던 거**에 대해서 기억나는 모든 거야.

어휘 및 표현

I used to eat Junk food 정크푸드를 먹곤 했어   **When I came home** 집에 돌아왔을 때   **It felt like a hassle to go back** 다시 돌아가기 귀찮았어

최근 경험 최근에 한 기억에 남는 전화통화 경험

Q63 ──────── 🎧 MP3 IM3-AL_Q_63

Let's talk about a recent phone call you remember. **Whom** did you talk to, and **what kind of topic** did you talk about? What made that phone call **so special?** Please tell me about that phone call in as much detail as possible.

당신이 기억하는 최근에 전화통화에 대해 말해봅시다. 누구에게 전화를 했나요 그리고 무슨 종류의 토픽에 대해 이야기 했나요? 어떤 것이 당신의 전화통화를 특별하게 만들었나요? 가능한 세부적으로 전화통화에 대해 말해주세요.

──────── 🎧 MP3 IM3-AL_A_63

서론
시작문장/10%

- **Great,** you mean *a recent phone call I made?* I think it was yesterday.

본론
했던 일/40%

- **Frankly** speaking, I really enjoy watching all kinds of movies because it helps me release stress.
  - So whenever I watch a movie, I spend long time talking about the movie with my friend.
  - You know, I usually talk to Russell since he is an actor.
  - Which means, he knows a lot about movies, so he is a great person to talk with.

본론
반전/20%

- **As I mentioned before,** I talked to Russell about the movie yesterday.
  - Well, it was a musical film.
  - We sang the main song together on the phone.
  - After like 20 minutes? We totally lost track of time, we danced, jumped, I mean, we just went crazy.

본론
결과/20%

- I'm not going to lie to you Eva!
  - You know, it was the best movie I've ever seen.

결론
마무리문장/10%

- Okay Eva, this is *a recent phone call I made.*

- -

- 좋아, **최근 전화 통화?** 내 생각에는 어제였던 것 같아.

- 솔직히 말하면, 난 모든 종류의 영화를 보는 것을 좋아해 왜냐하면 스트레스를 해소하는 데 도움이 돼.
  - 그래서 내가 영화를 볼 때마다, 난 친구와 함께 영화에 대해 이야기하는 데 긴 시간을 보내.
  - 있잖아, 나는 보통 Russell과 얘기해 왜냐하면 그는 배우거든.
  - 그 말은 그는 영화에 대해 많이 알고 있단 얘기이며, 같이 이야기하기에 좋은 사람이야.

- 내가 전에도 언급했듯이, 난 어제도 Russell과 어제 영화에 대해 이야기했어.
  - 음, 그건 뮤지컬영화였어.
  - 우리는 전화로 같이 메인 노래를 불렀어.
  - 20분 후쯤? 우리는 시간 가는 것을 잊고 춤추고 뛰었어. 내 말은, 우리는 정말 제정신이 아니었어.

- 에바야 난 거짓말하는 게 아니야!
  - 있잖아 에바야, 그건 내가 봤던 것 중에 최고의 영화였어.

- 오케이 에바, 이게 **내가 걸었던 최근 전화 통화**야.

어휘 및 표현
a recent phone call I made 최근 했던 전화통화   **I think it was yesterday** 어제였던 것 같아
We sang the main song together on the phone 전화로 함께 메인 노래를 불렀어

최근 경험 <small>최근 자유시간을 즐긴 경험</small>

Q64 ────────────────────────────── 🎧 MP3 IM3-AL_Q_64

Think about the last time you had some free time. **When** was it? **Who** were you with? **Where** did you go? **What** did you do? How did you **feel** on that day? Tell me everything you did on that day in detail.

가장 마지막으로 여가 시간을 보냈던 때에 대해서 생각해 보세요. 언제 였나요? 누구와 함께 갔나요? 어디에 갔나요? 무엇을 했나요? 그 날에 어떤 느낌을 느꼈나요? 당신이 그날 했던 것에 대하여 세부적으로 말해 보세요.

────────────────────────────── 🎧 MP3 IM3-AL_A_64

서론
시작문장/10%

- **Alright!** Let me tell you *the last time I had some free time.*

본론
했던 일/40%

- I clearly remember that it was like 2 weeks ago.
  - You know, I went to the nearest park with my friend to enjoy our Saturday.
  - In the park, there was a huge bike track where you could see lots of people exercising.
  - So we started to ride our bikes there.

본론
반전/20%

- Well, after like 500 meters? I was already out of breath.
  - But after riding about 2 km, I finally found my optimal pace. And yeah, I could burn a lot of calories.
  - But um, all of a sudden, it started to rain. I mean, the weather was so sunny, but it poured!
  - So, I just lost balance and fell over.

본론
결과/20%

- **Oh my god,** it was so painful.
  - So, I called an ambulance and I stayed in the hospital for 2 days.

결론
마무리문장/10%

- Alright Eva, I guess this is pretty much about *the last time I had some free time.*

- -

- **그래! 가장 마지막으로 여가 시간을 보냈던 때**에 대해서 말해 줄게.

- 나는 2주 전이었던 것으로 명확하게 기억해.
  - 있잖아, 난 토요일을 즐기기 위해 내 친구들과 함께 가장 가까운 공원에 갔어.
  - 공원에는, 많은 사람들이 운동하고 있는 큰 자전거 트랙이 있었어.
  - 그래서, 우리는 거기에 자전거를 타기 시작했어.

- 음, 500m쯤 후에? 난 숨이 차기 시작했어.
  - 그러나 약 2km 달린 후에, 나는 마침내 최적의 속도를 찾았어.
  - 그리고 난 많은 칼로리를 태울 수 있었어.
  - 그러나 갑자기, 비가 내리기 시작했어. 내 날은, 날씨는 정말 좋았었는데 갑자기 비가 퍼부었어!
  - 그래서, 난 균형을 잃었고 넘어졌어.

- 이럴 수가, 그건 정말 고통스러웠어.
  - 그래서, 난 앰뷸런스를 불렀고 이틀 동안 병원에서 입원했어.

- 그래 에바, 이게 **가장 마지막으로 여가 시간을 보냈던 때야.**

─────────────────────────────────────

어휘 및 표현
the last time I had some free time 마지막으로 보냈던 여가시간   to enjoy our Saturday 토요일을 즐기기 위해
we started to ride our bikes there 자전거 타길 시작했어

최근 경험 어제 인터넷으로 방문한 웹사이트 경험

Q65 ———————————————————— 🎧 MP3 IM3-AL_Q_65

Do you remember what you did on the Internet yesterday? **Which website** did you visit? **Why** did you visit that website? Please tell me about the things you did on that website yesterday.

어제 인터넷으로 무엇을 했는지에 대해 기억하나요? 당신은 어떤 웹사이트에 방문했나요? 왜 그 웹사이트에 방문했죠? 어제 웹사이트에서 했던 것들에 대하여 말해 주세요.

———————————————————— 🎧 MP3 IM3-AL_A_65

서론
시작문장/10%
- Okay Eva, *what I did on the Internet yesterday*?

본론
했던 일/40%
- As I mentioned before, I do lots of things on the Internet!
  - You know, I visited one of the shopping websites yesterday.
  - And I bought lots of cosmetics and perfumes online.

본론
반전/20%
- Also, I visited a Starbucks homepage to order a coffee for next morning.
  - To be honest, I always go to a coffee shop and order Latte in the morning but sometimes I need to stand in a long line.
  - So I used an app to order online.

본론
결과/20%
- Obviously, most people in the world use the Internet every single day.
  - I mean, can you live without your cell phone for a day?

결론
마무리문장/10%
- Um yeah, I think this is all I remember Eva.

- -

- 오케이 에바, **어제 인터넷으로 한 것?**

- 내가 전에도 언급했듯이, 난 인터넷으로 많은 것들을 해!
  - 있잖아, 난 어제 쇼핑 웹사이트 중 한곳을 방문했어.
  - 그리고 난 온라인으로 많은 화장품과 향수를 샀어.

- 또한, 내일 아침 커피를 주문하기 위해 스타벅스 홈페이지 방문을 했어.
  - 솔직히 말하면, 난 항상 커피숍에 가서 아침에 라테를 주문해. 하지만 때때로 난 긴 줄을 설 필요가 있어.
  - 그래서 난 온라인으로 주문하기 위해 앱을 사용했어.

- 명백하게, 전 세계의 대부분의 사람들은 매일매일 인터넷을 사용해.
  - 내 말은, 하루라도 핸드폰 없이 살 수 있니?

- 음 예, 이게 내가 기억하는 모든 거야 에바.

어휘 및 표현

I visited one of the shopping websites 쇼핑 사이트 중 한 곳을 방문했어 **So I used an app to order online** 난 앱을 사용해서 온라인으로 주문했어
I bought lots of cosmetics and perfumes online 온라인으로 화장품과 향수를 샀어
most people in the world use the Internet every single day 대부분 사람들이 매일 인터넷을 사용해
can you live without your cell phone for a day? 핸드폰 없이 하루를 살 수 있어?

20강

유형 03 (경험)

스크립트 훈련2

인상 깊었던 경험 기억에 남는 해변 경험

Q66 ——————————————————————————— 🎧 MP3 IM3-AL_Q_66

Tell me about a memorable trip to the beach. **When** was it, and **who** were you with? **Which beach** were you at? **What** did you do there? What made this trip to the beach **so special?** Please tell me everything you did at the beach from the moment you arrived there.

해변에서 기억에 남는 여행에 대해 말해 주세요. 언제 였고 누구와 함께 갔나요? 당신은 어떤 해변에 있었나요? 거기에서 무엇을 했나요? 해변으로의 이 여행이 무엇이 특별하게 만들었나요? 거기에 도착했던 순간부터 해변에서 했던 일까지 모든 것을 말해 주세요.

🎧 MP3 IM3-AL_A_66

서론
시작문장/10%

본론
했던 일/40%

본론
반전/20%

본론
결과/20%

결론
마무리문장/10%

- Okay Eva, *when it comes to a memorable trip to the beach,* I got a lot to tell you Eva.

- When I was 27, I went to Hawaii with my friends.
  - Well, Hawaii was the perfect place to go for a vacation and do some outdoor activities.
  - Speaking of the beach, it was undeniably beautiful, and the water was crystal clear.
  - Also, there was a huge park with many different areas where people played soccer, cricket and so on.
  - So, bunch of my friends also played volleyball there.

- You know, we had so much fun.
  - After playing volleyball, we were about to eat something, but it started to rain.
  - I mean, the weather was so sunny, but it poured!
  - Guess what! We were completely soaked.

- I don't know why but, we enjoyed being in that situation.
  - So we turned the music on, and we totally lost track of time.
  - I mean, we danced, jumped, and we just went crazy.
  - Also, we grabbed a beer together. I mean, it was a great way to wrap up all of the fun.

- Um yeah, I think this is all I remember *about a memorable trip to the beach,* Eva.

- -

- 오케이 에바, **해변에서 기억에 남는 여행에 대해서 말한다면,** 난 너에게 말할 게 있어 에바.

- 27살이었을 때, 난 내 친구들과 하와이에 갔어.
  - 음, 하와이는 휴가를 위해 가기에 완벽한 장소이며, 많은 야외 활동을 할 수 있어.
  - 해변에 대해 말해본다면, 정말 아름다웠고 바다는 크리스탈처럼 깨끗했어.
  - 또한, 난 사람들은 축구, 크리켓 등 운동할 수 있는 장소가 많은 큰 공원이 있었어.
  - 그래서, 많은 내 친구들은 거기서 배구를 했어.

- 있잖아, 우리는 정말 재밌었어.
  - 배구를 한 후에, 우리는 뭔가를 먹으려고 했는데 비가 내리기 시작했어.
  - 내 말은, 날씨는 화창했는데, 갑자기 비가 쏟아졌어!
  - 우리는 완벽하게 젖었어.

- 이유는 잘 모르겠지만, 우리는 그 상황을 즐겼어.
  - 그래서, 우리는 음악을 틀었고 시간이 가는 줄도 몰랐어.
  - 내 말은, 우리는 춤췄고, 뛰었고, 제정신이 아니었어.
  - 또한, 우리는 함께 맥주를 마셨어. 내 말은, 그건 하루를 마무리하기 완전 좋은 방법이었어.

- 음 예, 이게 **해변에서 기억에 남는 여행**에 대한 거야.

어휘 및 표현
bunch of my friends also played volleyball there 친구들과 발리볼도 했어   After playing volleyball 발리볼 후에
So we turned the music on 그래서 우린 음악을 틀었어

인상 깊었던 경험 인터넷에서 본 가장 기억에 남는 동영상

Q67 ─────────────────────────── 🎧 MP3 IM3-AL_Q_67

Tell me about the most memorable video that you have watched on the Internet. Maybe the video was **something funny,** or **something related to work, school,** or **leisure.** Tell me everything about that video in as much detail as possible.

인터넷에서 봤던 가장 기억에 남는 영상에 대해 말해 주세요. 그 영상은 아마 재미있었거나 일, 학교 혹은 여가와 관련되어 있을 것입니다. 가능한 세부적으로 그 영상에 대해 말해 주세요.

─────────────────────────── 🎧 MP3 IM3-AL_A_67

서론
시작문장/10%

- <u>Alright</u>! Let me tell you **about the <u>most</u> memorable video I've watched on <u>YOUTUBE</u>.**

본론
했던 일/40%

- **As I mentioned <u>before</u>,** I <u>really</u> enjoy watching music videos on <u>YOUTUBE</u>.
  - <u>Especially</u>, I enjoy watching <u>all</u> kinds of <u>music</u> videos.
  - Speaking of the <u>most</u> memorable video, I've watched an <u>Eminem</u> music video last week.
  - You know, I watched the video with my friend <u>Ryan</u> since he knew a <u>lot</u> about music.
  - You know, the music was <u>great</u>, and we had <u>so</u> much fun.

본론
반전/20%

- **You know,** the <u>highlight</u> of the video was when Eminem sang '<u>Without</u> me'.
  - When we <u>heard</u> the music, we <u>totally</u> lost track of time, we <u>danced</u>, jumped, I mean, we just went <u>crazy</u>.

본론
결과/20%

- While we were <u>watching</u> **the video,** we <u>also</u> grabbed a beer.
  - <u>Actually</u>, it was the <u>best</u> music video I've <u>ever</u> seen.

결론
마무리문장/10%

- <u>Alright</u> Eva, I guess this is <u>pretty</u> much about **the <u>most</u> memorable video I've watched on <u>YOUTUBE</u>.**

- **그래! 유튜브에서 봤던 가장 기억에 남는 영상**에 대해서 말해 줄게.

- 내가 전에도 언급했듯이, 난 유튜브에서 뮤직비디오 보는 것을 정말로 좋아해.
  - 특히, 난 모든 종류의 뮤직비디오를 보는 것을 좋아해.
  - 가장 기억에 남는 비디오에 대해 말해본다면, 나는 저번 주에 에미넴 뮤직비디오를 봤어.
  - 있잖아, 나는 내 친구 라이언과 영상을 봤어 왜냐하면 그는 음악에 대해 많이 알았기 때문이야.
  - 있잖아, 음악은 훌륭했고, 우리는 정말 즐거웠어.

- 있잖아, 영상의 하이라이트는 에미넴이 'Without me'를 불렀을 때였어.
  - 우리가 음악을 들었을 때, 정말 시간 가는 줄 몰랐고, 우린 춤을 추고, 뛰었어 내 말은 우리는 제정신이 아니었어.

- 우리가 영상을 보는 동안, 우리는 맥주도 마셨어.
  - 사실은, 내가 봤던 최고의 뮤직비디오였어.

- **그래 에바, 이게 유튜브에서 봤던 가장 기억에 남는 영상** 이야.

어휘 및 표현
I've watched an Eminem music video 에미넴 뮤직 비디오를 봤어   the highlight of the video was when Eminem sang 'Without me'
비디오의 하이라이트는 에미넴이 'without me'를 불렀을 때야   When we heard the music 우리가 음악을 들었을 때

인상 깊었던 경험 기억에 남는 해외여행 경험

Q68

Tell me your most memorable experience while traveling overseas. Maybe **something funny** or **unexpected happened. Where** did you go and **who** were you with? Please tell me the story from the beginning to the end.

해외여행을 하는 동안 가장 기억에 남는 경험에 대해 말해 주세요. 아마 웃기거나 예상치 못하게 일어났던 일일 것입니다. 언제 갔고 누구와 함께 갔나요? 처음부터 끝까지 해당 이야기에 대해 말해 주세요.

MP3 IM3-AL_A_68

서론
시작문장/10%

- Okay Eva, *experience about my international trips?* Perfect, I will tell you when I went to New Zealand.

본론
했던 일/40%

- Speaking of international trips, New Zealand is the perfect place for a vacation.
  - You know, the main reason why I went there was that, I could spend the time alone.
  - Plus, I preferred going on a trip alone since I could enjoy the peace and quiet.
  - Actually, the beach in New Zealand was undeniably beautiful.
  - So, I fell asleep while I was relaxing at the beach.

본론
반전/20%

- When I woke up, I realized that I was in trouble.
  - Oh my god! I lost my wallet. Oh my god, I felt like a homeless person.

본론
결과/20%

- So, I asked for a help to the people that were at the beach.
  - Luckily, people searched for my wallet for 2 hours and found it!
  - In return, I bought a nice dinner for them.
  - You know, people in New Zealand were so friendly.

결론
마무리문장/10%

- Um yeah, I think this is all I remember *about my international trip,* Eva.

- -

- 오케이 에바, **해외여행에 관한 경험?** 좋아, 내가 뉴질랜드를 갔던 때에 대해서 말해 줄게.

- 해외여행에 대해 말해본다면, 뉴질랜드가 휴가를 보내기에 완벽한 장소야.
  - 있잖아, 내가 뉴질랜드에 갔던 주요한 이유는 내가 혼자 시간을 보낼 수 있었기 때문이야.
  - 또한, 난 평화로움과 조용함을 즐길 수 있기 때문에 나는 혼자 여행 가는 것을 좋아했어.
  - 실제로 뉴질랜드에 있는 해변은 정말 아름다웠어.
  - 그래서, 난 해변에서 쉬는 동안 잠이 들었어.

- 내가 깼을 때, 난 곤경에 처했다는 것을 깨달았어.
  - 이럴 수가! 난 지갑을 잃어버렸어. 이럴 수가, 난 노숙자가 된 기분이었어.

- 그래서 난 해변에 있는 사람들에게 도움을 요청했어.
  - 운 좋게도, 사람들은 내 지갑을 2시간 동안 찾았고, 마침내 발견했어!
  - 답례로, 난 그들에게 저녁식사를 대접했어.
  - 있잖아, 뉴질랜드에 있는 사람들은 정말 친절했어.

- 음 예, 이게 **해외여행에 대해** 기억하는 거야. 에바.

어휘 및 표현

I preferred going on a trip alone 혼자 여행 가는 것을 선호해   **I fell asleep while I was relaxing at the beach** 해변에서 쉬는 동안 잠이 들었어
I asked for a help to the people that were at the beach 해변에 있던 사람들에게 도움을 요청했어
I bought a nice dinner for them 그들에게 좋은 저녁을 사줬어

인상 깊었던 경험 공원에서 있었던 기억에 남는 경험

Q69 ————————————————————————— 🎧 MP3 IM3-AL_Q_69

Have you ever had a special experience at a park? **When** was it and **what** happened? **Who** were you with? Why is it **so special?** Please tell me about that story from the beginning to the end.

공원에서 일어난 특별한 경험을 겪은 적이 있나요? 언제였고 무슨 일이 있었죠? 누구와 함께 갔나요? 왜 그렇게 특별했나요? 경험에 대해 처음부터 끝까지 상세히 말해주세요.

——————————————————————————————————— 🎧 MP3 IM3-AL_A_69

서론
시작문장/10%

• <u>Great,</u> you mean *my special experience at a park?*

본론
했던 일/40%

• **You know,** when I'm <u>stressed</u> out, I go out and <u>run.</u>
  - <u>2</u> years ago, I went to the <u>nearest</u> park in my neighborhood to <u>run.</u>
  - Because there used to be a <u>huge</u> running track.
  - You know, I <u>always</u> prepare my <u>MP3</u> player when I run because I <u>enjoy</u> listening to music.
  - I started to run and after like <u>500</u> meters? <u>Jesus,</u> it started to <u>rain.</u>
  - I mean, the weather was <u>so</u> sunny, but it <u>poured</u>!

본론
반전/20%

• **After like <u>10min,</u>** my MP3 player stopped <u>working.</u>
  - <u>Oh</u> my god, it was <u>annoying</u> because it was a <u>new</u> MP3 player that I got for my <u>birthday</u> present.

본론
결과/20%

• **So quickly,** I ran to the <u>service</u> center which was located in the <u>middle</u> of the town.
  - <u>Luckily,</u> the engineer fixed it.
  - But I <u>ended</u> up spending <u>$1000</u> USD.

결론
마무리문장/10%

• <u>Okay</u> Eva, this is *my special experience at the park.*

- -

• **좋아, 공원에서 나의 특별한 경험?**

• 있잖아, 난 스트레스 받을 때, 나가서 뛰어.
  - 그래서, 2년 전에, 우리 동네에 있는 가장 가까운 공원에 뛰러 갔어.
  - 왜냐하면 거기에는 큰 러닝트랙이 있었거든.
  - 있잖아, 나는 음악 듣는 것을 좋아하기 때문에 뛸 때 항상 MP3 플레이어를 준비해.
  - 난 뛰기 시작했고 약 500m 후에? 이럴 수가, 비가 오기 시작했어.
  - 내 말은, 날씨가 정말 화창했었는데 비가 쏟아졌어!

• 한 10분 후에, MP3 플레이어가 갑자기 작동을 멈췄어.
  - 이럴 수가, 내가 생일 선물로 받았던 새 MP3 플레이어였기 때문에 난 짜증 났어.

• 그래서 빠르게, 시내 중심에 위치해 있던 서비스센터에 달려갔어.
  - 운 좋게도, 엔지니어가 고쳐줬어.
  - 하지만, 난 1000달러를 쓰고 말았어.

• 오케이 에바, 이게 **공원에서 나의 특별한 경험**이야.

————————————————————————————————————

어휘 및 표현
when I'm stressed out 내가 스트레스 받을 때   **I always prepare my MP3 player when I run** 뛸 때 난 항상 MP3 플레이어를 챙겨
My MP3 player stopped working 내 MP3 플레이어가 작동을 멈췄어   **I ran to the service center** 서비스센터로 달려갔어
Luckily, the engineer fixed it 다행히 엔지니어가 고쳤어

인상 깊었던 경험 머물었던 호텔에서 가장 기억에 남는 경험

Q70 ────────────────────────────── 🎧 MP3 IM3-AL_Q_70

Think about a memorable hotel you stayed at. **Where** was it located? **Who** did you go there with? **What made you visit** to that hotel? Was there **something interesting** happened? Please tell me about that story from the beginning to the end.

당신이 머물렀던 기억에 남을만한 호텔에 대해서 생각해 보세요. 어디에 위치해 있었나요? 누구와 거기에 갔었나요? 왜 그 호텔을 방문했나요? 흥미로운 일이 있었나요? 처음부터 끝까지 말해 주세요.

────────────────────────────── 🎧 MP3 IM3-AL_A_70

서론
시작문장/10%

- <u>Okay</u> Eva, *a memorable hotel I <u>stayed</u> at?* Well, it must be the <u>W</u> hotel.

본론
했던 일/40%

- **Whenever I visited the W hotel,** it made me feel <u>so</u> great.
  - Because the rooms were <u>extremely</u> clean, and the people were <u>so</u> friendly.
  - In <u>order</u> to celebrate 1year <u>anniversary</u> with my girlfriend, we went to W hotel in the <u>Philippines</u>.
  - You know, the <u>hotel</u> gave us such a <u>great</u> service, and we had <u>so</u> much fun.

본론
반전/20%

- **When we <u>checked</u> out,** we grabbed a cab to go to the <u>airport</u>.
  - But you know, I <u>realized</u> that I was in <u>trouble</u>.
  - When we were just about to arrive at the <u>airport</u>, I realized that I left my <u>luggage</u> at the hotel.
    Can you <u>imagine</u> that?

본론
결과/20%

- **So,** I asked the driver to go <u>back</u>.
  - <u>Oh</u> my god, I felt like a <u>homeless</u> person.
  - <u>Luckily</u>, the hotel staff searched for my luggage for <u>2</u> hours and <u>found</u> it! In <u>return</u>, I gave him <u>200</u> dollars.
  - <u>Actually</u>, it was the <u>best</u> customer service I've <u>ever</u> had.

결론
마무리문장/10%

- Um <u>yeah</u>, I think this is <u>all</u> I remember *about a <u>memorable</u> hotel I stayed at.*

- -

- 오케이 에바, **내가 머물렀던 기억에 남을만한 호텔?** 음, 그건 W호텔이야.

- 내가 W 호텔에 방문할 때마다 기분이 좋았어.
  - 왜냐하면, 방은 정말 깨끗했고, 사람들은 정말 친절했어.
  - 여자친구와 1주년을 기념하기 위하여, 우리는 필리핀에 있는 W 호텔에 갔어.
  - 있잖아, 호텔은 좋은 서비스를 제공했고 우리는 재미있게 보냈어.

- 우리가 체크아웃을 했을 때, 공항에 가기 위해 택시를 잡았어.
  - 그러나 있잖아, 난 곤경에 처했다는 것을 깨달았어.
  - 우리가 공항에 막 도착했을 때, 난 내가 짐을 호텔에 놓고 왔다는 것을 깨달았어. 상상이 가니?

- 그래서, 난 운전기사에게 돌아가 달라고 요청했어.
  - 이럴 수가, 난 노숙자가 된 것 같은 기분이었어.
  - 다행히도, 호텔 직원이 2시간 동안 노력한 끝에 내 짐을 찾았어! 보답으로, 난 그에게 200달러를 줬어.
  - 사실은, 내가 이때까지 겪었던 것 중 최고의 서비스였어.

- 음 예, 이게 **내가 머물렀던 기억에 남을만한 호텔**에 대한 거야.

──

어휘 및 표현
In order to celebrate 1year anniversary with my girlfriend 여자친구와의 1년을 기념하기 위해
the hotel gave us such a great service 호텔은 정말 훌륭한 서비스를 제공했어

인상 깊었던 경험 학창시절 인터넷을 이용해 수행한 프로젝트 경험

Q71 ────────────────────────── 🎧 MP3 IM3-AL_Q_71

In the past, **how** did you use the Internet to get your project done at school? **When** was it? **What** was the project about? **Was it useful** to use the Internet? Please give me all the details.

과거에, 학교에서 프로젝트를 수행하기 위해 인터넷을 어떻게 사용했나요? 언제 였나요? 어떤 프로젝트 였나요? 인터넷이 유용했나요? 세부적으로 말해 주세요.

── 🎧 MP3 IM3-AL_A_71

서론
시작문장/10%

본론
했던 일/50%

• <u>Great,</u> you mean *the <u>school</u> project done by using the <u>Internet</u>?*

• **When I was a <u>university</u> student,** my favorite class was <u>music</u>.
  - <u>Back</u> then, I <u>really</u> enjoyed listening to <u>all</u> kinds of music.
  - When it came to my school <u>project</u>, I had to study the <u>music</u> trends in 1990s.
  - So, I used <u>YOUTUBE</u> to find some <u>music</u> videos in 1990s.
  - <u>Actually,</u> I did the project with my friend <u>Ryan</u> because he knew a <u>lot</u> about music.

본론
결과/30%

• **As you can <u>expect,</u>** we could find <u>all</u> kinds of music videos in 1990s on <u>YOUTUBE</u>.
  - You know, <u>YOUTUBE</u> was the <u>best</u> free music sharing service I've <u>ever</u> used.

결론
마무리문장/10%

• <u>Okay</u> Eva, this is *about the <u>school</u> project done by using the <u>Internet</u>.*

- -

• 좋아, **인터넷으로 했던 학교 프로젝트?**

• 내가 대학생이었을 때, 내가 가장 좋아하는 과목은 음악이었어.
  - 그땐, 난 모든 종류의 음악을 듣는 것을 좋아했어.
  - 학교 프로젝트에 관련해서는, 난 1990년 대 음악 트렌드를 공부해야만 했어.
  - 그래서, 1990년대 뮤직비디오를 찾는 데 유튜브를 사용했어.
  - 사실은, 내 친구 Ryan과 함께 프로젝트를 했고 왜냐하면 그는 음악에 대해 많이 알았기 때문이야.

• 네가 예상했듯이, 우리는 유튜브에서 1990년대 모든 종류의 뮤직비디오를 찾을 수 있었어.
  - 있잖아, 유튜브는 내가 사용했던 최고의 무료 음악 공유 서비스였어.

• 오케이 에바, 이게 **인터넷으로 했던 학교 프로젝트야.**

어휘 및 표현
I had to study the music trends in 1990s 1990년대 음악 트렌드를 공부했어야 해   **Back then** 그땐   **we could find all kinds of music videos** 우린 모든 종류의 뮤직 비디오를 찾을 수 있었어   **YOUTUBE was the best free music sharing service** 유투브는 최고의 무료 음악 공유 서비스였어

인상 깊었던 경험 가족/친구 집에 방문했던 경험

Q72
🎧 MP3 IM3-AL_Q_72

Think about a time when you visited one of your friends or relatives. **When** was it? **What** did you do when you visited them? Why was it **so special**? Please tell me everything from the beginning to the end.

어린 시절에 당신의 친척 또는 친구에게 방문한 경험에 대해 말해 주세요. 언제 였나요? 그들을 방문했을 때 당신은 무엇을 했나요? 왜 그 경험이 특별했나요? 처음부터 끝까지 모든 것을 말해 주세요.

🎧 MP3 IM3-AL_A_72

서론
시작문장/10%

- <u>Alright</u>! *I remember that I was <u>invited</u> to a party a couple of <u>weeks</u> ago.*

본론
했던 일/40%

- Like <u>2</u> weeks ago, I was <u>invited</u> to a house party from my friend.
  - In <u>fact</u>, he lived in a <u>huge</u> house and it had <u>5</u> floors and a <u>terrace</u> garden.
  - Just like you can <u>imagine</u>, the house was <u>packed</u> with <u>lots</u> of people.
  - You know, people did <u>many</u> kinds of things such as playing <u>beer</u> pong, listening to <u>music</u> and stuff like that.

본론
반전/20%

- While we were having <u>fun</u>, all of a sudden, the <u>power</u> went out and we <u>freaked</u> out.
  - In order to <u>solve</u> this problem, my friend <u>quickly</u> found <u>lots</u> of candles and lit them.

본론
결과/20%

- <u>To</u> be honest, it was such a <u>memorable</u> experience.
  - So, we <u>enjoyed</u> being in that situation drinking and <u>dancing</u>.
  - I mean, we drank like there's <u>no</u> tomorrow.
  - The <u>only</u> thing I remember is that I kept <u>dancing</u> and laughing.

결론
마무리문장/10%

- <u>Alright Eva</u>, I guess this is <u>pretty</u> much about *the <u>house</u> party I've been to.*

- -

- **그래! 난 몇 주 전에 파티에 초대받았던 것을 기억해.**

- 한 2주 전에, 난 친구로부터 파티에 초대받았어.
  - 사실, 그는 큰 집에 살았어 5층짜리 건물이고 테라스 정원이 있었어.
  - 네가 예상할 수 있듯이, 많은 사람들로 가득 차 있었어.
  - 있잖아, 사람들은 비어퐁 게임, 음악 듣기와 같은 많은 것들은 했어.

- 우리는 즐겁게 시간을 보내고 있었는데, 갑자기 정전이 됐고 우리는 당황했어.
  - 이러한 문제를 해결하기 위해, 내 친구는 신속하게 많은 촛불을 찾아서 불을 붙였어.

- 솔직히 말하면, 기억에 남을만한 경험이었어.
  - 그래서, 우리는 술 마시고 춤추면서 그 상황에 있는 것을 즐겼어.
  - 내 말은, 내일 없는 것처럼 술을 마셨어.
  - 내가 기억하는 유일한 것은 내가 계속 춤추고 웃었다는 거야.

- 그래 에바, 이게 **내가 갔었던 파티**에 대한 거야.

어휘 및 표현
I was invited to a house party from my friend 난 친구로부터 하우스파티에 초대 받았어

인상 깊었던 경험 집에서 먹은 요리 중 기억에 남는 경험

Q73 ──────────────────────────── 🎧 MP3 IM3-AL_Q_73

Think about a memorable experience you had while eating something at home. **What** did you eat? Did you **like the food?** Why was it **so memorable?** Please tell me everything about that story from the beginning to the end.

집에서 무엇인가를 먹는 동안 겪었던 기억에 남을만한 경험에 대해 생각해 보세요. 무엇을 먹었나요? 그 음식이 좋았나요? 왜 기억에 남았나요? 그 이야기에 대해서 처음부터 끝까지 말해 주세요.

🎧 MP3 IM3-AL_A_73

서론
시작문장/10%

• <u>Okay</u> Eva, *maybe I can tell you about my* <u>memorable</u> dinner experience.

본론
했던 일/40%

• **Actually,** it was my mom's <u>birthday</u>.
  - For my mom's birthday <u>present</u>, I decided to <u>cook</u> for her.
  - So, I went <u>grocery</u> shopping and bought some <u>meats</u>, vegetables and etcetera.

본론
반전/20%

• **While I was trying to cook,** I don't know why, but the <u>microwave</u> oven just stopped <u>working</u>.
  - Oh my god, it was <u>really</u> annoying.
  - So <u>quickly</u>, I <u>called</u> an engineer and he came in like <u>10</u>min.
  - I guess, he worked on it for about an <u>hour</u>, but <u>sadly</u>, he couldn't fix it.

본론
결과/20%

• **In order <u>not</u> to ruin my mom's birthday,** I went to the <u>convenience</u> store.
  - And I bought some <u>noodles</u> for our dinner.
  - <u>Luckily</u>, my mom <u>enjoyed</u> being in that situation and we finished our <u>dinner</u>.

결론
마무리문장/10%

• **Um <u>yeah</u>,** I think this is <u>all</u> I remember *about my* <u>memorable</u> dinner experience.

• 오케이 에바, **난 기억에 남는 저녁식사 경험에 대해서 말할 수 있을 것 같아.**

• 사실, 엄마 생일이었어.
  - 엄마 생일 선물로, 난 요리를 해드리기로 결정했어.
  - 그래서, 난 장을 보러 갔어 그리고 고기, 야채 등을 샀어.

• 내가 요리를 시도하고 있을 동안에, 이유를 모르겠지만 갑자기 전자레인지가 작동을 멈췄어.
  - 이럴 수가, 정말 짜증 났어.
  - 그래서 빠르게, 난 엔지니어를 불렀고 10분 안에 왔어.
  - 그는 1시간쯤 걸렸지만 고치지 못했어.

• 엄마의 생일을 망치지 않기 위해, 난 편의점에 갔어.
  - 그리고 저녁식사로 라면을 샀어.
  - 운이 좋게도 우리 엄마는 그 상황을 즐겼고 우리는 저녁을 먹었어.

• 음 예, 이게 **기억에 남는 저녁식사 경험**이야.

어휘 및 표현
I decided to cook for her 그녀를 위해 요리하기로 결심했어   **I went grocery shopping** 장을 보러 갔어
The microwave oven just stopped working 전자레인지가 고장났어   **but sadly, he couldn't fix it** 하지만 슬프게도, 그는 고치지 못했어
And I bought some noodles 라면을 샀어

문제 해결 경험 집에서 일어난 문제를 해결한 경험

Q74 ———— 🎧 MP3 IM3-AL_Q_74

Pick one of the problems you have experienced at home. **What** exactly **happened?** Please tell me how the problem **started** and how it **ended.** Please tell me how you **solved** that problem in detail.

당신이 집에서 경험했던 문제 중 하나를 골라 보세요. 정확히 어떤 일이었나요? 문제가 어떻게 시작했고 어떻게 끝났는지 말해 주세요. 문제를 어떻게 해결했는지 세부적으로 말해 주세요.

———————————————————————— 🎧 MP3 IM3-AL_A_74

서론
시작문장/10%
- <u>Okay</u> Eva, *one of the* <u>problems</u> *I had at home?*

본론
했던 일/40%
- <u>Actually,</u> I live in a <u>3</u>-story house.
  - As you can <u>imagine</u>, on the first floor, there is a <u>huge</u> living room and a cozy couch.
  - And there is a <u>kitchen</u> on the second floor.
  - A <u>few</u> weeks ago, for my <u>birthday</u> present, my girlfriend bought me a <u>coffee</u> maker.
  - So, I <u>decided</u> to make some <u>coffee</u>.

본론
반전/20%
- But <u>oh my god Eva</u>, you are <u>not</u> going to believe what <u>happened</u>.
  - I mean, it was a <u>new</u> coffee maker, but it was <u>broken</u>.
  - So, I called the <u>store</u> and told them about my <u>broken</u> coffee maker.
  - And they sent me an engineer and he <u>came</u> in like 10min.
  - But he couldn't <u>fix</u> it and I was <u>so</u> mad.

본론
결과/20%
- So I called the store <u>again,</u> but they <u>never</u> answered the phone and I <u>started</u> to lose my <u>patience</u>.
  - Even after they <u>answered</u>, <u>apologized</u> and offered an <u>exchange</u>, I just <u>strongly</u> asked them for a <u>refund</u>.
  - You know, it was the <u>worst</u> customer service I've <u>ever</u> had.

결론
마무리문장/10%
- Um <u>yeah</u>, I think this is <u>all</u> I remember *about the* <u>biggest</u> *problem I had at home,* Eva.

- -

- 오케이 에바, **집에서 겪었던 문제 중에 하나?**

- 사실은, 난 3층 집에 살아.
  - 네가 상상할 수 있듯, 첫 번째 층에서는 큰 거실과 안락한 소파가 있어.
  - 그리고 2층에는 부엌이 있어.
  - 몇 주 전에, 내 생일선물로 여자친구는 커피 메이커를 사줬어.
  - 그래서, 난 커피를 만들기로 결정했어.

- 그러나 이럴 수가 에바, 무슨 일이 일어났는지 믿지 못할 거야.
  - 내 말은, 새로운 커피 메이커였는데 부서졌어.
  - 그래서 난 상점에 전화했고, 부서진 내 커피 메이커에 대해 설명했어.
  - 그리고 그들은 엔지니어를 보냈고 약 10분 만에 왔어.
  - 하지만 그는 고치지 못했고 난 정말 화가 났어.

- 그래서 난 다시 가게에 전화했지만, 그들은 전화를 받지 않았어. 난 인내심을 잃기 시작했어.
  - 그들이 전화를 받아 사과를 하고 교환을 해주겠다 했음에도 불구하고, 난 강하게 환불을 요청했어.
  - 있잖아, 그건 내가 겪은 최악의 고객 서비스였어.

- 음 예, 이게 **집에서 겪었던 가장 큰 문제 중에 하나야.**

———————————————————————————————————————

어휘 및 표현

I decided to make some coffee 커피를 만들기로 했어   **They sent me an engineer** 엔지니어를 보내주었어

They never answered the phone 그들은 내 전화를 받지 않았어

Even after they answered, apologized and offered an exchange 그들이 전화를 받아 사과를 하고 교환을 해주겠다 했음에도 불구하고

문제 해결 경험 그 산업이 직면한 문제를 해결한 경험

Q75 ──────────────────── 🎧 MP3 IM3-AL_Q_75

Tell me about **some difficulties or challenges** that industry had before. What were the **challenges** that industry **dealt with?** How did they **solve** that problem? Please tell me about that story from the beginning to the end.

해당 산업이 직면한 어려움에 대해 말해주세요. 어떤 문제가 있었나요? 어떻게 해결했나요? 해당 이야기에 대해 상세히 말해주세요.

🎧 MP3 IM3-AL_A_75

서론
시작문장/10%
- **Great,** you mean *some difficulties or* <u>challenges</u> *that the* <u>coffee</u> *industry had before?*

본론
했던 일/40%
- <u>Recently in Korea,</u> the <u>coffee</u> industry is getting <u>increasingly</u> popular.
  - When it comes to <u>coffee</u>, Koreans <u>normally</u> take one to three cups of <u>coffee</u> a day.
  - In the past, people <u>preferred</u> to go to the coffee shops since they could <u>enjoy</u> the peace and <u>quiet</u>.
  - But <u>now</u>, the <u>coffee</u> shops are <u>always</u> packed with <u>lots</u> of people.
  - I mean, people <u>always</u> need to wait in a <u>long</u> line.

본론
반전/20%
- In <u>order</u> to fix this problem, they made <u>coffee</u> makers.
  - Well, using a <u>coffee</u> maker is <u>very</u> convenient.
  - I mean, you <u>don't</u> have to get dressed up to get a bit of <u>caffeine</u>.

본론
결과/20%
- So <u>now</u>, when it comes to the home <u>appliances</u>, I guess the <u>coffee</u> maker became the <u>biggest</u> change in our lives.
  - I mean, <u>most</u> Koreans are using it since it's getting <u>increasingly</u> popular.

결론
마무리문장/10%
- <u>Okay</u> Eva, this is *how the* <u>coffee</u> *industry solved their* <u>problem</u>.

- **좋아,** 예전에 커피 산업이 직면한 어려움이나 문제 말하는 거지?

- 최근 한국에서는, 커피 산업이 점점 인기 있어지고 있어.
  - 커피에 대해서 말한다면, 한국인들은 보통 하루에 커피를 한 잔에서 3잔은 마시거든.
  - 과거에는, 사람들이 커피숍 가는 것을 선호했어 왜냐하면 그들은 평화로움과 조용함을 즐길 수 있었기 때문이지.
  - 하지만 지금은, 커피숍은 항상 많은 사람들로 가득 차 있어.
  - 내 말은 사람들은 항상 줄을 서서 주문을 해야 해.

- 이 문제를 해결하기 위해, 커피 메이커를 만들었어.
  - 음, 커피 메이커는 매우 편리해.
  - 내 말은 커피를 사기 위해서 옷을 차려입고 나가지 않아도 돼.

- 그래서 요즘, 생활 가전제품에 대해 말한다면, 커피 메이커가 우리 삶의 가장 큰 변화가 되었다고 생각해.
  - 내 말은, 대부분의 한국인들이 그걸 사용해 왜냐하면 점점 더 인기 있어지고 있기 때문에.

- 오케이 에바, 이건 **커피 산업이 어떻게 문제를 해결했는지**에 관한 거야.

어휘 및 표현
Koreans normally take one to three cups of coffee a day 한국사람들은 보통 하루에 1-3잔의 커피를 마셔
Using a coffee maker is very convenient 커피 메이커를 사용하는 것은 매우 편리해
You don't have to get dressed up to get a bit of caffeine 커피를 사기위해 옷을 차려 입고 나가지 않아도 돼

문제 해결 경험 인터넷을 사용하며 발생한 문제의 해결 경험

Q76

MP3 IM3-AL_Q_76

Have you ever experienced **any problems when you were using the Internet?** Perhaps a website that you wanted to open suddenly stopped working. **What exactly happened?** How did you **solve the situation?** Please tell me about the story from the beginning to the end.

당신이 인터넷을 사용할 때 문제를 겪은 적이 있나요? 아마 열려고 했던 웹사이트가 갑자기 멈췄을 것입니다. 정확히 어떤 일이 발생했죠? 그 문제를 어떻게 해결했나요? 처음부터 끝까지 해당 이야기에 대해 말해 주세요.

MP3 IM3-AL_A_76

서론
시작문장/10%

- <u>Okay</u> Eva, *any <u>problems</u> when I was using the <u>Internet</u>?*

본론
했던 일/40%

- **Hey Eva!** Did I tell you that I <u>usually</u> go to the park to spend time <u>alone</u>?
  - <u>Last</u> Tuesday, I went to the park at <u>night</u> since I could <u>enjoy</u> the peace and quiet.
  - I mean, the <u>main</u> reason why I like to visit the park at <u>night</u> is that I can spend time <u>alone</u>.
  - You know, it was a <u>perfect</u> spot for just sitting and <u>watching</u> a movie alone.
  - Well, I used <u>YOUTUBE</u> since it's <u>free</u> to use.

본론
반전/20%

- While I was <u>enjoying</u> the movie, I <u>accidently</u> spilled coffee on the <u>laptop</u>.
  - <u>Oh</u> my god, it was <u>so</u> annoying.

본론
결과/20%

- So **quickly,** I called an engineer, but it was late at <u>night</u>.
  - The <u>next</u> day, I went to the <u>service</u> center.
  - You know what? I <u>ended</u> up spending $<u>1000</u> USD.

결론
마무리문장/10%

- **Um <u>yeah</u>,** I think this is all I <u>remember</u> Eva.

- -

- 오케이 에바, **내가 인터넷을 사용하고 있었을 때 생긴 문제?**

- 에바! 내가 시간을 혼자 보내기 위해 공원에 간다고 말했었어?
  - 지난주 화요일에, 나는 밤에 공원에 갔어 왜냐하면 평화로움과 조용함을 즐기려고.
  - 내 말은, 밤에 공원에 가는 것을 좋아하는 가장 큰 이유는 혼자 시간을 보낼 수 있기 때문이야.
  - 있잖아, 공원은 혼자 앉아서 영화를 보기 완벽한 장소였어.
  - 음, 나는 유튜브를 사용했는데 왜냐하면 그건 무료이기 때문이야.

- 내가 영화를 보는 동안, 난 실수로 노트북에 커피를 쏟았어.
  - 이럴 수가, 그건 정말 짜증 났어.

- 그래서 빠르게, 엔지니어에게 전화했지만 늦은 밤이었어.
  - 다음 날, 난 서비스 센터에 갔어.
  - 그거 알아? 난 1000달러를 쓰는 것으로 끝났어.

- 음 예, 이게 내가 기억하는 거야.

어휘 및 표현

I used YOUTUBE since it's free to use 난 무료이기 때문에 유튜브를 사용했어   **it was late at night** 늦은 밤이었어
While I was enjoying the movie 내가 영화를 보던 중

문제 해결 경험 대중교통 이용 시 발생한 문제의 해결 경험

Q77 ──────────────── 🎧 MP3 IM3-AL_Q_77

Think about a time when you had trouble while using public transportation. **When** was it and **who** were you with? **What exactly happened?** How did you **deal with the situation?** Please give me all the details.

대중교통을 이용하는 동안 문제를 겪었을 때에 대해 생각해 보세요. 언제 였나요 그리고 당신은 누구와 함께 갔나요? 무슨 일이 일어났나요? 그 상황을 어떻게 해결했나요? 자세하게 말해 주세요.

──────────────── 🎧 MP3 IM3-AL_A_77

서론
시작문장/10%
· <u>Great</u>, you mean *the time I had <u>trouble</u> while using public <u>transportation</u>?*

본론
했던 일/40%
· **When it comes to public <u>transportation</u>,** people <u>usually</u> use the bus.
  - <u>Generally</u>, it has central heating and air-<u>conditioning</u>, so it's <u>cool</u> during summer and <u>warm</u> during winter.
  - <u>One</u> day, I got on the bus because I had a <u>job</u> interview.

본론
반전/20%
· **I <u>don't</u> know why,** but the bus just <u>stopped</u>.
  - So, the <u>driver</u> called an engineer.
  - After like <u>30</u> min, the engineer <u>still</u> didn't show up and I <u>started</u> to lose my <u>patience</u>.

본론
결과/20%
· <u>Oh my god!</u> I just got off the bus and took a <u>cab</u>.
  - And you know, I <u>ended</u> up paying <u>$100</u> USD.

결론
마무리문장/10%
· <u>Okay</u> Eva, this is *about the time I had <u>trouble</u> while using public <u>transportation</u>.*

- -

· **좋아, 내가 대중교통을 사용하면서 겪었던 문제** 말하는 거지?

· **대중교통에 대해서 말한다면,** 사람들은 보통 버스를 사용해.
  - 일반적으로, 중앙난방과 에어컨이 있어서 여름에는 시원하고 겨울에는 따뜻해.
  - 어느 날, 난 면접이 있어서 버스를 탔어.

· **이유는 모르겠는데,** 버스가 갑자기 멈췄어.
  - 그래서, 버스기사님은 엔지니어를 불렀어.
  - 30분 후가 지났는데도, 엔지니어는 여전히 나타나지 않았고 나는 인내심을 잃기 시작했어.

· **이럴 수가!** 난 버스에서 내렸고 택시를 잡았어.
  - 그리고 있잖아, 난 100달러를 내고 말았어.

· **오케이 에바, 이게 내가 대중교통을 사용하면서 겪었던 문제야.**

어휘 및 표현
people usually use the bus 사람들은 주로 버스를 이용해　　**I had a job interview** 면접이 있었어　　**But the bus just stopped** 하지만 버스가 멈췄어
The engineer still didn't show up 엔지니어는 아직 나타나지 않았어　　**I just got off the bus and took a cab** 버스에서 내려 택시를 탔어

문제 해결 경험 재활용 관련 기억에 남는 에피소드

Q78 ───────────────────────────────── 🎧 MP3 IM3-AL_Q_78

I would like to ask you about an unexpected incident regarding recycling. **When** was it? **Who** were you with? **What exactly happened?** How did you **solve the situation?** Tell me everything about that day from the beginning to the end.

재활용과 관련한 예상치 못했던 사건에 대해서 물어보고 싶습니다. 언제 였나요? 누구와 함께 갔나요? 정확히 무슨 일이 있었나요? 당신은 어떻게 문제를 해결했나요? 그 날에 대해서 처음부터 끝까지 말해 주세요.

🎧 MP3 IM3-AL_A_78

서론
시작문장/10%

- <u>Alright!</u> Let me tell you *about an incident regarding <u>recycling</u>.*

본론
했던 일/40%

- **Speaking of recycling in <u>Korea,</u>** people <u>recycle</u> in the recycling centers.
  - <u>Seriously,</u> I prefer to go there at night since it's <u>always</u> packed with <u>lots</u> of people.
  - <u>Last</u> week, I went to the <u>recycling</u> center near my place at like <u>10pm.</u>

본론
반전/20%

- **While I was <u>recycling,</u> all of a sudden,** the <u>power</u> went out and I <u>freaked</u> out.
  - So, I <u>ran</u> down the stairs.
  - Because it was <u>so</u> dark, I just lost <u>balance</u> and fell over.

본론
결과/20%

- <u>Oh</u> my god, it was <u>so</u> painful, and I was <u>crying.</u>
  - So, I called an <u>ambulance</u> and I stayed in the hospital for <u>2</u> days.

결론
마무리문장/10%

- <u>Alright</u> Eva, I guess this is <u>pretty</u> much about *an <u>incident</u> regarding recycling.*

- 그래! **재활용과 관련된 사건**에 대해서 말해줄게.

- 한국 재활용에 대해 말해본다면, 사람들은 재활용센터에서 재활용을 해.
  - 솔직히, 난 그곳에 밤에 가는 것을 좋아해 왜냐하면 항상 많은 사람들로 가득 차 있기 때문이야.
  - 저번 주에, 난 우리 집에서 가까운 재활용센터에 밤 10시쯤 갔어.

- 재활용을 하고 있었는데, 갑자기 정전이 됐고 난 당황했어.
  - 그래서 난 계단 밑으로 뛰어 내려갔어.
  - 왜냐하면 거긴 너무 어두웠기 때문에, 난 균형을 잃고 넘어졌어.

- 이럴 수가, 정말 아팠고, 난 울었어.
  - 그래서, 난 앰뷸런스를 불렀고 병원에 이틀 동안 입원했어.

- 그래 에바, 이게 **재활용과 관련된 사건**이야.

어휘 및 표현
an incident regarding recycling 재활용 관련된 사건   people recycle in the recycling centers 사람들은 재활용센터에서 재활용을 해

21강

모의고사

유형 01 (묘사)
유형 02 (세부묘사)
유형 03 (경험)

묘사, 경험 모의고사 준비

롤플레이를 제외한 문제를 풀어 보시면서 훈련하세요!

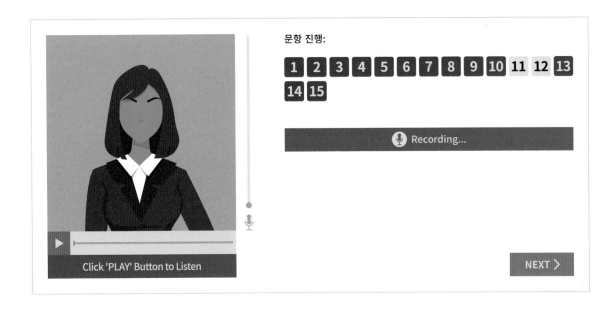

묘사	세부묘사	경험
2 5 8	3 14 15	4 6 7 9 10 13

묘사, 경험 모의고사

실제 시험처럼 각 문제의 MP3를 듣고, 훈련을 해보세요.

Q79   Let's start the interview now. Please tell me a little about yourself.

Q80   You indicated in the survey that you like **listening to music.** What kind of music do you listen to? Who are some of your favorite musicians or composers?

Q81   How did you **first get interested in music?** Please **compare the music** that you used to listen when you were **young** and the music you listen **today.** Also, how has your interest in music changed over the years?

Q82   Please tell me about a time when you went to listen to some live music. Was it at a concert or a live café? **Who did you go there with? How did you like the music** you listened to there? Please tell me about that day from the beginning to the end.

Q83   I would like to ask you about **gatherings in your country. What** do people in your country do when they get together? **Where** do they go? How do they normally **celebrate** their gatherings? Please tell me in detail.

Q84   Think about your last gathering. **Who** were you with? **Where** did you go? Please tell me about how you spent your day on your last gathering in as much detail as possible.

Q85   Tell me about a memorable moment you had at a gathering. **When** was it? **What kinds of gathering** was it? **What** exactly **happened** on that day? **Why** was it **memorable?** Please tell me everything from the beginning to the end.

Q86   You indicated in the survey that you go to **bars.** Describe one of your favorite bars that you usually visit. **What** does it look like? **Why** do you like to visit that bar? Please tell me everything about that place in detail.

Q87   Do you remember the first bar you went to? **When** was it and **who** did you go there with? What was so special about that bar? Was there **something interesting happened** that made that experience more special?

Q88   Tell me about a memorable incident that happened at a bar. **When** was it? **Who** were you with? **What** exactly happened there? Was there **something interesting** going on? Why was it **so special?** Tell me everything about that day at the bar from the beginning to the end.

Q89   Let's say that something wrong can happen to our health. What are **some health problems** that we can have? Please describe **what can be happening** when someone loses his/her health. **How can we fix** those health problems? Please **provide some solutions** to stay healthy.

Q90   **What are some hot products or services** that people talk about these days? Why are they mentioned by people so often these days? Give me all the details.

Q91   What are **some major changes in people's shopping habits?** Where do people normally shop and what do they normally buy?

1번 자기소개

Q79

Let's start the interview now. Please tell me a little about yourself.

이제 인터뷰를 시작해 봅시다. 자기소개를 해주세요.

서론
시작문장/10%

본론
단락별 핵심문장/80%

- Oh hi Eva! *Let me briefly introduce myself.*

- **As you can imagine,** I'm Korean and I live in Seoul.
  - I'm very outgoing and like socializing.
  - Well, in my free time, I really enjoy watching all kinds of movies because it helps me release stress.
  - You know, I suppose I tend to watch movies a few times a month.

- Plus, I love working out at the park.
  - Because there is a huge running track where you can see lots of people exercising.
  - Whenever I go out and run, it makes me feel so great and it means a lot to me.

결론
마무리문장/10%

- **Alright Eva,** this is all I can say about *myself.* Thank you.

- 오 안녕 에바! 내 소개를 간단히 해볼게.

- 네가 예상했듯, 난 한국인이고 서울에 살아.
  - 난 매우 활발하고 사람 만나는 것을 좋아해.
  - 음, 여가 시간에는 모든 종류의 영화를 보는 것을 좋아해 왜냐하면 그건 스트레스 해소하는 데 도움이 되거든.
  - 있잖아, 난 한 달에 몇 번 영화를 보는 경향이 있어.

- 추가로, 난 공원에서 운동하는 것을 좋아해.
  - 왜냐하면 거기에는 많은 사람들이 운동하는 것을 볼 수 있는 큰 러닝트랙이 있어.
  - 내가 거기에 가서 뛸 때마다, 기분이 좋고 그건 나에게 많은 의미가 있어.

- 그래 에바, 이게 **나에 대한 소개**야. 고마워

어휘 및 표현

I love working out at the park 난 공원에서 운동하는 것을 좋아해   I'm very outgoing and like socializing 난 굉장히 활발하고 사람 만나는 것을 좋아해

2번 좋아하는 음악 묘사

Q80 ──────────────────────── 🎧 MP3 IM3-AL_Q_80

You indicated in the survey that you like **listening to music.** What kind of music do you listen to? Who are some of your favorite musicians or composers?

당신은 음악 듣는 것을 좋아한다고 서베이에서 답했습니다. 어떤 종류의 음악을 듣나요? 좋아하는 가수 혹은 작곡가는 누구인가요?

──────────────────────────── 🎧 MP3 IM3-AL_A_80

서론
시작문장/10%

본론
단락별 핵심문장/80%

- Oh <u>yeah</u>, *I like listening to <u>music</u>!* You know, I think I listen to music <u>every</u> single day.

- When it <u>comes</u> to music, I <u>really</u> enjoy listening to <u>hip</u>-hop because it helps me <u>release</u> stress.
  - Well, when I listen to music, I <u>usually</u> go to the park or somewhere <u>quiet</u>.
  - Speaking of the park, it's a <u>perfect</u> spot for listening to music alone while looking at the <u>beautiful</u> flowers.

- As for my <u>favorite</u> singer, it <u>has</u> to be Eminem since I <u>love</u> hip-hop.
  - No matter <u>how</u> many people are going, I <u>always</u> attend his concerts.
  - Because it makes me feel <u>so</u> great when I listen to his songs.

- In <u>addition</u>, I love K-POP since it's getting <u>increasingly</u> popular.
  - You know, I guess listening to music is the <u>best</u> way to get rid of stress.

결론
마무리문장/10%

- Well, <u>okay</u> Eva, this is <u>pretty</u> much about *my <u>favorite</u> music and singer.*

- -

- 오 예, **난 음악 듣는 것을 좋아해!** 있잖아, 난 매일매일 음악을 들어.

- 음악에 대해서 말한다면, 난 힙합 듣는 것을 좋아해. 왜냐하면 힙합은 스트레스 해소에 도움을 많이 줘.
  - 내가 음악을 들을 때, 난 공원이나 조용한 곳에 보통 가
  - 공원에 대해 말한다면, 공원은 아름다운 꽃을 보면서 혼자 음악을 듣기에 좋은 장소야.

- 좋아하는 가수를 얘기한다면, 에미넴이야 왜냐하면 나는 힙합을 좋아하거든.
  - 얼마나 많은 사람들이 오는 것은 상관없이 난 항상 그의 콘서트에 참석했어.
  - 왜냐하면 내가 그의 음악을 들을 때 기분이 좋아지기 때문이야.

- 추가로, K-pop은 계속 인기 있어지고 있기 때문에 K-pop을 좋아해.
  - 있잖아, 나는 음악을 듣는 것이 스트레스를 없앨 수 있는 가장 좋은 방법이라고 생각해.

- 음, 오케이 에바, 이게 **내가 좋아하는 음악과 가수야.**

어휘 및 표현
I think I listen to music every single day 난 매일 음악을 듣는 것 같아   **somewhere quiet** 조용한 곳
No matter how many people are going 아무리 많은 사람들이 간다고 해도
listening to music is the best way to get rid of stress 음악을 듣는 것이 스트레스를 해소할 수 있는 가장 큰 방법이야

3번 음악 취향 변화

Q81 ———————————————————————— 🎧 MP3 IM3-AL_Q_81

How did you **first get interested in music?** Please **compare the music** that you used to listen when you were **young** and the music you listen **today.** Also, how has your interest in music changed over the years?

당신은 어떻게 처음 음악에 대해서 관심 갖게 되었나요? 어렸을 때 듣던 음악과 현재 듣는 음악에 대해 비교해 주세요. 또한, 관심이 몇 년 동안 어떻게 변해왔나요?

———————————————————————— 🎧 MP3 IM3-AL_A_81

서론
시작문장/10%

- Oh <u>yeah</u>, *compare the music I <u>used</u> to listen to when I was young and now?* You know, I'll choose <u>ballad</u> and <u>hip</u>-hop.

본론
단락별 핵심문장/80%

- When <u>I</u> was little, I used to listen to <u>ballad</u> music.
  - Whenever I listened to <u>ballad</u>, it made me feel <u>so</u> great and it meant a <u>lot</u> to me.
  - In fact, I've <u>always</u> lived in <u>very</u> quiet areas, so I <u>really</u> liked listening to quiet music.

- However, my <u>music</u> taste has changed a <u>lot</u> over the years.
  - Now, I <u>enjoy</u> listening to <u>hip</u>-hop.
  - You know, going to a <u>hip</u>-hop concert is <u>so</u> much fun. We can <u>dance</u>, jump and sing together.

- When it <u>comes</u> to some similarities, both music can help me <u>release</u> stress.
  - For the <u>differences</u>, I guess where we listen to those types of <u>music</u> is different.
  - You know, we can listen to ballad in some <u>quiet</u> areas and hip-hop at some <u>clubs</u> or bars.

결론
마무리문장/10%

- <u>Alright</u> Eva, this is <u>all</u> I can say about *the music I <u>used</u> to listen and now.* Thank you.

- -

- 오 예, **어렸을 때 듣던 음악과 지금 듣는 음악의 비교?** 있잖아, 난 발라드와 힙합을 고를 거야.

- 난 어렸을 때, 난 발라드를 듣곤 했어.
  - 발라드를 들을 때마다, 난 기분이 너무 좋았고 그건 나에게 많은 의미가 있었어.
  - 사실, 나는 매우 조용한 장소에서 살아왔고 그래서 난 조용한 음악 듣는 것을 좋아했어.

- 하지만 내 음악 취향은 몇 년에 걸쳐 변해왔어.
  - 지금, 난 힙합을 듣는 것을 좋아해.
  - 있잖아, 힙합 콘서트에 가는 것은 정말 재미있어. 우리는 춤추고 뛰고 같이 노래 부를 수 있어.

- 몇몇 유사점에 대해서 말한다면, 두 음악은 스트레스를 해소하는 데 도움이 돼.
  - 차이점에 대해서는 그러한 타입의 음악을 듣는 장소가 달라.
  - 있잖아, 발라드는 조용한 장소에서 듣고 힙합은 클럽이나 바에서 들어.

- 그래 에바, 이 정도면 **내가 들었던 음악과 지금 듣는 음악**에 대한 거야. 고마워.

어휘 및 표현

my music taste has changed a lot over the years 내 음악 취향은 몇 년에 걸쳐 변해왔어   **For the differences** 차이점으로는
I guess where we listen to those types of music is different 음악 종류에 따라 듣는 장소가 달라

4번 라이브 음악을 들었던 경험

Q82
🎧 MP3 IM3-AL_Q_82

Please tell me about a time when you went to listen to some live music. Was it at a concert or a live café? **Who** did you go there with? **How did you like the music** you listened to there? Please tell me about that day from the beginning to the end.

라이브 음악을 들었던 때에 대해 말해주세요. 콘서트 혹은 라이브 카페였나요? 누구와 함께 갔나요? 당신이 거기서 들었던 음악은 어땠나요? 처음부터 끝까지 그 날에 대해 말해 주세요.

🎧 MP3 IM3-AL_A_82

서론
시작문장/10%

- <u>Alright!</u> Let me tell you *the time I went to a hip-hop concert.*

본론
했던 일/40%

- **When it <u>comes</u> to a concert,** I went to <u>Eminem</u> concert 3 weeks ago.
  - You know, I took my friend <u>Kevin</u> since he knows a <u>lot</u> about music.
  - <u>Plus</u>, we could get a discount since we got <u>membership</u> cards.
  - As I expected, it was filled with <u>lots</u> of people.
  - So, we needed to stand in a <u>long</u> line.

본론
반전/20%

- **When we got in,** as I <u>expected</u>, there were <u>full</u> of people dancing.
  - After like <u>20</u> minutes? We <u>totally</u> lost track of time, we <u>danced</u>, jumped, I mean, we just went <u>crazy</u>.
  - You know, the music was <u>fantastic</u>, and we had <u>so</u> much fun.

본론
결과/20%

- And <u>after</u> the festival, we went to a bar and <u>grabbed</u> a beer.
  - You know, we drank like there's <u>no</u> tomorrow. The <u>only</u> thing I remember is that I kept <u>dancing</u> and laughing.
  - I mean, it was a <u>great</u> way to wrap up <u>all</u> of the fun.

결론
마무리문장/10%

- <u>Alright</u> Eva, I guess this is <u>pretty</u> much about *the time I went to a hip-hop concert.*

- -

- 그래! **힙합 콘서트에 갔던 때**에 대해서 말해줄게.

- 콘서트에 대해서 말한다면, 3주 전에 에미넴 콘서트에 갔어.
  - 있잖아, 내 친구 케빈을 데리고 갔어 왜냐하면 그는 음악에 대해 많이 알거든.
  - 추가로 우리는 멤버십 카드가 있기 때문에 할인을 받을 수 있었어.
  - 내가 예상했듯이, 많은 사람들로 가득 차 있었어.
  - 그래서, 우리는 엄청 긴 줄을 서서 기다렸어.

- 우리가 들어갔을 때, 내가 예상했듯이 많은 사람들이 춤추고 있었어.
  - 20분 후쯤? 우리는 시간 가는 줄 모르고 춤추고 뛰었어. 내 말은 정신이 나갔었지.
  - 있잖아, 음악이 환상적이었고 우리는 정말 재미있었어.

- 그리고 축제 후에, 우리는 바에 가서 맥주를 마셨어.
  - 있잖아, 우리는 내일이 없는 것처럼 술을 마셨어. 내가 기억하는 유일한 것은 내가 계속 춤추고 웃었단 거야.
  - 내 말은, 그건 하루를 마무리하기 정말 좋은 방법이었어.

- 그래 에바, 이게 **힙합 콘서트에 갔던 때**야.

어휘 및 표현
As I expected 내가 예상했듯 **the music was fantastic** 음악은 환상적이었어

5번 우리나라 모임 묘사

Q83 ──────────────────────────── 🎧 MP3 IM3-AL_Q_83

I would like to ask you about **gatherings in your country. What** do people in your country do when they get together? **Where** do they go? How do they normally **celebrate** their gatherings? Please tell me in detail.

당신 나라에 있는 모임에 대해서 물어보고 싶습니다. 사람들은 모였을 때 무엇을 하나요? 어디에 가나요? 그들은 보통 모임에서 어떻게 축하하나요? 자세하게 말해 주세요.

🎧 MP3 IM3-AL_A_83

서론
시작문장/10%

본론
단락별 핵심문장/80%

- Well, *gatherings in my country?* You know, they <u>usually</u> meet their friends and do <u>lots</u> of things.

- Well, I'm <u>pretty</u> sure that people commonly have <u>social</u> gatherings in their <u>free</u> time.
  - Whenever I visit the park, I see <u>lots</u> of people playing <u>sports</u>, listening to <u>music</u> and stuff like that.
  - In <u>fact</u>, I also go to the park with my friends since it's a <u>perfect</u> spot for just sitting and relaxing.

- Moreover, <u>most</u> Koreans love <u>shopping</u>.
  - <u>All</u> you need to know is that the <u>shopping</u> malls are <u>always</u> packed with <u>lots</u> of people on every weekend.

- <u>Lastly,</u> in order to <u>release</u> stress, people <u>usually</u> grab a beer together.
  - Therefore, you will <u>probably</u> see lots of people drinking in public during Korean <u>summers</u>.

결론
마무리문장/10%

- <u>Alright Eva,</u> this is <u>all</u> I can say about *how people spend their <u>free</u> time in Korea.* <u>Thank</u> you.

- -

- 음, **우리나라의 모임?** 있잖아, 그들은 보통 친구들을 만나서 많은 것들을 해.

- 음, 사람들은 보통 여가 시간에 모임을 가져.
  - 내가 공원에 갈 때마다, 난 운동을 하거나, 음악을 들으며 여가를 보내는 사람들을 봐.
  - 사실, 공원은 편하게 앉아서 쉬는 곳이기 때문에 내 친구들과 공원에 가.

- 게다가, 대부분의 한국인들은 쇼핑하는 것을 좋아해.
  - 중요한 점은 쇼핑몰이 매주 주말에 항상 많은 사람들로 가득 차 있다는 거야.

- 마지막으로, 스트레스를 풀기 위해서, 사람들은 함께 맥주를 마셔.
  - 그러므로, 너는 많은 사람들이 여름에 야외에서 술 마시는 것을 볼 수 있을 거야.

- 그래 에바, 이게 **사람들이 여가시간에 한국에서 어떻게 시간을 보내는지**에 대한 거야. 고마워.

어휘 및 표현

people commonly have social gatherings in their free time 사람들은 여가 시간에 모임을 가져　**most Koreans love shopping** 대부분의 한국사람들은 쇼핑을 좋아해　**on every weekend** 매주 주말　**people usually grab a beer together** 사람들은 주로 함께 술을 마셔　**you will probably see lots of people drinking in public during Korean summers** 한국 여름에 야외에서 술 마시는 사람들을 볼 거야

6번   지난 모임을 사람들과 즐긴 경험

Q84 ────────────────────────────────── 🎧 MP3 IM3-AL_Q_84

Think about your last gathering. **Who** were you with? **Where** did you go? Please tell me about how you spent your day on your last gathering in as much detail as possible.

지난 모임에 대해 생각해 보세요. 누구와 함께 있었나요? 어디에 갔나요? 지난 모임이 있었던 그 날을 어떻게 보냈는지에 대해 세부적으로 말해 주세요.

────────────────────────────────── 🎧 MP3 IM3-AL_A_84

서론
시작문장/10%

본론
했던 일/40%

본론
반전/20%

본론
결과/20%

결론
마무리문장/10%

- <u>Great</u>, you mean *my <u>last</u> gathering?* Yeah, it was <u>2</u> months ago at <u>ABC</u> lounge bar.

- As I <u>recall</u>, it was my friend's <u>birthday</u> party.
  - In order to celebrate his <u>birthday</u>, bunch of our friends went to the bar.
  - You know, it was the <u>most</u> famous bar which was located in the <u>middle</u> of the town.
  - <u>Plus</u>, there were <u>many</u> other things we could do at the bar such as playing <u>darts</u> or beer pong.
  - Well, we had <u>so</u> much fun.

- While we were <u>enjoying</u> our time, the birthday boy spilled <u>beer</u> on my cell phone.
  - <u>Oh</u> my god, it was <u>annoying</u> at first, but I pretended like it was ok.

- So <u>quickly</u>, my friend called an engineer and he came in like <u>10</u>min.
  - I guess, he <u>worked</u> on it for about an <u>hour</u>. And you know, I ended up spending <u>$300</u> USD.
  - You know, I was <u>very</u> upset but, it was ok.
  - Because it was his <u>birthday</u>.

- <u>Okay</u> Eva, this is *what <u>happened</u> on my last gathering.*

- -

- 좋아, **내 마지막 모임** 말이지? 응, 2주 전에 ABC 라운지 바를 갔었어.

- 회상해 보면, 내 친구의 생일 파티였어.
  - 그의 생일을 축하하기 위해, 많은 친구들이 바에 갔어.
  - 있잖아, 그건 시내 중심에 있었던 가장 유명한 바였어.
  - 추가로, 비어퐁 게임, 음악 듣기와 같이 우리가 할 수 있는 많은 것들이 있었어.
  - 우리는 즐거운 시간을 보냈어.

- 즐겁게 시간을 보내고 있었는데, 생일 주인공이 내 핸드폰에 맥주를 쏟았어.
  - 이럴 수가, 난 처음에는 짜증 났지만 괜찮은 척했어.

- 그래서 빠르게, 내 친구는 엔지니어를 불렀고 그는 10분 만에 왔어.
  - 내 생각에 엔지니어는 그것을 고치는 데 한 시간이 걸렸어.
  - 그리고 있잖아, 난 300달러를 결국 쓰고 말았어.
  - 난 정말 화가 났지만 괜찮았어.
  - 왜냐하면 그의 생일이었거든.

- 오케이 에바, 이게 **내 마지막 모임에서 있었던 일**에 대한 거야.

──────────────────────────────────

어휘 및 표현
bunch of our friends went to the bar 많은 친구들이 바에 갔어   we could do at the bar such as playing darts or beer pong 다트, 비어퐁 게임을 했어   the birthday boy spilled beer on my cell phone 생일인 친구가 내 핸드폰에 맥주를 쏟았어

Q85 ———————————————————

🎧 **MP3 IM3-AL_Q_85**

Tell me about a memorable moment you had at a gathering. **When** was it? **What kinds of gathering** was it? **What** exactly **happened** on that day? **Why** was it **memorable?** Please tell me everything from the beginning to the end.

당신이 모임에서 있었던 기억에 남을 만한 때에 대해서 말해 주세요. 언제 였나요? 어떤 종류의 모임이었나요? 정확히 그 날에 무슨 일이 있었나요? 왜 기억에 남았나요? 처음부터 끝까지 모든 일에 대해서 말해 주세요.

🎧 **MP3 IM3-AL_A_85**

서론
시작문장/10%

- <u>Alright</u>! Let me tell you *about a <u>recent</u> gathering I had with my friends.*

본론
했던 일/40%

- **When I was little,** I <u>used</u> to watch movies with <u>bunch</u> of my friends.
  - <u>Also</u>, there was a <u>huge</u> movie theater and it was in the <u>tallest</u> building in the city.
  - As I <u>recall</u>, I went there with my friends to watch an <u>action</u> movie.
  - Well, one of my friends already bought tickets <u>online</u>.

본론
반전/20%

- **When we <u>arrived</u> at the movie theater,** we <u>realized</u> that my friend bought the <u>wrong</u> tickets.
  - Oh my god, it was annoying at <u>first</u>, but we pretended like it was ok.

본론
결과/20%

- **So,** I went to the <u>ticket</u> booth and explained the <u>whole</u> situation.
  - <u>Thankfully</u>, they offered an <u>exchange</u> for the <u>next</u> movie.
  - <u>Moreover</u>, there was <u>no</u> additional payment.
  - <u>Actually</u>, it was the <u>best</u> customer service I've <u>ever</u> had.
  - To sum up, the movie was <u>great</u>, and we had <u>so</u> much fun.

결론
마무리문장/10%

- **Alright Eva,** I guess this is <u>pretty</u> much about *a <u>recent</u> gathering I had with my friends.*

- -

- 그래! **내 친구와 있었던 최근 모임**에 대해 말해줄게.

- 내가 어렸을 때, 난 많은 친구들과 함께 영화를 보곤 했어.
  - 또한, 큰 영화관이 있었고, 도시에서 가장 큰 건물에 있었어.
  - 회상해 보면, 난 액션 영화를 보기 위해 친구와 영화관에 갔어.
  - 음, 내 친구 중에 한 명은 이미 온라인으로 표를 샀어.

- 우리가 영화관에 도착했을 때, 우리는 내 친구가 잘못된 티켓을 샀다는 것을 깨달았어.
  - 이럴 수가, 그건 처음에는 짜증 났지만, 우리는 괜찮은 척했어.

- 그래서, 난 티켓부스에 갔고, 전체 상황을 설명했어.
  - 고맙게도, 그들은 다음 영화로 교환을 해주었어.
  - 게다가 추가로 돈을 지불하지도 않았어.
  - 실제로, 그건 내가 겪었던 최고의 고객 서비스였어.
  - 요약해 보면, 영화는 좋았고, 우리는 재미있었어.

- 그래 에바, 이게 **내 친구와 있었던 최근 모임**이야.

어휘 및 표현
one of my friends already bought tickets online 친구 중 한 명이 온라인으로 티켓을 샀어

8번 술집/바 묘사

Q86

You indicated in the survey that you go to **bars.** Describe one of your favorite bars that you usually visit. **What** does it look like? **Why** do you like to visit that bar? Please tell me everything about that place in detail.

당신은 바에 가는 것을 좋아한다고 했습니다. 당신이 주로 방문하는 좋아하는 바 중에 하나에 대해서 말해 주세요. 그 장소는 어떻게 생겼나요? 왜 그 바에 방문하는 것을 좋아하나요? 그 장소에 대하여 세부적으로 말해 주세요.

서론
시작문장/10%

본론
단락별 핵심문장/80%

결론
마무리문장/10%

- <u>That's</u> a good question, *one of my favorite <u>bars</u>,* right? I go to ABC bar literally <u>everyday</u>.

- In <u>fact</u>, it's the <u>most</u> famous bar which is located in the <u>middle</u> of the town.
  - When I enter the bar, the <u>first</u> thing I can see is a <u>flat</u> screen TV and a <u>long</u> cozy couch.
  - Whenever I hit that bar, I can see <u>bunch</u> of people talking and <u>drinking</u>.

- **Actually,** I've <u>always</u> visited <u>very</u> quiet bars, so I'm trying to visit places that are <u>new</u> to me.
  - Because there are <u>many</u> other things you can do at the bar such as playing darts or <u>beer</u> pong.
  - But you know, the bar is <u>always</u> filled with lots of people, so I <u>prefer</u> going there late at <u>night</u>.

- **Whenever I visit the bar,** I have good times with my <u>buddies</u>.
  - And you know, it makes me feel <u>so</u> great and it means a <u>lot</u> to me.
  - Well, I guess it's one of the <u>best</u> ways to <u>release</u> stress.

- So <u>overall</u>, this is about *one of my <u>favorite</u> bars that I <u>usually</u> visit.*

- -

- 좋은 질문이야, **좋아하는 바 중에 하나,** 맞지? 난 거의 매일 ABC 바에 가.

- 사실은, 거긴 시내 중심에 위치해 있는 가장 유명한 바 중에 하나야.
  - 내가 바에 들어갈 때마다, 내가 처음 볼 수 있는 것은 평면 TV와 안락한 소파야.
  - 내가 바에 갈 때마다, 많은 사람들이 이야기하고 술 마시는 것을 볼 수 있어.

- 사실은, 난 항상 매우 조용한 바를 다녔어, 그래서 난 새로운 장소들을 방문하려고 노력하고 있어.
  - 왜냐하면 다트, 비어퐁 게임과 같이 바에서 할 수 있는 많은 것들이 있거든.
  - 그러나 있잖아, 바는 항상 많은 사람들로 가득 차 있고, 그래서 나는 거기를 늦은 밤에 가는 것을 좋아해.

- 내가 바에 방문할 때마다, 난 내 친구들과 좋은 시간을 보내.
  - 그리고 있잖아, 정말 기분이 좋고 많은 의미를 줘.
  - 음, 내 생각엔 그건 스트레스를 풀 수 있는 가장 좋은 방법 중에 하나야.

- 그래서 전반적으로, 이게 **내가 방문하는 좋아하는 바 중에 하나**야.

어휘 및 표현
I go to ABC bar literally everyday 난 거의 매일 ABC 바에 가   **I've always visited very quiet bars** 항상 조용한 바만 다녔어
It's one of the best ways to release stress 스트레스 해소하기 좋은 방법 중에 하나야

9번 처음 갔던 술집/바의 경험

Q87

Do you remember the first bar you went to? **When** was it and **who** did you go there with? What was **so special** about that bar? Was there **something interesting happened** that made that experience more special?

당신이 처음 갔던 바에 대해서 기억하나요? 언제였나요 그리고 누구와 거기에 갔나요? 그 바에 대해서 특별한 점이 무엇이었나요? 그 경험을 특별하게 만드는 재미있는 사건이 있었나요?

서론
시작문장/10%

- Okay Eva, *experience at the first bar I went to?* Perfect, it was ABC jazz bar in town.

본론
했던 일/40%

- Well, I'm pretty sure that the bar was around 20-minutes away from my place.
  - You know, the bar was extremely clean, and the people were so friendly and that's why I used to visit there.
  - I think I went there with my friend John like 2 weeks ago.
  - Actually, he was a great person to go with because he enjoyed drinking all kinds of whiskey.
  - And yeah, as you can imagine, we drank a lot.

본론
반전/20%

- After only being there for 30 minutes, we got so drunk.
  - I mean, we drank like there's no tomorrow. The only thing I remember is that we kept dancing and laughing.

본론
결과/20%

- Well, the next day? I ended up staying in my bed all day.
  - I'm not going to lie to you. I mean, I couldn't remember half of the night.
  - I was so ashamed of myself.
  - But you know? It was kinda fun and I feel like drinking again.

결론
마무리문장/10%

- Um yeah, I think this is all I remember *about an experience at the first bar I went to,* Eva.

- -

- 오케이 에바, 내가 처음 바에 갔을 적의 경험? 물론이지, 그건 시내에 있는 ABC 재즈 바였어.

- 음, 바는 아마 우리 집에서 대략 20분 정도 거리였어.
  - 있잖아, 바는 정말 깨끗했고, 사람들은 정말 친절했어 그게 내가 거기에 방문했던 이유야.
  - 나는 한 2주 전에 내 친구 John과 함께 그곳에 갔어.
  - 사실은, 그는 같이 가기에 좋은 사람이었어 왜냐하면 그는 모든 종류의 위스키를 마시는 것을 좋아했거든.
  - 그리고, 너도 상상할 수 있듯이, 우리는 많이 마셨어.

- 거기에서 30분 후에, 우리는 완전히 취했어.
  - 내 말은, 우리는 내일이 없는 것처럼 마셨어. 내가 기억하는 유일한 것은 계속 춤추고 웃었던 거였어.

- 음, 다음 날? 난 침대에 하루 종일 있어야 했어.
  - 진짜 거짓말 하나 안 하고, 난 그날 밤의 반은 기억이 안 나.
  - 난 너무 창피했어.
  - 근데 그거 알아? 정말 재미있었고 난 또다시 술을 마시고 싶어.

- 음 예, 이게 내가 처음 바에 갔을 적의 경험이야, 에바.

어휘 및 표현
he enjoyed drinking all kinds of whiskey 그는 모든 종류의 위스키를 마셨어   **I couldn't remember half of the night** 그날 밤의 반은 기억이 안 나
I was so ashamed of myself 너무 창피했어

10번 술집/바에서 기억에 남는 경험

Q88
🎧 MP3 IM3-AL_Q_88

Tell me about a memorable incident that happened at a bar. **When** was it? **Who** were you with? **What** exactly happened there? Was there **something interesting** going on? Why was it **so special**? Tell me everything about that day at the bar from the beginning to the end.

바에서 있었던 기억에 남는 사건에 대해 말해 주세요. 그것은 언제였나요? 누구와 함께 있었죠? 거기에서 정확히 무엇을 했나요? 재미있는 일들이 진행되고 있었나요? 왜 그건 특별했나요? 시작부터 끝까지 바에서 있었던 모든 일에 대해 말해 주세요.

🎧 MP3 IM3-AL_A_88

서론
시작문장/10%

• <u>Great,</u> you mean *a <u>memorable</u> incident that happened at a <u>bar</u>?*

본론
했던 일/40%

• As I <u>mentioned</u> before, I <u>really</u> enjoy drinking <u>all</u> kinds of whiskey.
  - In my town, there was a <u>famous</u> bar and it was called the ABC lounge bar.
  - <u>Seriously,</u> I preferred to go there late at night since I could <u>enjoy</u> the peace and quiet.
  - And I went there last week <u>alone</u>, and I started to drink.
  - <u>Plus,</u> the main <u>reason</u> why I liked to drink at that bar was that the music was <u>so</u> good.
  - You know, the music was <u>great</u>, and I had <u>so</u> much fun.

본론
반전/20%

• **After only being there for <u>30</u> minutes,** I got <u>so</u> drunk.
  - I mean, I drank like there's <u>no</u> tomorrow.
  - After drinking, I tried to pay, but I <u>realized</u> that I was in trouble.
  - As you can <u>expect</u>, I lost my <u>wallet</u>. Oh my god, I <u>felt</u> like a homeless person.

본론
결과/20%

• **Ugh, I felt <u>sick</u>,** I mean, I had to <u>cancel</u> all my credit cards.
  - You know what? <u>Losing</u> a wallet is like starting a <u>new</u> life.
  - Well, the next day? I <u>ended</u> up staying in my bed all day.
  - But you know? It was <u>kinda</u> fun and I <u>feel</u> like drinking again.

결론
마무리문장/10%

• Okay Eva, this is *about a <u>memorable</u> incident that <u>happened</u> at a bar.*

• 좋아, 바에서 일어났던 기억에 남을만한 사건?

• 내가 전에 언급했듯이, 나는 정말로 모든 종류의 위스키를 마시는 것을 좋아해.
  - 우리 동네에는, 유명한 바가 있었고 그것은 ABC 라운지 바라고 불렸어.
  - 솔직히, 나는 밤늦게 거기에 가는 것을 좋아했어 왜냐하면 난 평화로움과 조용함을 즐길 수 있었거든.
  - 그리고 나는 혼자 저번 주에 갔고 술을 마시기 시작했어.
  - 추가로, 내가 바에서 술 마시는 것을 좋아했던 가장 중요한 이유는 음악이 정말 좋았다는 거야.
  - 있잖아, 음악은 최고였고 난 정말 즐거웠어.

• 30분 후쯤, 난 정말 술에 취했어.
  - 내 말은, 내일이 없는 것처럼 술을 마셨어.
  - 술을 마신 후에, 난 계산하려고 했는데 내가 곤경에 처했다는 것을 깨달았어.
  - 네가 예상했듯이, 난 지갑을 잃어버렸어. 이럴 수가, 난 노숙자가 된 기분이었어.

• 내 말은, 난 너무 짜증이 났고 내 모든 신용카드들을 취소해야만 했어.
  - 그거 알아? 지갑을 잃어버리는 것은 새로운 인생을 사는 것과 같아.
  - 음, 다음 날? 나는 결국 내 침대에서 하루 종일 있게 되었어.
  - 그거 알아? 재미있었고 나는 다시 술을 먹고 싶어.

• 오케이 에바, 이게 **내가 바에서 일어났던 기억에 남을만한 사건**이야.

어휘 및 표현
I went there last week alone, and I started to drink 난 혼자 가서 술을 마시기 시작했어   **the music was so good** 음악은 정말 좋았어

Q89

🎧 MP3 IM3-AL_Q_89

Let's say that something wrong can happen to our health. What are **some health problems** that we can have? Please describe **what can be happening** when someone loses his/her health. **How can we fix** those health problems? Please **provide some solutions** to stay healthy.

우리 건강은 항상 문제가 생길 수 있습니다. 우리가 가질 수 있는 건강상의 문제는 어떤 것들이 있나요? 우리의 건강이 나빠지면 어떠한 일이 발생하는지 묘사해주세요. 우리는 그 문제를 어떻게 고칠 수 있나요? 건강을 유지하기 위한 해결책을 제시해주세요.

🎧 MP3 IM3-AL_A_89

서론
시작문장/10%

- <u>Great,</u> you mean *some <u>health</u> problems that we can have?*

본론
단락별 핵심문장/80%

- **When it comes to some <u>health</u> problems,** studies have found <u>many</u> health problems <u>related</u> to stress.
  - The <u>main</u> reason why people are stressed out is that they work <u>too</u> much.
  - When they are stressed out, they may get <u>headaches</u>, <u>insomnia</u>, frequent colds and low <u>energy</u>.

- **In <u>order</u> to get rid of stress,** people need to enjoy their <u>free</u> time.
  - <u>Some</u> people spend their time in <u>very</u> quiet areas since they can <u>enjoy</u> the peace and quiet.
  - <u>Or</u>, people can enjoy watching <u>all</u> kinds of movies because it helps them <u>release</u> stress.
  - <u>As</u> for me, whenever I'm under stress, I go out and <u>run</u>.

결론
마무리문장/10%

- <u>Okay</u> Eva, this is about *<u>how</u> we can fix those health problems.*

- 좋아, 우리가 가질 수 있는 건강상 문제가 뭐냐고?

- 건강상 문제에 대해서 말한다면, 많은 건강상 문제는 스트레스와 관련이 있다는 연구 결과가 나왔어.
  - 사람들이 스트레스를 받는 가장 큰 이유는 일을 너무 많이 한다는 거거든.
  - 사람들은 스트레스를 받으면, 두통, 불면증, 잦은 감기와 기력이 없어지곤 해.

- 스트레스를 풀기 위해선, 사람들은 그들의 자유시간을 즐길 필요가 있어.
  - 몇몇 사람들은 평화와 한적함을 즐기기 위해 조용한 장소에 가.
  - 아니면, 사람들은 스트레스 해소에 도움이 되는 영화를 즐겨 보곤 해.
  - 나로 말한다면, 난 스트레스를 받으면, 밖에 나가서 뛰어.

- 오케이 에바, 이게 건강상 문제를 해결하는 것들이야.

어휘 및 표현
studies have found many health problems related to stress 많은 건강상 문제는 스트레스와 관련이 있다는 연구 결과가 나왔어
The main reason why people are stressed out is that they work too much 스트레스를 받는 가장 큰 이유는 과다 업무야
they may get headaches, insomnia, frequent colds and low energy 그들은 두통, 불면증, 잦은 감기 그리고 기력이 없어지곤 해

14번 최근 잘 팔리는 인기상품/서비스

Q90 ———————————————————————————— 🎧 MP3 IM3-AL_Q_90

What are some hot products or services that people talk about these days? Why are they mentioned by people so often these days? Give me all the details.

사람들이 요즘 이야기하고 있는 인기 있는 제품 또는 서비스는 무엇인가요? 요즘 그것들은 왜 사람들에 의해 요즘 종종 언급되죠? 상세하게 말해 주세요.

——————————————————————————————————— 🎧 MP3 IM3-AL_A_90

서론
시작문장/10%

본론
단락별 핵심문장/80%

- <u>That's</u> a good question, *some <u>hot</u> products or services?* Sure, I got it.

- When it comes to the <u>hottest</u> product, it must be the <u>new</u> cell phone from <u>ABC</u> electronics.
  - I mean, in the <u>past</u>, the cell phones were <u>only</u> used to make calls.
  - <u>However,</u> this cell phone from <u>ABC</u> electronics has <u>various</u> functions such as <u>voice</u> recognition and <u>powerful</u> speakers.

- <u>Speaking</u> of the powerful speakers, it is just <u>amazing</u> Eva.
  - You know, <u>most</u> Koreans enjoy listening <u>all</u> kinds of music, right?
  - When you listen to music using <u>this</u> cell phone, you will <u>feel</u> like you are in the <u>middle</u> of the concert hall.

- In <u>addition,</u> it is <u>only</u> sold at OPIc department store which is located <u>right</u> next to Seoul station.
  - If <u>you</u> like music, <u>this</u> cell phone is the one you should buy.

결론
마무리문장/10%

- So <u>overall,</u> this is about *some <u>hot</u> products or <u>services</u> that people talk about.*

- -

- 좋은 질문이야, 인기 있는 **제품 또는 서비스?** 물론이지, 알겠어.

- 가장 인기 있는 제품에 대해서 말한다면, ABC 전자상점의 최신 휴대폰이야.
  - 내 말은, 과거에는 핸드폰은 전화를 하기 위해서만 사용됐잖아.
  - 하지만 ABC 전자의 이 휴대폰은 음성인식 기능과 강력한 스피커와 같은 다양한 기능이 있어.

- 강력한 스피커에 대해 말해본다면, 그건 진짜 놀라워 에바.
  - 있잖아, 대부분은 한국인들은 모든 종류의 음악을 듣는 것을 즐겨 맞지?
  - 이 휴대폰을 사용해서 음악을 들으면, 아마 콘서트홀 중간에 있는 것과 같이 느껴질 거야.

- 게다가, 그건 서울역 바로 옆에 있는 오픽 백화점에서만 팔아.
  - 네가 음악을 좋아한다면, 이건 네가 꼭 사야 하는 핸드폰이야.

- 그래서 전반적으로, 이게 **사람들이 이야기하는 인기 있는 제품 또는 서비스에 관한 거야.**

어휘 및 표현
voice recognition and powerful speakers 음성인식과 강력한 스피커
you will feel like you are in the middle of the concert hall 콘서트홀 중앙에 있는 것같이 느낄거야
it is only sold at OPIc department store 오픽 백화점에서만 팔아   **this cell phone is the one you should buy** 네가 꼭 사야하는 핸드폰이야

15번 쇼핑 습관 변화

Q91

🎧 MP3 IM3-AL_Q_91

What are **some major changes in people's shopping habits?** Where do people normally shop and what do they normally buy?

당신의 쇼핑 습관에서 주요한 변화는 무엇입니까? 주로 어디로 쇼핑을 하러 가나요? 사람들이 주로 무엇을 사죠?

🎧 MP3 IM3-AL_A_91

서론
시작문장/10%

본론
단락별 핵심문장/80%

결론
마무리문장/10%

• Well, *some major changes in people's shopping habits?* You know, people usually buy things online.

• In the past, people used to go to the shopping malls.
  - In fact, there are lots of famous shopping centers in Korea.
  - So, most Koreans used to go there to buy things.

• However, the shopping malls are always packed on the weekends.
  - So people started to shop online using their phones.
  - The main reason why people shop online is to save time.

• So overall, this is about *some major changes in people's shopping habits.*

- -

• 음, 사람들의 쇼핑 습관에서 가장 큰 변화? 있잖아, 사람들은 온라인에서 보통 구매를 해.

• 과거에는, 사람들은 쇼핑몰에 가곤 했어.
  - 사실, 한국에는 많은 유명한 쇼핑센터가 있어.
  - 그래서, 대부분의 한국인들은 물건을 사기 가기 위해 거기에 가곤 했어.

• 하지만, 쇼핑몰은 항상 주말에 사람들로 가득 차 있어.
  - 그래서 사람들은 그들의 핸드폰을 사용하여 온라인으로 쇼핑을 하기 시작했어.
  - 사람들이 온라인 쇼핑을 하는 가장 큰 이유는 그들의 시간을 절약할 수 있기 때문이야.

• 그래서 전반적으로, 이게 사람들의 쇼핑 습관에서 가장 큰 변화야.

어휘 및 표현

people used to go to the shopping malls 사람들은 쇼핑몰에 가곤 했어
people started to shop online using their phones 사람들은 핸드폰을 사용하여 온라인 쇼핑을 시작했어
The main reason why people shop online is to save time 온라인 쇼핑의 가장 큰 이유는 시간을 절약할 수 있기 때문이야

22강 유형 04 (롤플레이)

이론

롤플레이의 이해

OPIc 질문들 중 실제 전화통화를 하는 '연기' 를 해야 하는 롤플레이 질문입니다.
롤플레이는 정보요청, 문제해결, 단순질문 롤플레이로 나뉩니다.
단, 난이도 5~6 선택 시, 롤플레이 질문의 개수는 2개가 출제됩니다.

롤플레이가 나오는 질문 번호를 외우세요!

롤플레이가 나오는 질문 번호를 외우세요!
IM3-AL 등급 목표 시, 난이도 5으로 설정하시면, 롤플레이는 총 2문제 출제!

1	2	3	4	5	6	7	8	9	10	11	12	13	14	15
자기소개	묘사	세부묘사	경험	묘사	경험	경험	묘사	경험	경험	정보요청	문제해결	문제해결경험	세부묘사	세부묘사

롤플레이의 종류

Background Survey에서 선택한 모든 주제 & 모든 출제 가능한 돌발 주제의 롤플레이를 모두 암기하는 것은 불가능합니다. 2가지 종류의 롤플레이에 필요한 Format을 제공합니다.

| 정보 요청 롤플레이 | ➡ | 주어진 대상에게 질문하는 롤플레이 |

| 문제 해결 롤플레이 | ➡ | 주어진 대상과 문제 해결을 위해 대안을 제시하는 롤플레이 |

 이미 문제 유형을 알기에, 문제를 듣기 전, 해당 롤플레이의 답변 Format 준비!

롤플레이의 답변 Format

롤플레이는 실제 전화통화 같은 자연스러운 '연기'가 필요한 문제입니다.
진짜녀석들 OPIc은 3가지 롤플레이에 필요한 답변 Format을 제공합니다.
또한, 묘사, 경험 유형을 통해 암기한 문장들의 사용이 필히 있어야 합니다.
(이미 익숙한 문장의 사용이 보다 더 자연스러운 답변을 만들어줍니다.)

서론 Introduction
답변비중 20-30%

인사말/상황설명
• 롤플레이 종류에 따라 다른 서론으로 시작!
• 실제 전화 통화하는 것 같은 자신감 있는 연기로 시작!

본론 Body
답변비중 60-70%

질문/대안
• 롤플레이 종류에 따라 다른 본론!
• 묘사, 경험, 롤플레이의 암기문장 모두 활용!
• 질문의 '키워드' 필수 포함

결론 Conclusion
답변비중 10%

마무리 문장
• 실제 전화 통화를 끊는 것 같은 자연스러운 마무리!

롤플레이의 암기문장

정확한 롤플레이의 답변을 위하여 본론에 필요한 암기문장을 제공합니다.

정보 요청 롤플레이 - 11번

MP3 IM3-AL_110~114

인사말
- 안녕, 난 사고 싶어 MP3 플레이어를. 뭣 좀 물어봐도 돼?
  Hi there, I would like to buy **an MP3 player.** Could I ask you some questions?

질문
- 첫 번째로, 어디에 있어? 내가 듣기론, 가깝다고 하던데 서울역과, 맞아?
  First of all, where is it? I heard that it is close to **Seoul station.** Is it right?

- 그리고, 얼마야? 받을 수 있어 할인을?
  And also, how much is it? Can you give me a discount?

- 마지막으로, 운영 시간은 어떻게 돼? 연중무휴야?
  Lastly, what are your opening hours like? Are you open 24/7?

마무리
- 알겠어 그럼, 많이 고마워. 나중에 보자.
  Alright then, thanks a lot. See you later.

문제 해결 롤플레이 - 12번

MP3 IM3-AL_115~120

상황 설명
- 있잖아, 할 말이 있어. 사실, 나 많이 아파 오늘. 못 만날 것 같아 오늘.
  Hey, I need to tell you something. Actually, I feel **awful** today. I don't think I can meet you today.

- 그래서, 대안을 제시해 줄게 이 문제를 풀 수 있는.
  So, let me give you some options to solve this problem.

대안
- 그럼, 내가 티켓 회사 전화해서 환불을 할 수 있어.
  Maybe, I can call **the ticket company** and get a refund.

- 아니면, 물어보지 그래? 너의 친구들 중 한 명에게.
  Or, why don't you ask **one of your friends**?

- 아니면, 마지막 방법으론 연기하는 거야 다음 주로 하자. 어때?
  Or, the only other way is to postpone it till **the following week.** What do you think?

마무리
- 다시 한번, 많이 미안해. 생각해보고 알려줘.
  Once again, I'm so sorry. Let me know what's best for you.

롤플레이 답변 준비 – 시험화면

난이도 5 설정 시, 롤플레이가 나오는 번호를 실제 시험화면으로 익숙해져야 합니다.

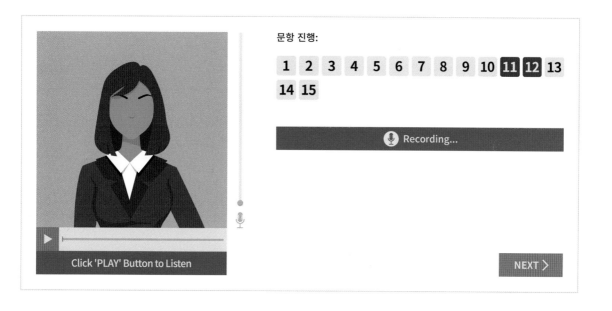

난이도 5 설정 시, 롤플레이 질문은 총 2문제(11, 12번)가 출제됩니다.

1. 이미 유형을 알고 있기에 'Play' 버튼 클릭 전, 사용할 롤플레이의 종류를 결정합니다.

2. 전화 통화 같은 자연스러운 연기 연습을 간단히 합니다.

3. 'Play' 버튼 클릭 후, 첫 번째 문제에서 롤플레이 질문의 키워드를 집중해서 듣습니다.

4. 'Replay' 버튼 클릭 후, 두 번째 문제는 듣지 않고 답변 Format을 다시 준비합니다.

5. 오른쪽 상단의 'Recording' 버튼 생성 시, '롤플레이 답변 Format' 대로 답변합니다.

 문제를 집중하여 듣고, 필히 실제 연기를 하는 것과 같은 자연스러운 답변!

롤플레이 질문 파악 전략 – 예시

질문 듣기 전, 이미 유형을 알기에 자연스러운 연기 연습에 집중해야 합니다.

정보 요청 예시 질문 - 해변가기

- I'd like to give you a situation and ask you to act it out. You want to visit **the beach** with your friend. Call your friend and ask **two to three questions** about the beach trip you are planning.

  ① the beach 키워드 캐치 → ② 답변 Format 준비 → ③ 답변

문제 해결 예시 질문 - 해변가기

- I'm sorry, but there is a problem you need to resolve. You have just heard from the news that **the weather will be bad.** Call your friend, explain the situation and offer **two to three alternatives** to solve this problem.

  ① weather will be bad 키워드 캐치 → ② 답변 Format 준비 → ③ 답변

자연스러운 '연기'를 위한 답변 Format 작성을 훈련합니다.

ⓐ 인사말/상황설명
문제에 따라 다른 상대, 롤플레이 종류에 따라 다른 인사말/상황설명으로 실제 전화통화같은 답변으로 시작합니다.

ⓑ 질문/대안
제공하는 답변 Format을 사용하며, 묘사, 경험에서 훈련한 문장들을 사용하여 질문/대안을 만듭니다.

ⓒ 마무리 문장
실제 전화통화를 하다 끊는 듯한 자연스러운 연기로 마무리를 짓습니다.

- 진짜녀석들 OPIc 묘사, 경험 답변 훈련과 같이 모든 단락에 <u>본인 실력 문장</u>을 필히 포함해 주시기 바랍니다.

롤플레이 답변 전략 – 예시(정보요청 롤플레이)

OPIc은 면접과 흡사한 시험으로 서론, 본론, 결론을 명확하게 지키며 답변합니다.

Q

I'd like to give you a situation and ask you to act it out. You want to visit **the beach** with your friend. Call your friend and ask **two to three questions** about the beach trip you are planning.

상황을 드릴 테니 연기해보세요. 당신은 친구와 해변에 가고 싶습니다. 친구에게 전화하여 계획하고 있는 해변 여행에 대해 2-3가지 질문을 하세요.

예시 답변 – 해변 가기 제안

서론
인사말/20%

• Hi there, I would like to *go to the <u>beach</u> with you this <u>weekend</u>*.

본론
질문/70%

• **First of all,** I prefer going to <u>HAEWOONDAE</u> beach in BUSAN.
  - I mean, speaking of HAEWOONDAE beach, it's a <u>perfect</u> spot for just sitting and <u>relaxing</u>.
  - <u>Plus</u>, the beach is undeniably <u>beautiful</u>, and the <u>water</u> is crystal clear.
  - So, what do you think?

• **Secondly,** what do you want to <u>do</u> there?
  - I mean, there are different areas where people play <u>soccer</u>, cricket and so on.
  - <u>Or</u> we can just <u>enjoy</u> the peace and quiet.
  - But <u>obviously</u>, I guess <u>most</u> people go there to swim.

• **Lastly,** let's stay at ABC <u>hotel</u>!
  - I mean, the rooms are <u>extremely</u> clean, and the people are <u>so</u> friendly.
  - You know, I'm <u>pretty</u> sure that I can get a discount since I got a <u>membership</u> card.
  - So, how about <u>that</u>?

결론
마무리문장/10%

• **Alright then,** <u>thanks</u> a lot. See you later.

정보 요청 롤플레이 답변의 고득점을 향한 스피킹 방법을 훈련합니다.

ⓐ **서론 – 인사말**
대상이 누구인지를 파악하고 필요하다면 대상에 맞는 키워드를 추가해줍니다.
실제 전화 통화같은 자연스러움이 묻어 있게 연기해야 합니다.

ⓑ **본론 – 질문**
진짜녀석들 OPIc 롤플레이 질문으로 답변을 구성합니다. 다만, 제시 대안으로 대체가 되지 않을 시, 배웠던 묘사, 경험에서 암기한 문장들을 사용하여 대안을 구성해줍니다.

ⓒ **결론 – 마무리 문장**
실제 전화 통화를 마무리하는 것과 같은 연기로 자연스럽게 마무리합니다.

• 진짜녀석들 OPIc 묘사, 경험 답변 훈련과 같이 모든 단락에 <u>본인 실력 문장</u>을 필히 포함해 주시기 바랍니다.

롤플레이 답변 전략 – 예시(문제 해결 롤플레이)

OPIc은 면접과 흡사한 시험으로 서론, 본론, 결론을 명확하게 지키며 답변합니다.

Q

I'm sorry, but there is a problem you need to resolve. You have just heard from the news that **the weather will be bad.** Call your friend, explain the situation and offer **two to three alternatives** to solve this problem.

안타깝게도 해결해야 할 문제가 생겼습니다. 당신은 뉴스에서 날씨가 안 좋을 것이란 소식을 접했습니다. 친구에게 전화하여 상황을 설명하고 2-3가지 대안을 제시하여 문제를 해결하세요.

예시 답변 - 해변 못 가는 문제해결

서론
상황설명/30%

- **Hey, I need to tell you something.** <u>Actually</u>, I just <u>heard</u> from the news that the weather will be <u>bad</u>.
  - I <u>don't</u> think we can go to the <u>beach</u>.
  - So, let me give you some <u>options</u> to solve this problem.

본론
대안/60%

- **Maybe,** I can call the <u>ABC</u> hotel and get a <u>refund</u>.
  - For me, it is <u>fully</u> refundable since I got a <u>membership</u> card.

- **Or,** if you <u>really</u> want to go, why don't you ask one of your <u>friends</u>?
  - You know, I <u>heard</u> that your friend is an <u>outgoing</u> person, and likes <u>socializing</u>.

- **Well or,** the <u>only</u> other way is to <u>postpone</u> it till the following week.
  - What do you think?

결론
마무리문장/10%

- **Once again,** I'm <u>so</u> sorry. Let me know what's <u>best</u> for you.

문제 해결 롤플레이 답변의 고득점을 향한 스피킹 방법을 훈련합니다.

ⓐ **서론 – 상황설명**
문제에 따라 상황설명이 주어지거나, 주어지지 않기도 합니다. 문제에서 상황설명이 주어진다면 문제에서 나온 상황설명을 사용하며, 주어지지 않는다면 진짜녀석들 OPIc에서 제공하는 상황설명으로 구성합니다. 상황에 걸맞은 연기가 더해져야 보다 더 자연스러운 시작이 됩니다.

ⓑ **본론 – 대안**
진짜녀석들 OPIc 롤플레이 대안으로 답변을 구성합니다. 다만, 제시 대안으로 대체가 되지 않을 시, 배웠던 묘사, 경험에서 암기한 문장들을 사용하여 대안을 구성해줍니다.

ⓒ **결론 – 마무리 문장**
실제 전화 통화를 마무리하는 것과 같은 연기로 자연스럽게 마무리합니다.

- 진짜녀석들 OPIc 묘사, 경험 답변 훈련과 같이 모든 단락에 <u>**본인 실력 문장**</u>을 필히 포함해 주시기 바랍니다.

23강

유형 04 (롤플레이)

암기문장 활용

조동사 의문문

의문사 + be동사 의문문

How + 수량 형용사

be동사 의문문

I feel awful

Let me give you some options

관용어구 (+ why)

to부정사 (명사적 용법)

롤플레이의 암기문장　조동사 의문문

롤플레이의 문법을 정확히 배우고 응용해 보세요.

Hi there, I would like to buy an MP3 player. Could I ask you some questions?

• [조동사 의문문] Could + 주어 + 동사 ~? : ~해도 되나요?

01. **'Can', 'Could'** 조동사를 넣어 질문을 만들 땐 **'~해도 됩니까?'** 로 해석되어 상대에게 허락, 가능을 물어볼 때 쓰임
02. 'Could'가 조금 더 정중한 표현
03. **'조동사 + 주어 + 동사원형'** 의 형태
04. Should, Will, May, Could 등의 다양한 조동사로 문장의 의미를 다채롭게 만들 수 있음

사용 방법

조동사 + 주어 + 동사원형 ~ ?

활용 및 응용

• Could I ask you some questions?

• May I leave the message, please?

• Can you come to my house tonight?

MEMO

롤플레이의 암기문장 의문사 + be동사 의문문

롤플레이의 문법을 정확히 배우고 응용해 보세요.

First of all, where is it? I heard that it is close to Seoul station. Is it right?

• [의문사+be동사 의문문] Where is it? : 어디에 있나요?

01. 'be' 동사를 넣어 질문을 만들 땐 **'be동사 + 주어'**의 형태
02. 구체적인 질문을 할 때는 **'의문사'**를 질문의 가장 처음에 위치
03. 의문사 종류에 다양한 서술형 질문 사용 가능!
04. am – I / are – you, 복수 주어 / is – 단수 주어
05. 과거의 경우 : am, is – was / are - were

사용 방법

의문사 + be동사 + 주어 ~ ?

활용 및 응용

• First of all, where is it?

• What are your opening hours like?

• When is the party?

MEMO

롤플레이의 암기문장 How + 수량형용사

롤플레이의 문법을 정확히 배우고 응용해 보세요.

And also, how much is it? Can you give me a discount?

• [How + 수량 형용사] How much ~? : 얼마나 ~인가요?

01. 수량 형용사는 명사의 수나 양을 수식하는 형용사 : **many, much**

02. 의문사 'how' 뒤에 수량 형용사가 오면 '**얼마나 ~인가요?**' 라는 의미로, 보통 금액이나 수량을 물을 때 사용

03. 금액을 물을 때는 '**how much**' 로만 의미를 전달 가능

04. 단, 셀 수 없는 명사가 올 때는 '**much**', 셀 수 있는 명사는 '**many**'

05. How + 수량 형용사 다음에는 의문문을 만들어 문장을 완성

사용 방법

How much / many + 명사 + 의문문 ~ ?

* 셀 수 없는 명사엔 much / 셀 수 있는 명사엔 many

활용 및 응용

• How much is it?

• How much (money) do I pay for this new phone?

• How many people are coming to the party tonight?

MEMO

롤플레이의 암기문장   be동사 의문문

롤플레이의 문법을 정확히 배우고 응용해 보세요.

Lastly, what are your opening hours like? Are you open 24/7?

• [be동사 의문문] Are you open ~? : 문 여나요?

01.   'be'동사로 시작하는 의문문으로 보통 'yes' or 'no'로 답변하는 질문
02.   'be동사 + 주어' 형태
03.   'be동사'가 이미 '동사'역할을 하고 있으므로 그 뒤에 일반동사나 다른 동사가 추가로 올 수 없으니 주의!
04.   시제나 주어의 수일치는 모두 be동사가 영향을 받아서 변형

사용 방법

be동사 + 주어 ~ ?

활용 및 응용

• Are you open 24/7?

• Am I the only one with a bottle of wine?

• Is one of your friends a singer?

MEMO

롤플레이의 암기문장　I feel awful

롤플레이의 문법을 정확히 배우고 응용해 보세요.

Hey, I need to tell you something. Actually, I feel awful today. I don't think I can meet you today.

• [I feel awful] : 나 몸이 너무 안 좋아

01.　'awful'은 '끔찍한'이라는 의미로 기분이나 몸 상태를 나타낼 때는 동사 'feel'과 자주 함께 사용됨

02.　일상 회화에서 몸이나 컨디션이 좋지 않을 때 사용할 수 있는 표현

03.　동일한 표현 : I'm not feeling well / I don't feel good / I feel sick

사용 방법

몸 상태가 좋지 않음을 상대에게 알릴 때 사용

활용 및 응용

• I feel awful today.

• I'm about to go to the doctor because I'm not feeling well.

• I feel sick because I stayed up all night drinking.

MEMO

롤플레이의 암기문장   Let me give you some options

롤플레이의 문법을 정확히 배우고 응용해 보세요.

So, let me give you some options to solve this problem.

• [Let me give you some options] : 대안을 제시 할게

01.   문제 상황에서 **해결 대안을 제시하기 직전에 사용**하기 좋은 표현

02.   유사한 표현으로는

  a. I'll give you some options

  b. Here are some options

  c. Let me give you some alternatives

사용 방법

문제 해결 방안을 제시하기 직전에 사용

활용 및 응용

• Let me give you some options to solve this problem.

• Well, here are some options to deal with this issue.

• Actually, let me give you some alternatives to handle this.

MEMO

롤플레이의 암기문장　관용어구 (+why)

롤플레이의 문법을 정확히 배우고 응용해 보세요.

Or **why don't you** ask one of your friends?

• [관용어구] Why don't you ~? : ~ 하는게 어때?

01. **'why don't you + 동사원형'** 형태의 문장은 관용어구로서 의견을 제시하는 뉘앙스로 'how about' 'what about'과 동일한 의미

02. 'why'가 들어간 관용어구 중 자주 쓰이는 표현으로는

　　a. Why not? : 좋아! (안될 게 뭐야)

　　b. Why bother? : 뭐 하러 그래? 굳이?

사용 방법

Why don't + 주어 + 동사원형 ~?

* 자주 쓰이는 관용어구 'why not?' 'why bother?'는 보통 이 자체로만 사용

활용 및 응용

• **Why don't you ask** your friend?

• **Why don't we throw** another party next Friday?

• Pool party? Hell yeah, **why not?**

MEMO

274

롤플레이의 암기문장　to부정사 (명사적 용법)

롤플레이의 문법을 정확히 배우고 응용해 보세요.

Or the only other way is **to postpone** it till the following week. What do you think?

• **[to부정사 (명사적 용법)] to postpone : 미루는 것**

01.　to 부정사는 **'to + 동사원형'**형태로 각 용법에 따라 의미가 달라짐
02.　여기서는 '명사'적 용법으로 명사의 역할을 하여 **'~하는 것'** 으로 해석
03.　'명사'역할을 하므로 주어, 목적어, 보어 자리에 위치할 수 있음

사용 방법

---

to + 동사원형

* 명사적 용법으로 주어, 목적어, 보어 자리에 위치

활용 및 응용

• The only other way is **to postpone** it till the following week.

• **To speak** fluent English is not so easy.

• We decided **to go** back to the hotel and just chill.

MEMO

24강

유형 04 (롤플레이)

암기문장 쉐도잉

1단계 : 사전학습

2단계 : 딕테이션

3단계 : 문장 끊어 읽기

4단계 : 전체 문장 읽기

5단계 : 반복 학습

암기문장 쉐도잉

암기문장 쉐도잉은 총 5단계로 나누어져 있습니다.
진짜녀석들 OPIc의 암기문장을 반복듣기 하면서 쉐도잉을 진행합니다.

1단계 사전학습	문장을 들은 후, 주어진 암기문장을 억양, 강세를 고려하여 큰소리로 읽습니다. ex.) Actually, It is incredibly **beautiful** and **peaceful.**
2단계 딕테이션	문장을 들은 후, 밑줄 친 부분을 적습니다. ex.) Actually, ____ is incredibly _____ and _____.
3단계 문장 끊어 읽기	문장을 들은 후, 청크 단위로 끊어 읽어 봅니다. ex.) Actually, / It is incredibly **beautiful** / and **peaceful.**
4단계 전체 문장 읽기	문장을 들은 후, 3단계를 여러 번 반복한 후, 전체 문장을 한숨에 읽어 봅니다. ex.) Actually, It is incredibly **beautiful** and **peaceful.**
5단계 반복학습	위 단계를 반복하여, 영어의 어순으로 된 한글 해석을 보며, 쉐도잉 연습을 합니다. ex.) 사실, 그 곳은 숨막히게 아름다워 그리고 평화로워.

암기문장 쉐도잉

정보요청 롤플레이 문장의 쉐도잉 연습을 하세요.

🎧 MP3 IM3-AL_110~114

1단계 : 사전학습

문장을 들은 후, 주어진 암기문장을 억양, 강세를 고려하여 큰소리로 읽습니다.

`IM3-AL_110` • **Hi there,** I would like to buy **an MP3 player.** Could I ask you some questions?

`IM3-AL_111` • **First of all,** where is it? I heard that it is close to **Seoul station.** Is it right?

`IM3-AL_112` • **And also,** how much is it? Can you give me a discount?

`IM3-AL_113` • **Lastly,** what are your opening hours like? Are you open 24/7?

`IM3-AL_114` • **Alright then,** thanks a lot. See you later.

2단계 : 딕테이션

문장을 들은 후, 밑줄 친 부분을 적습니다.

• **Hi there,** I would like to buy _____. Could I ask you some questions?

• **First of all,** where is it? I heard that it is close to _____. Is it right?

• **And also,** how much is it? Can you give me a discount?

• **Lastly,** what are your opening hours like? Are you open 24/7?

• **Alright then,** thanks a lot. See you later.

3단계 : 문장 끊어 읽기

문장을 들은 후, 청크 단위로 끊어 읽어 봅니다.

• **Hi there, /** I would like to buy **/ an MP3 player. /** Could I ask you some questions?

• **First of all, /** where is it? **/** I heard that it is close to **/ Seoul station.** Is it right?

• **And also, /** how much is it? **/** Can you give me a discount?

• **Lastly, /** what are your opening hours like? **/** Are you open 24/7?

• **Alright then, /** thanks a lot. See you later.

4단계 : 전체 문장 읽기

문장을 들은 후, 3단계를 여러 번 반복한 후, 전체 문장을 한숨에 읽어 봅니다.

• **Hi there,** I would like to buy **an MP3 player.** Could I ask you some questions?

• **First of all,** where is it? I heard that it is close to **Seoul station.** Is it right?

• **And also,** how much is it? Can you give me a discount?

• **Lastly,** what are your opening hours like? Are you open 24/7?

• **Alright then,** thanks a lot. See you later.

5단계 : 반복 학습

위 단계를 반복하여, 영어의 어순으로 된 한글 해석을 보며, 쉐도잉 연습을 합니다.

• 안녕, 난 사고 싶어 **MP3 플레이어**를. 뭣 좀 물어봐도 돼?

• 첫 번째로, 어디에 있어? 내가 듣기론, 가깝다고 하던데 **서울역**과, 맞아?

• 그리고, 얼마야? 받을 수 있어 할인을?

• 마지막으로, 운영 시간은 어떻게 돼? 연중무휴야?

• 알겠어 그럼, 많이 고마워. 나중에 보자.

암기문장 쉐도잉

문제해결 롤플레이 문장의 쉐도잉 연습을 하세요.

🎧 MP3 IM3-AL_115~120

1단계 : 사전학습

문장을 들은 후, 주어진 암기문장을 억양, 강세를 고려하여 큰소리로 읽습니다.

IM3-AL_115 • **Hey,** I need to tell you something. Actually, I feel <u>awful</u> today. I don't think I can meet you today.
IM3-AL_116 • **So,** let me give you some options to solve this problem.
IM3-AL_117 • **Maybe,** I can call <u>the ticket company</u> and get a refund.
IM3-AL_118 • **Or,** why don't you ask <u>one of your friends</u>?
IM3-AL_119 • **Or,** the only other way is to postpone it till <u>the following week</u>. What do you think?
IM3-AL_120 • **Once again,** I'm so sorry. Let me know what's best for you.

2단계 : 딕테이션

문장을 들은 후, 밑줄 친 부분을 적습니다.

• **Hey,** I need to tell you something. Actually, I feel _____ today. I don't think I can meet you today.
• **So,** let me give you some options to solve this problem.
• **Maybe,** I can call _____ and get a refund.
• **Or,** why don't you ask _____?
• **Or,** the only other way is to postpone it till _____. What do you think?
• **Once again,** I'm so sorry. Let me know what's best for you.

3단계 : 문장 끊어 읽기

문장을 들은 후, 청크 단위로 끊어 읽어 봅니다.

• **Hey,** / I need to tell you something. / Actually, I feel <u>awful</u> today. / I don't think I can meet you today.
• **So,** / let me give you some options / to solve this problem.
• **Maybe,** / I can call <u>the ticket company</u> and / get a refund.
• **Or,** / why don't you ask / <u>one of your friends</u>?
• **Or,** / the only other way is to / postpone it till <u>the following week</u>. / What do you think?
• **Once again,** / I'm so sorry. / Let me know what's best for you.

4단계 : 전체 문장 읽기

문장을 들은 후, 3단계를 여러 번 반복한 후, 전체 문장을 한숨에 읽어 봅니다.

• **Hey,** I need to tell you something. Actually, I feel <u>awful</u> today. I don't think I can meet you today.
• **So,** let me give you some options to solve this problem.
• **Maybe,** I can call <u>the ticket company</u> and get a refund.
• **Or,** why don't you ask <u>one of your friends</u>?
• **Or,** the only other way is to postpone it till <u>the following week</u>. What do you think?
• **Once again,** I'm so sorry. Let me know what's best for you.

5단계 : 반복 학습

위 단계를 반복하여, 영어의 어순으로 된 한글 해석을 보며, 쉐도잉 연습을 합니다.

• **있잖아,** 할 말이 있어. 사실, 나 **많이 아파** 오늘. 못 만날 것 같아 오늘.
• **그래서,** 대안을 제시해 줄게 이 문제를 풀 수 있는.
• **그럼,** 내가 **티켓 회사** 전화해서 환불을 할 수 있어.
• **아니면,** 물어보지 그래? **너의 친구들 중 한** 명에게.
• **아니면,** 마지막 방법으론 연기하는 거야 **다음 주로** 하자. 어때?
• **다시 한번,** 많이 미안해. 생각해보고 알려줘.

25강

유형 04 (롤플레이)

리스닝 훈련

롤플레이 질문 리스트

진짜녀석들 OPIc의 다양한 롤플레이 질문들의 MP3를 듣고 키워드 캐치를 훈련하세요.

🎧 MP3 IM3-AL_Q_92~103

**정보 요청
롤플레이**

I'd like to give you a situation and ask you to act it out. **One of your friends is having a party and you are invited to that party.** Call your friend and ask **when the party starts** and **what you need to bring there.** Ask two or three more questions about the party.

I'd like to give you a situation and ask you to act it out. **You are staying at a hotel and have a chance for a one-day trip in a new city.** Ask the front desk agent three or four questions about **what things you can do.**

I'd like to give you a situation and ask you to act it out. **You are at a clothing store and try to buy some clothes.** Ask the staff two to three questions about **the clothes you want to buy.**

I'd like to give you a situation and ask you to act it out. **You want to buy an MP3 player.** Call your friend and ask about the MP3 player that he or she is using. Ask three or four questions that will help you **decide if you want to get the same product your friend is using or not.**

I'd like to give you a situation and ask you to act it out. **You want to open a new bank account.** Go to the bank and ask the bank teller three to four questions about **opening a new account.**

I'd like to give you a situation and ask you to act it out. **You would like to buy a house to live in.** Call one of the real estate agencies and ask three or four questions about **buying a house to live in.**

- -

**문제 해결
롤플레이**

I'm sorry, but there is a problem you need to resolve. **Unfortunately, you just had a car accident, and you are not able to make it to the party.** Call your friend, explain the situation, and give two to three alternatives to solve the situation.

I'm sorry, but there is a problem you need to resolve. **You left your bag in the taxi that brought you back from the one-day trip.** Call the taxi company, explain the situation, describe your bag, and ask them **how you can get your bag back.**

I'm sorry, but there is a problem you need to resolve. **You found out that one of the shirts you bought has a problem.** Call the clothing store and explain the situation. Give two to three alternatives to **solve this problem.**

I'm sorry, but there is a situation that you need to solve. **You borrowed an MP3 player from your friend but unfortunately, you broke it.** Call your friend, explain the situation, and offer two to three alternatives to **resolve this matter.**

I'm sorry, but there is a problem you need to resolve. **You left your credit card behind at a shopping mall.** Call the shopping mall and explain the situation. Give two to three alternatives to **solve the problem.**

I'm sorry, but there is a problem you need to resolve. **You have moved into the new house but found out that one of the windows in your house was broken.** Call the repair shop, explain **why you need to get a new window as soon as possible.**

롤플레이 질문 리스트

진짜녀석들 OPIc의 다양한 롤플레이 질문들의 MP3를 듣고 키워드 캐치를 훈련하세요.

🎧 MP3 IM3-AL_Q_104~109

문제 해결 경험

That's the end of the situation. **Have you ever made plans for a trip or a party but had to cancel at the very last minute because of something that happened unexpectedly?** How did you **solve the problem?** Please tell me all the stories from the beginning to the end.

That's the end of the situation. Have you ever had that kind of situation before? **Have you ever lost something?** How did you **solve that situation?** Please tell me about what happened from the beginning to the end.

That's the end of the situation. **Have you ever had any experience of being unhappy with something that you bought or some service you received?** Maybe, something could have had a scratch or a rip on it. What was the problem, and how did you **solve the problem?** Please tell me everything in detail.

That's the end of the situation. **Please tell me about a time when a piece of equipment broke.** When was it and what exactly happened? How did you **fix the problem?** Tell me everything about that experience.

That's the end of the situation. **Have you ever had any problems using your bank card, bank account, or a credit card?** Maybe your credit card was not working properly for some reason. Please tell me everything that happened and how you **resolved the matter.**

That's the end of the situation. **Have you ever broken something at home?** If so, **what did you break? What exactly happened?** How did you **solve the problem?** Please give me all the details from the beginning to the end.

정보요청 롤플레이

진짜녀석들 OPIc의 다양한 롤플레이 질문들의 MP3를 듣고 키워드 캐치를 훈련하세요.

MP3 IM3-AL_Q_92

돌발 / 파티

친구에게 초대받은 파티에 대한 질문

I'd like to give you a situation and ask you to act it out. One of your friends is having a party and you are invited to that party. Call your friend and ask when the party starts and what you need to bring there. Ask two or three more questions about the party.

/ KEYWORD

MP3 IM3-AL_Q_93

돌발 / 호텔

직원에게 일일여행에 할 수 있는 활동 문의

I'd like to give you a situation and ask you to act it out. You are staying at a hotel and have a chance for a one-day trip in a new city. Ask the front desk agent three or four questions about what things you can do.

/ KEYWORD

MP3 IM3-AL_Q_94

서베이 / 쇼핑

구매하고 싶은 옷에 대해 직원에게 문의

I'd like to give you a situation and ask you to act it out. You are at a clothing store and try to buy some clothes. Ask the staff two to three questions about the clothes you want to buy.

/ KEYWORD

MP3 IM3-AL_Q_95

서베이 / 음악

구매하고 싶은 친구의 MP3플레이어에 대해 문의

I'd like to give you a situation and ask you to act it out. You want to buy an MP3 player. Call your friend and ask about the MP3 player that he or she is using. Ask three or four questions that will help you decide if you want to get the same product your friend is using or not.

/ KEYWORD

MP3 IM3-AL_Q_96

돌발 / 은행

은행직원에게 은행 계좌 개설을 위한 문의

I'd like to give you a situation and ask you to act it out. You want to open a new bank account. Go to the bank and ask the bank teller three to four questions about opening a new account.

/ KEYWORD

MP3 IM3-AL_Q_97

돌발 / 부동산

부동산에 구입하고 싶은 집에 대한 문의

I'd like to give you a situation and ask you to act it out. You would like to buy a house to live in. Call one of the real estate agencies and ask three or four questions about buying a house to live in.

/ KEYWORD

문제해결 롤플레이

진짜녀석들 OPIc의 다양한 롤플레이 질문들의 MP3를 듣고 키워드 캐치를 훈련하세요.

🎧 MP3 IM3-AL_Q_98

돌발 / 파티

차 사고로 파티에 늦게 될 상황설명 및 대안

I'm sorry, but there is a problem you need to resolve. Unfortunately, you just had a car accident, and you are not able to make it to the party. Call your friend, explain the situation, and give two to three alternatives to solve the situation.

/ KEYWORD

🎧 MP3 IM3-AL_Q_99

돌발 / 호텔

택시에 가방을 놓고 내려 택시회사에 전화하여 문제해결

I'm sorry, but there is a problem you need to resolve. You left your bag in the taxi that brought you back from the one-day trip. Call the taxi company, explain the situation, describe your bag, and ask them how you can get your bag back.

/ KEYWORD

🎧 MP3 IM3-AL_Q_100

서베이 / 쇼핑

구매한 옷에 불량이 있어 상점에 전화 후 문제해결

I'm sorry, but there is a problem you need to resolve. You found out that one of the shirts you bought has a problem. Call the clothing store and explain the situation. Give two to three alternatives to solve this problem.

/ KEYWORD

🎧 MP3 IM3-AL_Q_101

서베이 / 음악

친구 MP3플레이어를 고장 낸 상황의 대안 제시

I'm sorry, but there is a situation that you need to solve. You borrowed an MP3 player from your friend but unfortunately, you broke it. Call your friend, explain the situation, and offer two to three alternatives to resolve this matter.

/ KEYWORD

🎧 MP3 IM3-AL_Q_102

돌발 / 은행

카드를 쇼핑몰에 두고와 쇼핑몰에 전화 후 문제해결

I'm sorry, but there is a problem you need to resolve. You left your credit card behind at a shopping mall. Call the shopping mall and explain the situation. Give two to three alternatives to solve the problem.

/ KEYWORD

🎧 MP3 IM3-AL_Q_103

돌발 / 부동산

이사 후 깨져있는 창문때문에 수리점에 수리요청

I'm sorry, but there is a problem you need to resolve. You have moved into the new house but found out that one of the windows in your house was broken. Call the repair shop, explain why you need to get a new window as soon as possible.

/ KEYWORD

문제해결 경험

진짜녀석들 OPIc의 다양한 롤플레이 질문들(경험)의 MP3를 듣고 키워드 캐치를 훈련하세요.

🎧 MP3 IM3-AL_Q_104

돌발 / 파티

계획했던 파티 혹은 여행이 캔슬된 경험

That's the end of the situation. Have you ever made plans for a trip or a party but had to cancel at the very last minute because of something that happened unexpectedly? How did you solve the problem? Please tell me all the stories from the beginning to the end.

/ KEYWORD

🎧 MP3 IM3-AL_Q_105

돌발 / 호텔

무언가를 잃어버린 후, 해결한 경험

That's the end of the situation. Have you ever had that kind of situation before? Have you ever lost something? How did you solve that situation? Please tell me about what happened from the beginning to the end.

/ KEYWORD

🎧 MP3 IM3-AL_Q_106

서베이 / 쇼핑

구매한 무언가가 마음에 안 들었던 경험

That's the end of the situation. Have you ever had any experience of being unhappy with something that you bought or some service you received? Maybe, something could have had a scratch or a rip on it. What was the problem, and how did you solve the problem? Please tell me everything in detail.

/ KEYWORD

🎧 MP3 IM3-AL_Q_107

서베이 / 음악

기계/기기가 고장나 해결한 경험

That's the end of the situation. Please tell me about a time when a piece of equipment broke. When was it and what exactly happened? How did you fix the problem? Tell me everything about that experience.

/ KEYWORD

🎧 MP3 IM3-AL_Q_108

돌발 / 은행

은행 계좌, 카드 등 사용 중 문제가 생겨 해결한 경험

That's the end of the situation. Have you ever had any problems using your bank card, bank account, or a credit card? Maybe your credit card was not working properly for some reason. Please tell me everything that happened and how you resolved the matter.

/ KEYWORD

🎧 MP3 IM3-AL_Q_109

돌발 / 부동산

집에서 무언가를 부순 후 해결한 경험

That's the end of the situation. Have you ever broken something at home? If so, what did you break? What exactly happened? How did you solve the problem? Please give me all the details from the beginning to the end.

/ KEYWORD

26강

유형 04 (롤플레이)

스크립트 훈련1

정보요청 롤플레이

정보 요청(파티) 친구에게 초대받은 파티에 대한 질문

Q92 ────────────────────

I'd like to give you a situation and ask you to act it out. **One of your friends is having a party and you are invited to that party.** Call your friend and ask **when the party starts** and **what you need to bring there.** Ask two or three more questions about the party.

상황을 드릴 테니 연기해보세요. 친구 중에 한 명이 파티를 열고 있고 당신은 그 파티에 초대되었습니다. 친구에게 전화하여 파티가 언제 시작하고 거기에 무엇을 가져올 필요가 있는지에 대해 물어보세요. 파티에 대해 2~3개 이상의 질문을 물어보세요.

서론
인사말/20%

- **Hi** there, *I would like to join your party, but I don't know* much about the party.
  - If it's possible, could I ask you some questions?

본론
질문/70%

- **First of all,** when does the party start?
  - Actually, I heard that the party starts at 7pm. Is it right?

- **And also,** where is it?
  - Is it in the tallest building in the city?
  - Do I need an ID card to get in?

- **Lastly,** what do I need to bring?
  - When it comes to the party, people really enjoy listening to music.
  - Can I bring my powerful speakers?
  - Also, can I take my friend?
  - Actually, he knows a lot about music, so he is a great person to go with.

결론
마무리문장/10%

- **Alright then,** thanks a lot. See you later.

- -

- 안녕, 나는 파티에 가고 싶은데 내가 파티에 대해 아는 것이 없어.
  - 가능하다면, 뭐 좀 물어봐도 되지?

- 첫 번째로, 파티는 언제 시작해?
  - 사실 난 파티가 7시에 시작한다고 들었어. 맞지?

- 그리고 또한, 파티는 어디서 열려?
  - 도시에서 가장 큰 빌딩이지?
  - 들어가려면 신분증이 필요하지?

- 마지막으로, 내가 뭘 가져가야 해?
  - 파티에 대해서 말한다면, 사람들은 정말 음악을 듣는 것을 좋아해.
  - 내가 강력한 스피커를 가져가도 될까?
  - 또한, 내가 친구를 데려가도 돼?
  - 사실은 그는 음악에 대해 많이 알고 있어서 같이 가기에 좋은 사람이야.

- 알겠어 그럼, 고마워. 나중에 보자.

어휘 및 표현

when does the party start? 파티는 언제 시작해? **I heard that the party starts at 7pm** 7시에 시작한다고 들었어 **what do I need to bring?** 무엇을 가져가야 해? **Can I bring my powerful speakers?** 강력한 스피커를 가져가도 돼? **Also, can I take my friend?** 또한 친구를 데려가도 돼?

정보 요청(호텔) 직원에게 일일여행에 할 수 있는 활동 문의

Q93 ━━━━━━━━━━━━━━━━━━━━━━━━━━━━━━ 🎧 MP3 IM3-AL_Q_93

I'd like to give you a situation and ask you to act it out. **You are staying at a hotel and have a chance for a one-day trip in a new city.** Ask the front desk agent three or four questions about **what things you can do.**

상황을 드릴 테니 연기해보세요. 당신은 호텔에 머무르고 있고 새로운 도시에서 일일 투어를 할 수 있는 기회가 있습니다. 호텔 프론트에 당신이 할 수 있는 것들에 대하여 3~4개의 질문을 물어보세요.

━━ 🎧 MP3 IM3-AL_A_93

서론
인사말/20%

• Hi there, *I would like to plan for a* one*-day trip, but I* don't *know much about the city.*
  - If it's possible, could I ask you some questions?

본론
질문/70%

• In fact, I've always lived in very busy areas, so I'm trying to visit places that are very peaceful and quiet.
  - Actually, I heard that there is a beach and watching the sunset is kinda romantic.
  - And that's why the place is famous for couples. Is it right?

• And also, I want to go shopping.
  - I mean, I want the most famous shopping center in this city.
  - So, what are the opening hours like? Are they open 24/7?

• Lastly, I want some coffee.
  - You know, I heard that there is a beautiful old house which is now a café.
  - Is it always packed with lots of people?
  - Do I need to stand in a long line?

결론
마무리문장/10%

• Alright then, thanks a lot. See you later.

- -

• 안녕하세요. **일일 투어를 계획하고 싶은데요 이 도시에 대해서 아는 것이 없습니다.**
  - 가능하다면, 뭐 좀 여쭤봐도 될까요?

• 사실은 저는 매우 바쁜 지역에서 살아와서, 정말 평화롭고 조용한 곳에 방문하려고 합니다.
  - 사실은 해변이 있고 노을 보는 것이 꽤 로맨틱하다고 들었는데요.
  - 그래서 그 장소가 커플에게 유명한 장소인 거 맞죠?

• 그리고 또한, 저는 쇼핑을 가고 싶습니다.
  - 내 말은, 이 도시에서 가장 유명한 쇼핑센터에 가고 싶습니다.
  - 그래서, 오픈 시간이 어떻게 되죠? 연중무휴인가요?

• 마지막으로, 저는 커피를 먹고 싶습니다.
  - 저는 지금 카페인 아름답고 오래된 집이 있다고 들었는데요.
  - 거기는 항상 사람이 많나요? + 긴 줄을 서야 할까요?

• 알겠습니다 그럼, 감사합니다. 나중에 봐요.

━━━

어휘 및 표현
I would like to plan for a one-day trip 일일 투어를 계획하고 싶어요

정보 요청(상점) 구매하고 싶은 옷에 대해 직원에게 문의

Q94 ───────────────────────────── 🎧 MP3 IM3-AL_Q_94

I'd like to give you a situation and ask you to act it out. **You are at a clothing store and try to buy some clothes.** Ask the staff two to three questions about **the clothes you want to buy.**

상황을 드릴 테니 연기해보세요. 당신은 옷 가게에 있고 옷 몇 개를 사려고 합니다. 당신이 사고 싶은 옷에 대하여 2~3개의 질문을 직원에게 해보세요.

───────────────────────────── 🎧 MP3 IM3-AL_A_94

서론
인사말/20%

• <u>Hi</u> there, *I would like to buy some <u>clothes</u>, but I don't know much about your <u>store</u>.*
  - If it's <u>possible</u>, could I ask you some <u>questions</u>?

본론
질문/70%

• In <u>fact</u>, it is summer, and I would like to buy some <u>outdoor</u> clothes.
  - <u>First</u> of all, do you have swimsuits?
  - And <u>also</u>, I would like to buy some <u>gym</u> wear.

• And <u>also,</u> can you give me a <u>discount</u>?
  - You know, I'm <u>pretty</u> sure that I can get a discount since I got a <u>membership</u> card.
  - So, what are your <u>opening</u> hours like? Are they open 24/7?

• <u>Lastly,</u> where is your <u>store</u>?
  - I <u>heard</u> that it is in the <u>ABC</u> shopping center which is in the <u>middle</u> of the town. Right?

결론
마무리문장/10%

• <u>Alright</u> then, thanks a lot. See you later.

- -

• 안녕하세요, **옷을 좀 사려고 하는데요, 근데 제가 당신의 가게에 대해서 많이 아는 점이 없습니다.**

• 사실은, 여름이라서 몇몇 야외활동 옷을 사고 싶습니다.
  - 첫 번째로, 수영복이 있나요?
  - 그리고 또한 헬스장에서 입을 옷도 사고 싶어요.

• 그리고 또한, 할인을 받을 수 있을까요?
  - 있잖아요, 멤버십 카드가 있어서 할인을 받을 수 있다고 알고 있는데요.
  - 그래서, 오픈 시간이 어떻게 되나요? 연중무휴인가요?

• 마지막으로, 가게 위치는 어떻게 되나요?
  - 시내 중심에 있는 ABC 쇼핑센터 안에 있다고 들었는데요. 맞나요?

• 알겠습니다 그럼, 감사합니다. 나중에 봐요.

───

어휘 및 표현
I would like to buy some outdoor clothes 야외 활동 옷을 좀 사고 싶어요   **I would like to buy some gym wear** 운동복을 좀 사고 싶어요

정보 요청(MP3) 구매하고 싶은 친구의 MP3플레이어에 대해 문의

Q95 ───────────────────────────── 🎧 MP3 IM3-AL_Q_95

I'd like to give you a situation and ask you to act it out. **You want to buy an MP3 player.** Call your friend and ask about the MP3 player that he or she is using. Ask three or four questions that will help you **decide if you want to get the same product your friend is using or not.**

상황을 드릴 테니 연기해보세요. 당신은 MP3 플레이어를 사고 싶습니다. 친구에게 전화해서 친구가 사용하고 있는 MP3 플레이어에 대해 물어보세요. 친구가 사용하는 같은 제품을 얻을 수 있다면, 당신의 구매 결정을 도와줄 수 있는 3~4개의 질문을 물어보세요.

🎧 MP3 IM3-AL_A_95

서론
인사말/20%

• <u>Hi</u> there, *I would like to buy an <u>MP3</u> player, but I don't know <u>much</u> about it.*
  - If it's <u>possible</u>, could I ask you some <u>questions</u>?

본론
질문/70%

• <u>First of all,</u> I heard that your MP3 player has <u>various</u> functions such as taking <u>pictures</u> or playing games. Is it right?
  - <u>Plus</u>, I <u>really</u> enjoy listening to <u>music</u> at parks since it's the <u>perfect</u> spot for listening to <u>music</u>.
  - Does it have <u>powerful</u> speakers?

• <u>Speaking</u> of the store, <u>where</u> is it?
  - Is it in the <u>ABC</u> shopping center which is located in the <u>middle</u> of the town?

• <u>Lastly,</u> how much is it?
  - You know, I'm <u>pretty</u> sure that I can get a discount since I got a <u>membership</u> card.

결론
마무리문장/10%

• <u>Alright</u> then, thanks a lot. See you later.

- -

• **안녕, 내가 MP3 플레이어를 사고 싶은데, 아는 게 별로 없어.**
  - 가능하다면 몇 가지 질문을 해도 될까?

• 첫 번째로, 난 너의 MP3 플레이어가 사진 찍기, 게임하기 등과 같은 다양한 기능을 가지고 있다고 들었는데 맞지?
  - 추가로, 난 공원에서 음악을 듣는 것을 좋아해 왜냐하면 음악을 듣기에 좋은 장소이기 때문이야.
  - 그건 강력한 스피커를 구비하고 있어?

• 가게에 대해 말해본다면, 거기는 어디에 있어?
  - 시내 중심에 위치해 있는 ABC 쇼핑센터 맞지?

• 마지막으로, 그건 얼마야?
  - 있잖아, 난 멤버십 카드가 있어서 할인을 받을 수 있다고 알고 있어.

• 알겠어 그럼, 고마워. 나중에 보자.

어휘 및 표현
Does it have powerful speaker? 강력한 스피커가 있나요?

정보 요청(은행) 은행직원에게 은행 계좌 개설을 위한 문의

Q96

I'd like to give you a situation and ask you to act it out. **You want to open a new bank account.** Go to the bank and ask the bank teller three to four questions about **opening a new account.**

상황을 드릴 테니 연기해보세요. 당신은 은행 계좌 개설을 하고 싶습니다. 은행에 가서 계좌 개설에 대해 3~4개의 질문을 해보세요.

🎧 MP3 IM3-AL_A_96

서론
인사말/20%

• Hi there, *I would like to open a new bank account, but I don't know much about it.*
  - If it's possible, could I ask you some questions?

본론
질문/70%

• First of all, do I need to bring my ID card?
  - Well, speaking of my ID, I have a passport. Is it ok?

• Also, is there a branch nearby?
  - Well, I'm pretty sure that there is a branch around 20-minutes away from Seoul station. Is it right?

• Lastly, where are your ATMs located in that branch?
  - You know, I heard that, in total, I can find more than 50 ATMs. Is it right?
  - Because I don't want to stand in a long line.

결론
마무리문장/10%

• Alright then, thanks a lot. See you later.

• 안녕하세요, **계좌개설을 하고 싶은데 아는 게 많이 없습니다.**
  - 가능하다면, 뭐 좀 물어봐도 되나요?

• 첫 번째로, 제가 신분증을 가져가야 하나요?
  - 음, 제 신분증에 대해 말해본다면, 여권이 있습니다. 괜찮나요?

• 또한, 근처에 지점이 있나요?
  - 서울역에서 20분 거리에 지점이 있다고 확신하는데, 맞나요?

• 마지막으로, 그 지점에 ATM기는 어디에 있나요?
  - 있잖아요, 50개 이상의 ATM기가 있다고 들었는데요, 맞죠?
  - 왜냐하면 저는 긴 줄을 서고 싶지 않습니다.

• 알겠습니다 그럼, 감사합니다. 나중에 봐요.

어휘 및 표현
I would like to open a new bank account 계좌를 오픈하고 싶어요   **is there a branch nearby?** 근처에 지점이 있나요?
where are your ATMs located in that branch? 지점안에 ATM 기계는 어디에 있나요?

정보 요청(부동산) 부동산에 구입하고 싶은 집에 대한 문의

Q97 ─────────────────────────── 🎧 MP3 IM3-AL_Q_97

I'd like to give you a situation and ask you to act it out. **You would like to buy a house to live in.** Call one of the real estate agencies and ask three or four questions about **buying a house to live in.**

상황을 드릴 테니 연기해보세요. 살 집을 구입하고 싶습니다. 부동산 전화하여 집 구매에 대하여 3~4개의 질문을 물어 보세요.

─────────────────────────── 🎧 MP3 IM3-AL_A_97

서론
인사말/20%

본론
질문/70%

결론
마무리문장/10%

• <u>Hi</u> there, *I would like to buy a <u>house</u>, but I <u>don't</u> know much about this area.*
  - If it's <u>possible</u>, could I ask you some <u>questions</u>?

• <u>In the past</u>, I used to live in a <u>studio</u> apartment, but now, I would like to buy a <u>huge</u> house.
  - I mean, I want a house with a <u>master</u> bedroom, <u>three</u> bedrooms, and <u>two</u> baths.
  - So, what kinds of houses are <u>available</u>?

• <u>Also</u>, I want a house with a smart door lock because it's <u>handy</u>.
  - In <u>addition</u>, there must be a <u>central</u> heating and air-<u>conditioning</u>, so it's <u>cool</u> during summer and <u>warm</u> during winter.

• <u>Lastly</u>, how much should I save for a <u>down</u> payment?
  - <u>Plus</u>, where is your office? I <u>heard</u> that it is in the <u>ABC</u> tower. Is it right?

• <u>Alright</u> **then,** thanks a lot. See you later.

- -

• 안녕하세요, **집을 구매하고 싶은데요, 해당 지역에 대해서 많이 아는 것이 없습니다.**
  - 가능하다면, 뭐 좀 물어봐도 될까요?

• 과거에는, 원룸에서 살았는데요, 지금은 큰 집을 사고 싶습니다.
  - 제 말은, 화장실이 딸린 안방, 침실 3개, 욕실 2개인 집을 원합니다.
  - 그래서, 어떤 종류의 집이 가능할까요?

• 또한, 스마트 도어락이 있었으면 좋겠습니다. 왜냐하면 그건 편하니까요.
  - 게다가, 중앙난방과 에어컨이 있어야만 합니다. 그래야 여름에는 시원하고 겨울에는 따뜻하니까요.

• 마지막으로, 제가 계약금으로 얼마를 준비해야 하죠?
  - 추가로, 사무실은 어딘가요? 제가 듣기로는 ABC 타워 안이라고 들었는데요. 맞죠?

• 알겠습니다 그럼, 감사합니다. 나중에 뵐게요.

어휘 및 표현
what kinds of houses are available? 어떤 종류의 집이 가능한가요?
How much should I save for a down payment? 계약금은 얼마나 준비해야 하나요?

27 강   유형 04 (롤플레이)

스크립트 훈련2

문제해결 롤플레이

문제 해결(파티) 차 사고로 파티에 늦게 될 상황 설명 및 대안

Q98 ———————————————————————— 🎧 MP3 IM3-AL_Q_98

I'm sorry, but there is a problem you need to resolve. **Unfortunately, you just had a car accident, and you are not able to make it to the party.** Call your friend, explain the situation, and give two to three alternatives to **solve the situation.**

당신이 해결해야 할 문제가 있습니다. 불행히도, 당신은 교통사고를 당해서 파티에 참석하지 못할 것 같습니다. 친구에게 전화하여 상황을 설명하고 문제를 해결할 수 있는 2~3개의 대안에 대해 말해 주세요.

🎧 MP3 IM3-AL_A_98

서론
상황설명/30%

- **Hey,** I need to tell you something.
  - *Unfortunately, I just got into a <u>car</u> accident, and I'm <u>not</u> able to make it to the <u>party</u>.*
  - So, let me give you some <u>options</u> to solve this problem.

본론
대안/60%

- **Firstly, why don't you ask** <u>Alex</u>?
  - You know, when it <u>comes</u> to Alex, we spent <u>lots</u> of time with him and he is a <u>partygoer</u>.
  - <u>Plus</u>, he knows a <u>lot</u> about music, so he is a <u>great</u> person to go with.

- **Well or,** the <u>only</u> other way is to <u>postpone</u> it till the following week.
  - How about having a party at the <u>beach</u>?
  - You know, it's a <u>perfect</u> spot for just sitting and <u>relaxing</u>.
  - <u>Plus</u>, people can <u>also</u> do many kinds of things such as playing <u>sports</u>, listening to <u>music</u> and stuff like that.
  - What do you think?

결론
마무리문장/10%

- <u>**Seriously,**</u> I need to stay in the hospital for <u>2</u> days.
  - Once again, I'm <u>so</u> sorry.
  - Let me know what's <u>best</u> for you.

- -

- 안녕, 나 할 말이 있는데
  - **불행히도 내가 금방 교통사고를 당했어. 그래서 파티에 못 갈 것 같아.**
  - 그래서 내가 이 문제를 해결할 수 있는 몇 가지 해결책을 주려고 해.

- 첫 번째로, 알렉스한테 물어보는 게 어때?
  - 있잖아, 알렉스에 대해서 말한다면, 우리는 많은 시간을 알렉스와 보냈었고 그는 파티광이잖아.
  - 추가로, 그는 음악에 대해 많이 알고 그는 함께 가기에 좋은 사람이야.

- 음 아니면, 유일한 다른 방법은 그걸 다음 주까지 미루는 거야.
  - 해변에서 파티를 하는 건 어때?
  - 있잖아, 거긴 그냥 앉아서 쉬기에 완벽한 장소잖아.
  - 추가로, 사람들은 스포츠, 음악 듣기와 같은 많은 것들을 할 수 있어.
  - 어떻게 생각하니?

- 솔직히, 난 이틀 동안 병원에 입원해야 해.
  - 다시 한번, 정말 미안해.
  - 어느 게 너한테 제일 좋을지 말해줘.

어휘 및 표현
I just got into a car accident, and I'm not able to make it to the party 교통사고가 나서 파티에 못 갈 것 같아   he is a partygoer 그는 파티광이야

문제 해결(호텔) 택시에 가방을 놓고 내려 택시회사에 전화하여 문제 해결

Q99 ⏻ MP3 IM3-AL_Q_99

I'm sorry, but there is a problem you need to resolve. **You left your bag in the taxi that brought you back from the one-day trip.** Call the taxi company, explain the situation, describe your bag, and ask them how you can get your bag back.

당신이 해결해야 할 문제가 있습니다. 일일 투어에서 돌아오는 택시에서 당신을 가방을 두고 내렸습니다. 택시 회사에 전화하여 상황을 설명하고 당신의 가방을 설명하고 어떻게 가방을 돌려받을 수 있는 지 물어보세요.

⏻ MP3 IM3-AL_A_99

서론
상황설명/30%

• **Hi there,** is this <u>ABC</u> taxi company?
  - *<u>Unfortunately</u>, I left my <u>bag</u> in the taxi.*
  - If it's <u>possible</u>, could I ask you some <u>questions</u>?
  - You know, when I just <u>arrived</u> at the hotel, I <u>realized</u> that I left my bag in the <u>taxi</u>. Can you <u>imagine</u> that?

본론
대안/60%

• **So,** could you <u>please</u> tell the staff to search for my <u>bag</u>?
  - In <u>return</u>, I can give him <u>20</u> dollars!

• **Also,** where is your office? I <u>heard</u> that it is close to <u>ABC</u> hotel. Is it right?
  - <u>Plus</u>, what are your <u>opening</u> hours like? Are you open <u>24/7</u>?

결론
마무리문장/10%

• **Once again,** I'm <u>so</u> sorry.
  - Let me know as <u>soon</u> as possible.

- -

• 안녕하세요, ABC 택시 회사 맞나요?
  - **불행히도, 제가 2시간 전에 사용했던 택시에 가방을 두고 내렸습니다.**
  - 가능하다면, 질문 몇 가지를 해도 될까요?
  - 있잖아요, 제가 금방 호텔에 도착했을 때, 제가 택시에 가방을 두고 내렸다는 것을 알아차렸어요, 상상할 수 있나요?

• 그래서, 직원에게 내 가방을 찾아달라고 말해 주실 수 있나요?
  - 답례로, 20달러를 드릴 수 있습니다.

• 또한, 사무실이 어디인가요? ABC 호텔과 가깝자고 들었습니다. 맞죠?
  - 추가로, 영업시간이 어떻게 되나요? 연중무휴인가요?

• 다시 한번, 정말 죄송합니다. 가능한 한 빨리 알려주세요.

어휘 및 표현

is this ABC taxi company? ABC 택시 회사죠? **Unfortunately, I left my bag in the taxi** 불행히도, 택시에 가방을 두고 내렸어요
could you please tell the staff to search for my bag? 직원에게 제 가방을 찾아달라고 말해주실 수 있나요?
Let me know as soon as possible 가능한 한 빨리 알려주세요

문제 해결(상점) 구매한 옷에 불량이 있어 상점에 전화 후 문제 해결

Q100 🎧 MP3 IM3-AL_Q_100

I'm sorry, but there is a problem you need to resolve. **You found out that one of the shirts you bought has a problem.** Call the clothing store and explain the situation. Give two to three alternatives to **solve this problem.**

당신이 해결해야 할 문제가 있습니다. 당신이 샀던 셔츠들 중에 하나에 문제가 있다는 것을 발견하였습니다. 옷가게에 전화해서 상황을 설명해 주세요. 이 문제를 해결하기 위해 2~3개의 대안을 말해 주세요.

🎧 MP3 IM3-AL_A_100

서론
상황설명/30%

- **Hey,** I need to tell you something.
  - *Unfortunately, I found out that one of the <u>shirts</u> I bought has a <u>problem</u>.*
  - So, let me give you some <u>options</u> to solve this problem.

본론
대안/60%

- **You know,** it was a <u>birthday</u> present from my <u>girlfriend</u>.
  - Well, I'm <u>very</u> upset so, I <u>strongly</u> ask you for a <u>refund</u>.

- In **addition,** where is your <u>store</u>?
  - Is it in the <u>ABC</u> shopping center which is located in the <u>middle</u> of the town?
  - And <u>also</u>, what are your <u>opening</u> hours like? Are you open <u>24</u>/7?

결론
마무리문장/10%

- **Once again,** I'm <u>very</u> upset.
  - Let me know as <u>soon</u> as possible.

- 안녕하세요, 할 말이 있는데요.
  - **불행히도, 제가 샀던 셔츠들 중에 하나에 문제가 있다는 것을 발견했습니다.**
  - 이 문제를 해결하기 위한 몇 가지 옵션을 드리려고 하는데요.

- 있잖아요, 이건 내 여자친구의 생일 선물이었습니다.
  - 음, 저는 너무 화가 나서 환불을 강력하게 요청하고 싶습니다.

- 추가로, 가게는 어딘가요?
  - 시내 중간에 위치해 있는 ABC 쇼핑센터에 있나요?
  - 그리고 또한, 영업시간이 어떻게 되나요? 연중무휴인가요?

- 다시 한번, 정말 화가 나네요. 가능한 한 빨리 알려주세요.

어휘 및 표현
I found out that one of the shirts I bought has a problem 구매한 셔츠 중 하나가 문제가 있음을 발견했어요

문제 해결(MP3) 친구 MP3를 고장 낸 상황의 대안 제시

Q101 ─────────────── 🎧 MP3 IM3-AL_Q_101

I'm sorry, but there is a situation that you need to solve. **You borrowed an MP3 player from your friend but unfortunately, you broke it.** Call your friend, explain the situation, and offer two to three alternatives to **resolve this matter.**

당신이 해결해야 할 문제가 있습니다. 친구에게 MP3 플레이어를 빌렸는데 그게 부서졌습니다. 친구에게 전화해서 상황을 설명해 주세요. 이 문제를 해결하기 위해 2~3개의 대안을 말해 주세요.

🎧 MP3 IM3-AL_A_101

서론
상황설명/50%

- **Hey,** I need to tell you something.
  - _**Unfortunately, I broke your MP3 player.**_
  - You know, I went to the park and listened to <u>music</u> there using your MP3 <u>player</u>.
  - Well, I went there since I could <u>enjoy</u> the peace and quiet.
  - But um, when I was about to <u>leave</u>, it started to <u>rain</u>. I mean, the weather was <u>so</u> sunny, but it <u>poured</u>!
  - After like <u>10</u>min, your MP3 player stopped <u>working</u>.
  - I'm <u>so</u> sorry and let me give you some <u>options</u> to solve this problem.

본론
대안/40%

- **You know,** I can <u>quickly</u> call an engineer.
  - I guess, I will end up spending $<u>300</u> USD.
  - How about that?

- **Or,** why don't I buy you a <u>new</u> one?
  - You know, there is a <u>famous</u> electronic store which is located in the <u>middle</u> of the town.
  - You know, I'm <u>pretty</u> sure that I can get a discount since I got a <u>membership</u> card.

결론
마무리문장/10%

- **Once again,** I'm <u>so</u> sorry.
  - Let me know what's <u>best</u> for you.

- -

- 안녕, 할 말이 있어.
  - **불행히도, 난 너의 MP3 플레이어를 고장 냈어.**
  - 있잖아, 나는 공원에 갔고 MP3 플레이어를 사용해서 음악을 들었어.
  - 음, 난 평화로움과 조용함을 즐길 수 있었기에 공원에 갔어.
  - 근데 음, 내가 막 나가려고 했을 때, 비가 오기 시작했어. 내 말은, 날씨가 정말 화창했었는데 비가 쏟아졌어!
  - 10분 후에, MP3 플레이어가 갑자기 작동을 멈췄어.
  - 정말 미안해 그리고 이 문제를 해결하기 위한 몇 개의 옵션을 줄게.

- 있잖아, 난 빨리 엔지니어를 부를 수 있어.
  - 난 아마도 300달러를 쓰게 되고 말 거야.
  - 어때?

- 아니면, 내가 너에게 새 걸 사주는 건 어때?
  - 있잖아, 시내 중심에 위치해 있는 유명한 MP3 가게가 있거든.
  - 있잖아, 난 멤버십 카드가 있기 때문에 할인을 받을 수 있다고 생각해.

- 다시 한번, 정말 미안해.
  - 어느 게 너한테 최선인지 말해줘.

어휘 및 표현
why don't I buy you a new one? 내가 새 걸 사줄께   **How about that?** 어떻게 생각해?

문제 해결(은행) 카드를 쇼핑몰에 두고와 쇼핑몰에 전화 후 문제 해결

Q102 🎧 MP3 IM3-AL_Q_102

I'm sorry, but there is a problem you need to resolve. **You left your credit card behind at a shopping mall.** Call the shopping mall and explain the situation. Give two to three alternatives to **solve the problem.**

당신이 해결해야 할 문제가 있습니다. 쇼핑몰에 당신의 신용카드를 두고 왔습니다. 쇼핑몰에 전화해서 상황을 설명해 주세요. 이 문제를 해결하기 위해 2~3개의 대안을 말해 주세요.

🎧 MP3 IM3-AL_A_102

서론
상황설명/30%

- **Hey,** I need to tell you something.
  - I mean, after shopping, I went to the restaurant and I tried to pay, but I realized that I was in trouble.
  - *As you can expect, I left my credit card at your store.*

본론
대안/60%

- **So,** could you please tell the staff to search for my credit card?
  - In return, I can give him 20 dollars!

- **Also,** where is your store?
  - You know, I'm pretty sure that it was on the third floor in ABC shopping mall. Is it right?
  - Plus, what are your opening hours like? Are you open 24/7?

결론
마무리문장/10%

- **Once again,** I'm so sorry.
  - Let me know as soon as possible.

- 안녕하세요, 드릴 말씀이 있는데요.
  - 제가 쇼핑 후에, 식당에 갔다가 계산을 하려고 했는데 문제가 생겼다는 것을 깨달았습니다.
  - **그쪽이 예상하듯, 제가 상점에 신용카드를 놓고 왔습니다.**

- 그래서, 직원에게 제 신용카드를 찾아달라고 말해 주실 수 있나요?
  - 답례로, 20달러를 드릴 수 있습니다.

- 또한, 가게가 어디인가요?
  - 있잖아요, 저는 ABC 쇼핑몰 3층이었다고 알고 있는데, 맞죠?
  - 추가로, 영업시간이 어떻게 되나요? 연중무휴인가요?

- 다시 한번, 정말 죄송합니다. 가능한 한 빨리 알려주세요.

어휘 및 표현
I left my credit card at your store 당신 상점에 카드를 두고 왔어요

문제 해결(부동산) 이사 후, 깨져 있는 창문때문에 수리점에 수리 요청

Q103 ──────────── 🎧 MP3 IM3-AL_Q_103

I'm sorry, but there is a problem you need to resolve. **You have moved into the new house but found out that one of the windows in your house was broken.** Call the repair shop, explain **why you need to get a new window as soon as possible.**

당신이 해결해야 할 문제가 있습니다. 당신은 새 집으로 이상했는데 집에 있는 창문들 중 하나가 깨져있는 것을 발견하였습니다. 수리점에 전화해서 가능한 한 빨리 새 창문이 필요한 이유에 대해 설명해 주세요.

🎧 MP3 IM3-AL_A_103

서론
상황설명/30%

- **Hey,** I need to tell you something.
  - *You know, I have moved into the <u>new</u> house but found out that one of the <u>windows</u> was broken.*
  - So, I need to get a <u>new</u> window.

본론
대안/60%

- <u>**Actually,**</u> my house doesn't have <u>central</u> heating so it's <u>so</u> cold.
  - <u>Plus</u>, it's <u>raining</u>.
  - I mean, the weather was <u>so</u> sunny, but it is <u>pouring</u>!

- <u>**So,**</u> where is your <u>repair</u> shop?
  - Well, I'm <u>pretty</u> sure that it is around <u>20</u>-minutes away from my place.
  - <u>Plus</u>, what are your <u>opening</u> hours like? Are you open <u>24/7</u>?

결론
마무리문장/10%

- <u>**Alright**</u> **then,** let me know as <u>soon</u> as possible.

- 안녕하세요, 드릴 말씀이 있는데요.
  - **있잖아요, 제가 새집에 이사 왔는데 창문 중에 하나가 깨진 것을 발견하였습니다.**
  - 그래서, 전 새 창문이 필요합니다.

- 사실은, 저희 집이 중앙난방이 없어서 춥습니다.
  - 추가로, 비까지 와요.
  - 제 말은, 날씨는 정말 화창했는데 갑자기 비가 오고 있어요.

- 그래서, 수리점은 어디인가요?
  - 음, 우리 집에서 20분 정도 거리에 있는 것으로 알고 있는데요.
  - 추가로, 영업시간이 어떻게 되나요? 연중무휴인가요?

- 다시 한번, 정말 죄송합니다. 가능한 한 빨리 알려주세요.

어휘 및 표현
I have moved into the new house 새 집으로 이사를 왔어요   **So, I need to get a new window** 그래서 난 새 창문이 필요해요
where is your repair shop? 수리점은 어디죠?

28강

유형 04 (롤플레이)

스크립트 훈련3

문제해결 경험

문제 해결 경험(파티) 계획했던 파티 혹은 여행이 캔슬된 경험

Q104

🎧 MP3 IM3-AL_Q_104

That's the end of the situation. **Have you ever made plans for a trip or a party but had to cancel at the very last minute because of something that happened unexpectedly? How did you solve the problem?** Please tell me all the stories from the beginning to the end.

상황이 종료되었습니다. 여행 또는 파티 계획을 세웠다가 예상치 못한 일 때문에 마지막 순간에 취소했어야만 했던 경험이 있나요? 그 문제를 어떻게 해결했나요? 처음부터 끝까지 그 이야기에 대해 말해 주세요.

🎧 MP3 IM3-AL_A_104

서론
시작문장/10%

본론
했던 일/40%

- <u>Alright</u>! Let me tell you *the time I had to <u>cancel</u> for my trip to the <u>beach</u>.*

- **When I was 21,** I planned a beach trip to <u>BUSAN</u> with my friends.
  - Because BUSAN is the <u>perfect</u> place to go for a vacation since there are <u>lots</u> of beautiful beaches.
  - Speaking of the beach in <u>BUSAN</u>, the water is <u>crystal</u> clear.
  - So I went to the <u>shopping</u> mall to buy my new <u>swimsuit</u>.
  - Because I guess <u>most</u> people go there to swim.

본론
반전/20%

- After <u>shopping,</u> we grabbed a <u>cab</u> to go to BUSAN.
  - When we were <u>just</u> about to leave, it started to <u>rain</u>.
  - I mean, the weather was <u>so</u> sunny, but it <u>poured</u>!

본론
결과/20%

- **Guess what!** We were <u>completely</u> soaked.
  - Well, what could we do? We <u>ended</u> up going back <u>home</u>.

결론
마무리문장/10%

- <u>Okay</u> Eva, this is about *a trip that I <u>cancelled</u> at the <u>very</u> last minute.*

- 그래! 내가 **해변 여행을 취소해야 했던 때에 대해서 말해줄게.**

- 21살이었을 때, 난 친구들과 부산 바다 여행을 계획했어.
  - 왜냐하면 부산은 아름다운 해변이 많아서 휴가를 가기에 완벽한 장소였거든.
  - 부산에 있는 해변에 대해 말해본다면, 바다는 크리스탈처럼 깨끗해.
  - 그래서, 난 수영복을 사기 위해 쇼핑몰에 갔어.
  - 왜냐하면 대부분의 사람들이 수영하기 위해 부산에 가거든.

- 쇼핑을 하고 나서, 우리는 부산에 가기 위해 택시를 탔어.
  - 우리가 막 떠나려고 할 때, 비가 내리기 시작했어.
  - 내 말은 날씨는 매우 화창했었는데 갑자기 비가 퍼부었어.

- 이럴 수가! 우리는 완전히 젖었어.
  - 음, 우리는 무엇을 할 수 있었을까? 우리는 그냥 집에 가는 것으로 끝이 났어.

- 오케이 에바, **이게 내가 제일 마지막 순간에 취소했던 여행에 대한 거야.**

어휘 및 표현
I planned a beach trip to BUSAN with my friends 친구들과의 부산 해변 여행을 계획했어
I went to the shopping mall to buy my new swimsuit 수영복을 사기 위해서 쇼핑몰에 갔어

문제 해결 경험(호텔) 무언가를 잃어버린 후 해결한 경험

Q105 ──────
🎧 MP3 IM3-AL_Q_105

That's the end of the situation. Have you ever had that kind of situation before? **Have you ever lost something?** How did you **solve that situation?** Please tell me about what happened from the beginning to the end.

상황이 종료되었습니다. 이러한 상황을 전에 겪어본 적이 있나요? 뭔가를 잃어버렸던 적이 있나요? 어떻게 그 상황을 해결했나요? 처음부터 끝까지 무슨 일이 일어났었는지 말해 주세요.

🎧 MP3 IM3-AL_A_105

서론
시작문장/10%

• <u>Okay</u> Eva, let me tell you *when I lost my* <u>wallet</u>.

본론
했던 일/40%

• **When I was <u>28</u>,** I went to the <u>most</u> famous bar with my buddies which was located in the <u>middle</u> of the town.
  - <u>Actually</u>, it was my <u>birthday</u>.
  - Speaking of that bar, it is <u>always</u> packed with <u>lots</u> of people since the <u>atmosphere</u> is excellent.
  - You know, me and my friends <u>really</u> enjoy drinking <u>all</u> kinds of whiskey.
  - So, we drank like there's <u>no</u> tomorrow.

본론
반전/20%

• **After <u>only</u> being there for <u>30</u> minutes,** I got <u>so</u> drunk.
  - The <u>only</u> thing I remember is that I kept <u>dancing</u> and laughing.
  - Well, the next day? I <u>realized</u> that I was in <u>trouble</u>.
  - As you can <u>expect</u>, I lost my <u>wallet</u>. Oh my god, I felt like a <u>homeless</u> person.

본론
결과/20%

• **So,** I <u>grabbed</u> a cab to go to that bar.
  - <u>Luckily</u>, the bar staff searched for my wallet for <u>2</u> hours and found it!
  - In <u>return</u>, I gave him <u>10</u> dollars.

결론
마무리문장/10%

• **Um <u>yeah</u>,** I think this is <u>all</u> I remember Eva.

- -

• 오케이 에바, **내가 지갑을 잃어버렸을 때를 말해 줄게.**

• 28살 때, 나는 시내 중심에 있었던 가장 유명한 바에 내 친구들과 갔어.
  - 사실, 내 생일이었어.
  - 그 바에 대해 말한다면, 분위기가 좋아서 항상 많은 사람들로 가득 차 있어.
  - 있잖아, 내 친구들과 나는 정말로 모든 종류의 위스키를 마시는 것을 좋아해.
  - 그래서, 우리는 내일이 없는 것처럼 술을 마셨어.

• 30분 후쯤, 난 정말 술에 취했어.
  - 내가 기억하는 유일한 것은 내가 계속 춤추고 웃었단 거야.
  - 음, 다음 날? 내가 곤경에 처했다는 것을 깨달았어.
  - 네가 예상했듯이, 난 지갑을 잃어버렸어. 이럴 수가, 난 노숙자가 된 기분이었어.

• 그래서, 난 그 바에 가기 위해 택시를 잡았어.
  - 운 좋게도, 그 바 직원이 2시간 동안 지갑을 찾았고, 결국 발견했어!
  - 답례로, 난 그 직원에게 10달러를 줬어.

• 음 예, 이게 기억하는 모든 거야 에바.

어휘 및 표현
the atmosphere is excellent 분위기가 최고였어

문제 해결(상점) 구매한 무언가가 마음에 안 들었던 경험

Q106 ──────── 🎧 MP3 IM3-AL_Q_106

That's the end of the situation. **Have you ever had any experience of being unhappy with something that you bought or some service you received?** Maybe, something could have had a scratch or a rip on it. What was the problem, and how did you **solve the problem?** Please tell me everything in detail.

상황이 종료되었습니다. 당신이 샀던 것 혹은 받은 서비스에 대해 불만족스러웠던 경험이 있나요? 아마도, 물건에 스크레치 혹은 찢어진 것이 있었을 수도 있습니다. 문제가 무엇이었나요 그리고 어떻게 그 문제를 해결했나요? 자세하게 모든 것을 말해 주세요.

🎧 MP3 IM3-AL_A_106

서론
시작문장/10%
본론
했던 일/40%

- Okay Eva, *experience of being* <u>unhappy</u> *with something that I* <u>bought</u>?

- **You know,** it was my <u>birthday</u>.
  - A <u>few</u> days ago, for my birthday <u>present</u>, my brother bought me a <u>laptop</u> online.
  - You know, it was the <u>biggest</u> online electronic website and he bought me the <u>latest</u> model.
  - <u>Speaking</u> of my new laptop, it had <u>various</u> functions such as the <u>voice</u> recognition.
  - <u>Plus</u>, it had powerful <u>speakers</u>.

본론
반전/20%

- **After like <u>10</u> days,** I got the <u>laptop</u>, but it was <u>broken</u>!
  - Oh my god! Can you <u>imagine</u> that?

본론
결과/20%

- **So,** I called the <u>store</u> and <u>told</u> them about my broken laptop.
  - Because I was <u>so</u> mad, they <u>apologized</u> and offered an <u>exchange</u>.
  - But I was <u>very</u> upset so, I <u>strongly</u> asked them for a <u>refund</u>.

결론
마무리문장/10%

- **You know,** that's the <u>main</u> reason why I don't buy things <u>online</u>!

- -

- 오케이 에바, **내가 샀던 것에 대하여 불만족스러웠던 경험?**

- 있잖아, 내 생일이었어.
  - 며칠 전에, 내 생일 선물로 남동생은 온라인으로 나에게 노트북을 사줬어.
  - 있잖아, 가장 큰 온라인 전자상점 사이트였고, 그는 나에게 가장 최신 모델을 사줬어.
  - 내 노트북에 대해 말해본다면, 음성인식과 같은 다양한 기능을 가지고 있었어.
  - 추가로, 강력한 스피커가 있었어.

- 10일 후쯤, 난 노트북을 받았는데 근데 그건 부서져 있었어.
  - 이럴 수가! 상상이 가니?

- 그래서, 난 가게에 전화했고 내 부서진 노트북에 대해 말했어.
  - 왜냐하면 난 정말 화가 났고, 그들은 사과하고 교환을 제공했어.
  - 그러나 난 정말 화가 났기 때문에 난 그들에게 환불을 요청했어.

- 있잖아, 이게 내가 왜 온라인으로 물건을 사지 않는 가장 큰 이유야.

어휘 및 표현
my brother bought me a laptop online 남동생이 온라인으로 노트북을 사줬어
It was the biggest online electronic website 가장 큰 온라인 전자상점 웹사이트였어
he bought me the latest model 그는 가장 신상품을 사줬어   **I don't buy things online!** 난 온라인으로 물건을 사지 않아

문제 해결 경험(MP3) 기계/기기가 고장나 해결한 경험

Q107 ———

🎧 MP3 IM3-AL_Q_107

That's the end of the situation. **Please tell me about a time when a piece of equipment broke.** When was it and what exactly happened? How did you **fix the problem?** Tell me everything about that experience.

상황이 종료되었습니다. 기계가 고장 났을 때에 대해 말해 주세요. 언제였나요 그리고 정확히 무슨 일이었나요? 문제를 어떻게 해결했나요? 자세하게 모든 것을 말해 주세요.

🎧 MP3 IM3-AL_A_107

서론
시작문장/10%

본론
했던 일/40%

본론
반전/20%

본론
결과/20%

결론
마무리문장/10%

• <u>Great</u>, you mean *a time when a piece of equipment <u>broke</u>?*

• **Well,** it <u>all</u> happened <u>last</u> Saturday.
  - As I <u>remember</u>, it was my second-year <u>anniversary</u> with my girlfriend.
  - You know, there was a <u>beautiful</u> old house which is now a <u>bar</u>.
  - Well, the bar was <u>extremely</u> clean, and the people were <u>so</u> friendly.
  - So, I went there with my <u>girlfriend</u> to celebrate our <u>anniversary</u>.

• **While we were <u>enjoying our time,</u>** my girlfriend spilled <u>wine</u> on my cell phone.
  - Oh my god, it was <u>annoying</u> at first, but in order <u>not</u> to ruin our anniversary, I pretended like it was ok.

• So **quickly,** we went to the <u>service</u> center and the engineer <u>worked</u> on it for about an <u>hour</u>.
  - Guess what? I <u>ended</u> up spending <u>$500</u> USD.

• <u>Alright Eva,</u> I guess this is <u>pretty</u> much about what I <u>remember</u>.

- -

• 좋아, **기기가 고장 났을 때 말이지?**

• 음, 지난주 토요일에 모든 일이 일어났어.
  - 내가 기억하기로는, 내 여자친구와 2주년 기념일이었어.
  - 있잖아, 그건 아름다운 오래된 집이었는데 지금은 바야.
  - 음, 그 바는 정말 깨끗했고, 사람들은 정말 친절했어.
  - 그래서, 난 내 여자친구와 기념일을 축하하기 위해 거기에 갔어.

• 우리는 즐겁게 시간을 보내고 있었는데, 여자친구가 핸드폰에 와인을 쏟았어.
  - 이럴 수가, 난 처음에는 짜증 났지만 우리 기념일을 망치지 않기 위해 괜찮은 척했어.

• 그래서 빠르게, 우리는 서비스 센터를 불렀고 엔지니어는 그것을 고치는 데 한 시간이 걸렸어.
  - 그리고 있잖아, 난 500달러를 결국 쓰고 말았어.

• 그래 에바, 이게 **내가 기억하는 모든 것**에 대한 거야.

어휘 및 표현
it all happened last Saturday 지난주 토요일에 일어났어
it was my second-year anniversary with my girlfriend 내 여자친구와 2주년 기념일이었어

문제 해결 경험(은행) 은행 계좌, 카드 등 사용 중 문제가 생겨 해결한 경험

Q108 ━━━━━━━━━━━━━━━━━━━━━━━━━━━ 🎧 MP3 IM3-AL_Q_108

That's the end of the situation. **Have you ever had any problems using your bank card, bank account, or a credit card?** Maybe your credit card was not working properly for some reason. Please tell me everything that happened and how you **resolved the matter.**

상황이 종료되었습니다. 은행 카드, 은행 계좌 또는 신용카드를 사용하면서 문제를 겪은 적이 있나요? 아마도 신용카드가 어떤 이유로 적절하게 작동되지 않았을 것 입니다. 일어났던 모든 것과 문제를 어떻게 해결했는지 말해 주세요.

━━ 🎧 MP3 IM3-AL_A_108

서론
시작문장/10%

- Alright! Let me tell you *the problem I had at the bank.*

본론
했던 일/40%

- **When it** comes to the bank, I usually go to ABC bank and it's like 2km from where I live.
  - You know, I suppose I tend to visit there a few times a month.
  - I mean, the main reason why I go to the bank is that there are lots of ATMs.
  - When it comes to the machine, I guess the ATM is the biggest change in our lives.
  - Anyway, I went there to take out some cash.
  - You know, it was just after the holiday so, the bank was packed with lots of people.
  - So, I had to stand in a long line.

본론
반전/20%

- **When I was using the ATM,** it just stopped working!
  - Oh my god, it was annoying at first, but I pretended like it was ok.
  - So quickly, someone called an engineer and he came in like 10min.

본론
결과/20%

- **After like 30 min,** I was still waiting, and I started to lose my patience.
  - So, I just decided to leave the bank.
  - And I just went to a convenience store to take out the cash.

결론
마무리문장/10%

- **Um yeah,** I think this is all I remember about *the problem I had at the bank.* Eva.

- -

- 그래! 내가 은행에서 겪었던 문제에 대해서 말해 줄게.

- 은행에 대해서 말한다면, 난 보통 ABC 은행에 가고 내가 사는 곳에서 약 2km 떨어져 있어.
  - 있잖아, 난 한 달에 몇 번씩 거기에 방문하는 경향이 있어.
  - 내 말은, 내가 은행에 가는 주요한 이유는 많은 ATM기가 있기 때문이야.
  - 기계에 관해서는, 난 ATM기가 내 인생에서 가장 큰 변화라고 생각해.
  - 어쨌든, 난 현금을 인출하기 위해 거기에 갔어.
  - 그땐 휴일 직후였고, 은행은 항상 많은 사람들로 가득 차 있었어.
  - 난 긴 줄을 서야만 했어.

- 내가 ATM기를 사용하고 있었을 때, 갑자기 작동이 멈췄어!
  - 이럴 수가, 그건 처음에는 정말 짜증 났지만, 난 괜찮은 척했어.
  - 그래서 빠르게, 엔지니어를 불렀고, 그는 10분 만에 왔어.

- 30분 후에, 난 여전히 기다리고 있었고 난 인내심을 잃기 시작했어.
  - 그래서 난 거기를 떠나기로 결정했어.
  - 그리고 난 현금을 인출하기 위해 편의점으로 갔어.

- 음 예, **이게 은행에서 겪었던 문제야 에바.**

어휘 및 표현
Anyway, I went there to take out some cash 어쨌든, 현금 인출을 하기 위해 갔어   **it was just after the holiday** 휴일 직후 였어

문제 해결 경험(부동산) 집에서 무언가를 부순 후 해결한 경험

Q109 ——

🎧 MP3 IM3-AL_Q_109

That's the end of the situation. **Have you ever broken something at home?** If so, **what did you break? What exactly happened?** How did you **solve the problem?** Please give me all the details from the beginning to the end.

상황이 종료되었습니다. 집에서 무언가를 부순 경험이 있나요? 그렇다면, 무엇을 부쉈나요? 정확히 어떤 일이 일어났나요? 어떻게 문제를 해결하였나요? 처음부터 끝까지 자세하기 말해 주세요.

🎧 MP3 IM3-AL_A_109

서론
시작문장/10%

- Okay Eva, *experience about a time I broke something at home?*

본론
했던 일/40%

- **When I was little,** I used to live in a studio apartment, but now I live in a 3-story house.
  - On my last summer vacation, I stayed home alone.
  - The main reason why I like to stay at home is that I can spend time alone.
  - You know, in my house, there is a huge living room on the second floor.
  - And the first thing you can see is a flat screen TV and a cozy couch.
  - I was having a coffee while watching a movie.

본론
반전/20%

- While I was watching a movie, all of a sudden, the power went out and I freaked out.
  - I was so scared, so I ran down the stairs.
  - But it was too dark, so I lost balance and fell over.
  - And the coffee mug broke.

본론
결과/20%

- **Oh my god,** the broken coffee mug was very expensive.
  - So, I bought a new coffee mug and I ended up spending $300.

결론
마무리문장/10%

- Okay Eva, *this is about a time I broke something at home.*

- -

- 오케이 에바, **집에서 무언가를 부순 경험?**

- 내가 어렸을 때, 난 원룸에 살곤 했어, 근데 지금은 3층 집에 살아.
  - 지난 여름휴가때, 난 집에 혼자 머물렀어.
  - 내가 집에 있는 것을 좋아하는 가장 큰 이유는 내가 혼자 시간을 보낼 수 있기 때문이야.
  - 있잖아, 우리 집에는 2층에 큰 거실이 있어.
  - 네가 볼 수 있는 첫 번째 것은 평면 TV와 안락한 소파야.
  - 난 영화를 보면서 커피를 마시고 있었어.

- 내가 영화를 보고 있을 동안에, 갑자기, 정전이 됐고, 난 당황했어.
  - 난 정말 무서웠고 그래서 난 계단 밑으로 뛰어 내려갔어.
  - 그러나, 너무 어두웠기 때문에, 난 균형을 잃고 넘어졌어.
  - 그리고 커피 머그가 깨졌어.

- 이럴 수가, 깨진 머그잔은 정말 비싼 거였어.
  - 그래서, 난 새 커피 머그를 샀고, 결국 300달러를 지불하는 것으로 끝이 났어.

- 오케이 에바, **이게 집에서 무언가를 부순 경험이야.**

어휘 및 표현
I was having a coffee while watching a movie 영화를 보면서 커피를 마셨어   **I was so scared** 난 엄청 무서웠어
And the coffee mug broke 커피머그가 깨졌어   **the broken coffee mug was very expensive** 깨진 커피머그는 엄청 비쌌어

29강

유형 04 (롤플레이)

모의고사

롤플레이 모의고사 준비

난이도 5 설정 시, 롤플레이 질문은 총 2문제(11, 12번)가 출제됩니다.
13번은 문제해결 경험으로 출제되므로 롤플레이 모의고사에 포함됩니다.

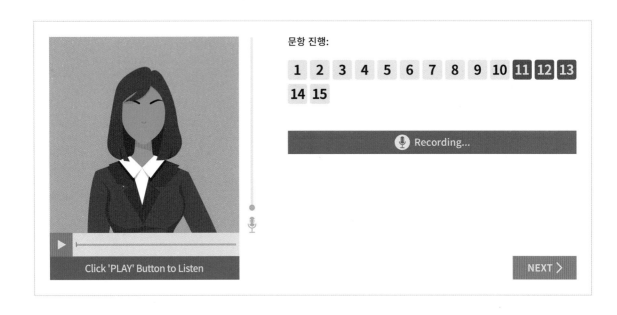

	11 12 13
유형	롤플레이
주제	11번: 알 수 없음 & 12, 13번: 이미 알고 있음
준비시간	20초
답변Format	인사말/상황설명 – 질문/대안 – 마무리 문장
집중내용	자연스러운 연기

롤플레이 모의고사

실제 시험처럼 각 문제의 MP3를 듣고, 훈련을 해보세요.

🎧 MP3 IM3-AL_Q_110~124

Q110   I'd like to give you a situation and ask you to act it out. **You want to buy some tickets to go watch a concert tonight.** Call the ticket booth and ask two to three questions about **how to get tickets.**

Q111   I'm sorry, but there is a problem you need to resolve. **On the concert day, you are so sick that you can't even get out of the bed.** Call your friend and explain the situation. Then give two or three alternatives to **solve this problem.**

Q112   That's the end of the situation. **Have you ever bought some concert tickets or made plans for a trip but had to cancel at the last minute because something unexpected happened?** Please tell me everything about what had happened **how you dealt with it.**

Q113   I'd like to give you a situation and ask you to act it out. **You have a job interview at a company tomorrow, but you don't know much about the company.** Call the company and ask three or four **questions about the company.**

Q114   I'm sorry, but there is a problem you need to resolve. **Unfortunately, something happened to you and you cannot make it to the interview.** Call the company and explain what happened to you. Then, give two to three alternatives to **make some arrangements for a schedule change.**

Q115   That's the end of the situation. **Have you ever had to cancel an appointment or a meeting for some reason?** What exactly happened, and **how did you deal with the situation?** Please give me all the details.

Q116   I'd like to give you a situation and ask you to act it out. **You are going on an international trip.** Call one of the hotels in that country and ask how the weather is like there. Also, you want to know **what clothes you need to bring.** Please ask two or three more questions to **complete the plans for your trip.**

Q117   I'm sorry, but there is a problem you need to resolve. **You bought some clothes while your international trip but unfortunately, the weather doesn't match with the clothes you bought.** Call the clothing store and explain the situation. Please tell them **you want to get some other clothes.**

Q118   That's the end of the situation. **Have you ever had any trouble due to an unexpected weather?** Where were you? **What happened** and **who** were you with? **How did you deal with the situation?** Please tell me everything about what happened on that day.

Q119   I'd like to give you a situation and ask you to act it out. **You would like to get some coffee from a new coffee shop that has opened recently.** Call the coffee shop and ask three to four questions about **their menu and how to order the coffee.**

Q120   I'm sorry, but there is a problem you need to resolve. **You got your coffee delivered to your house. Unfortunately, you find out that you've got the wrong order.** Call the coffee shop and explain the situation. Then, give two to three alternatives to **solve the problem.**

Q121   That's the end of the situation. **Have you ever been in a situation that you had ordered something but got the wrong order?** Where were you and **what did you order? What exactly happened** and how did you **deal with the situation?** Please describe the event in detail.

Q122   I'd like to give you a situation and ask you act it out. **One of your relatives is going on a trip for two days. Their house will be empty, and you've been asked to watch the house while they are gone.** Call your relative and ask three or four questions about what **you have to do for two days.**

Q123   I'm sorry, but there is a problem you need to resolve. **You are at your relative's house, but you can't get into the house because you don't have the key.** Call your relative and ask two to three questions to **solve the problem.**

Q124   That's the end of the situation. **Have you ever had an incident that you couldn't keep a promise with a family member or a friend? When** was it? **What was the main reason you couldn't keep the promise? What did you do to solve the problem?** Please give me all the details.

정보 요청(콘서트) 콘서트 티켓 구매를 위한 문의

Q110 ———
🎧 MP3 IM3-AL_Q_110

I'd like to give you a situation and ask you to act it out. **You want to buy some tickets to go watch a concert tonight.** Call the ticket booth and ask two to three questions about **how to get tickets.**

상황을 드릴 테니 연기해보세요. 당신은 오늘 밤에 콘서트를 보기 위해 티켓을 구매하려고 합니다. 티켓부스에 전화하여 티켓 구매 방법에 대해서 2~3개의 질문을 해보세요.

🎧 MP3 IM3-AL_A_110

서론
인사말/20%

- Hi there, *I would like to buy some* tickets *for a* concert *tonight.*
  - If it's possible, could I ask you some questions?

본론
질문/70%

- First of all, where is the ticket booth?
  - Perhaps, it's the most famous concert hall which is located in the middle of the town. Is it right?
  - And as I remember, on the first floor, there is a reception desk.
  - I mean, do I need an ID card to get in?

- And also, how many people are going?
  - All I know is that the concert hall is always packed with lots of people.

- Lastly, how much is the concert ticket? Can you give me a discount?
  - You know, I'm pretty sure that I can get a discount since I got a membership card.

결론
마무리문장/10%

- Alright then, thanks a lot. See you later.

- -

- 안녕하세요, 저는 오늘 밤 콘서트 티켓을 구매하고 싶은데요.
  - 가능하다면, 뭐 좀 물어봐도 될까요?

- 첫 번째로, 티켓부스는 어디에 있나요?
  - 아마도 시내 중심에 위치해 있는 가장 유명한 콘서트홀 맞죠?
  - 제가 기억하기로는 1층에는 리셉션 데스크가 있습니다.
  - 제 말은, 입장하려면 신분증이 필요한가요?

- 그리고 또한, 몇 명이 거기에 가나요?
  - 제가 아는 것은 콘서트홀은 많은 사람들로 가득 차 있다는 것입니다.

- 마지막으로, 티켓 가격은 어떻게 되나요? 할인을 받을 수 있나요?
  - 제가 멤버십 카드가 있어서 할인을 받을 수 있다고 알고 있어요.

- 알겠습니다 그럼, 감사합니다. 나중에 뵐게요.

어휘 및 표현
where is the ticket booth? 티켓부스는 어디에 있나요?　　how many people are going? 사람이 몇 명이나 오나요?

문제 해결(콘서트) 아파서 콘서트를 못 가는 문제 해결

Q111 ──────────── 🎧 MP3 IM3-AL_Q_111

I'm sorry, but there is a problem you need to resolve. **On the concert day, you are so sick that you can't even get out of the bed.** Call your friend and explain the situation. Then give two or three alternatives to **solve this problem.**

당신이 해결해야 할 문제가 있습니다. 콘서트 당일에, 너무 아파서 심지어 침대 밖에 나올 수도 없습니다. 친구에게 전화해서 상황을 설명해 보세요. 그리고 문제를 해결하기 위해 2~3개의 대안을 주세요.

🎧 MP3 IM3-AL_A_111

서론
상황설명/30%

- <u>Hey,</u> I need to tell you something.
  - *<u>Actually</u>, I feel <u>awful</u> today.*
  - I mean, I <u>can't</u> even get out of bed.
  - I <u>don't</u> think I can go to the <u>concert</u> with you today.
  - So, let me give you some <u>options</u> to solve this problem.

본론
대안/60%

- <u>Maybe,</u> I can call the <u>ticket</u> company and get a <u>refund</u>.
  - If they can't <u>give</u> one, I'll give you the money back.

- **Well,** why don't you ask <u>Chris</u>?
  - You know, when it <u>comes</u> to Chris, as you know, he is a <u>partygoer</u>.
  - <u>Plus</u>, he knows a <u>lot</u> about music, so he is a <u>great</u> person to go with.

- **Well or,** the <u>only</u> other way is to <u>postpone</u> it till the next concert.
  - Why don't you come to <u>my</u> place?
  - You know, there is a <u>flat</u> screen TV and a <u>cozy</u> couch.
  - I mean, we <u>really</u> enjoy watching <u>all</u> kinds of movies, right?

결론
마무리문장/10%

- <u>Seriously,</u> I need to stay in the <u>hospital</u> for 2 days.
  - Once again, I'm <u>so</u> sorry.
  - Let me know what's <u>best</u> for you.

- -

- 안녕, 나 할 말이 있어.
  - **사실, 오늘 너무 몸이 안 좋아.**
  - 내 말은, 난 침대 밖으로도 못 나오겠어.
  - 내가 너와 함께 오늘 콘서트에 갈 수 없을 것 같아.
  - 그래서 내가 이 문제를 해결할 수 있는 몇 가지 해결책을 주려고 해.

- 아마, 내가 티켓 회사에 전화해서 환불을 요청할 수 있을 것 같아.
  - 그들이 환불을 해줄 수 없다면, 내가 너에게 돈을 돌려줄게.

- 음, 크리스한테 물어보는 게 어때?
  - 있잖아, 크리스에 대해 말한다면, 그는 파티광이잖아.
  - 추가로, 그는 음악에 대해 많이 알고 그는 함께 가기에 좋은 사람이야.

- 음 아니면, 유일한 다른 방법은 그걸 다음 콘서트까지로 미루는 거야.
  - 우리 집에 오는 건 어때?
  - 있잖아, 평면 TV와 안락한 소파가 있어.
  - 우리는 모든 종류의 영화를 보는 것을 좋아하잖아, 맞지?

- 솔직히, 난 이틀 동안 병원에 입원해야 할 것 같아.
  - 다시 한번, 정말 미안해.
  - 어느 게 너한테 제일 좋을지 말해줘.

어휘 및 표현
I mean, I can't even get out of bed 내 말은, 침대 밖에로도 못 나오겠어

문제 해결 경험(콘서트) 티켓/여행 계획의 취소 경험

Q112

MP3 IM3-AL_Q_112

That's the end of the situation. **Have you ever bought some concert tickets or made plans for a trip but had to cancel at the last minute because something unexpected happened?** Please tell me everything about what had happened **how you dealt with it.**

상황이 종료되었습니다. 여행 계획을 하거나 콘서트 티켓을 샀었는데, 예기치 못한 일이 생겨서 마지막 순간에 취소해야만 했던 적이 있나요? 어떻게 그 문제를 다루었는지 자세하게 말해 주세요.

MP3 IM3-AL_A_112

서론
시작문장/10%

- Alright! Let me tell you *what happened at the movie theater.*

본론
했던 일/40%

- **You know,** I really enjoy watching all kinds of movies because it helps me release stress.
  - When I was little, I used to watch movies at home, but now I go to movie theaters.
  - Last Friday, I went to the nearest movie theater with my brother.
  - Well, I'm pretty sure that the theater was around 20-minutes away from my place.

본론
반전/20%

- When I arrived at the movie theater, I realized that my brother bought the wrong tickets.
  - Oh my god, it was annoying at first, but I pretended like it was ok.

본론
결과/20%

- So, I went to the ticket booth and explained the whole situation.
  - But it was Friday night, and the movie theater was packed with lots of people.
  - As you can imagine, the other movies were fully booked!
  - Well, what could we do? We ended up going back home.
  - And we watched a movie at home, and it was alright.

결론
마무리문장/10%

- Alright Eva, I guess this is pretty much about *what happened at the movie theater.*

- -

- **그래!** 영화관에서 있었던 일에 대해 말해줄게.

- 있잖아, 난 모든 종류의 영화를 보는 것을 좋아해 왜냐하면 내가 스트레스 푸는 데 도움이 되기 때문이야.
  - 내가 어렸을 때, 난 영화를 집에서 보곤 했어. 하지만 지금은 영화관에 가.
  - 지난주 금요일에, 난 내 남동생과 가장 가까운 영화관에 갔어.
  - 음, 난 그 영화관이 우리 집에서 약 20분 정도 떨어져 있다고 알고 있어.

- 우리가 영화관에 도착했을 때, 나는 내 남동생이 잘못된 티켓을 샀다는 것을 깨달았어.
  - 이럴 수가, 그건 처음에는 짜증 났지만, 난 괜찮은 척했어.

- 그래서, 난 티켓부스에 갔고, 전체 상황을 설명했어.
  - 그러나, 금요일 밤이었고, 영화관은 많은 사람들로 가득 차 있었어.
  - 내가 상상할 수 있듯이, 다른 영화들은 다 예약이 차 있었어.
  - 우리가 뭘 할 수 있겠어? 우리는 집에 돌아가는 것으로 끝이 났어.
  - 우리는 영화를 집에서 봤고, 나쁘지 않았어.

- 그래 에바, 이게 영화관에서 있었던 일이야.

어휘 및 표현
And we watched a movie at home, and it was alright 그리고 우린 집에서 영화를 봤고, 나쁘지 않았어

정보 요청(면접) 면접 보러 갈 회사에 전화하여 정보 요청

Q113

🎧 MP3 IM3-AL_Q_113

I'd like to give you a situation and ask you to act it out. **You have a job interview at a company tomorrow, but you don't know much about the company.** Call the company and ask three or four **questions about the company.**

상황을 드릴 테니 연기해보세요. 내일 회사 면접이 있습니다. 그러나 그 회사에 대해서 아는 것이 많이 없습니다. 회사에 전화하여 그 회사에 대해 3~4개 질문을 물어보세요.

🎧 MP3 IM3-AL_A_113

서론
인사말/20%

- **Hi there,** is this <u>ABC</u> movie theater?
  - *My name is Jean and I have a <u>job</u> interview at your company <u>tomorrow</u>.*
  - If it's <u>possible</u>, could I ask you some <u>questions</u>?

본론
질문/70%

- <u>First of all,</u> what do I need to <u>wear</u>?
  - Since it's a <u>movie</u> theater so can I wear something <u>casual</u>?

- And <u>also,</u> do I need to bring my <u>ID</u>?
  - Because I <u>heard</u> that there is a <u>reception</u> desk and I need an <u>ID</u> card to get in. Is it right?

- <u>Lastly,</u> where <u>exactly</u> is your company?
  - You know, I <u>heard</u> that it's the <u>tallest</u> building in the city and it's called the <u>ABC</u> tower. Is it right?
  - What <u>floor</u> is it?

결론
마무리문장/10%

- <u>Alright then,</u> <u>thanks</u> a lot. See you later.

- 안녕하세요, ABC 영화관 맞나요?
  - **제 이름은 Jean이고 내일 면접이 있습니다.**
  - 가능하다면, 뭐 좀 물어봐도 될까요?

- 첫 번째로, 제가 무엇을 입어야 할까요?
  - 영화관인데 캐주얼을 입어도 될까요?

- 그리고 또한, 제가 신분증을 가져가야 하나요?
  - 왜냐하면 리셉션 데스크가 있다고 들었고 신분증이 필요하다고 들었습니다. 맞죠?

- 마지막으로, 정확히 회사 위치가 어디인가요?
  - 있잖아요, 저는 도시에서 가장 큰 건물이고 ABC 타워라고 들었습니다. 맞죠?
  - 몇 층인가요?

- 알겠습니다. 감사합니다. 나중에 뵐게요.

어휘 및 표현

I have a job interview at your company tomorrow 내일 당신 회사에 면접이 있어요   **What floor is it?** 몇 층인가요?

문제 해결(면접) 무슨 일이 생겨 면접에 못 가게 된 상황의 대안 제시

Q114 —————————————————— 🎧 MP3 IM3-AL_Q_114

I'm sorry, but there is a problem you need to resolve. **Unfortunately, something happened to you and you cannot make it to the interview.** Call the company and explain what happened to you. Then, give two to three alternatives to **make some arrangements for a schedule change.**

당신이 해결해야 할 문제가 있습니다. 불행히도, 무슨 일이 생겨서 인터뷰를 갈 수 없게 되었습니다. 회사에 전화해서 상황을 설명해 보세요. 그리고 스케줄을 변경하기 위해 2~3개의 대안을 주세요.

🎧 MP3 IM3-AL_A_114

서론
상황설명/30%

- <u>Hey</u>, I need to <u>tell</u> you something.
  - My name is <u>Jean</u> and I have a <u>job</u> interview at your <u>company</u> today.
  - *But <u>something</u> happened and I'm in the <u>hospital</u> now.*
  - I mean, I woke up late this <u>morning</u> and I <u>realized</u> that I'd <u>miss</u> the train, so I <u>ran</u> down the stairs.
  - I don't know <u>why</u>, but I just lost <u>balance</u> and fell over.
  - So, I <u>don't</u> think I can make it to the <u>interview</u>.
  - So, let me give you some <u>options</u> to solve this problem.

본론
대안/60%

- If it's <u>possible,</u> can I <u>postpone</u> it to next week?
  - What do you think?

결론
마무리문장/10%

- Seriously, I <u>need</u> to stay in the hospital for <u>2</u> days.
  - Once again, I'm <u>so</u> sorry.
  - Let me know what's <u>best</u> for you.

- -

- 안녕하세요. 드릴 말씀이 있는데요.
  - 제 이름은 진이고 오늘 면접이 있습니다.
  - **근데 일이 있어서 지금 병원에 있습니다.**
  - 제 말은, 오늘 아침에 늦게 일어났어요, 그래서 기차를 놓칠 것 같음을 깨닫고 계단을 뛰어 내려갔어요.
  - 이유는 모르겠는데, 균형을 잃고 넘어졌습니다.
  - 그래서, 인터뷰에 못 갈 것 같습니다.
  - 그래서, 이 문제를 해결할 수 있는 몇 가지 옵션을 드리려고 합니다.

- 가능하다면, 다음 주로 미룰 수 있을까요?
  - 어떻게 생각하세요?

- 솔직히, 저는 병원에서 이틀 동안 입원해야 합니다.
  - 다시 한번, 정말 죄송합니다.
  - 무엇이 당신에게 최선인지 알려 주세요.

어휘 및 표현
something happened and I'm in the hospital now 일이 생겨 지금 병원에 있습니다   **I woke up late this morning** 오늘 아침에 늦게 일어났어요
I don't think I can make it to the interview 인터뷰에 못 갈 것 같습니다

문제 해결 경험(면접) 중요한 약속/미팅을 취소한 경험

Q115 — 🎧 MP3 IM3-AL_Q_115

That's the end of the situation. **Have you ever had to cancel an appointment or a meeting for some reason? What exactly happened,** and **how did you deal with the situation?** Please give me all the details.

상황이 종료되었습니다. 어떤 이유로 약속이나 회의를 취소한 적이 있나요? 정확히 어떤 일이 일어났나요 그리고 그 상황에 어떻게 대처하였나요? 자세하게 말해 주세요.

🎧 MP3 IM3-AL_A_115

서론
시작문장/10%

- <u>Okay</u> Eva, *Have I ever had to <u>cancel</u> an appointment for some <u>reason?</u>*

본론
했던 일/40%

- **You know,** I had a <u>job</u> interview last week.
  - <u>Actually</u>, the company was located in the <u>middle</u> of the town.
  - Well, I'm <u>pretty</u> sure that the company was around <u>50</u>-minutes away from my place.
  - So I <u>grabbed</u> a cab to go to the interview.

본론
반전/20%

- When I was just <u>about</u> to arrive at the company, I <u>realized</u> that I left my <u>wallet</u> at home. Can you <u>imagine</u> that?
  - So, I <u>asked</u> the driver to go back. <u>Luckily</u>, I searched for <u>2</u> hours and <u>found</u> it!

본론
결과/20%

- In <u>order</u> not to be late for the <u>interview</u>, I <u>asked</u> the driver to go as <u>fast</u> as he could.
  - And I <u>arrived</u> there <u>just</u> on time.
  - In <u>return</u>, I gave him <u>20</u> dollars.

결론
마무리문장/10%

- Um <u>yeah</u>, I think this is <u>all</u> I remember about my <u>job</u> interview. Eva.

- -

- 오케이 에바, **어떤 이유로 약속을 취소한 적 있냐고?**

- 있잖아, 난 저번 주에 면접이 있었어.
  - 사실, 회사는 시내 중심에 위치해 있었어.
  - 음, 회사는 우리 집에서 약 50분 정도 떨어져 있었다고 확신해.
  - 난 면접을 가기 위해 택시를 잡았어.

- 내가 회사에 막 도착했을 때, 난 지갑을 집에 두고 왔다는 것을 깨달았어. 상상이 되니?
  - 그래서, 난 기사님께 되돌아가달라고 부탁했어. 운 좋게도, 난 2시간 동안 찾았고 그걸 마침내 발견했어!

- 면접에 늦지 않기 위하여, 기사님께 최대한 빨리 가달라고 부탁했어.
  - 그리고 난 거기에 정시에 도착했어.
  - 답례로, 난 그에게 20달러를 드렸어.

- 음 예, 내가 기억하는 면접에 대한 거야. 에바.

어휘 및 표현
asked the driver to go as fast as he could 가능한 한 빨리 가달라고 기사님에게 부탁했어   **I arrived there just on time** 시간에 맞춰 도착했어

정보 요청(호텔) 챙겨갈 옷, 그 나라 날씨에 대해 호텔에 전화하여 문의

Q116

MP3 IM3-AL_Q_116

I'd like to give you a situation and ask you to act it out. **You are going on an international trip.** Call one of the hotels in that country and ask **how the weather is like there.** Also, you want to know **what clothes you need to bring.** Please ask two or three more questions to **complete the plans for your trip.**

상황을 드릴 테니 연기해보세요. 당신은 해외여행에 가려고 합니다. 그 나라에 있는 호텔 중 하나에 전화해서 거기 날씨는 어떤지 물어보세요. 또한, 당신은 어떤 옷을 가져가야 할지 알고 싶습니다. 여행 계획을 끝내기 위해서 2~3개 이상의 질문을 물어보세요.

MP3 IM3-AL_A_116

서론
인사말/20%

- Hi there, ***I'm visiting your country next week, but I don't know much about your country.***
  - If it's possible, could I ask you some questions?

본론
질문/70%

- **First of all,** how is the weather like there?
  - Actually, I heard that it started to rain from yesterday. Is it right?
  - You know, I'm planning to go to the beach because watching the sunset is kinda romantic.

- **And also,** what kind of clothes should I bring?
  - I mean, is it very cold at night?
  - I mean, I prefer to go to the beach at night since I can enjoy the peace and quiet.

- **Plus,** where is your hotel? I heard that it is close to the airport. Is it right?
  - So, how far is it from the airport?

- **Lastly,** how much is the suite room?
  - And um, do you have central heating and air-conditioning?
  - You know, I have a VIP membership card.
  - So, can you give me a discount?

결론
마무리문장/10%

- **Alright then,** thanks a lot. See you later.

- 안녕하세요, **제가 당신 나라를 다음 주에 방문하려고 하는데요, 아는 것이 많이 없습니다.**
  - 가능하다면, 몇 가지 여쭤봐도 될까요?

- 첫 번째로, 거기 날씨는 어떤가요?
  - 사실, 어제부터 비가 온다고 들었는데요, 맞나요?
  - 있잖아요, 저는 해변에 가는 것을 계획하고 있습니다. 왜냐하면 노을 보는 것은 꽤 로맨틱하기 때문이죠.

- 그리고 또한, 어떤 옷을 제가 가져가야 하나요?
  - 내 말은, 밤에 거기는 춥나요?
  - 제 말은 평화로움과 조용함을 즐길 수 있기 때문에 저는 밤에 해변을 가는 것을 선호하거든요.

- 추가로, 호텔의 위치는 어디인가요? 공항과 가깝다고 들었는데 맞죠?
  - 그래서, 공항에서 얼마나 먼가요?

- 마지막으로, 스위트룸 가격은 얼마인가요?
  - 그리고 중앙난방과 에어컨이 있죠?
  - 저는 VIP 멤버십 카드가 있습니다.
  - 그래서, 제가 할인을 받을 수 있을까요?

- 알겠습니다 그럼, 감사합니다. 나중에 봅시다.

어휘 및 표현

I'm visiting your country next week 당신 나라를 다음 주에 방문하려 합니다 **how is the weather like there?** 날씨는 어떤가요?
what kind of clothes should I bring? 어떤 종류의 옷을 가져가야 하나요? **how far is it from the airport?** 공항에서 얼마나 걸리나요?
how much is the suite room? 스위트룸은 얼만가요?

문제 해결(호텔) 여행 도중 구입한 옷이 날씨와 맞지않아 상점에 전화 후 해결

Q117 ──────────────── 🎧 MP3 IM3-AL_Q_117

I'm sorry, but there is a problem you need to resolve. **You bought some clothes while your international trip but unfortunately, the weather doesn't match with the clothes you bought.** Call the clothing store and explain the situation. Please tell them **you want to get some other clothes.**

당신이 해결해야 할 문제가 있습니다. 해외여행 동안 몇 개의 옷을 사왔는데 불행히도 날씨는 당신이 샀던 옷과 맞지 않습니다. 옷 가게에 전화해서 상황을 설명해 보세요. 다른 옷이 필요하다는 것을 말해 주세요.

🎧 MP3 IM3-AL_A_117

서론
상황설명/30%

• Hey, I need to tell you something.
  - You know, I bought a T-shirt at your store yesterday.
  - Because I heard that the weather is so sunny in your country.
  - So, I went to the beach at night since I could enjoy the peace and quiet.
  - *But you know what? It was too cold.*

본론
대안/60%

• If it's possible, can I get a refund?
  - Seriously, I can't wear this T-shirt.

• Well or, the only other way is to exchange my clothes.
  - You know, if there is additional payment, I will pay for it.
  - What do you think?

결론
마무리문장/10%

• Once again, I'm so sorry.
  - Let me know what's best for you.

- -

• 안녕하세요, 할 말이 있는데요.
  - 있잖아요, 전 어제 당신 상점에서 티셔츠 하나를 샀습니다.
  - 왜냐하면 날씨가 매우 화창하다고 들었기 때문입니다.
  - 저는 평화로움과 조용함을 즐기기 위해 밤에 해변에 갔습니다.
  - **그거 알아요? 너무 추웠습니다.**

• 가능하다면, 환불을 받을 수 있을까요?
  - 솔직히, 저는 이 티셔츠를 입을 수 없습니다.

• 음 아니면, 다른 유일한 방법은 제 옷을 교환하는 것입니다.
  - 추가적으로 내야 할 돈이 있다면, 그것을 지불할 수 있습니다.
  - 어떻게 생각하세요?

• 다시 한번, 정말 죄송합니다.
  - 어느 게 최선인지 말해주세요.

어휘 및 표현
I can't wear this T-shirt 이 티셔츠는 입을 수 없어요   **the only other way is to exchange my clothes** 다른 유일한 방법은 제 옷을 교환하는 거예요

문제 해결 경험(호텔) 예상치 못한 날씨로 인해 겪은 문제의 해결 경험

Q118 —

🎧 MP3 IM3-AL_Q_118

That's the end of the situation. **Have you ever had any trouble due to an unexpected weather? Where** were you? What happened and who were you with? **How did you deal with the situation?** Please tell me everything about what happened on that day.

상황은 종료되었습니다. 예상치 못한 날씨 때문에 어려움을 겪은 적이 있나요? 당신은 어디에 있었나요? 무슨 일이 있었고 누구와 함께 있었나요? 그 상황을 어떻게 처리했나요? 그 날에 일어났던 일을 모두 말해 주세요.

🎧 MP3 IM3-AL_A_118

서론
시작문장/10%

- <u>Great,</u> you mean *a time I had trouble due to an <u>unexpected</u> weather?*

본론
했던 일/40%

- **For me, I** <u>really</u> enjoy going to <u>music</u> festivals because it helps me <u>release</u> stress.
  - And I <u>always</u> take my friend Ryan since he knows a <u>lot</u> about music.
  - <u>Last</u> summer, we went to the <u>most</u> famous <u>beach</u> festival in Korea.
  - As you can <u>imagine</u>, the festival was <u>packed</u> with <u>lots</u> of people.
  - When we <u>got</u> in, as I <u>expected</u>, there were <u>full</u> of people dancing.
  - After like <u>20</u> minutes? We <u>totally</u> lost track of time, we <u>danced</u>, jumped, I mean, we just went <u>crazy</u>.

본론
반전/20%

- **You know,** the music was <u>great</u>, and we had <u>so</u> much fun.
  - But um, <u>all</u> of a sudden, it started to <u>rain</u>. I mean, the weather was <u>so</u> sunny, but it <u>poured</u>!
  - Guess what! We were <u>completely</u> soaked.
  - Oh my god, it was <u>annoying</u> at first, but I pretended like it was ok.

본론
결과/20%

- **In order <u>not</u> to ruin our day,** we went to a bar and <u>grabbed</u> a beer
  - I mean, the bar was <u>extremely</u> clean, and the <u>people</u> were <u>so</u> friendly.

결론
마무리문장/10%

- **Um <u>yeah</u>,** I think this is <u>all</u> I remember about *a time I had <u>trouble</u> due to an <u>unexpected</u> weather.* Eva.

- -

- **좋아, 예상치 못한 날씨 때문에 어려움을 겪은 적 말하는 거지?**

- 나로 말할 것 같으면, 스트레스를 해소하는 데 도움이 되기 때문에 뮤직 페스티벌에 가는 것을 정말 좋아해.
  - 나는 내 친구 Ryan을 항상 데리고 가 왜냐하면 그는 음악에 대해 많이 알기 때문이야.
  - 지난여름에, 우리는 한국에서 가장 유명한 해변 페스티벌에 갔어.
  - 네가 상상할 수 있듯, 페스티벌은 많은 사람들로 가득 차 있었어.
  - 우리가 들어갔을 때, 예상했듯이, 춤을 추고 있는 많은 사람들로 가득 차 있었어.
  - 20분 후쯤? 우리는 시간이 가는 줄도 몰랐고 춤췄고, 뛰었고, 제정신이 아니었어.

- 있잖아, 음악은 좋았고, 우리는 정말 즐거웠어. 그러나 갑자기, 우리는 비가 내리기 시작했어.
  - 내 말은, 날씨는 화창했었는데, 갑자기 비가 쏟아졌어!
  - 우리는 완벽하게 젖었어.
  - 이럴 수가, 처음에는 짜증 났지만 난 괜찮은 척했어.

- 그날을 망치지 않기 위하여, 우리는 바에 가서 맥주를 마셨어.
  - 내 말은, 바는 정말 깨끗했고, 사람들은 정말 친절했어.

- **음 예, 이게 예상치 못한 날씨 때문에 어려움을 겪은 적에 대해 기억하는 모든 거야. 에바.**

어휘 및 표현
I really enjoy going to music festivals 뮤직페스티벌 가는 것을 즐겨   **I always take my friend** 난 항상 친구를 데려가

정보 요청(커피숍) 새로 생긴 커피숍에서 커피 주문 관련 문의

Q119 ———————————————————— 🎧 MP3 IM3-AL_Q_119

I'd like to give you a situation and ask you to act it out. **You would like to get some coffee from a new coffee shop that has opened recently.** Call the coffee shop and ask three to four questions about **their menu and how to order the coffee.**

상황을 드릴 테니 연기해보세요. 당신은 최근에 오픈한 커피숍에서 커피를 주문하고 싶습니다. 커피숍에 전화해서 메뉴와 커피 주문 하는 법에 대해 3~4개의 질문을 해보세요.

🎧 MP3 IM3-AL_A_119

서론
인사말/20%

• **Hi there,** I <u>heard</u> that your <u>coffee</u> shop has opened recently. Is it right?
  - ***I would like to get some <u>coffee</u> at your <u>coffee</u> shop.***
  - If it's <u>possible</u>, could I ask you some <u>questions</u>?

본론
질문/70%

• **First of all,** how much is <u>Latte</u>?
  - Well, I <u>always</u> order Latte in the <u>morning</u>.
  - Is it <u>always</u> filled with lots of <u>people</u>?
  - Then I <u>prefer</u> going there <u>early</u> in the morning. What do you think?

• **Plus,** do you have an <u>app</u> to order online?
  - You know, I <u>don't</u> want to stand in a <u>long</u> line.

• In <u>addition</u>, where is your <u>coffee</u> shop?
  - I <u>heard</u> that it is in the ABC <u>tower</u>. Is it right?

결론
마무리문장/10%

• <u>Alright</u> **then,** <u>thanks</u> a lot. See you later.

• 안녕하세요, 최근에 커피숍을 오픈했다고 들었는데요, 맞죠?
  - 커피를 주문하고 싶은데요.
  - 가능하다면, 몇 가지 질문을 해도 될까요?

• 첫 번째로, 라테 가격은 얼마죠?
  - 음, 전 항상 아침에 라테를 주문합니다.
  - 항상 많은 사람들로 가득 차 있죠?
  - 그렇다면 아침 일찍 방문하는 것을 선호하는데요, 어떻게 생각하세요?

• 또한, 온라인으로 주문할 수 있는 앱이 있나요?
  - 전 긴 줄을 서서 기다리고 싶지 않아요.

• 추가로, 커피숍이 어디에 있나요?
  - ABC타워 안에 있다고 들었습니다. 맞죠?

• 알겠습니다 그럼, 고맙습니다. 나중에 뵐게요.

어휘 및 표현
I heard that your coffee shop has opened recently 최근에 커피숍을 오픈했다고 들었어요
do you have an app to order online? 온라인으로 주문할 수 있는 앱이 있나요?

문제 해결(커피숍) 잘못 배달된 커피 주문의 대안 제시

Q120 ———————————————————————— 🎧 MP3 IM3-AL_Q_120

I'm sorry, but there is a problem you need to resolve. **You got your coffee delivered to your house. Unfortunately, you find out that you've got the wrong order.** Call the coffee shop and explain the situation. Then, give two to three alternatives to **solve the problem.**

당신이 해결해야 할 문제가 있습니다. 당신의 집으로 배달된 커피를 받았습니다. 불행히도, 당신이 잘못 주문했다는 것을 발견했습니다. 커피숍에 전화해서 상황을 설명해 주세요. 이 문제를 해결할 수 있는 2~3가지 대안에 대해 말해 주세요.

—————————————————————————————————————— 🎧 MP3 IM3-AL_A_120

서론
상황설명/30%

- **Hey**, I need to tell you <u>something</u>.
  - *You know, I got my <u>coffee</u> but <u>unfortunately</u>, I found out that I've got the <u>wrong</u> order.*
  - Well, it is <u>very</u> annoying.
  - So, let me give you some <u>options</u> to solve this <u>problem</u>.

본론
대안/60%

- **If it's <u>possible</u>,** can I get a <u>refund</u>?
  - Seriously, I <u>always</u> order Latte, but I got a hot <u>chocolate</u>.

- **Well or,** the <u>only</u> other way is to <u>exchange</u> my coffee.
  - You know, if there is <u>additional</u> payment, I can pay for it.
  - What do you think?

결론
마무리문장/10%

- <u>Alright</u> then.
  - Let me know as <u>soon</u> as possible.

- -

- 안녕하세요, 할 말이 있는데요.
  - 있잖아요, 제가 커피를 받았는데 불행히도, 제가 잘못 주문했다는 것을 발견했습니다.
  - 음, 정말 짜증 나는데요.
  - 그래서, 이 문제를 해결할 수 있는 몇 가지 옵션을 제안하려고 합니다.

- 가능하다면, 환불을 받을 수 있을까요?
  - 실은, 저는 항상 라테를 주문합니다, 그런데 핫초코를 받았어요.

- 음 아니면, 다른 유일한 방법은 제 커피를 교환하는 것입니다.
  - 추가적으로 내야 할 돈이 있다면, 그것을 지불할 수 있습니다.
  - 어떻게 생각하세요?

- 알겠습니다
  - 그럼. 최대한 빨리 말해주세요.

어휘 및 표현
I found out that I've got the wrong order 내가 주문을 잘못한 것을 알아차렸어   **it is very annoying** 굉장히 짜증나나
I can pay for it 내가 지불할게

문제 해결 경험(커피숍) 음식이 잘못 주문되었던 경험과 해결책

Q121 ──────────────────── 🎧 MP3 IM3-AL_Q_121

That's the end of the situation. **Have you ever been in a situation that you had ordered something but got the wrong order? Where** were you and **what did you order? What exactly happened and how did you deal with the situation?** Please describe the event in detail.

상황은 종료되었습니다. 당신이 어떤 것을 주문했으나 잘못된 것을 받았던 경험이 있나요? 어디서 그리고 무엇을 주문했나요? 정확히 어떤 일이 있었고 어떻게 그 상황을 처리했나요? 그 사건에 대해 자세히 묘사해 주세요.

🎧 MP3 IM3-AL_A_121

서론
시작문장/10%

• <u>Alright!</u> Let me tell you *a time I got the <u>wrong</u> order at a restaurant.*

본론
했던 일/40%

• In <u>order</u> to celebrate my <u>dad's</u> birthday, my <u>family</u> went to <u>Korean</u> restaurant which was located in the <u>middle</u> of the town.
  - You know, the restaurant was <u>extremely</u> clean, and the people were <u>so</u> friendly.
  - As you can <u>imagine</u>, the restaurant was <u>packed</u> with <u>lots</u> of people.

본론
반전/20%

• After like <u>30 min</u>, I <u>still</u> haven't received my <u>order</u> and I <u>started</u> to lose my <u>patience</u>.
  - Oh my god, it was <u>annoying</u> at first, but In order <u>not</u> to ruin my dad's <u>birthday</u>, I pretended like it was ok.
  - But I <u>realized</u> that I ordered the <u>wrong</u> food.

본론
결과/20%

• So, I <u>called</u> the waiter and explained the <u>whole</u> situation.
  - <u>Thankfully</u>, they offered a better food. <u>Moreover</u>, they <u>corrected</u> my order. It was <u>complimentary</u>.
  - <u>Actually</u>, it was the <u>best</u> customer service I've ever had.

결론
마무리문장/10%

• <u>Okay</u> Eva, this is *about a time I got the <u>wrong</u> order at a restaurant.*

- -

• **그래! 레스토랑에서 주문을 잘못했던 적에 대해 말해줄게.**

• 우리 아빠 생일을 축하하기 위해, 우리 가족은 시내 중심에 위치해 있는 한식당에 갔어.
  - 있잖아, 레스토랑은 정말 깨끗했고, 사람들은 정말 친절했어.
  - 네가 예상했듯이, 레스토랑은 많은 사람들로 가득 차 있었어.

• 30분 후에도, 난 여전히 내 주문을 받지 못하였고 인내심을 잃기 시작했어.
  - 이럴 수가, 난 처음엔 짜증 났지만, 우리 아빠의 생일을 망치지 않기 위해 괜찮은 척했어.
  - 근데 내가 음식을 잘못 주문한 것을 깨달았어.

• 그래서, 난 웨이터를 불렀고, 전체 상황을 설명했어.
  - 고맙게도, 그들은 더 좋은 음식을 제공했어. 게다가 그들은 내 주문을 정정해 줬어. 그건 무료였어.
  - 실제로, 내가 겪었던 최고의 고객 서비스였어.

• 오케이 에바, **이게 내가 레스토랑에서 주문을 잘못했던 경험이야.**

어휘 및 표현
I realized that I ordered the wrong food 잘못된 음식을 주문한 것을 깨달았어   Moreover, they corrected my order 게다가, 내 주문을 정정해줬어
It was complimentary 무료였어

정보 요청(친척집) 2일 동안 빈 친척집을 봐주기 위해 해야 할 일 질문

Q122 ─────

I'd like to give you a situation and ask you act it out. **One of your relatives is going on a trip for two days. Their house will be empty, and you've been asked to watch the house while they are gone.** Call your relative and ask three or four questions about **what you have to do for two days.**

상황을 드릴 테니 연기해보세요. 당신은 친척들 중 한 명은 이틀 동안 여행에 갈 것입니다. 그들의 집은 빌 것이고 당신은 그들은 집을 비운 동안 집을 지켜달라고 부탁 받았습니다. 친척에게 전화해서 이틀 동안 해야 할 일에 대해서 3~4개의 질문을 해보세요.

서론
인사말/20%

- **Hi Ryan, I** heard that you are going on a trip for two days.
  - *And you want me to watch the house for two days. Is it right?*
  - If it's possible, could I ask you some questions?

본론
질문/70%

- First of all, one of the biggest issues is taking out the trash.
  - How do you recycle?
  - When it comes to my town, there are many recycling centers which are normally located in the middle of the town.
  - How about your town?

- Plus, where is the grocery store and what should I buy there?
  - Well, I'm pretty sure that the nearest grocery store is around 20-minutes away from your place.
  - Actually, I'm pretty sure that I can get a discount since I'm a regular.

- In addition, when it comes to your house, there are three bedrooms, and two baths.
  - Do I have to vacuum all the rooms?

결론
마무리문장/10%

- Alright then, thanks a lot. See you later.

- 안녕 라이언, 이틀 동안 여행 간다고 들었어.
  - **그리고 이틀 동안 집을 내가 봐주길 원하는 거 맞지?**
  - 가능하다면, 뭐 좀 물어봐도 될까?

- 첫 번째로, 가장 큰 문제 중에 하나는 쓰레기를 버리는 거야.
  - 어떻게 재활용을 해?
  - 우리 동네에 대해서 말한다면 보통 시내 중심에 위치해 있는 재활용센터들이 많이 있어.
  - 너희 동네는 어때?

- 추가로, 식료품점은 어디 있고 내가 거기서 뭘 사야 해?
  - 음, 난 가장 가까운 식료품점이 너희 집에서 약 20분 거리라고 알고 있어.
  - 실제로, 난 거기 단골이라서 할인을 받을 수 있다고 꽤 확신해.

- 게다가, 너희 집에 관해서, 3개의 침실과 2개의 욕실이 있어.
  - 내가 모든 방을 청소해야 돼?

- 알겠어 그럼, 고마워. 나중에 보자.

어휘 및 표현

one of the biggest issues is taking out the trash 가장 큰 이슈 중 하나는 쓰레기 버리는 거야   **what should I buy there?** 그곳에서 뭘 사야해?
Do I have to vacuum all the rooms? 모든 방을 청소해야 해?

문제 해결(친척집) 열쇠가 없어 친척집에 못 들어가는 상황의 대안 제시

Q123 ━━━━━━━━━━━━━━━━━━ 🎧 MP3 IM3-AL_Q_123

I'm sorry, but there is a problem you need to resolve. **You are at your relative's house, but you can't get into the house because you don't have the key.** Call your relative and ask two to three questions to **solve the problem.**

당신이 해결해야 할 문제가 있습니다. 당신은 친척 집에 갔습니다. 그러나 키가 없어서 집에 들어갈 수 없습니다. 친척집에 전화해서 문제를 해결하기 위해 2~3개의 대안을 물어보세요.

━━━━━━━━━━━━━━━━━━━━━━━━━━━━━━ 🎧 MP3 IM3-AL_A_123

서론
상황설명/60%

• <u>Hey</u>, I need to tell you something.
 - *You know, I'm at your <u>house</u>, but I <u>can't</u> get into the house because I <u>don't</u> have the key.*
 - Guess what? it <u>started</u> to rain. I mean, the weather was <u>so</u> sunny, but it's <u>pouring</u>!
 - And I am <u>completely</u> soaked.
 - Well, it is <u>very</u> annoying.
 - So, let me give you some <u>options</u> to solve this <u>problem</u>.

본론
대안/30%

• <u>Obviously,</u> people can <u>easily</u> call the <u>lock</u> smith if they <u>lose</u> their <u>keys</u>.
 - You know, I was in the <u>same</u> situation before, and I <u>ended</u> up spending $<u>200</u> USD.
 - So, can you give me their <u>numbers</u>?

결론
마무리문장/10%

• <u>Alright</u> then.
 - Let me know as <u>soon</u> as possible.

- -

• 안녕, 할 말이 있어.
 - **있잖아, 난 집에 왔는데 키가 없어서 집을 들어갈 수가 없어.**
 - 있잖아, 근데 비가 내리기 시작했어.
 - 내 말은 날씨는 매우 화창했었는데 갑자기 비가 퍼부었어.
 - 그리고 난 완전히 젖었어.
 - 음, 난 정말 짜증 나.
 - 내가 이 문제를 해결할 수 있는 몇 가지 옵션을 알려줄게.

• 명백하게, 사람들이 키를 잃어버린다면 락스미스를 쉽게 부를 수 있거든.
 - 있잖아, 난 전에 같은 상황이 있었는데, 난 결국 200달러를 쓰는 것으로 끝이 났어.
 - 그래서, 그들 번호를 알려줄 수 있어?

• 알겠어 그럼.
 - 가능한 한 빨리 알려줘.

━━━━━━━━━━━━━━━━━━━━━━━━━━━━━━━━━━━

어휘 및 표현
I can't get into the house because I don't have the key 열쇠가 없어서 집 안으로 못 들어가겠어
people can easily call the lock smith if they lose their keys 사람들이 키를 잃어버린다면 락스미스를 쉽게 부를 수 있어
So, can you give me their numbers? 그들 번호를 좀 줄래?

문제 해결 경험(친척집) 가족/친구와의 약속을 못 지켰던 경험과 해결책

Q124 ——————————— 🎧 MP3 IM3-AL_Q_124

That's the end of the situation. **Have you ever had an incident that you couldn't keep a promise with a family member or a friend? When** was it? **What was the main reason you couldn't keep the promise?** What did you do to **solve the problem?** Please give me all the details.

상황이 종료되었습니다. 가족 또는 친구 구성원과의 약속을 지킬 수 없었던 사건이 있었던 적이 있나요? 언제 였나요? 약속을 지킬 수 없었던 가장 큰 이유는 무엇이었나요? 그 문제를 해결하기 위해 어떤 것을 했나요? 상세히 말해주세요.

🎧 MP3 IM3-AL_A_124

서론
시작문장/10%
- **Okay Eva,** experience about *an <u>incident</u> that I couldn't <u>keep</u> a promise with a friend?*

본론
했던 일/40%
- **When I was little,** I <u>used</u> to go to the park to <u>run</u> with my friend John.
  - Because there was a <u>huge</u> park and there was a <u>huge</u> running track where you could see <u>lots</u> of people exercising.
  - I've known him since I was <u>10</u>, and I <u>always</u> ran with my friend John.
  - As <u>usual</u>, we <u>planned</u> to run at the park.
  - But you know, on that day, I felt <u>really</u> awful.

본론
반전/20%
- **While I was on <u>my</u> way to the <u>park,</u>** I don't know <u>why</u>, but I lost <u>balance</u> and fell over.
  - Oh my god, it was <u>so</u> painful, and I was crying. So, I <u>called</u> an ambulance.

본론
결과/20%
- **Because my friend was <u>so</u> mad,** I <u>apologized</u> him.
  - Well, the <u>only</u> other way was to <u>postpone</u> it till the following week.
  - So, he just <u>ended</u> up coming to the <u>hospital</u> to visit me.
  - In return, I <u>bought</u> him a good dinner.

결론
마무리문장/10%
- **Um <u>yeah,</u>** I think this is <u>all</u> I remember *about an <u>incident</u> that I <u>couldn't</u> keep a promise with a friend.* Eva.

- -

- **오케이 에바,** 내가 **친구**와 약속을 지킬 수 없었던 사건에 대한 경험?

- 내가 어렸을 때, 친구 존과 함께 공원에서 뛰곤 했어.
  - 왜냐하면 큰 공원이 있었는데 거기에는 많은 사람들이 운동하는 것을 볼 수 있는 큰 러닝트랙이 있었어.
  - 난 그를 10살 때부터 알아왔고, 난 항상 내 친구 존과 함께 뛰었어.
  - 평소와 같이, 우리는 공원에서 뛰기로 했어.
  - 그러나, 있잖아 그날에, 난 매우 몸이 안 좋았어.

- 내가 공원에 가고 있던 중에, 난 이유를 모르겠는데 균형을 잃고 넘어졌어.
  - 이럴 수가, 그건 고통스러웠고, 난 울고 있었어. 그래서, 앰뷸런스를 불렀어.

- 존은 매우 화났기 때문에, 난 그에게 사과했어.
  - 음, 유일한 다른 방법은 다음 주까지 공원 가는 것을 연기하는 거였어.
  - 그래서, 그는 날 병문안 와주었어.
  - 답례로, 난 그에게 좋은 저녁식사를 대접했어.

- 음 예, 이게 내가 **친구**와 약속을 지킬 수 없었던 사건에 대해 기억하는 거야. 에바.

어휘 및 표현
As usual, we planned to run at the park 평소와 같이, 우린 공원에서 뛰기로 했어
he just ended up coming to the hospital to visit me 날 위해 병문안을 와 줬어

30강

시험 전 정리

시험 준비

시험 화면

시험 준비

실제 시험과 같은 순서로 준비하였습니다.

1. 첫 화면

2. Background Survey

1. 어느 분야에 종사하고 계십니까?
- 일 경험 없음

2. 학생이십니까?
- 아니오
- 수강 후 5년 이상 지남

3. 어디에서 살고 계십니까?
- 개인 주택이나 아파트에 홀로 거주

4. 여가 활동으로 무엇을 하십니까?
- 콘서트 보기 ■ 공원 가기 ■ 해변 가기
- 술집/바에 가기 ■ 카페/커피전문점 가기 ■ 쇼핑하기

5. 취미나 관심사는 무엇입니까?
- 음악 감상하기

6. 주로 어떤 운동을 즐기십니까?
- 조깅 ■ 걷기

7. 어떤 휴가나 출장을 다녀온 경험이 있습니까?
- 집에서 보내는 휴가 ■ 국내 여행 ■ 해외 여행

3. Self Assessment

희망 등급	난이도
IL	**난이도 1** 나는 10단어 이하의 단어로 말할 수 있습니다. **난이도 2** 나는 기본적인 물건, 색깔, 요일, 음식, 의류, 숫자 등을 말할 수 있습니다. 나는 항상 완벽한 문장을 구사하지 못하고 간단한 질문도 하기 어렵습니다.
IM1	**난이도 3** 나는 나 자신, 직장, 친한 사람과 장소, 일상에 대한 기본적인 정보를 간단한 문장으로 전달할 수 있습니다. 간단한 질문을 할 수 있습니다.
IM2	**난이도 4** 나는 나 자신, 일상, 일/학교와 취미에 대해 간단한 대화를 할 수 있습니다. 나는 이 친근한 주제와 일상에 대해 쉽게 간단한 문장들을 만들 수 있습니다. 나는 또한 내가 원하는 질문도 할 수 있습니다.
IM3 – AL	**난이도 5** 나는 친근한 주제와 가정, 일, 학교, 개인과 사회적 관심사에 대해 자신 있게 대화할 수 있습니다. 나는 일어난 일과 일어나고 있는 일, 일어날 일에 대해 합리적으로 자신 있게 말할 수 있습니다. 필요한 경우 설명도 할 수 있습니다. 일상 생활에서 예기치 못한 상황이 발생하더라도 임기응변으로 대처할 수 있습니다. **난이도 6** 나는 개인적, 사회적 또는 전문적 주제에 나의 의견을 제시하여 토론할 수 있습니다. 나는 다양하고 어려운 주제에 대해 정확하고 다양한 어휘를 사용하며 자세히 설명할 수 있습니다.

4. Pre-Test Setup

5. 시험 시작!

시험 화면(15개 문제 준비)

실제 시험 화면과 비슷한 이미지로 구성하였습니다.

15개 문제의 'Play' 버튼 클릭 전 유형, 답변 Format 생각 정리

A. 준비시간 – 20초

(매 문제마다 'Play' 버튼 클릭 전 20초간 문제의 유형, 답변 Format을 생각하는 시간을 가집니다.)

B. 답변 시간 – 1분 ~ 2분

(답변 시간이 중요하진 않지만 적어도 1분, 최대 2분간 답변 Format을 생각하시며 답변하시기 바랍니다.)

1번 – 자기소개

흔히 스피킹 시험의 첫 번째 문제는 긴장하여 망칠 확률이 높으므로 굳이 자기소개를 위한 스크립트 준비는 필요가 없습니다.
다만 배운 문장들을 토대로 즉흥적으로 답변합니다.

2번 – 묘사

묘사 유형임을 인지하고 'Play' 버튼 클릭 전, 3가지 묘사 종류를 생각합니다. 답변 Format을 생각하거나 시작문장의 연습을 해도 괜찮습니다.

3번 – 세부묘사

2번에서 이미 주제를 알았기에 세부묘사의 준비는 해당 주제와 관련된 묘사 문장을 생각합니다.

4번 – 경험

이 또한 주제를 이미 알고 있기에 'Play' 전 어떤 경험을 사용할지, 답변 Format을 제대로 짠 후 답변합니다.

5번 – 묘사

다시 새로운 주제의 묘사 유형입니다. 마찬가지로 'Play' 버튼 클릭 전 묘사 종류를 생각합니다.

6번 – 경험

이 또한 주제를 이미 알고 있기에 'Play' 전 어떤 경험을 사용할지, 답변 Format을 제대로 짠 후 답변합니다.

7번 – 경험

같은 주제의 추가 경험이므로 'Play' 전 어떤 경험을 사용할지, 답변 Format을 제대로 짠 후 답변합니다.

8번 – 묘사

다시 새로운 주제의 묘사 유형입니다. 마찬가지로 'Play' 버튼 클릭 전 묘사 종류를 생각합니다.

9번 – 경험

이 또한 주제를 이미 알고 있기에 'Play' 전 어떤 경험을 사용할지, 답변 Format을 제대로 짠 후 답변합니다.

10번 – 경험

같은 주제의 추가 경험이므로 'Play' 전 어떤 경험을 사용할지, 답변 Format을 제대로 짠 후 답변합니다.

11번 – 정보요청 롤플레이

인사말 – 질문 – 마무리문장의 Format을 잘 생각한 후, 'Play' 버튼 클릭 후, 문제의 키워드를 잘 캐치합니다.

12번 – 문제해결 롤플레이

상황설명 – 대안 – 마무리문장의 Format을 잘 생각한 후, 'Play' 버튼 클릭 후, 문제의 키워드를 잘 캐치합니다.

13번 – 문제해결 경험

12번 문제해결 롤플레이와 연관성이 있는 문제해결 경험으로 필히 해결점을 제시해 줍니다.

14번 – 세부묘사

다시 새로운 주제의 세부묘사 유형이며 비교, 이슈, 뉴스, 어려움 등의 난이도 높은 문제입니다.

15번 – 세부묘사

14번 주제의 세부묘사 유형이며 비교, 이슈, 뉴스, 어려움 등의 난이도 높은 문제입니다.

APPENDIX

진짜녀석들 OPIc IM3-AL MP3 질문 리스트(유형)

묘사 질문 MP3

🎧 MP3 IM3-AL_Q_1~19

개방공간 묘사

You indicated in the survey that you like to go to **the beach.** Describe your favorite beach for me. Where is it? What does it look like? How often do you visit that beach? Please tell me in detail.

You indicated in the survey that you go on **international trips.** I would like you to describe one of the countries or cities you usually visit. What does the place look like? Why do you like to visit there? How are the people like there? Please tell me in detail.

You indicated in the survey that you go to **the parks** with your friends. Please tell me about one of the parks that you usually visit. Where is it located? What does it look like? Please describe your favorite park in detail.

I would like you to describe **the geography of your country.** Are there mountains, lakes or rivers? Please describe the geographical features of your country in as much detail as possible.

I would like to ask you about **a country that is nearby your country.** What is the name of that country? What is special about that country? How are the people there? Please give me all the details.

- -

독립공간 묘사

You indicated in the survey that you go to cafes or coffee shops. What cafes or coffee shops are there in your neighborhood? Which café do you like to go to and why? Please describe one of your favorite cafes in detail.

I would like to ask you about your **favorite shopping mall.** Where is it located and what does it look like? Describe one of your favorite shopping malls in as much detail as possible.

A lot of people like to eat out during the weekends. I would like to know **one of your favorite restaurants** in your area. Where is it located? What does it look like? Also, what kind of food do they serve and why do you like to visit there? Please tell me in detail.

I would like to ask you where you live. Please describe your **house** in detail. What does it look like? How many rooms are there? Also, which room is your favorite room and why?

I would like to ask you about **the banks** in your country. What do they typically look like? Where are they usually located? Please tell me about the banks in your country.

- -

일반적 묘사

What do people normally **do on the Internet?** Do they play games, listen to music, or watch movies? Please tell me about the things people do online.

I would like to know **what you like most about your cell phone.** Maybe you like the camera or other functions. Tell me why you like these kinds of features.

I would like to ask you about **how recycling is practiced** in your country. What do people especially do? Please tell me about all the different kinds of items that you recycle.

How do people in your country move around? **What types of transportation** do people usually use? Why do they use those types of transportation? Please tell me how people move around.

Please tell me about **some holidays in your country.** What do people in your country do to celebrate these holidays? Please tell me about some holidays in your country.

I would like you to **describe one of your family members or friends.** What is he or she like? What is special about that person?

I'd like you to describe **a healthy person you know of.** Who is he or she? What makes that person healthy? Why do you think that way? Please tell me everything about the things that make that person healthy.

I would like to ask you about **how people in your country dress.** What kind of clothes do they wear? Tell me about fashion styles in your country in as much detail as possible.

Please tell me about **the weather and seasons in your country.** What is the weather like in each season? Which season do you like? Please tell me in detail.

진짜녀석들 OPIc IM3–AL MP3 질문 리스트(유형)

세부 묘사 질문 MP3

일반

🎧 MP3 IM3-AL_Q_20~47

전자기기
집에서 사용 전자기기

What types of home appliances are used in your house? It must be a refrigerator, a microwave, or a dishwasher. Tell me about **the appliances used for various tasks in your home.**

산업
일하고 싶은 기업

What kinds of companies do young people in your country want to work? Why do they want to work at those companies? Please give me some examples of the industry or company.

가족/친구
대화 주제

What kinds of topics do you commonly talk about with your family or friends? When was the last time you talked to them? What did you talk about? Please give me all the details.

휴일
특별한점

Tell me about **some holidays in your country.** What do people normally do during those holidays? What are some special things about those holidays? Give me all the details.

산업
진로를 위해 하는 일

I would like to know **what people do to get a job** in your country. Do they go to school? And what do they do when they get a job? Do they get any training at the company? Tell me everything they do to get a job.

비교 변화 차이점

하우징
과거현재 비교

I would like to ask you about **houses in your country.** Perhaps houses have changed over the years. **How is the structure of the houses different from the past?**

레스토랑
음식점 비교

You can expect set menus at chain restaurants such as Outback. On the other hand, **small local restaurants** have their own menus, and you may not know what to expect. **Talk about the difference between those two.**

전화기
예전지금 전화기 비교

Do you remember the phone you used for the first time? What is **the difference between the phone you used back then and the phone you use now?**

재활용
과거현재 비교

How is recycling you practiced when you were young different from what you do today? What are **the differences** and **similarities?** Please tell me about how recycling has changed over the years.

공원
어른,아이들
공원활동 시설비교

Now, describe the differences in activities between children and adults at the park. What are **the differences?** How are **the facilities** at parks different for children and adults?

모임
과거-현재 모임 차이

Let's talk about the ways of gatherings. It has changed over the years. **How was it in the past? How is it now?** What are **the differences and the similarities?** Please give me all the details.

건강
유지방법 차이

In the past, tell me **how your parents' generation kept their health. How is it different from what your generation does?** Give me all the details.

인터넷
연령별 인터넷 이용 차이

How is Internet usage different among generations? What do **younger people** commonly **do online?** What do **older people do online?** Please give me all the details.

가족/친구
두명 유사점/차이점

Now, I would like you to pick two of your family members or friends and tell me about **their differences and similarities.** Please give me all details.

전자기기
우리 삶의 변화

Home appliances have changed our lives. **How was life before the appliances different from life now?** Tell me the biggest change that has had an impact on our lives. Please give me specific details.

레스토랑
건강식 메뉴 변화 추세

People have become a lot more health-conscious than in the past. So, lots of restaurants are changing their menus for those customers. Talk about **the changes you notice about a restaurant related to this trend.**

식품
식품 구매 방식 변화

How has the way people bought food changed over the years? Where did people buy food in the past, and where do they **buy it now?**

지형/이웃국가
국가 변화 추세

Tell me about a country that is **a geographically similar to your country.** What are **the changes** that the country has gone through in recent years? Please give me all the details.

진짜녀석들 OPIc IM3-AL MP3 질문 리스트(유형)

세부 묘사 질문 MP3

뉴스기사

🎧 MP3 IM3-AL_Q_20~47

식품
식품 오염 뉴스

Food can become contaminated because of bacteria. It can cause consumer illness. **I would like you to tell me about an incident you heard on the news** regarding food contamination. What was **the problem?** How was it dealt with?

재활용
최근 재활용 뉴스

Let's talk about **one of the recycling issues** that you heard in the news recently. **What was the news about?** What is being done to **solve the issue?** Please give me all the details about that issue on recycling.

지형/이웃국가
이웃국가 정치경제 기사

I would like to ask you about **an article** you read about **the country you have mentioned before.** What was the issue about? Also, how was it **related to the politics or the economy of that country?**

이슈 어려움

건강
최근 언급 건강관련 이슈

There must be some issues related to our health in the news these days. Do people in your country talk about that topic a lot? Please **describe common health-related concerns people have.**

공원
관련 이슈 및 해결책

I would like to ask you about **one of the issues about parks in your country.** What are some challenges public parks are faced with these days? Discuss what has caused these concerns. **What steps do we take in order to solve this problem?**

인터넷
이슈,보안문제

Let's talk about some issues that people talk about regarding the Internet. What are their concerns, and why are those concerns a problem? Are there any security problems? If so, talk about the issue.

전화기
사회적 문제

Now, **let's talk about some issues related to cell phones. Why** do people talk about that topic? Why is it **a problem?** Please give me all the details.

하우징
임대 어려움

There must be **a problem when people rent a house. Why do you think those problems occur? How do** people in your country **solve those problems?**

모임
계획과정 어려운 점

It is not easy to make plans for gatherings. **What are some issues related to making plans for gathering? How** do people **deal with those problems?**

휴일
휴일관련 걱정거리

Let's talk about some issues or concerns that people in your country have regarding holidays. What steps do people need to take in order to **solve this problem?**

진짜녀석들 OPIc IM3-AL MP3 질문 리스트(유형)

묘사 모의고사 질문 MP3

🎧 MP3 IM3-AL_Q_48~53

2번
집휴가 묘사

You indicated in the survey that **you take vacations at home.** Who do you normally meet and spend time during your vacations at home?

3번
집휴가 비교

What do people in your country normally do during vacations at home? **How has their ways of spending vacations changed over the years?** Please tell me in detail.

5번
걷는 장소 묘사

You indicated in the survey that you like to **take a walk.** Where do you normally take a walk? What does the place look like? And where is it located? Please describe the place you normally take a walk.

8번
콘서트 묘사

You indicated in the survey that **you often go to concerts.** What type of concerts do you enjoy going to? And why do you like going to concerts? Please tell me in detail.

14번
국내여행
(과거/현재 어려워진 점)

How is traveling today different from the past? What are some difficulties that people go through regarding going on domestic trips? Has traveling become more difficult in any way? If so, tell me why.

15번
국내여행
(여행객 우려/걱정)

What are **some issues people have related to traveling?** What do people need to do in order to solve those problems?

진짜녀석들 OPIc IM3-AL MP3 질문 리스트(유형)

경험 질문 MP3

어릴적 경험

I would like to ask you about a restaurant you used to go when you were a child. **Who** did you go there with? **What** was the **place like?** What did you **eat?** **What** do you remember most about that restaurant? Tell me about that experience in as much detail as possible.

Now, think about what you did during your **free time as a child.** You may have spent time with your parents or with your friends. I would like you to tell me about **how** you mostly **spent** your free time when you were a child.

Please tell me about a visit to a friend or one of your relatives in your childhood. **Who** did you visit? **Where** did you go and **whom** did you go there with? **What** did you do there? Why was it so special?

I would like to ask you about a holiday from your childhood. **What** did you do? **Who** did you spend time with? What was **so special** about that holiday? Tell me everything about that holiday in detail.

Think about a trip you went on when you were little. **Where** did you go, and **whom** did you go there with? What made that trip **memorable?** Tell me everything you remember about that trip in detail.

- -

최근 경험

When was the last time you went for shopping? Tell about a time you went to buy **some clothes. Where** did you go, and **whom** did you go there with? **What** did you buy? What was **so special** about that shopping experience?

I would like to ask you about the most recent holiday you celebrated. **When** was it, and **who** were you with? **How** did you celebrate that holiday? Why was that holiday **memorable?** Tell me why that holiday was particularly unforgettable?

Tell me about a time you ate out at recently. **What kind of restaurant** did you go to? What did you **eat? When** was it and **whom** did you go with? Did you like **the food** there? Tell me everything about that experience in detail.

I would like to ask you about **a take-out or delivery restaurant** you got food from recently. **What** kind of restaurant was it and what was their **menu?** What did you **order?** Did you like **the food** there? Tell me everything in detail.

Let's talk about a recent phone call you remember. **Whom** did you talk to, and **what kind of topic** did you talk about? What made that phone call **so special?** Please tell me about that phone call in as much detail as possible.

Think about the last time you had some free time. **When** was it? **Who** were you with? **Where** did you go? **What** did you do? How did you **feel** on that day? Tell me everything you did on that day in detail.

Do you remember what you did on the Internet yesterday? **Which website** did you visit? **Why** did you visit that website? Please tell me about the things you did on that website yesterday.

진짜녀석들 OPIc IM3-AL MP3 질문 리스트(유형)

경험 질문 MP3

인상깊었던 경험

Tell me about a memorable trip to the beach. **When** was it, and **who** were you with? **Which beach** were you at? **What** did you do there? What made this trip to the beach **so special?** Please tell me everything you did at the beach from the moment you arrived there.

Tell me about the most memorable video that you have watched on the Internet. Maybe the video was **something funny,** or **something related to work, school,** or **leisure.** Tell me everything about that video in as much detail as possible.

Tell me your most memorable experience while traveling overseas. Maybe **something funny** or **unexpected happened. Where** did you go and **who** were you with? Please tell me the story from the beginning to the end.

Have you ever had a special experience at a park? **When** was it and **what** happened? **Who** were you with? Why is it **so special?** Please tell me about that story from the beginning to the end.

Think about a memorable hotel you stayed at. **Where** was it located? **Who** did you go there with? **What made you visit** to that hotel? Was there **something interesting** happened? Please tell me about that story from the beginning to the end.

In the past, **how** did you use the Internet to get your project done at school? **When** was it? **What** was the project about? **Was it useful** to use the Internet? Please give me all the details.

Think about a time when you visited one of your friends or relatives. **When** was it? **What** did you do when you visited them? Why was it **so special?** Please tell me everything from the beginning to the end.

Think about a memorable experience you had while eating something at home. **What** did you eat? Did you **like the food?** Why was it **so memorable?** Please tell me everything about that story from the beginning to the end.

- -

문제해결 경험

Pick one of the problems you have experienced at home. **What** exactly **happened?** Please tell me how the problem **started** and how it **ended.** Please tell me how you **solved** that problem in detail.

Tell me about **some difficulties or challenges** that industry had before. What were the **challenges** that industry **dealt with?** How did they **solve** that problem? Please tell me about that story from the beginning to the end.

Have you ever experienced **any problems when you were using the Internet?** Perhaps a website that you wanted to open suddenly stopped working. **What exactly happened?** How did you **solve the situation?** Please tell me about the story from the beginning to the end.

Think about a time when you had trouble while using public transportation. **When** was it and **who** were you with? **What exactly happened?** How did you **deal with the situation?** Please give me all the details.

I would like to ask you about an unexpected incident regarding recycling. **When** was it? **Who** were you with? **What exactly happened?** How did you **solve the situation?** Tell me everything about that day from the beginning to the end.

진짜녀석들 OPIc IM3-AL MP3 질문 리스트(유형)

묘사, 세부묘사, 경험 모의고사 질문 MP3

🎧 MP3 IM3-AL_Q_79~91

1번   Let's start the interview now. Please tell me a little about yourself.

2번   You indicated in the survey that you like **listening to music.** What kind of music do you listen to? Who are some of your favorite musicians or composers?

3번   How did you **first get interested in music?** Please **compare the music** that you used to listen when you were **young** and the music you listen **today.** Also, how has your interest in music changed over the years?

4번   Please tell me about a time when you went to listen to some live music. Was it at a concert or a live café? **Who did you go there with? How did you like the music** you listened to there? Please tell me about that day from the beginning to the end.

5번   I would like to ask you about **gatherings in your country. What** do people in your country do when they get together? **Where** do they go? How do they normally **celebrate** their gatherings? Please tell me in detail.

6번   Think about your last gathering. **Who** were you with? **Where** did you go? Please tell me about how you spent your day on your last gathering in as much detail as possible.

7번   Tell me about a memorable moment you had at a gathering. **When** was it? **What kinds of gathering** was it? **What** exactly **happened** on that day? **Why** was it **memorable?** Please tell me everything from the beginning to the end.

8번   You indicated in the survey that you go to **bars.** Describe one of your favorite bars that you usually visit. What does it look like? Why do you like to visit that bar? Please tell me everything about that place in detail.

9번   You indicated in the survey that you go to **bars.** Describe one of your favorite bars that you usually visit. What does it look like? Why do you like to visit that bar? Please tell me everything about that place in detail.

10번   Tell me about a memorable incident that happened at a bar. **When** was it? **Who** were you with? **What** exactly happened there? Was there **something interesting** going on? Why was it **so special?** Tell me everything about that day at the bar from the beginning to the end.

13번   Let's say that something wrong can happen to our health. What are **some health problems** that we can have? Please describe **what can be happening** when someone loses his/her health. **How can we fix** those health problems? Please **provide some solutions** to stay healthy.

14번   **What are some hot products or services** that people talk about these days? Why are they mentioned by people so often these days? Give me all the details.

15번   What are **some major changes in people's shopping habits?** Where do people normally shop and what do they normally buy?

진짜녀석들 OPIc IM3-AL MP3 질문 리스트(유형)

롤플레이 질문 MP3

정보 요청 롤플레이

I'd like to give you a situation and ask you to act it out. **One of your friends is having a party and you are invited to that party.** Call your friend and ask **when the party starts** and **what you need to bring there.** Ask two or three more questions about the party.

I'd like to give you a situation and ask you to act it out. **You are staying at a hotel and have a chance for a one-day trip in a new city.** Ask the front desk agent three of four questions about **what things you can do.**

I'd like to give you a situation and ask you to act it out. **You are at a clothing store and try to buy some clothes.** Ask the staff two to three questions about **the clothes you want to buy.**

I'd like to give you a situation and ask you to act it out. **You want to buy an MP3 player.** Call your friend and ask about the MP3 player that he or she is using. Ask three or four questions that will help you **decide if you want to get the same product your friend is using or not.**

I'd like to give you a situation and ask you to act it out. **You want to open a new bank account.** Go to the bank and ask the bank teller three to four questions about **opening a new account.**

I'd like to give you a situation and ask you to act it out. **You would like to buy a house to live in.** Call one of the real estate agencies and ask three or four questions about **buying a house to live in.**

- -

문제 해결 롤플레이

I'm sorry, but there is a problem you need to resolve. **Unfortunately, you just had a car accident, and you are not able to make it to the party.** Call your friend, explain the situation, and give two to three alternatives to solve the situation.

I'm sorry, but there is a problem you need to resolve. **You left your bag in the taxi that brought you back from the one-day trip.** Call the taxi company, explain the situation, describe your bag, and ask them **how you can get your bag back.**

I'm sorry, but there is a problem you need to resolve. **You found out that one of the shirts you bought has a problem.** Call the clothing store and explain the situation. Give two to three alternatives to **solve this problem.**

I'm sorry, but there is a situation that you need to solve. **You borrowed an MP3 player from your friend but unfortunately, you broke it.** Call your friend, explain the situation, and offer two to three alternatives to **resolve this matter.**

I'm sorry, but there is a problem you need to resolve. **You left your credit card behind at a shopping mall.** Call the shopping mall and explain the situation. Give two to three alternatives to **solve the problem.**

I'm sorry, but there is a problem you need to resolve. **You have moved into the new house but found out that one of the windows in your house was broken.** Call the repair shop, explain **why you need to get a new window as soon as possible.**

진짜녀석들 OPIc IM3-AL MP3 질문 리스트(유형)

롤플레이 질문 MP3

문제 해결 경험

That's the end of the situation. **Have you ever made plans for a trip or a party but had to cancel at the very last minute because of something that happened unexpectedly?** How did you **solve the problem?** Please tell me all the stories from the beginning to the end.

That's the end of the situation. Have you ever had that kind of situation before? **Have you ever lost something?** How did you **solve that situation?** Please tell me about what happened from the beginning to the end.

That's the end of the situation. **Have you ever had any experience of being unhappy with something that you bought or some service you received?** Maybe, something could have had a scratch or a rip on it. What was the problem, and how did you **solve the problem?** Please tell me everything in detail.

That's the end of the situation. **Please tell me about a time when a piece of equipment broke.** When was it and what exactly happened? How did you **fix the problem?** Tell me everything about that experience.

That's the end of the situation. **Have you ever had any problems using your bank card, bank account, or a credit card?** Maybe your credit card was not working properly for some reason. Please tell me everything that happened and how you **resolved the matter.**

That's the end of the situation. **Have you ever broken something at home?** If so, **what did you break? What exactly happened?** How did you **solve the problem?** Please give me all the details from the beginning to the end.

진짜녀석들 OPIc IM3–AL MP3 질문 리스트(유형)

롤플레이 모의고사 질문 MP3

롤플레이 11번	I'd like to give you a situation and ask you to act it out. **You want to buy some tickets to go watch a concert tonight.** Call the ticket booth and ask two to three questions about **how to get tickets.**
롤플레이 12번	I'm sorry, but there is a problem you need to resolve. **On the concert day, you are so sick that you can't even get out of the bed.** Call your friend and explain the situation. Then give two or three alternatives to **solve this problem.**
롤플레이 경험 13번	That's the end of the situation. **Have you ever bought some concert tickets or made plans for a trip but had to cancel at the last minute because something unexpected happened?** Please tell me everything about what had happened **how you dealt with it.**
롤플레이 11번	I'd like to give you a situation and ask you to act it out. **You have a job interview at a company tomorrow, but you don't know much about the company.** Call the company and ask three or four **questions about the company.**
롤플레이 12번	I'm sorry, but there is a problem you need to resolve. **Unfortunately, something happened to you and you cannot make it to the interview.** Call the company and explain what happened to you. Then, give two to three alternatives to **make some arrangements for a schedule change.**
롤플레이 경험 13번	That's the end of the situation. **Have you ever had to cancel an appointment or a meeting for some reason?** What exactly happened, and **how did you deal with the situation?** Please give me all the details.
롤플레이 11번	I'd like to give you a situation and ask you to act it out. **You are going on an international trip.** Call one of the hotels in that country and ask how the weather is like there. Also, you want to know **what clothes you need to bring.** Please ask two or three more questions to **complete the plans for your trip.**
롤플레이 12번	I'm sorry, but there is a problem you need to resolve. **You bought some clothes while your international trip but unfortunately, the weather doesn't match with the clothes you bought.** Call the clothing store and explain the situation. Please tell them **you want to get some other clothes.**
롤플레이 경험 13번	That's the end of the situation. **Have you ever had any trouble due to an unexpected weather? Where** were you? **What happened** and **who** were you with? **How did you deal with the situation?** Please tell me everything about what happened on that day.
롤플레이 11번	I'd like to give you a situation and ask you to act it out. **You would like to get some coffee from a new coffee shop that has opened recently.** Call the coffee shop and ask three to four questions about **their menu and how to order the coffee.**
롤플레이 12번	I'm sorry, but there is a problem you need to resolve. **You got your coffee delivered to your house. Unfortunately, you find out that you've got the wrong order.** Call the coffee shop and explain the situation. Then, give two to three alternatives to **solve the problem.**
롤플레이 경험 13번	That's the end of the situation. **Have you ever been in a situation that you had ordered something but got the wrong order? Where** were you and **what did you order? What exactly happened** and how did you **deal with the situation?** Please describe the event in detail.
롤플레이 11번	I'd like to give you a situation and ask you act it out. **One of your relatives is going on a trip for two days. Their house will be empty, and you've been asked to watch the house while they are gone.** Call your relative and ask three or four questions about what **you have to do for two days.**
롤플레이 12번	I'm sorry, but there is a problem you need to resolve. **You are at your relative's house, but you can't get into the house because you don't have the key.** Call your relative and ask two to three questions to **solve the problem.**
롤플레이 경험 13번	That's the end of the situation. **Have you ever had an incident that you couldn't keep a promise with a family member or a friend? When** was it? **What was the main reason you couldn't keep the promise?** What did you do to **solve the problem?** Please give me all the details.

진짜녀석들 OPIc IM3-AL 핵심 암기 문장 리스트

진짜녀석들 OPIc의 유형별 암기 문장을 모아두었으니 적어도 80% 이상은 암기하시기 바랍니다.

🎧 MP3 IM3-AL_1~66

묘사
&
세부묘사

1. That's a good question, <u>my favorite coffee shop</u>? Sure, I got it.
2. Well, <u>music</u>? You know, <u>I listen to music in my free time</u>.
3. Oh yeah, <u>vacation</u>? You know, I love <u>traveling around my country</u>.
4. Alright Eva, this is all I can say about <u>my favorite beach</u>. Thank you.
5. Well, okay Eva, this is pretty much about it.
6. So overall, this is about <u>my favorite park</u>.
7. When it comes to <u>my favorite coffee shop</u>, it's like <u>2km</u> from <u>where I live</u>.
8. Well, I'm pretty sure that <u>the park</u> is around <u>20-minutes away</u> from <u>my place</u>.
9. Speaking of <u>the beach</u>, it's a perfect spot for just <u>sitting and relaxing</u> while looking at <u>the beautiful flowers</u>.
10. Also, there is <u>a huge running track</u> where you can see lots of people <u>exercising</u>.
11. I mean, there is <u>a huge park</u> with many different areas where people <u>play soccer</u>, <u>cricket</u> and so on.
12. In addition, there is <u>a beautiful old house</u> which is now <u>a café</u> where you can have <u>afternoon tea</u>.
13. Actually, <u>the beach</u> is undeniably beautiful, and the water is crystal clear.
14. Oh! I must say that <u>watching the sunset</u> is kinda romantic and that's why <u>the place</u> is famous for <u>couples</u>.
15. Well, <u>summer</u> is the perfect time to go to <u>the park</u> and do <u>some outdoor activities</u>.
16. In my opinion, getting back to nature, just relaxing outside is essential for human beings.
17. Seriously, I prefer to go <u>there at night</u> since I can enjoy <u>the peace and quiet</u>.
18. You know, I suppose I tend to <u>visit there a few times a month</u>.
19. Whenever I visit <u>there</u>, I can see bunch of people <u>talking and relaxing</u>.
20. In fact, I've always lived in <u>very quiet areas</u>, so I'm trying to visit places <u>that are new to me</u>.
21. You know, people do many kinds of things such as <u>playing sports</u>, <u>listening to music</u> and stuff like that.
22. However, there are many other things you can do such as <u>reading books</u> or <u>just relaxing</u>.
23. Well, I guess most people go there to walk/run and to swim.
24. All you need to know is that <u>the shopping mall</u> is always packed with lots of people.
25. Whenever I go <u>there</u>, it makes me feel so great and it means a lot to me.
26. In addition, I always end up <u>going there</u> since it's free to visit.
27. First of all, the building has <u>5</u> floors and <u>a terrace garden</u>.
28. Firstly, <u>the shopping mall</u> is a <u>10</u>-story building, so it definitely stands out.
29. You know, I must say that it's the tallest building in the city and it's called <u>the ABC tower</u>.
30. In fact, it's the most famous <u>shopping center</u> which is located <u>in the middle of the town</u>.
31. As you can imagine, on the first floor, there is <u>a reception desk</u> and you need <u>an ID card</u> to get in.
32. Also, on the second to fourth floors, there are lots of <u>luxury stores</u>.
33. Plus, on the ninth floor, there is <u>a gym</u> where I <u>work out</u>.
34. As you can expect, on the top floor, there is <u>a coffee shop</u> and <u>a cozy bar</u> where you can <u>chill</u>.
35. When it comes to my house, our place has <u>a master bedroom</u>, three bedrooms, and <u>two</u> baths.
36. When you go there, in total, you can find more than <u>50 ATMs</u>.
37. The first thing I can see is <u>a flat screen TV</u> and <u>a cozy couch</u>.
38. The most interesting thing about <u>this place</u> is that every single thing is automated.
39. You know, it has <u>a smart door lock</u> so it's handy.
40. Generally, it has central heating and air-conditioning so it's cool during summer and warm during winter.
41. Obviously, people can easily call <u>the engineer</u> if <u>the elevator</u> is not working.
42. I mean, <u>the room</u> is extremely clean, and the people are so friendly and that's why I love <u>to go there</u>.
43. But you know, it is always filled with lots of people, so I prefer going there <u>early in the morning</u>.
44. As you walk in, you will probably see <u>my brother</u> being a couch potato.
45. Well, I always order <u>Latte</u> <u>in the morning</u> but sometimes I need to stand in a long line.
46. In order to lose weight, I <u>run on a treadmill</u> every day.
47. When it comes to my friend, I spend lots of time with <u>John</u> and I've known <u>him</u> since I was <u>10</u>.
48. Actually, <u>he</u> knows a lot about <u>music</u>, so he is <u>a great person</u> to go with
49. In order to prepare for summer, I spend lots of time <u>at the gym</u> because I need to <u>lose weight</u>.
50. Moreover, I really enjoy <u>watching</u> all kinds of <u>movies</u> because it helps me release stress.
51. You know, I'm pretty sure that I can get a discount since I got <u>a membership card</u>.
52. As you can imagine, <u>recycling</u> is <u>mandatory</u> in Korea and people recycle trash such as paper, glass, metal and etcetera. When I was young, I used to <u>wear something casual</u>, but now, I <u>wear something formal</u>.
53. The main reason why I like to stay at home is that I can <u>spend time alone</u>.
54. To be honest, I don't know why, but I kinda feel like <u>drinking</u>.
55. I mean, most <u>Koreans</u> are using it since it's getting increasingly popular.
56. When I was little, I used to <u>live in a studio apartment</u>, but now I <u>live in a 3-story house</u>.
57. In the past, <u>the cell phones</u> were only used to <u>make calls</u>. However, <u>the cell phones</u> today have <u>various</u>
58. <u>functions</u> such as <u>taking pictures</u> or <u>playing games</u>.
59. When it comes to the home appliances, I guess <u>the vacuum</u> is the biggest change in our lives.
60. However, <u>taste buds</u> have changed a lot over the years.
61. But now, it has become a daily routine that people are very used to.
62. But now, people have become a lot more health-conscious than in the past.
63. On the other hand, <u>they</u> are a little different in some ways.
64. Speaking of issues, people can experience various problems when they talk about <u>renting a house</u>.
65. However, one of the biggest issues about <u>parks</u> is <u>garbage problems</u>.
66. Frankly speaking, there are not many issues when it comes to <u>recycling</u>.

진짜녀석들 OPIc IM3-AL 핵심 암기 문장 리스트

진짜녀석들 OPIc의 유형별 암기 문장을 모아두었으니 적어도 80% 이상은 암기하시기 바랍니다.

경험
&
롤플레이

67. I got it Eva, <u>experience about my trip</u>?
68. **Great,** you mean <u>my beach experience</u>?
69. **Alright!** Let me tell you <u>my first concert experience</u>.
70. **Um yeah,** this is all I remember Eva. Thank you.
71. **Okay Eva,** this is <u>my park experience</u>.
72. **Alright Eva,** I guess this is pretty much about it.
73. **Well, after like 500 meters?** I was already out of breath.
74. **But after running about 2 km,** I finally found my optimal pace. And yeah, I could <u>burn a lot of calories</u>.
75. **You know what,** I could lose weight and I became super happy. So, whenever I'm under stress, I <u>go out and run</u>.
76. **When we got in,** as I expected, there were full of people <u>dancing</u>.
77. **After like 20 minutes?** We totally lost track of time, we danced, jumped, I mean, we just went crazy.
78. **And after the festival,** we went to <u>a bar and grabbed a beer</u>. I mean, it was a great way to wrap up all of the fun.
79. **You know,** the <u>movie</u> was great, and we had so much fun.
80. **But um,** when we were about to <u>eat something</u>, it started to rain. I mean, the weather was so sunny, but it poured!
81. **Guess what!** We were completely soaked. Well, what could we do? We ended up <u>going back home</u>.
82. **After only being there for 30 minutes,** I got so drunk.
83. **I mean,** I drank like there's no tomorrow. The only thing I remember is that I kept <u>dancing and laughing</u>.
84. **Well, the next day?** I ended up <u>staying in my bed all day</u>. But you know? It was kinda fun and I feel like drinking again.
85. **After shopping,** I tried to pay, but I realized that I was in trouble.
86. **As you can expect,** I lost <u>my wallet</u>. Oh my god, I felt like a homeless person.
87. **Ugh, I felt sick,** I mean, I had to <u>cancel all my credit cards</u>. You know what? <u>Losing a wallet</u> is like starting a new life.
88. **After like 3 hours,** I realized that <u>I'd miss the last train</u>, so I ran down the stairs.
89. **I don't know why,** but I just lost balance and fell over.
90. **Oh my god,** it was so painful, and I was crying. So, I called an ambulance and I stayed in the hospital for <u>2 days</u>.
91. **After like 30 min,** I still haven't received my order and I started to lose my patience.
92. **In order not to ruin our anniversary,** I just decided to <u>leave there</u>.
93. **You know what,** everywhere was fully booked! So, we just went to <u>a convenience store</u> for <u>our dinner</u>.
94. **While we were having fun, all of a sudden,** the power went out and we freaked out.
95. **In order to solve this problem,** I quickly <u>found candles and lit them</u>.
96. **To be honest,** it was such a memorable experience. So, we enjoyed being in that situation <u>talking</u> and <u>finishing our meal</u>.
97. **When we checked out,** we grabbed a cab to go to <u>the airport</u>.
98. **When we were just about to arrive at the airport,** I realized that I left <u>my luggage</u> at <u>the hotel</u>. Can you imagine that?
99. **So,** I asked the driver to go back. Luckily, <u>the hotel staff</u> searched for <u>my luggage</u> for <u>2 hours</u> and found it! In return, I gave him <u>20 dollars</u>.
100. **While we were enjoying the music,** my friend spilled <u>coffee</u> on <u>my laptop</u>.
101. **Oh my god,** it was annoying at first, but I pretended like it was ok.
102. **So quickly,** my friend called an engineer and <u>he</u> came in like <u>10</u>min.
103. **I guess,** he worked on it for about <u>an hour</u>. And you know, I ended up spending <u>$1,000 USD</u>.
104. **For my birthday present,** <u>my girlfriend</u> bought me <u>a coffee maker</u>. After like <u>10</u> days, I got <u>the coffee maker</u>, but it was broken!
105. **So,** I called <u>the store</u> and told them about my broken <u>coffee maker</u>.
106. **Because I was so mad,** they apologized and offered an exchange. But I was very upset, so I strongly asked them for a refund.
107. **When I arrived at the movie theater,** I realized that I bought the wrong <u>ticket</u>.
108. **So,** I went to <u>the ticket booth</u> and explained the whole situation.
109. **Thankfully,** they offered an exchange for <u>the next movie</u>. Moreover, there was no additional payment. Actually, it was the best customer service I've ever had.
110. **Hi there,** I would like to buy <u>an MP3 player</u>. Could I ask you some questions?
111. **First of all,** where is it? I heard that it is close to <u>Seoul station</u>. Is it right?
112. **And also,** how much is it? Can you give me a discount?
113. **Lastly,** what are your opening hours like? Are you open 24/7?
114. **Alright then,** thanks a lot. See you later.
115. **Hey,** I need to tell you something. Actually, I feel <u>awful</u> today. I don't think I can meet you today.
116. **So,** let me give you some options to solve this problem.
117. **Maybe,** I can call <u>the ticket company</u> and get a refund.
118. **Or,** why don't you ask <u>one of your friends</u>?
119. **Or,** the only other way is to postpone it till <u>the following week</u>. What do you think?
120. **Once again,** I'm so sorry. Let me know what's best for you.

진짜녀석들 OPIc IM3-AL 어휘 및 표현 리스트

묘사 및 세부묘사 답변에 사용된 유용한 어휘 및 표현들을 암기하시기 바랍니다.

3 times a week 일주에 3번
a bit of caffeine 카페인
a country that is nearby my country 우리나라와 가까운 나라
a few times a month 한 달에 몇 번
a flip phone 폴더폰
a geographically similar to my country 우리나라와 지리적으로 비슷한 나라
a healthy person I know 내가 아는 건강한 사람
a huge concert hall 큰 콘서트장
a huge difference 큰 차이
a huge house for everyone to live in 모든 사람들이 살기에 큰 집
a problem when people rent a house 집 렌트 시 겪는 문제
after a stressful day at work 업무로부터 힘들었던 하루 끝에
after shopping 쇼핑 후에
After taking a walk 산책 후
after work 일이 끝나고
an article related to~ ~에 관련된 기사
And that means~ 그 말은
around 20-minutes away from my place 우리 집에서 약 20분 거리
as it has 7 floors 7층으로 되어있기 때문에
as you can expect 네가 예상하듯
As you may know 네가 알다시피
As you walk in 네가 걸어 들어오면
bank tellers 은행원
Basically 기본적으로
beautiful beach view 아름다운 해변 경치
both of them love to drink 둘 다 술 마시는 것을 좋아해
by that reason 이러한 이유로
can't stop spending money at that mall 쇼핑몰에서 돈 쓰는 것을 멈출 수 없어
cell phone industry 핸드폰 산업
changing their menus 메뉴를 바꾸는 것
couch potato 하루 종일 TV만 보는 사람
create strong and unique passwords 강력하고 독특한 비밀번호
differences and similarities 차이점과 유사점
different Internet usage among generations 세대 간 다른 인터넷 사용
do lots of things on the Internet 인터넷으로 많은 것들을 한다
do the same things 같은 것을 하다
drink beers like there's no tomorrow 내일이 없는 것처럼 술을 마셔
easily adapt their menus 메뉴를 쉽게 조정하다
end up ~ing ~로 결국 끝나다
every 3 months 3개월마다
every single day 매일
family dinner 가족 식사
feature 기능
filling out our social media profile 소셜미디어 프로필 작성
food contamination 음식 오염
for a day 하루동안
for a few days 며칠 동안
For instance 예를 들어
for tourists 관광객에게
For younger people 젊은 사람들은
freezing cold 얼도록 추운
from my work 내가 일하는 곳에서
gain too much weight 살이 많이 찌다
get rid of stress 스트레스를 없애다

going to the beach on Christmas 크리스마스에 해변을 가는 것
going to the gym 헬스장에 가는 것
good-looking 잘생긴
gym clothes 운동복
he is an outgoing person and likes socializing 그는 활발하고 사람 만나는 것을 좋아해
he just became a personal trainer 이제 막 트레이너가 되었어
health-conscious 건강에 신경을 쓰는
high cost 높은 비용
hit the gym and work out together 헬스장에 가서 같이 운동을 해
home appliances 가전제품
houses today 오늘날의 집들
How do you start your day? 하루를 어떻게 시작하나요?
how people in my country dress 우리나라 사람들이 옷 입는 법
how recycling has changed 재활용이 변한 점
how to lose weight 살을 빼는 방법
how to maintain their health 그들의 건강을 유지하는 법
I recently bought a new bed 난 최근에 새 침대를 샀어
I started to shop online 난 온라인으로 쇼핑하는 것을 시작했어
I strongly recommend you visit there 그곳을 방문할 것을 강력히 추천해
I take him with me 그를 데려가
I use an app to order online 난 온라인으로 주문하기 위해 앱을 사용해
I usually take my girlfriend 난 보통 여자친구를 데려간다
I usually take vacations at home 난 종종 집에서 휴가를 보내
I'm a regular 난 단골이야
if I had to choose one 한 가지를 고른다면
If there is any chance to visit Korea on Christmas
크리스마스에 한국을 방문할 기회가 있다면
in high peak seasons 성수기에
in my neighborhood 우리 동네에 있는
in order to solve this problem 이 문제를 풀기 위해서
In order to stay healthy 건강하게 유지하기 위해
In result 결과적으로
international trips 해외여행
is essential for ~에 필수적이다
is surrounded by water 바다로 둘러싸여 있어
it has powerful speakers 강력한 스피커가 있어
it has to be ~ ~이어야만 해
it has to be my TV 내 TV이어야만 해
it is better to change 바꾸는 것이 좋다
it is important to eat low-calorie foods 낮은 칼로리 음식을 먹는 것이 중요하다
It must be~ ~이어야만 해
it's cheaper and reliable 저렴하고 믿을만 해
it's fast and convenient 빠르고 편리해
it's gotta be Thailand 태국이어야만 해
it's like 600km away 대략 600km 정도야
it's scorching hot 타는 듯이 더워
it's such a romantic place 로맨틱한 장소야
it's the perfect way to release stress 스트레스 풀기 가장 좋은 방법이야
it's unlike any other Starbucks 다른 스타벅스와는 다르게
Korea is a mountainous country 한국은 산이 많은 나라야
Korea is a peninsula 한국은 반도야
Korea is surrounded by the oceans 한국은 바다로 둘러싸여져 있다
Koreans normally take one to three coffees a day
한국인들은 하루에 1~3잔씩 보통 커피를 마셔

진짜녀석들 OPIc IM3-AL 어휘 및 표현 리스트

묘사 및 세부묘사 답변에 사용된 유용한 어휘 및 표현들을 암기하시기 바랍니다.

Koreans work late in the office 한국사람들은 늦게까지 일울한다
lots of cosmetics and perfumes 많은 화장품과 향수들
lots of families come out to play sports 많은 가족들이 나와서 운동을 해
lots of Koreans are moving to rural areas 많은 한국사람들은 지방으로 이사를 가
love going to bars and drink 바에 가서 술 마시는 것을 즐겨
most Koreans are concerned about their health
대부분의 한국사람들은 건강을 걱정해
most Koreans have a big family 대부분의 한국인들은 대 가족이야
my favorite beach 내가 좋아하는 해변
New year's Eve 새해 전날
Not only that ~뿐만 아니라
old school buddies 오래된 친구
on the other hand 반면에
on the weekends 주말에
on their phone 핸드폰으로
once or twice a month 한 달에 한 두 번
once or twice a year 일년에 1-2번
one of my buddies 친구 중 한 명
one of my friends 내 친구 중 한 명
one of the best ways to make friends 친구들을 사귀는 가장 좋은 방법 중 하나
one of the issues about parks in Korea 한국 공원의 이슈 중 하나
one of the most efficient ways to release stress
스트레스를 해소하는 가장 효율적인 방법 중 하나
one of the recycling issues 재활용 이슈 중 하나
one of the rising industries in Korea 한국에서 그건 뜨고 있는 산업 중에 하나
order online 온라인으로 주문하다
ordering coffee online 온라인으로 커피를 주문하는 것
otherwise 그렇지 않으면
our generation 우리 세대
people are so addicted to their phones 사람들은 핸드폰에 너무 중독이 되었어
people became a phone addict 핸드폰 중독자가 되었어
people could only get their coffee at coffee shops
커피숍에서만 커피를 마실 수 있었어
people enjoy their free time at the parks
사람들은 공원에서 여가 시간을 보내는 것을 좋아해
people find it difficult to decide where to meet 어디서 만날지 정하는 것을 어려워해
people only recycled food waste 음식물 쓰레기만 재활용했어
people preferred to spend time alone 혼자 시간을 보내는 것을 즐겼다
people who are interested in the music industry 음악 산업에 관심 있는 사람들
physically, mentally and socially well balanced
신체적으로, 정신적으로, 사회적으로 잘 균형 잡힌
pre-built 미리 만들어진
public transportation 대중 교통
quite often 꽤 종종
rather than using a cell phone 핸드폰을 사용하는 것보다
recycle like 2 to 3 times a week 일주에 2-3번 재활용을 해
recycling center 재활용 센터
recycling policy is pretty strict in Korea 한국 재활용 정책은 엄격해
regarding ~에 관하여
riding bikes is another idea 자전거를 타는 것도 또 다른 아이디어야
romantic spot 로맨틱한 장소
security 보안
shopaholic 쇼핑중독
since it's very cheap 엄청 저렴하기 때문에

so many people waiting in a long line 긴 줄을 기다리고 있는 많은 사람들
social gatherings 모임
some holidays in my country 우리나라 휴일
some issues or concerns people have regarding holidays
휴일 관련한 사람들의 이슈 및 걱정
some issues or concerns people have related to traveling
여행 관련된 이슈 및 사람들의 걱정
some issues people talk about regarding the Internet
사람들이 얘기하는 인터넷 관련 이슈
some issues people talk about related to cell phones
사람들이 말하는 핸드폰 관련 이슈
some issues related to making plans for gathering 모임 계획에 관련된 이슈
some issues related to our health 건강 관련 이슈
something was wrong with the food 음식에 문제가 있었어
spend lots of time with~ ~와 많은 시간을 보내다
steal people's personal information 개인 정보를 훔치다
swimming and tanning at the beach 해변에서 수영하고 태닝하는 것
taking cabs 택시를 타는 것
talking and laughing with people helps him stay healthy
사람들과 대화하고 웃는 것이 그를 건강하게 해
taste them 맛을 봐
tend to ~하는 경향이 있다
Thanksgiving Day 추석
that's where I take a walk 내가 산책하는 장소
that's why~ ~하는 이유야
the beaches were famous for gatherings 해변이 모임 하기에 유명하다
the cell phones were only used to make calls
핸드폰들은 오직 전화를 거는 데만 사용되었어
the companies that young people want to work 젊은 사람들이 일하고 싶어하는 회사
the country is getting dirtier 나라가 점점 더러워지다
the country is losing the number of tourists 관광객 수가 줄어든다
the food was contaminated by bacteria 음식은 박테리아로 오염되었어
the geography of my country 우리나라 지리
the grocery stores 식료품점
the houses are cheaper and reliable 집들은 저렴하고 믿을 만 해
the industries that they are interested in 그들이 관심 있는 산업들
the news I heard last summer 작년 여름에 들었던 뉴스
the phone I used back then and now 예전과 지금 사용하는 핸드폰
the phone will dial or text to people 핸드폰이 사람에게 전화를 걸거나 문자를 해줘
the price is quite affordable 가격이 꽤 합리적이야
the structure of the houses 집의 구조
the traffic is congested 교통이 혼잡해
the types of appliances that are used in my house 우리 집에서 사용하는 가전제품 종류
the voice recognition 음성인식
the way of spending their vacations 그들의 휴가를 보내는 방식
the way people buy food 사람들이 음식을 사는 방법
the ways of gatherings 모임의 방식
the weather and seasons in my country 우리나라 날씨와 계절
their ways of spending vacations 휴가를 보내는 그들의 방법
there are 4 distinct seasons in Korea 한국에는 뚜렷한 4계절이 있어
there are lots of hackers 해커가 많다
these days 요즘
they are missing out on so many things 많은 것들을 놓친다
they attend K-POP concerts 케이팝 콘서트에 가

349

진짜녀석들 OPIc IM3-AL 어휘 및 표현 리스트

묘사 및 세부묘사 답변에 사용된 유용한 어휘 및 표현들을 암기하시기 바랍니다.

they have set menus 세트메뉴가 있어
they like to stay healthy 그들은 건강을 유지하고 싶어해
they prefer their PCs PC사용을 선호해
they rather go on trips in low peak seasons 차라리 비수기에 여행을 가
they serve good food 좋은 음식을 제공해
they shop many things online 온라인으로 쇼핑을 많이 해
Think about it 생각해봐
This is pretty interesting 매우 흥미롭네요
three to four times a week 한 주에 3·4번
throw parties 파티를 열다
throw trash on the streets 길거리에 쓰레기를 버리다4
too many people are visiting 너무 많은 사람들이 방문해
tourism places 관광 명소
two kinds of companies to talk about 말하고 싶은 2가지 종류의 회사
type of concerts I enjoy going to 내가 자주 가는 콘서트 종류
types of transportation 교통 수단 종류
undeniably 명백하게
unfortunately 불행히도
using a cell phone 핸드폰을 사용하면서
very convenient 매우 편리해
VIP room where I need an ID card to get in 들어가기 위해 신분증이 필요한 VIP룸
we can make our own coffee at home 집에서 커피를 만들 수 있어
we could be fined 우리는 벌금을 낼 수 있어
we need to back-up our data 데이터 백업을 해야 해
we need to have more parks 더 많은 공원이 필요하다
we need to make more places to entertain 즐길 수 있는 장소를 더 만들 필요가 있어
We need to separate the trash carefully 주의 깊게 분리수거 해야 해
wearing a makeup is common in Korea 메이크업을 하는 것은 한국에서 흔해
what adults and children do at parks 어른과 아이가 공원에서 하는 것
what I like most about my cell phone 내가 핸드폰에서 가장 좋아하는 것
what I talk about with my friends 친구들과 하는 대화
what people do to get a job 사람들이 직업을 갖기 위해 하는 것
what people normally do on the Internet 사람들이 보통 인터넷으로 하는 것
when I'm stressed out 내가 스트레스 받을 때
When I'm with him 내가 그와 함께 있을 때
When it comes to ~에 대해서 말한다면
When they are busy or too cold to run 그들이 바쁘거나 뛰기에 너무 추울 때
when you visit my place 우리 집을 방문하면
whenever I go to concerts 콘서트를 갈 때면
where I live 내가 사는 곳
working out is very important for a healthy life 운동하는 것은 건강한 삶에 있어 정말 중요해
you don't have to get dressed up 차려 입지 않아도 돼
young people celebrate Christmas the most 젊은 사람들은 크리스마스를 가장 축하해

진짜녀석들 OPIc IM3-AL 어휘 및 표현 리스트

경험 답변에 사용된 유용한 어휘 및 표현들을 암기하시기 바랍니다.

a recent phone call I made 최근 했던 전화통화
a restaurant I've been to lately 최근에 간 레스토랑
After playing volleyball 발리볼 후에
an incident regarding recycling 재활용 관련된 사건
And I bought some noodles 라면을 샀어
As I expected 내가 예상했듯
As I recall 내가 기억하기론
Back then 그땐
bunch of my friends also played volleyball there 친구들과 발리볼도 했어
bunch of our friends went to the bar 많은 친구들이 바에 갔어
but sadly, he couldn't fix it 하지만 슬프게도, 그는 고치지 못했어
But the bus just stopped 하지만 버스가 멈췄어
can you live without your cell phone for a day? 핸드폰 없이 하루를 살 수 있어?
come to think of it 돌이켜 생각해보면
due to amazing food 맛있는 음식 때문에
Even after they answered, apologized and offered an exchange 그들이 전화를 받아 사과를 하고 교환을 해주겠다 했음에도 불구하고
For the differences 차이점으로는
he enjoyed drinking all kinds of whiskey 그는 모든 종류의 위스키를 마셨어
he was good at sports 그는 운동을 잘했어
his father was very rich 그의 아버지는 엄청 부자였어
I always prepare my MP3 player when I run 뛸 때 난 항상 MP3 플레이어를 챙겨
I asked for a help to the people that were at the beach 해변에 있던 사람들에게 도움을 요청했어
I bought a nice dinner for them 그들에게 좋은 저녁을 사줬어
I bought lots of cosmetics and perfumes online 온라인으로 화장품과 향수를 샀어
I couldn't remember half of the night 그날 밤의 반은 기억이 안나
I decided not to go 안 가기로 결심했어
I decided to cook for her 그녀를 위해 요리하기로 결심했어
I decided to make some coffee 커피를 만들기로 했어
I fell asleep while I was relaxing at the beach 해변에서 쉬는 동안 잠이 들었어
I go to ABC bar literally everyday 난 거의 매일 ABC 바에 가
I guess it was like 3 days ago 한 3일 전쯤 인 것 같아
I guess where we listen to those types of music is different 음악 종류에 따라 듣는 장소가 달라
I had a job interview 면접이 있었어
I had to study the music trends in 1990s 1990년대 음악 트렌드를 공부했어야 해
I just got off the bus and took a cab 버스에서 내려 택시를 탔어
I love working out at the park 난 공원에서 운동하는 것을 좋아해
I preferred going on a trip alone 혼자 여행 가는 것을 선호해
I ran to the service center 서비스센터로 달려갔어
I think I listen to music every single day 난 매일 음악을 듣는 것 같아
I think it was yesterday 어제였던 것 같아
I used to eat Junk food 정크푸드를 먹곤 했어
I used to only eat Korean food 난 한식만 먹곤 했어
I used YOUTUBE since it's free to use 난 무료이기 때문에 유튜브를 사용했어
I visited one of the shopping websites 쇼핑 사이트 중 한 곳을 방문했어
I waited another 20min 20분을 더 기다렸어
I was invited to a house party from my friend 난 친구로부터 하우스파티에 초대 받았어
I was so ashamed of myself 너무 창피했어
I was so disappointed 난 너무 실망했어
I was so hyped 엄청 흥분했어
I went grocery shopping 장을 보러 갔어
I went there last week alone, and I started to drink 난 혼자 가서 술을 마시기 시작했어
I'm a shopaholic 난 쇼핑중독이야
I'm very outgoing and like socializing 난 굉장히 활발하고 사람 만나는 것을 좋아해
I've always visited very quiet bars 항상 조용한 바만 다녔어

진짜녀석들 OPIc IM3-AL 어휘 및 표현 리스트

경험 답변에 사용된 유용한 어휘 및 표현들을 암기하시기 바랍니다.

I've watched an Eminem music video 에미넴 뮤직 비디오를 봤어

In order to celebrate 1year anniversary with my girlfriend 여자친구와의 1년을 기념하기 위해

It felt like a hassle to go back 다시 돌아가기 귀찮았어

it is only sold at OPIc department store 오픽 백화점에서만 팔아

it was late at night 늦은 밤이었어

it was my parent's wedding anniversary 부모님 결혼기념일이었어

It's one of the best ways to release stress 스트레스 해소하기 좋은 방법 중에 하나야

Koreans normally take one to three cups of coffee a day 한국사람은 보통 하루에 1-3잔의 커피를 마셔

listening to music is the best way to get rid of stress 음악을 듣는 것이 스트레스를 해소할 수 있는 가장 큰 방법이야

Luckily, the engineer fixed it 다행히 엔지니어가 고쳤어

most Koreans love shopping 대부분의 한국사람들은 쇼핑을 좋아해

most people in the world use the Internet every single day 대부분 사람들이 매일 인터넷을 사용해

my family went to Thailand for our summer vacation 우리 가족은 여름휴가로 태국을 갔어

My MP3 player stopped working 내 MP3 플레이어가 작동을 멈췄어

my music taste has changed a lot over the years 내 음악 취향은 몇 년에 걸쳐 변해왔어

my parents took me to the shopping mall 부모님이 쇼핑몰에 데려가셨어

No matter how many people are going 아무리 많은 사람들이 간다고 해도

on every weekend 매주 주말

one of my friends already bought tickets online 친구 중 한 명이 온라인으로 티켓을 샀어

people commonly have social gatherings in their free time 사람들은 여가 시간에 모임을 가져

people recycle in the recycling centers 사람들은 재활용센터에서 재활용을 해

people started to shop online using their phones 사람들은 핸드폰을 사용하여 온라인 쇼핑을 시작했어

people used to go to the shopping malls 사람들은 쇼핑몰에 가곤 했어

people usually grab a beer together 사람들은 주로 함께 술을 마셔

people usually use the bus 사람들은 주로 버스를 이용해

So I used an app to order online 난 앱을 사용해서 온라인으로 주문했어

So we turned the music on 그래서 우린 음악을 틀었어

somewhere quiet 조용한 곳

studies have found many health problems related to stress 많은 건강상 문제는 스트레스와 관련이 있다는 연구 결과가 나왔어

the atmosphere was excellent 분위기는 최고였어

the birthday boy spilled beer on my cell phone 생일인 친구가 내 핸드폰에 맥주를 쏟았어

The engineer still didn't show up 엔지니어는 아직 나타나지 않았어

the highlight of the video was when Eminem sang 'Without me' 비디오의 하이라이트는 에미넴이 'Without me'를 불렀을 때야

the hotel gave us such a great service 호텔은 정말 훌륭한 서비스를 제공했어

the hotel was amazing too 호텔 또한 굉장했어

the last time I had some free time 마지막으로 보냈던 여가시간

The main reason why people are stressed out is that they work too much 스트레스를 받는 가장 큰 이유는 과다 업무야

The main reason why people shop online is to save time 온라인 쇼핑의 가장 큰 이유는 시간을 절약할 수 있기 때문이야

The microwave oven just stopped working 전자레인지가 고장났어

the music was fantastic 음악은 환상적이였어

the music was so good 음악은 정말 좋았어

there aren't many people around that beach 해변 주위에 사람들이 많지 않아

they may get headaches, insomnia, frequent colds and low energy 그들은 두통, 불면증, 잦은 감기 그리고 기력이 없어지곤 해

They never answered the phone 그들은 내 전화를 받지 않았어

They sent me an engineer 엔지니어를 보내주었어

this cell phone is the one you should buy 네가 꼭 사야하는 핸드폰이야

to enjoy our Saturday 토요일을 즐기기 위해

Using a coffee maker is very convenient 커피 메이커를 사용하는 것은 매우 편리해

using my laptop 노트북을 사용하며

voice recognition and powerful speakers 음성인식과 강력한 스피커

we could do at the bar such as playing darts or beer pong 다트, 비어퐁 게임을 했어

we could find all kinds of music videos 우린 모든 종류의 뮤직 비디오를 찾을 수 있었어

we got into the store 상점으로 들어갔어

we really had a great time there 정말 즐거웠어

We sang the main song together on the phone 전화로 함께 메인 노래를 불렀어

we spent lots of time collecting our favorite clothes 좋아하는 옷을 고르는데 시간을 소비했어

we started to ride our bikes there 자전거 타길 시작했어

we went to a fancy Italian restaurant 근사한 이탈리안 레스토랑에 갔어

When I came home 집에 돌아왔을 때

when I was a child 내가 어렸을 때

when I'm stressed out 내가 스트레스 받을 때

When we heard the music 우리가 음악을 들었을 때

While I was enjoying the movie 내가 영화를 보던 중

you are not going to believe what happened! 무슨 일이 있었는지 못 믿을거야

You don't have to get dressed up to get a bit of caffeine 커피를 사기위해 옷을 차려 입고 나가지 않아도 돼

you will feel like you are in the middle of the concert hall 콘서트홀 중앙에 있는 것같이 느낄거야

you will probably see lots of people drinking in public during Korean summers 한국 여름에 야외에서 술 마시는 사람들을 볼 거야

YOUTUBE was the best free music sharing service 유투브는 최고의 무료 음악 공유 서비스였어

진짜녀석들 OPIc IM3-AL 어휘 및 표현 리스트

롤플레이 답변에 사용된 유용한 어휘 및 표현들을 암기하시기 바랍니다.

Also, can I take my friend? 또한 친구를 데려가도 돼?

And the coffee mug broke 커피머그가 깨졌어

And we watched a movie at home, and it was alright
그리고 우린 집에서 영화를 봤고, 나쁘지 않았어

Anyway, I went there to take out some cash 어쨌든, 현금 인출을 하기 위해 갔어

As usual, we planned to run at the park 평소와 같이, 우린 공원에서 뛰기로 했어

asked the driver to go as fast as he could 가능한 한 빨리 가달라고 기사님에게 부탁했어

Can I bring my powerful speakers? 강력한 스피커를 가져가도 돼?

could you please tell the staff to search for my bag?
직원에게 제 가방을 찾아달라고 말해주실 수 있나요?

Do I have to vacuum all the rooms? 모든 방을 청소해야 해?

do you have an app to order online? 온라인으로 주문할 수 있는 앱이 있나요?

Does it have powerful speaker? 강력한 스피커가 있나요?

he bought me the latest model 그는 가장 신상품을 사줬어

he is a partygoer 그는 파티광이야

he just ended up coming to the hospital to visit me 날 위해 병문안을 와 줬어

How about that? 어떻게 생각해?

how far is it from the airport? 공항에서 얼마나 걸리나요?

how is the weather like there? 날씨는 어떤가요?

how many people are going? 사람이 몇 명이나 오나요?

how much is the suite room? 스위트룸은 얼만가요?

How much should I save for a down payment? 계약금은 얼마나 준비해야 하나요?

I always take my friend 난 항상 친구를 데려가

I arrived there just on time 시간에 맞춰 도착했어

I can pay for it 내가 지불할게

I can't get into the house because I don't have the key
열쇠가 없어서 집 안으로 못 들어가겠어

I can't wear this T-shirt 이 티셔츠는 입을 수 없어요

I don't buy things online! 난 온라인으로 물건을 사지 않아

I don't think I can make it to the interview 인터뷰에 못 갈 것 같습니다

I found out that I've got the wrong order 내가 주문을 잘못한 것을 알아차렸어

I found out that one of the shirts I bought has a problem
구매한 셔츠 중 하나가 문제가 있음을 발견했어요

I have a job interview at your company tomorrow
내일 당신 회사에 면접이 있어요

I have moved into the new house 새 집으로 이사를 왔어요

I heard that the party starts at 7pm 7시에 시작한다고 들었어

I heard that your coffee shop has opened recently
최근에 커피숍을 오픈했다고 들었어요

I just got into a car accident, and I'm not able to make it to the party
교통사고가 나서 파티에 못 갈 것 같아

I left my credit card at your store 당신 상점에 카드를 두고 왔어요

I mean, I can't even get out of bed 내 말은, 침대 밖에로도 못 나오겠어

I planned a beach trip to BUSAN with my friends
친구들과의 부산 해변 여행을 계획했어

I realized that I ordered the wrong food 잘못된 음식을 주문한 것을 깨달았어

I really enjoy going to music festivals 뮤직페스티벌 가는 것을 즐겨

I was having a coffee while watching a movie 영화를 보면서 커피를 마셨어

I was so scared 난 엄청 무서웠어

I went to the shopping mall to buy my new swimsuit
수영복을 사기 위해서 쇼핑몰에 갔어

I woke up late this morning 오늘 아침에 늦게 일어났어요

I would like to buy some gym wear 운동복을 좀 사고 싶어요

I would like to buy some outdoor clothes 야외 활동 옷을 좀 사고 싶어요

I would like to open a new bank account 계좌를 오픈하고 싶어요

I would like to plan for a one-day trip 일일 투어를 계획하고 싶어요

I'm visiting your country next week 당신 나라를 다음 주에 방문하려 합니다

is there a branch nearby? 근처에 지점이 있나요?

is this ABC taxi company? ABC 택시 회사죠?

it all happened last Saturday 지난주 토요일에 일어났어

it is very annoying 굉장히 짜증나

It was complimentary 무료였어

it was just after the holiday 휴일 직후였어

it was my second-year anniversary with my girlfriend
내 여자친구와 2주년 기념일이었어

It was the biggest online electronic website 가장 큰 온라인 전자상점 웹사이트였어

Let me know as soon as possible 가능한 한 빨리 알려주세요

Moreover, they corrected my order 게다가, 내 주문을 정정해줬어

my brother bought me a laptop online 남동생이 온라인으로 노트북을 사줬어

one of the biggest issues is taking out the trash
가장 큰 이슈 중 하나는 쓰레기 버리는 거야

people can easily call the lock smith if they lose their keys
사람들이 키를 잃어버린다면 락스미스를 쉽게 부를 수 있어

So, can you give me their numbers? 그들 번호를 좀 줄래?

So, I need to get a new window 그래서 난 새 창문이 필요해요

something happened and I'm in the hospital now
일이 생겨 지금 병원에 있습니다

the atmosphere is excellent 분위기가 최고였어

the broken coffee mug was very expensive 깨진 커피머그는 엄청 비쌌어

the only other way is to exchange my clothes
다른 유일한 방법은 제 옷을 교환하는 거예요

Unfortunately, I left my bag in the taxi 불행히도, 택시에 가방을 두고 내렸어요

what do I need to bring? 무엇을 가져가야 해?

What floor is it? 몇 층인가요?

what kind of clothes should I bring? 어떤 종류의 옷을 가져가야 하나요?

what kinds of houses are available? 어떤 종류의 집이 가능한가요?

what should I buy there? 그곳에서 뭘 사야해?

when does the party start? 파티는 언제 시작해?

where are your ATMs located in that branch? 지점안에 ATM 기계는 어디에 있나요?

where is the ticket booth? 티켓부스는 어디에 있나요?

where is your repair shop? 수리점은 어디죠?

why don't I buy you a new one? 내가 새 걸 사줄게

MEMO

MEMO

MEMO

MEMO

MEMO

ㄹ진짜 녀석들